THE
KING
OVER THE
WATER

THE
KING OVER THE WATER

A Complete History of the Jacobites

DESMOND
SEWARD

BIRLINN

First published in 2019 by
Birlinn Limited
West Newington House
10 Newington Road
Edinburgh
EH9 1QS

ISBN 978 1 78027 606 9

British Library Cataloguing in Publication Data
A catalogue record for this book is available from the British Library.

Designed and typeset by Initial Typesetting Services, Edinburgh
Printed and bound by Clays Ltd, Elcograf S.p.A.

For
Hugo and Elizabeth
and for
Kit, Lettie and Millie

Although God hath given Mee three Kingdomes, yet in these He hath not now left Me any place, where I may with Safety & Honour rest my Head.

King Charles I, *Eikon Basilike, or The King's Book*[1]

Contents

PART ONE
JAMES II – THE LOST THRONE

PART TWO
JAMES III – A SECOND RESTORATION?

PART THREE
WHIG TYRRANY

Part Four
A KING IN WAITING

Part Five
CHARLES III AND GEORGE III

PART SIX
TWILIGHT

List of Illustrations and diagrams

Colour plates

Black-and-white plates

Diagrams

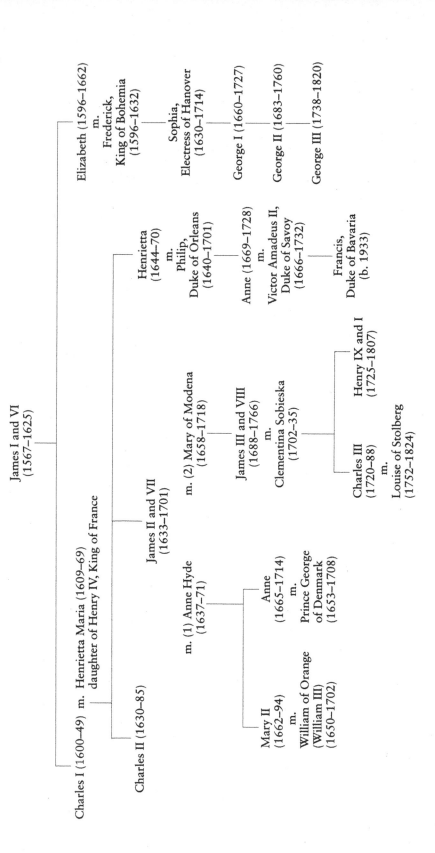

James I and VI
(1567–1625)

Charles I (1600–49) m. Henrietta Maria (1609–69)
daughter of Henry IV, King of France

Elizabeth (1596–1662)
m.
Frederick,
King of Bohemia
(1596–1632)

Sophia,
Electress of Hanover
(1630–1714)

George I (1660–1727)

George II (1683–1760)

George III (1738–1820)

Charles II (1630–85)

James II and VII
(1633–1701)

Henrietta
(1644–70)
m.
Philip,
Duke of Orleans
(1640–1701)

Anne (1669–1728)
m.
Victor Amadeus II,
Duke of Savoy
(1666–1732)

Francis,
Duke of Bavaria
(b. 1933)

m. (2) Mary of Modena
(1658–1718)

James III and VIII
(1688–1766)
m.
Clementina Sobieska
(1702–35)

Henry IX and I
(1725–1807)

Charles III
(1720–88)
m.
Louise of Stolberg
(1752–1824)

m. (1) Anne Hyde
(1637–71)

Anne
(1665–1714)
m.
Prince George
of Denmark
(1653–1708)

Mary II
(1662–94)
m.
William of Orange
(William III)
(1650–1702)

Prologue – into Exile

I call to God to witness that I go not on my own motive; but
if I stay in the kingdom I am very well informed of my destiny,
and that no king ever came out of the Tower but to his grave.

James II[1]

In the small hours of 23 December 1688, a tall, thin, middle-aged man and an equally tall youth, accompanied by two other men, stole out from the backdoor of a large house in Rochester High Street. In the darkness, the little group crept silently through the garden, then down to the River Medway, where a small boat was waiting.

Rowing out into the estuary they hoisted the sail but found wind and tide against them, so for a time they took refuge on board a man-of-war whose captain could be trusted. It was evening before they reached their destination, a big sloop called the *Henrietta*, with a skipper who was also a naval officer. He set sail immediately.

The tall man was King James II and VII, who would never again set foot on English or Scots soil, and the youth was his natural son, James FitzJames, Duke of Berwick. The other two were courtiers.

The king had left a note, written just before he fled, *His Majesties Reasons for Withdrawing Himself from Rochester*, which at his wish was printed and published soon after. In it he complains of his son-in-law (and nephew) William of Orange replacing his Whitehall guards by Dutch troops, then 'sending to me at One a Clock, after Midnight, when I was in Bed, a kind of an Order by three Lords, to begone out of mine own Palace before Twelve, that same Morning'. How can he feel his life is safe with a man who treats him like this, who says he does not believe the Prince of Wales is the king's son, who makes him appear 'as black as Hell to my own People, and to all the World besides'?

He explains that he is leaving his kingdom 'to be within call whenever the Nation's Eyes shall be opened', when he hopes a new Parliament will agree to 'Liberty of Conscience for all Protestant Dissenters; and that those of my own [Catholic] Perswasion may be so far considered and have such a share of it, as they may live peaceably and quietly as Englishmen and Christians'.

Yet this was the policy – too tolerant rather than intolerant – that had led to his downfall.

For many, the moment when the *Henrietta* sailed for France with King James on board marked the end of Britain's rule by her ancient, natural and rightful line of sovereigns. It was also the beginning of Jacobitism.

Introduction:
Jacobites – English, Scots and Irish

. . . if thou wilt restore me and mine to the Ancient rights and
glory of my Predecessours.

King Charles I, *Eikon Basilike*[1]

The Jacobites were men and women who refused to accept the 'Glorious'
Revolution of 1688 in which William of Orange deposed James II. For
seventy years, English, Scots and Irish, did their best to restore the wronged
House of Stuart – first James, then his son, and then his grandson.

The events of 1688 were not so much a revolution as an aristocratic coup
d'etat that ended in a one-party state while, far from always trying to set
the clock back, the Jacobites came to offer an escape from rule by a corrupt
oligarchy. Until forty years ago they were dismissed as a handful of kilted
anachronisms from the wilder areas of the Celtic Fringe. Nowadays they are
taken much more seriously, but the new insights are restricted to academics.

Most recent books about the Jacobite movement have concentrated on
the rising of 1745–6 that ended at Culloden, but these fail to tell the whole
story in England, Scotland and Ireland, from James II's flight in 1688 until his
grandson Henry IXs death in 1807. This is to omit the context that explains
the Jacobites' motivation.

Their cause involved the entire British Isles, and if English, Scots and Irish
Jacobites had somewhat different aims, they were all part of the same movement. Because of Scotland's heroic contribution they are often seen as purely
Scottish, ignoring the Irish war of 1689–91 and plans for risings in England and
Ireland that were on the cards until well into the 1750s. Too many historians
tend to forget that the Jacobites of each kingdom (and in a diaspora reaching
from Russia to America) had the same objective – a Stuart Restoration.

Support for their would-be counter-revolution was underestimated by
historians who until the late twentieth century failed to recognise their

importance over many decades in British politics. Contemporaries did not make the same mistake. In 1738 Robert Walpole warned the House of Commons that Jacobites 'are, I am afraid, more numerous than most gentlemen imagine'. They were taken very seriously indeed by the major European powers – the policies of the first two Georges in Germany ensuring that Hanover never lacked for enemies abroad. France, Spain, Sweden, Russia and Prussia all contemplated restoring the Stuarts – France considered restoring them in Ireland as late as 1796.

The Jacobite movement should be seen as the saga it was – a tale of loyalty and hope, yet in the end of bitter disillusion, lived by men and women who sacrificed all they had to restore the banished royal family. Few causes have aroused a more gallant response from the peoples of these islands than the Honest Cause, whether they were fighting for it at Killiecrankie, Prestonpans or Culloden, at the Boyne, Aughrim or Fontenoy, or dying for it on the scaffold.

To understand them better, I have written from a Jacobite perspective, which is why instead of 'Pretenders' I refer to the 'kings over the water' as 'James III', 'Charles III' ('Bonnie Prince Charlie') and 'Henry IX', as their supporters called them. The book's sub-title, *A Complete History of the Jacobites*, has been chosen to show that it deals with support for the exiled sovereigns in England and Ireland as well as in Scotland, but does not imply that Jacobitism ended at Henry's death in 1807. Even if no subsequent Head of the House of Stuart has ever claimed the throne, for a handful of diehards the cause is still alive today.

Chronology

1688

September   The Nine Years War begins
November   'The Protestant Wind' – William of Orange invades England
December   James II flees to France

1689

February   William and Mary declared King and Queen of England
March   James II lands in Ireland with French troops
William and Mary declared King and Queen of Scots
April   Jacobites besiege Derry
In Scotland Viscount Dundee begins the Highland War
May   James II summons the 'Patriot Parliament' at Dublin
July   Jacobite victory at Killiecrankie – but Dundee is killed
Derry relieved
August   Marshal Schomberg invades Ulster
Scottish Jacobites defeated at Dunkeld
November   Schomberg retreats from Dundalk

1690

February   Nonjuror priests and bishops deprived in England
May   Jacobite army defeated at the Haugh of Cromdale
June   William III invades Ulster
June   Williamite fleet defeated by French at Beachy Head
July   James II's Irish army defeated at the Boyne by
     William III
King James flees to France
August   William III besieges Limerick
After four weeks, William abandons the siege

1691

January	English Jacobite plot discovered – execution of John Ashton
July	Irish Jacobites defeated by Ginkel at Aughrim
August	Ginkel begins second Siege of Limerick
October	Limerick surrenders
	Treaty of Limerick ends the Jacobite war in Ireland
	End of Scotland's Highland War

1692

February	Massacre of the MacDonalds of Glencoe
May	French invasion fleet defeated at La Hogue

1694

December	Death of Mary II – William III reigns alone

1696

February	Discovery of English Jacobite plot to murder William

1697

January	Execution of Sir John Fenwick
September	Treaty of Ryswick – Louis XIV recognises William as King of Great Britain
	End of the Nine Years War

1701

April	Act of Succession – Hanover family become heirs to the throne
September	Death of James II – Louis XIV recognises James III and VIII

1702

March	Abjuration Act – compulsory oath denying claims of James III
	Death of William III, succeeded by Queen Anne
	England and Scotland enter the War of the Spanish Succession

1705

August   Colonel Hooke's mission to assess Jacobite support in
              Scotland

1706

December   Scots Parliament passes Act of Union with England

1707

January   Act of Union ratified by Parliament
April   Hooke's second mission to Scotland – to organise a rising

1708

March   James III and VIII's invasion fleet fails to land in Scotland

1710

February   Trial of the High Tory Dr Sacheverell – riots in London
October   Election – Tories win majority in House of Commons

1711

October   Articles of London – Britain makes peace with France

1713

April   Treaty of Utrecht signed – end of War of the Spanish
              Succession

1714

March   James III refuses to convert to Anglicanism
August   Death of Queen Anne, succeeded by George of Hanover

1715

March   Lord Bolingbroke escapes to France
September   Death of Louis XIV, the Jacobites' most powerful friend
              Earl of Mar proclaims King James III and VIII
October   English Jacobites proclaim James king in Northumberland
              West Country Jacobites fail to rise
November   Battle of Preston – English and Scots Jacobites surrender
              Battle of Sheriffmuir – Mar misses his chance

1716

January	James III and VIII lands at Peterhead and joins Mar's army
	Jacobites abandon Perth
February	James returns to France, accompanied by Mar
March	James moves his court to Avignon

1717

February	James leaves Avignon for Italy
	Swedish plot to invade England discovered
May	King James establishes his court at Urbino
June	Duke of Ormonde asks Tsar Peter to help James

1718

March	James betrothed to Princess Clementina Sobieska
May	Death of Queen Mary of Modena
October	Princess Clementina arrested en route for her marriage

1719

March	Spanish armada to restore James driven back by storms
April	Earl Marischal's expedition lands on Lewis – the Nineteen
	Captain Wogan rescues Princess Clementina
June	Jacobite defeat at Glenshiel – end of the Nineteen
September	James III marries Princess Clementina

1720

August	South Sea 'Bubble' bursts – George I makes a scandalous profit
December	Birth at Rome of Charles Edward Stuart, Prince of Wales

1721

April	Sir Robert Walpole becomes Prime Minister
Spring	Christopher Layer visits King James in Rome

1722

May	Discovery of Bishop Atterbury's plot to restore James

1723

May	Christopher Layer executed for treason
	Bishop Atterbury banished

1725

March   Birth in Rome of Henry, Duke of York

1727

June   Death of George I, succeeded by George II

1731

January   Lord Cornbury visits his cousin King James in Rome

1733

March   Uproar over Walpole's Excise Bill
June   The Cornbury Plot to restore James III
November   France refuses to support the Cornbury Plot

1735

January   Death of Queen Clementina

1736

September   Porteous Riots – Jacobite involvement suspected

1739

October   War of Jenkins' Ear between Britain and Spain begins

1740

December   War of the Austrian Succession begins

1742

February   Sir Robert Walpole resigns the premiership

1743

January   Death of Cardinal Fleury, opponent of Jacobitism

1744

February   The Forty-Four? French invasion fleet wrecked by storms

1745

April   Irish Brigade takes a leading role in France's victory at
                    Fontenoy

July	The Forty-Five – Prince Charles sails for Scotland
August	Standard of James III and VIII raised at Glenfinnan
September	Prince Charles captures Edinburgh
	Jacobites destroy Cope's army at Prestonpans
November	Charles and his Jacobite army invade England
December	Jacobite army begins retreat to Scotland at Derby

1746

January	Jacobite army defeats General Hawley at Falkirk
April	Jacobites defeated at Culloden by Cumberland
Summer	Charles hunted through the Highlands
September	Charles reaches France in safety

1747

| June | Henry, Duke of York, becomes a cardinal |

1748

October	Treaty of Aix-la-Chapelle
November	Charles arrested in Paris – agrees to leave France
December	Charles goes to papal territory at Avignon

1749

| February | Charles returns to Paris in secret |

1750

| September | Charles meets English Jacobite leaders in London |
| | Charles joins the (nonjuring) Church of England |

1751

| February | Charles meets Frederick II of Prussia in Berlin |

1752

| June | Clementina Walkinshaw goes to live with Charles |

1753

| March | Betrayal of Elibank Plot by the spy 'Pickle' |
| June | Dr Archibald Cameron executed – last Jacobite execution |

1754

April   Prince Charles quarrels with the English Jacobites

1756

May   Outbreak of the Seven Years War

1759

February   The Fifty-Nine? France plans to restore James III
November   French invasion fleet destroyed at Quiberon Bay

1760

October   Death of George II, succeeded by George III

1766

January   Death of James III and VIII, succeeded by Charles III
                 Papacy refuses to recognise Charles as king

1772

April   Charles marries Louise of Stolberg, the last Stuart queen

1774

October   Charles establishes his court in Florence

1775

April   Tensions erupt into the American Revolution
                 Charles declines to become king in North America

1780

December   Queen Louise flees from Charles

1783

December   Charles visited by Gustav III of Sweden

1784

June   Charles creates his daughter Charlotte, Duchess of Albany

1785

December   Charles returns to Rome

1788

January   Death of Charles III, succeeded by Henry IX

1789

November   Death of Charlotte, Duchess of Albany

1807

July   Death of Henry IX, the last Stuart of the royal line

1824

January   Death of Countess of Albany (the Dowager Queen Louise)

PART ONE

James II – The Lost Throne

1

James, Duke of York – Heir to the Throne?

This is the heir; come let us kill him, and seize on his inheritance.

Matthew, xxi:33

History is full of wicked uncles who rob a nephew of his inheritance. Wicked nephews are rarer. The outstanding example is William, Prince of Orange, who stole the crown of Great Britain from his mother's brother, King James II – not only his uncle but his father-in-law.

Early in autumn 1677 Princess Mary, elder daughter of James, Duke of York, who was the heir to the throne, burst into tears when told she must marry her cousin William. She cried until bedtime and all next day. Fifteen years old, her only education other than embroidery had been to play the spinet, apart from reading her Bible and that pious work *The Whole Duty of Man*. Although brought up as a Protestant by command of her uncle Charles II, she did not want to leave her Catholic father and stepmother.

Twelve years older than Mary, four our inches shorter, skeletal, round-shouldered, eagle-nosed and racked by asthma, William seldom spoke and rarely smiled. Even Bishop Burnet, who admired him, deplored his coldness and reserve. Despite a Stuart mother, his English was poor, and he spoke with a thick Dutch accent. Nevertheless, the marriage took place in November.

Three years before, the French ambassador had told Mary's father to fear such a marriage as he feared death – warning that the Prince of Orange would one day become England's idol and take away his crown. When that day came, James quoted a line from the Bible: 'I repent that I gave my daughter to him for he sought to slay me.'[1]

Protestant inheritance, Catholic heir

As a boy James had been imprisoned by Parliament, escaping just before the execution of his father Charles I in 1649. In exile, service with the French army under the great Marshal Turenne taught him to think in terms of military discipline for the rest of his life. He took part in the savage skirmishes in and around Paris that crushed the Fronde – France's last challenge to absolutism before the Revolution.

Soon after the Restoration, in 1660, he married Anne Hyde, the daughter of his brother Charles II's chief minister, the Earl of Clarendon, by whom he had two children – Mary, who married the Prince of Orange, and Anne, who married Prince George of Denmark. Two years after the death of his first wife in 1671, he took a new one, Mary of Modena.

In 1676 he became a Catholic, but in secret. Four years later, however, he told his friend George Legge that he could no longer hide his religion and had resolved by God's grace never to do so damnable a thing. If helpful in the next world, such firmness would be a handicap in this one.

His conversion was greeted with a horror that found expression in the Popish Plot of 1678. This was an imaginary conspiracy invented by Titus Oates who claimed that, bankrolled by Spain, the Pope and the Jesuits were about to invade England, kill King Charles and every Protestant, and put James on the throne. Forty innocent Catholics went to the scaffold. During what became known as 'the Exclusion Crisis' of 1679–81, the Whigs, who used the plot to dominate the House of Commons, passed a bill to stop James from succeeding his brother. If he became king, 'a total change of religion within these kingdoms would ensue'.

Seventeenth-century England's fear of Catholicism cannot be exaggerated – the nearest modern parallel is Islamophobia. On 5 November, 'Gunpowder Treason Day', parsons thanked God for saving 'our Church and State from the secret contrivances and hellish malice of Popish Conspirators'. The recent Fire of London was supposedly among the contrivances, while people still shuddered at the memory of the fires of Smithfield lit by Bloody Mary, terrifyingly recalled in Foxe's *Booke of Martyrs*, or at how Irish Catholics had massacred Protestants in 1641. It was easy for them to believe that there really had been a Popish Plot.

Catholics formed two per cent of the population at most (if 25 per cent in some areas of Lancashire), but included a fifth of the peerage and a tenth of the gentry, which made them seem more numerous than they really were. These 'recusants' kept secret chapels in their manor houses – the only places other than embassies where Mass could be heard – insisting on their tenants and servants being Catholics too. A tenant farmer or kitchen maid with a grudge might ruin them by reporting the presence of a chaplain. They also ran a highly efficient network for smuggling priests into the country and moving them from one safe house to another, and for sending children to be educated abroad.

Despite the dread of Catholics, eventually their more level-headed fellow countrymen saw through Titus Oates's lies, realising that the Popish Plot had never existed. The Tories (as they were starting to be known) grew alarmed by Whig ambitions, and the Lords threw out the Exclusion Bill. Once again James was heir to the throne.

In his portraits, James's hatchet-face with its lantern jaw is stiff and humourless. So was the man. Yet his arch-critic Gilbert Burnet thought him truthful, loyal and fair minded, if 'bred with strange notions of the obedience due to princes'.[2] He inspired respect among many who met him. 'I do affirm he was the most honest and sincere man I ever knew, a great and good Englishman', wrote the Earl of Ailesbury, one of his gentlemen in waiting.[3] The diarist John Evelyn agreed, declaring he was somebody on whose word you could rely, while Samuel Pepys, who worked with James at the Admiralty, always remained a devoted supporter.

Frequently harsh, James did have a kindly side. When he became king, learning that the dramatist William Wycherley had spent seven years in a debtor's prison, he paid Wycherley's debts and gave him a pension of £200 because he had so much enjoyed his play *The Plain Dealer*.

James's second wife, Mary of Modena, fifteen years old when they married, was a great beauty, with dark Italian eyes, jet black hair and a shapely figure, who, despite shedding tears on first seeing him, grew to love him deeply. High-spirited, intelligent, fluent in English, French and Latin, she developed into a Catholic of the narrow sort, beloved by Papists but loathed by Protestants.

Mary's devotion to James was surprising since he was unfaithful. During his first marriage he had had two sons by the pale, sharp-witted Arabella Churchill, the elder of whom was created Duke of Berwick. In 1680 Catherine Sedley, even plainer and notable only for a wit as savage as Nell Gwynne's and making her lover feel sinful', became his main mistress. James's brother laughed that his women were so ugly that the priests must have given them to him as a penance. To be fair, someone who saw Arabella's legs when she fell off her horse could not believe that 'such exquisite limbs' belonged to Miss Churchill's face.

James's other amusement was horses and hounds. Pursuing the fox instead of the hare, he enjoyed hard riding as much as hound work and pioneered English fox hunting. When in London he went to the theatre, but without the same enthusiasm as his brother.

A Tory Church of England

During Charles II's last years, when the Whigs were a broken faction, the old Cavalier party or Tories (which meant most landed gentry and Anglican clergy) rallied to James as heir to the throne. They saw him as a bulwark against another Civil War and, despite his Catholicism, as a defender of their Church.

An attractive form of Christianity, with its dignified liturgy, scholar divines and parson poets, a shared persecution during the Civil War and the Interregnum had endeared the Church of England to the Cavalier gentry, who had sheltered its priests, heard its outlawed services and taken its Sacrament at their manor houses behind locked doors. At the Restoration in 1660, 'Church and King' had become every Tory squire's slogan.

The Church of England presided over the nation's faith and morals. As most academics, schoolmasters and tutors were Churchmen, it largely shaped public opinion, with even the humblest parson's sermon making an impact since everybody was bound by law to attend their parish church on Sunday. In its modest way it was almost as intolerant as the Church of Rome, loathing the Dissenters who had harried it during the Interregnum (that period of Republican rule between Charles I and II), seeing Quakers as lunatics and Papists as tools of the devil. Furthermore, a 'Test Act' proscribed that no non-Anglican could hold municipal office or become a Justice of the Peace unless he had taken Communion in his parish church, with the result that local government was monopolised by the Tory gentry.

Significantly the Anglican clergy had developed a cult of the Stuarts, commemorating the anniversary of His Sacred Majesty Charles I's martyrdom. Some, it was said, spoke less in their sermons about Jesus Christ than they did about the Royal Martyr. They preached 'passive obedience' – that disobedience to a king could never be justified under any circumstances. Whosoever wore the crown was holy. As 'The Vicar of Bray' recalls,

Unto my Flock I daily Preach'd,
Kings are by God appointed,
And Damn'd are those who dare resist,
Or touch the Lord's Anointed.

Not only parsons thought like this. So did Tory squires, sons of the Cavaliers, who, even when questioning royal policy, regarded the monarchy as an inviolable inheritance bestowed by God.

2

King James II and VII,
1685–1688

When Royal James possest the Crown
And Popery grew in fashion

'The Vicar of Bray'

James became king following the death of his brother, Charles II, in February 1685, and was crowned at Westminster Abbey on 23 April by Archbishop Sancroft of Canterbury, swearing to defend the Church of England though declining to take Communion. The coronation service was magnificent, with noble music that included anthems by Blow and Purcell. But there were ill omens. Too big, the crown slipped down over the king's face and the canopy borne above him collapsed. Even so, both Houses of Parliament seemed devoted to their new sovereign. A thanksgiving service was added to the Book of Common Prayer for 'the day when His Majesty began his happy reign'.

Two failed rebellions

In April, the Earl of Argyll, who had been sentenced to death in 1681 for treason but had escaped, returned to Scotland and tried to raise a rebellion with a few hundred men, sending round the 'fiery cross' (a burning cross at the sight of which clansmen were supposed to make ready for war). He did not deign to say whom he wanted as king, merely flying a banner inscribed 'No Popery'. Few joined him, not even Cameronian fanatics (Scottish Covenantors who followed the teachings of the Presbyterian Richard Cameron). His rising was speedily crushed and on 30 June 1685 at Edinburgh's Mercat Cross he died face upward beneath the 'maiden' – a Scottish forerunner of the guillotine.

Argyll had intended his rising to coincide with a rebellion by James, Duke of Monmouth, Charles II's natural son. A glamorous if shallow figure, whom at one time some had hoped might become king, Monmouth landed at Lyme Regis on 11 June to raise a force of West Country peasants. Declaring that he had a better right to the crown, he called his uncle James a usurper and accused him of planning to destroy Protestantism, poisoning King Charles and starting the Fire of London.

England rallied to James, however, and the duke's motley army was cut to pieces by Lord Churchill at Sedgemoor on 6 July. The duke himself was swiftly caught, tried, condemned and beheaded. Many of his followers were punished without mercy by Judge Jeffreys in the ensuing 'Bloody Assizes'.

Both rebellions had been feeble affairs, but James was uneasy, doubling his army to 20,000 men. He also recruited Catholic officers whom he dispensed from the Test Act that forced them to take the Anglican Sacrament and deny transubstantiation. When Parliament protested, he prorogued it with an angry speech, the first sign that in the teeth of most Englishmen's disapproval he favoured Papists. 'My dear Lord, who could be the framer of this speech?', old Lord Bellasis, a Catholic, asked his kinsman the Earl of Ailesbury. 'I date my ruin and that of all my persuasion from this day.'[1]

A Catholic yet tolerant king

In late autumn 1685 Huguenots began to flee from Louis XIV's persecution, and although James referred publicly to 'barbarous cruelties used in France against the Protestants', few Englishmen accepted his disapproval at face value. It was doubly unfortunate that persecution across the Channel should coincide with a more public expression of his faith by the king, who now went daily with great pomp to Mass in the queen's chapel at St James's – and then to a new Catholic chapel at Whitehall that opened its doors on Christmas Day 1686.

He forbade the fining of recusants for non-attendance at Anglican services and appointed a Jesuit, Sir Edward Petre, as Clerk of the Closet, the royal household's senior clerical post. An Essex baronet whose life James had saved during the Popish Plot, Fr Petre was a vain mediocrity. The king appointed another Jesuit, John Warner, as his spiritual adviser. To control his womanising (Sedley having been pensioned off), Fr Warner made him practise the

Jesuit 'Exercises', whose terrifying meditation on Hell may have contributed to his later nervous collapse.

Encouraged by Petre, James started appointing Catholic peers to the Privy Council, and early in 1687 he dismissed his Protestant brothers-in-law, the Earls of Clarendon and Rochester, from their posts as Lord Lieutenant of Ireland and Lord Treasurer. Catholic schools and chapels opened in London, and monks, friars and Jesuits were seen wearing their habits.

In contrast, Protestant prelates could be roughly treated. In summer 1686 Henry Compton, Bishop of London, already deprived of his place on the Privy Council and his post as Dean of the Chapel Royal, was suspended by Judge Jeffreys's new Commission for Ecclesiastical Causes for refusing to discipline a parson who preached anti-Catholic sermons. A tough ex-cavalry officer, Compton was a dangerous enemy.

Yet, save for Petre and the Earl of Faversham, Protestants still held the main household offices. Nor was anybody dismissed because of his or her religion; Protestants in the household outnumbered Catholics by eighteen to one. Catholic gentlemen who applied for court posts were told there were no vacancies.[2]

Nonetheless, James's Whitehall felt like a Catholic court. Each morning he processed with the queen to hear Mass in the new Chapel Royal, and if there were not many Papists in the household, there were plenty of Papist courtiers. When Sir William Trumbull, recalled from being ambassador in Paris, went to the king's *lever* in 1686, he found him 'in his nightgown at the fireside with a company of Irish and unknown faces, so that the only person in the room I had ever seen was my old Lord Craven'.[3]

A Catholic adviser, who as an Irishman was disliked even more than Fr Petre, Colonel Richard Talbot from Kildare was a veteran from the mid-century Irish wars. He had survived the Drogheda massacre when Parliamentarian forces under Oliver Cromwell stormed the besieged city, killing most of the garrison and numerous civilians, and had been arrested for plotting to murder Cromwell – who personally interrogated him – but escaped, and went on to serve with James in the army of Marshal Turenne. A tall, charming womaniser, gambler and duellist called 'Fighting Dick' by his friends but 'Lying Dick' by those whom he crossed, he was clever and ruthless. Created Earl of Tyrconnell and commander-in-chief of the Irish army, with James's encouragement he began replacing Protestant officers across the Irish Sea with Catholics.

The Lord President of the Council, the handsome Earl of Sunderland who turned Catholic purely to curry favour with James, was no less detested. Fawning on those above him, a bully to those below, without principles, loyalty or gratitude, he cynically encouraged the king to ignore criticism. 'Pen cannot describe worse of him than he deserved', wrote Ailesbury.[4]

There was a growing suspicion that besides planning to force everyone to convert, King James intended to copy Louis XIV and make Britain an absolute monarchy – in popular thinking, 'arbitrary government' went hand in hand with Popery.

Moreover, on becoming queen, Mary of Modena had developed an intolerant streak. Anyone who refused to change their religion she thought either stupid or perverse, and she threw hairbrushes at Protestant ladies of the court unable to accept her arguments in favour of the One True Faith.

Yet in 1685 James had granted the Jewish community in London freedom to practise their religion. Early in 1687 he issued a declaration of indulgence in Scotland that allowed Catholics to hear Mass, hitherto a crime punishable by death on a third offence.

He then came up with a plan for England that in its day was breathtaking. This was to ally with Dissenters (Presbyterians, Baptists, Congregationalists, Independents or Quakers), who like Catholics suffered restrictions on worship and were excluded from public office by the Test Acts. Accordingly, in April 1687 he issued a Declaration of Liberty of Conscience for his English subjects. While admitting he would prefer everybody to be a Catholic, he declared, 'matters ought not to be constrained nor people forced in matters of mere religion'. Promising to protect the Church of England, James gave everyone 'leave to meet and serve God after their own way and manner' in private houses or chapels. Nobody need take the oaths previously required for public office.

The plan was entirely his own idea. 'Our Blessed Saviour whipt people out of the Temple, but I never heard he commanded any should be forced into it', he later told his son. 'I make no doubt if once Liberty of Conscience be well fixed, many conversions [to Catholicism] will ensue.' His motive was not so much tolerance as a desire to win people over to his Church.[5] 'James did not fill the gaols of London over the course of his reign; he emptied them, with two successive [general] pardons in March 1686 and September 1688', the historian Scott Sowerby stresses. 'He extended individual pardons to many of the dissidents who had fled to exile in the Netherlands at the end of his brother's reign.'[6]

Whatever the Declaration's merits, his tactlessness and inability to grasp legal argument were grave handicaps. Yet it attracted supporters in modest numbers from all the Nonconformist sects, whom the king asked for advice. They included the Baptist (and ex-Cromwellian colonel) Benjamin Sawley, the Presbyterian Vincent Alsop, the Congregationalist Stephen Lobb and the Quaker Sir William Penn. There were even one or two High Churchmen, such as Thomas Cartwright, Bishop of Chester and Denis Granville, Dean of Durham, although they were inspired by loyalty rather than thirst for toleration.

Between April 1687 and October 1688, 200 public addresses, mainly from the sorely persecuted Baptists and Quakers, were sent to the king, thanking him for the Declaration, all of which were printed in the *London Gazette*. Only six came from Anglicans while most Presbyterians, who made up the majority of Dissenters, rejected it. But Lord Halifax was too cynical in cautioning 'You are therefore to be hugged now only that you may be the better squeezed at another time.'[7] James was absolutely sincere.[8]

Anglicans, clerical and lay, who disliked Dissenters almost as much as they did Papists, were outraged by the denial of their role as national Church. When the Prayer Book blamed the Great Rebellion on 'traitorous, heady and high-minded men who under the pretence of Religion ... contrived and well-nigh effected the utter destruction of this Church and Kingdom', it meant Dissenters. Abolishing the Test Act would deprive the Tory gentry of their monopoly of local government.

James made matters worse by aggressively promoting his co-religionists. He installed Papists as masters or fellows of colleges at Oxford and Cambridge, appointed others to high public office and made Petre a privy councillor when most Englishmen regarded Jesuits as devils in human form. In 1685, a Papal Nuncio, Count D'Adda, was received in state. 'Dada' reported to Rome when Lord Rochester was sacked that 'rumour runs among the people how the minister was ejected for not being Catholic and opposing the extermination of Protestantism'. The Pope advised moderation. So did Lords Bellasis and Arundel, two sensible Catholic privy councillors who favoured dropping the Penal Laws but keeping the Test Act.

The king would not compromise. In April 1688 he re-issued the Declaration of Liberty of Conscience, ordering it to be read from every pulpit. Archbishop Sancroft of Canterbury and six other prelates told him, deferentially but firmly, that they could not allow this. In response, he sent them to the Tower of London to await trial for sedition – although the penalty they faced was not imprisonment but a fine.

To obtain a Parliament that would repeal the Test Acts, he planned to create sixty new peers and tried to find biddable MPs by pressuring the relatively few voters to elect the Crown's candidates. This was to be done in the shires by lord lieutenants, and in towns and cities by the corporations, a high proportion of whose members were Dissenters. Many lord lieutenants resigned in protest.

On 30 June the 'Seven Bishops' tried for seditious libel were acquitted amid wild rejoicing. Even the royal army camped on Hounslow Heath cheered. Nonetheless, everybody thought a French invasion was coming soon and that they would forced to convert to Catholicism or have their throats cut by Irish soldiers.

3

The Dutch Invasion, 1688

A great king, who had a good army and a strong fleet, did
choose rather to abandon all, than to expose himself to any
danger with that part of the army that was still firm to him, or
stay and see the issue of a parliament

Bishop Burnet, *History of his Own Times*[1]

On 10 June 1688 the queen gave birth to a Prince of Wales, James Francis
Edward Stuart, who replaced Princess Mary as heir to the throne. The king
saw this as a sign of divine approval. His subjects did not, horrified by the
prospect of another Popish monarch.

A rumour circulated that the baby was an impostor, smuggled into
Whitehall in a warming pan, and even the level-headed Burnet suspected
the queen of pretending to bear a child out of jealousy of her stepdaughters.
The painter Sir Godfrey Kneller demolished the story, but not until 1697.
'Vat de devil, de Prince of Wales the son of a brickbatt woman?' he cried. 'Be
Got, it is a lie! . . . His fader and moder have sat to me about thirty-six times
a-piece, and I know every line and bit in their faces. I say, the child is so like
them both that there is not a feature in his face but what belongs to father
and mother.'[2]

Even so, the 'warming-pan theory' was widely believed. Among those who
credited it was the king's younger daughter, Princess Anne – she wrote to her
elder sister Mary across the North Sea, convincing her that the story was true.

The secret enemy – William of Orange

One quarter from which the king never anticipated danger was Holland. He
was on excellent terms with his nephew, even if he resented William giving

refuge to the troublesome Burnet, who had gone into exile in 1685. Nor did he chide him for an affair with one of his daughter's ladies in waiting, Elizabeth Villiers. The two men regularly exchanged letters. Meanwhile Dyckvelt, the Dutch States General's envoy and William's agent, was secretly encouraging the English to see William as their saviour. Eventually, a group known as the 'Immortal Seven', which included men of great influence – such as the Earl of Danby, once Charles II's key adviser, and Bishop Compton – wrote to the prince, asking him to come and rescue Protestant England.

Desperate to save Europe from French domination, William, who feared that his father-in-law might go to Louis XIV's aid with his new army, had been planning to invade England since 1687. The Nine Years War broke out in 1688, tying up Louis's forces in Germany. The Seven's letter gave him his cue, and he assembled an invasion force.

Still euphoric after the Prince of Wales's birth, James refused to believe his nephew would attack him until the Dutch fleet set sail in October. He panicked, begging the bishops to tell England they supported their king. In response they demanded that he enforce the Penal Laws and the Test Act, and call a free Parliament. He agreed, but rushed in more Irish troops. Then, learning that William's ships had been driven back by gales, he cancelled the writs for a Parliament and his concessions.

During these weeks 'God Save the King' (modelled on a French anthem in praise of Louis XIV) was sung for the first time at the St James's Palace chapel. It remained a Stuart anthem for over half a century.[3] 'Send him victorious' became a cry for help when news arrived that his nephew's invasion was coming after all.

On 5 November a 'Protestant Wind' blew William's fleet, bigger than any Spanish armada, into Torbay with 15,000 Dutch, German and Swiss troops. William spent a week at Exeter, finding horses for his cavalry, but James failed to attack. The Dutchman announced that he came to save the religion, laws and liberties of England – 'not only we ourselves, but all good subjects of these Kingdoms, do vehemently suspect the pretended Prince of Wales was not born by the Queen.' Then he led his army towards London.

James's army had grown to 35,000, twice the size of his son-in-law's, led by professionals from whom political unreliables had supposedly been weeded out. He might have won had he entrusted command to General John Churchill instead of the inept Earl of Faversham, and had Churchill stayed loyal.[4] But at Salisbury he was struck down by a nose bleed lasting for three days. He behaved so oddly that some observers thought he was suffering from a tumour on the brain.

Senior officers went over to the enemy. Crucially, they included Churchill and – not such a loss – James's other son-in-law, George of Denmark, who was soon joined by Princess Anne. Hoping to make a stand on the Thames, the king retreated. Finally he lost his nerve altogether and took refuge at Whitehall. His breakdown is unlikely to have been syphilis, as has been sometimes suggested, but was probably a minor stroke or mental collapse – or both. Belated awareness of the incompetence of his commander-in-chief, Faversham, may have contributed, even his confessor's warnings of fire and brimstone.[5]

Reinforced every day by English recruits, William's army advanced towards London under strict discipline; there was no looting. On 7 December William reached Hungerford, a little market town on the Berkshire–Wiltshire border, where he waited at the Bear Hotel, giving no hint of his plans. He guessed that James's nerve would break.

Abandoned by those whom he trusted, even by his children, his army disintegrating, rebellion everywhere, the City in uproar, James called a meeting of all privy councillors and peers in London. They told him to negotiate with William, whose terms were surprisingly moderate. Protestants must take command of the Tower and all fortresses, Parliament must be called with neither side's army within twenty miles of London while it sat, and when William came to London he must have the same number of guards as the king.

James called a new Parliament for January 1689, convinced it would undo all he had done for Catholics. He thought that if he stayed, he might at best keep his throne, but only as 'a Duke of Venice', with the Prince of Wales declared a bastard or brought up a Protestant and destined for Hell. Or he might end in the Tower. He had surely read what his father wrote in *Eikon Basilike* – 'there are but few steps between the Prisons and Graves of Princes'.[6] He ordered the queen to leave for France secretly with their son, preparing his own escape.

Flight

Confident that loyal officers could muster 3,000 horse and even more foot, on 10 December Lord Ailesbury begged James not to flee but to march north, brushing aside 'broomsticks and whishtail militia', and go to Scotland, where 'that kingdom will be entirely yours'. (On his deathbed, James sent Ailesbury a message in which he wishes he 'had never rendered my soul to God my Creator in a foreign country'.)

At 3 a.m. on 11 December 1688 James left his Whitehall bedroom through a secret passage and crossed the Thames by wherry to Lambeth, purposefully dropping the Great Seal in the river. Relays of fast horses took him to a ship bound for France. However, it ran aground on the Kentish coast and was boarded by a mob of fishermen who mistook him for 'a hatchet-faced Jesuit'. He was stripped to his shirt and searched, and had tobacco smoke blown in his face.

Rescued by Lord Ailesbury, he returned to London. As his coach drove to Whitehall he was cheered by the crowds, who thought his presence would guarantee law and order and save them from having their throats cut by Irish soldiers – who were rumoured to be approaching. Momentarily he was so reassured that he thought he might keep his throne.

Learning that William had installed himself at Windsor Castle, James sent Lord Faversham to invite him to London and to talk – he could use St James's Palace as headquarters and bring as many troops as he liked. William, who by now had no intention of parleying, put Faversham under arrest, then ordered his cousin, Count Solms, to take the Dutch Blue Guards to London and occupy Whitehall.

The Earl of Craven, who commanded the Coldstream Guards on duty at the palace, begged the king to let them defend it to the last man, but James refused, and they were replaced by Dutchmen. Placed under arrest, the king was told he must go to Ham House (his manor beside the Thames at Richmond), but asked to go to Rochester instead. Guessing why, William, who wanted him out of the country as fast as possible, granted his request. The back door of the house where he was kept was deliberately left unguarded.

After dinner on 22 December, James told Ailesbury, who had escorted him to Rochester, that if he stayed in England, 'I shall certainly be sent to the Tower, and no king ever went out of that place but to his grave.' He was leaving to save his life. 'Can you advise me to stay?' When Ailesbury said he did not dare to give an opinion, the king embraced him in a tacit farewell.[7]

The future Bishop Burnet, who accompanied William on his invasion, believed James had been destroyed by the 'spiteful humours of a revengeful Italian lady' (the queen) and 'the ill laid, and worse managed, projects of some hot meddling priests'.[8]

Ailesbury differed, commenting that the king was ruined by 'a fool and a knave'. 'God damn Father Petre!' he heard Mr Dixie, the royal coachman, cry 'with bloody oaths' as he whipped on his horses after the king's downfall. 'I said to him, "Dixie, what harm hath he done you?" "Damn him!", he replied again, "but for him we had not been here." He spoke so much truth that I had not the force to chide him.'[9] If Petre was the fool, the knave was Sunderland who, when asked why he gave James disastrous counsels, 'replied with a sneer that but for those counsels the Prince of Orange had never landed and succeeded'.[10]

For all the talk of 'revolution principles' and 'liberty', the real reason why James lost his throne was England's neurotic terror of Catholicism, a terror exploited by ambitious politicians.

4

Revolution or Old Truth?

Old Principles I did revoke,
Set Conscience at a Distance

'The Vicar of Bray'

On Christmas morning, off the French coast near Boulogne, a frigate hailed an English sloop and asked for news of the King of England. In the dark the only man on deck shouted back, 'I *am* the King of England.' About 6 a.m., after a stormy voyage, he landed at the tiny port of Ambleteuse. His wife (who had left Whitehall disguised as a laundress) and his son had suffered an even more wretched journey.

They were pleasantly surprised by Louis XIV's welcome and their new palace, the château of St Germain-en-Laye, a few miles west of Paris – the greatest château in France after Versailles. Richly furnished, in lovely country, it made a sumptuous refuge. Louis gave them £45,000 a year, with £10,000 for immediate expenses, treating them as reigning sovereigns. Louis's generosity was not altogether selfless. He knew William would do his best to stop him seizing the territory he coveted to complete France's 'natural frontiers', and as ruler of England the Dutchman had become the soul of a Grand Alliance that included Holland, the Holy Roman Empire and Spain – the League of Augsburg. However, Louis believed that a second Stuart Restoration could defeat them.

Soon St Germain contained leading men from England, Scotland and Ireland, who had left mansions and estates, parsonages and livings. Called 'Jacobites' from the Latin for James, they took the White Rose of York as a badge because he had once been Duke of York. Life was pleasant – a round of hunting parties, balls and picnics. There were many young people in a court a thousand strong, children of courtiers or pensioners. Concerts were given in the chapel, the theatre or the royal apartments by musicians who included François Couperin. Optimism prevailed, everyone looked forward to the second Restoration.[1]

It is not true, as Thomas Macaulay says, that Protestant courtiers were banished to the attics and when they died were refused burial according to their Church's rites. That tale comes from *A View of the Court of St Germain* by a Whig spy, published at London in 1696, which claims that a Scottish bishop was 'reduced to the necessity of abjuring his Religion for want of Bread' – a lie.[2] Admittedly, major court posts at St Germain did go to Catholics, with John Drummond, Earl (later Duke) of Melfort becoming secretary of state and Lord Caryll being made Queen Mary's secretary. A Scottish convert, widely disliked, Melfort led the 'Non-Compounder' party, abetted by John Caryll, an elderly Sussex recusant whom Ailesbury called 'a grand bigot . . . doubting, positive and peevish'. In their view, James should punish everyone involved in the Revolution.

The Interregnum

Across the Channel the Tories (which meant most peers, gentry and clergy) were shocked by the royal family's flight and by the sight of Dutch Guards at Whitehall. They had wanted William to curb James's Catholicism, not to oust him. Sons of Cavaliers, their anchors were the Crown, Anglicanism and the Common Law. James might be misguided, but they venerated the monarchy. Half a century later, Lord George Murray wrote how he had heard his father, the Duke of Atholl, with 'many people of integrity' in both England and Scotland, say that 'not one in a thousand had the least notion of a Revolution and the royal line being excluded when the Prince of Orange was invited over'[3]

Only twenty years before, a Dutch fleet had sailed up the Thames to Gravesend after burning the British fleet at anchor in the Medway. Many questioned the motives of James's enemies. 'The transaction was, in almost every part, discreditable to England', even the Whig Macaulay admits. 'The Revolution was in a great measure effected by men who cared little about their political principles.'[4] But they were very clever, very determined men.

The peers had summoned a 'Convention Parliament' when the king was still at Rochester. Consisting of the House of Lords and MPs elected in Charles II's reign, this met on 22 January 1689. In the Lords, Archbishop

Sancroft moved that James be replaced by a regency, a motion supported by forty-nine in a hundred peers, but which the Whigs rejected as unworkable. Sancroft then moved that James be brought back under strict restraint. Again, the Whigs refused to countenance the motion.

Bewilderment was evident on 30 January 1689, Charles the Martyr's Day, when at St Margaret's, Westminster, the Commons heard Dr John Sharp, Dean of Norwich, ask God to bless James, giving thanks for 'the wonderful deliverance of these kingdoms from the Great Rebellion'. Then he preached a sermon damning subjects who dethroned their king. Yet only a short time before, James had suspended Sharp for refusing to read the Declaration of Indulgence.

The debate went on for weeks, many Tories wanting a regency, some Whigs a republic. Opinion hardened in favour of offering the throne to Princess Mary, but William threatened to go home to Holland and leave everybody at James's mercy unless he were made king for life.

On 13 February, Parliament passed a Bill of Rights largely drafted by John Somers, a brilliant Whig lawyer whose father had fought for Cromwell. Pretending that James had abdicated, the bill implied he was a criminal, listing thirteen of his 'infractions', with thirteen clauses limiting royal power. It resolved that 'William and Mary, Prince and Princess of Orange be, and be declared, King and Queen of England'. Both partners in this 'double-bottomed monarchy' (Burnet's term) would reign, but only William was to rule. On the same day, in the Banqueting House at Whitehall, the couple accepted the throne. They were crowned at Westminster Abbey in April by Henry Compton, Bishop of London. Parliament 'had tried to patch up the ancient constitution and to get it working again with as few changes as possible.'[5]

'Glorious Revolution'?

Whether this was coup d'etat or conservative revolution is still debated. Whigs called it 'glorious', others disagreed. If it limited the powers of the Crown, many failed to see the benefits. They recalled Charles I the Martyr's warning – 'the Devill of Rebellion doth commonly turn himself into an Angell of Reformation; and the old Serpent can pretend new Lights'[6]

A Toleration Act followed, allowing Dissenters to worship in their own chapels and run their own schools but not to hold public office – a poor substitute for James's Declaration. Even so, it outraged High Churchmen, who saw it as betraying the Anglican claim to be the national Church. However, it insisted on enforcing laws against recusants, such as that forbidding them to come within ten miles of London. As the historian Paul Kléber Monod puts it, 'the Revolution was the victory, not of timeless conceptions of "liberty", but of virulent anti-Catholicism'[7]

While most Englishmen thought they had escaped a rekindling of the fires of Smithfield, they were uneasy. Some suspected the revolution was a coup by 'Rye House plotters and haunters of conventicles' who wanted a republic with William and Mary as figureheads. Churchmen were horrified. Deposing a king could never be right – even Nero had been accepted by St Paul. To abandon James was to abandon his father, the Martyr.

The nonjurors

Many clergy (and laymen) believed in 'passive obedience' – the Crown must be obeyed because its authority came from God via descent from Adam, mankind's first king. In practice, this could be surprisingly flexible. When the Seven Bishops resisted the Declaration of Indulgence they saw themselves as saving James from evil advisers. But there could be no compromise with usurpation.

Thomas Cartwright, Bishop of Chester, went into exile, joining James in France, while Archbishop Sancroft and five of the six bishops imprisoned with him in 1688 refused to swear allegiance to William and Mary. They were joined by four other prelates and 400 clergy (one in six parsons). These 'nonjurors', some among England's finest minds, were deprived of dioceses or livings, giving up palaces or parsonages for homelessness and want. When they could, they worshipped with like-minded congregations in makeshift chapels.

More than 200 clergy who had been educated at Cambridge were deprived. A third of the Fellows of St John's College refused the oath, resulting in a Whig purge, although most survived and the college remained a Jacobite bastion. In January 1692, undergraduates from St John's rioted in protest when the university's vice chancellor declared his loyalty to William and Mary.[8] Their attitude was summed up by a Sussex parson, Thomas Eades of Chiddingly, who, evicted for refusing the oath, wrote his own epitaph:

A faithful shepherd that did not pow'rs fear
But kept Old Truth, and would not let her go

Nor turn out of the way for friend or foe.
He was suspended in the Dutchman's days
Because he would not walk in their strange ways ...

Churchmen were shocked by Parliament imposing its will on bishops, realising the revolution had destroyed the alliance between Church and State. Most clergy who took the Oath of Allegiance did so from fear of losing their livings, nine out of ten 'swearing clergy' being Jacobites at heart. Thomas White, Bishop of Peterborough, who framed the oath, compared it to 'a plate of cucumbers dressed with oil and vinegar, and yet fit for nothing but to throw out of the window'.

Wherever possible, William replaced nonjuror prelates by Latitudin-arians (forerunners of today's Liberals) such as John Tillotson who became Archbishop of Canterbury and Gilbert Burnet, the new Bishop of Salisbury, but they were a minority. Their appointment fuelled suspicions that the king, a convinced Calvinist, had little sympathy for the Church of England.

Nonjurors, who thought Latitudinarianism blasphemous, grew steadily more 'Catholic', if they had no time for Popery. They included men like Jeremy Collier. Brilliantly gifted, although one of England's first drama critics, his real forte was theology and in other times he might have been a bishop. But, as Macaulay put it in 1841, 'he belonged to that section of the Church of England which lies farthest from Geneva and nearest to Rome.'[9]

In 1689 Collier published *The Desertion discuss'd in a Letter to a Country Gentleman,* refuting a pamphlet by Bishop Burnet which claimed that James's flight had left the throne vacant. Collier argued that because the king had good reason for 'apprehension' his 'withdrawal' could not be abdication, and that it contradicted law and nature to pronounce the throne void. The government sent him to Newgate Prison. Dr Charles Leslie, an Irish nonjuror whom Burnet called 'the violentest Jacobite [of all]', was an even more savage critic of the new regime, eloquently demolishing Whig opponents.

Nonjuror laymen included a dozen peers who were heavily taxed for refusing the oath. 'I cannot violate my duty to the King [James] my master', explained the Earl of Arran. 'I must distinguish between his Popery and his Person: I dislike the one; but have sworn and do allegiance to the other.'[10]

Among these peers, in spirit if not in deed, was Henry Somerset, Duke of Beaufort, President of the Council of Wales and lord lieutenant of four English counties, who at his great house of Badminton gave dinner everyday to his household's 200 members. He had tried to hold the West Country for

James in 1688 and as a (bastard) Plantagenet despised the Dutch usurper, if reluctantly he swore allegiance. For over sixty years his descendants stayed loyal to the Stuarts.

A hundred families of landed gentry, including sixty MPs or former MPs, have been identified as nonjurors. Refusing the oath cost them all chance of a career in politics, the Church or the Bar, of commissions in the army or navy. There was also a strong middle- and working-class contingent, especially in London and Manchester.[11]

The legal fraternity's higher ranks held serious misgivings. The Lord Chief Justice of the King's Bench, Sir Edward Herbert, followed James to France, as did the Chief Baron of the Exchequer, Sir Edward Atkyns. Other distinguished lawyers, too, saw the king's deposition as breaching England's constitution, which in future would be based on a lie (the fiction of his abdication) besides denying primogeniture and the Common Law rule of inheritance.

William III and Mary II

Refusing to be a powerless 'Duke of Venice', William played the parties against each other, at first ruling with Tory ministers. He ignored his unpopularity. 'This people was not made for me', he remarked, 'nor was I made for this people.' Fog disagreed with his health so he and Mary moved out of Whitehall to Hampton Court, before building a new palace at Kensington. 'The gaiety and the diversions of a court disappeared', admits Burnet.[12]

Courtiers sneered at his accent and the Dutch favourites he entertained in his banqueting house at Hampton Court, angered by the titles and presents he gave them. Hans William Bentinck, Earl of Portland, Arnold van Keppel, Earl of Albemarle and William Nassau Zuylestein, Lord Rochford, grew so rich that they were called the 'Dutch blood-suckers'. Jacobites insisted that William's relationship with Bentinck was homosexual, a 'Coronation Ode' claiming somewhat implausibly how 'buggering of Benting' compensated for castration at birth by a clumsy midwife.[13]

Towering over William, at twenty-seven Mary was a large, red-faced woman who took even Whigs aback by her high spirits on arriving from Holland. She 'put on a great air of gaiety' that shocked even Burnet. 'I thought a little more seriousness had done as well, when she came into her father's palace, and was to be set on his throne next day.'[14] John Evelyn was horrified at how 'she came into Whitehall laughing and jolly, as to a wedding'[15] Jacobites compared her to Lear's daughter, 'cruel, lustful Goneril', so much that performances of

King Lear were banned. A satire, *Tarquin and Tullia* by Arthur Maynwaring, likened her to the savage Tullia who, having made her husband kill her father, King Servius Tullius, drove her chariot over his body.[16]

In reality, Mary's memoirs show her as kind and gentle, if under her spouse's thumb. The Duchess of Marlborough said she 'wanted bowels', meaning she lacked spirit. Her adviser, Bishop Burnet, tells us she 'set herself to make up what was wanting in the King, by a great vivacity and cheefulness', but 'though she gave a wonderful content to all that came near her, yet few came'.[17] 'God knows what she suffered inwardly and to a high degree', Ailesbury told the Earl of Nottingham, when he deplored her behaviour towards her parent.[18] She dreaded 'my father might fall by our arms'.[19] Nottingham believed that had she outlived William she would have tried to bring about a Restoration.

As Mary was James's daughter and William was half Stuart, the dynastic principle had a fig leaf. But although they chose ministers from both parties and called new elections in 1690 to stop Whigs persecuting Tories, Tory MPs were bent on making life as difficult as possible for Dutch Billy and 'Goneril'.

Understandably, Roman Catholics pitied a king who lost his crown for trying to better their lot. In April 1689 armed recusant squires began meeting at the Earl of Derwentwater's house in Northumberland, and until the mid 1690s a secret Catholic army north of the Trent stockpiled arms, ready to join a Jacobite invasion.

John Stevens, a Catholic gentleman of Lord Clarendon's bedchamber, is best known for his journal of the Jacobite war in Ireland, but he also describes his reaction to the Revolution – that of fellow recusants: 'At Highgate I first saw some of the Prince of Orange's foreigners, who [were] quartered and kept guard there and next found them possessed of all the guards in London. I found the face of affairs quite altered, the usurper in quiet possession of the Royal Palaces . . . the most general and barbarous rebellion the world has seen, except what the same people had shown in this unparalleled monarch's father's day.'[20]

One Catholic who did not keep a low profile was a convert, John Dryden, the age's greatest writer. After refusing allegiance to William and Mary, and losing his post as poet laureate, until his death in 1700 he published a stream of plays and poems defending James. He made his views clear – 'an Honest Man ought to be contented with that Form of Government, and with those Fundamental Constitutions of it, which he receiv'd from his Ancestors, and under which he himself was Born'.[21]

Opposition to the new regime burst out in print from secret presses, rang-
ing from ballads and pamphlets to learned works packed with Greek and
Hebrew quotations. 'Women were on the watch to give the alarm by their
screams if an officer appeared near the workshop', says Macaulay. 'The press
was immediately pushed into a closet behind the bed: the types were flung
into the coal-hole, and covered with cinders: the compositor disappeared
through a trapdoor in the roof, and made off over the tiles of the neighbouring houses.'

Macaulay was especially shocked by a pamphlet entitled *A Form of Prayer
and Humiliation* that claimed the Church of England lay in ruins because
her priests had perjured themselves. James was the stone rejected by the
builders whom God would surely restore. 'Raise up the former government
both in Church and State, that we may no longer be without King, without
priest, without God in the World', it prayed. 'Do some great thing for him,
which we in particular know not how to pray for' – meaning, strike William
and Mary dead.[22]

In Drury Lane taverns such as The Dog or The Blue Posts, Tories sang the
old Cavalier song, 'When the King enjoys his Own again', and it was sung at
a whole network of other public houses in London that catered for Jacobites.
Among the singers were hundreds of ex-officers from James's army who had
been cashiered, besides people from all walks of life. For them, England and
the ancient magic of the Crown were indivisible.

For the first two years after the Revolution William and Mary's tenure
of the throne was insecure. Despite a draconian purge, the army contained
officers who wanted another Restoration. Even Macaulay admits there was a
reaction in James's favour. If English Jacobites would not rise unless he came
back with an army, they hoped for good news from Scotland or Ireland.

5

Hope and Despair – Scotland, 1689–1691

Away to the hills, to the caves, to the rocks –
Ere I own a usurper, I'll couch with the fox;
And tremble, false Whigs, in the midst of your glee,
You have not seen the last of my bonnet and me!

Sir Walter Scott, *The Doom of Devorgoil*

On 18 March 1689 Major-General Viscount Dundee galloped out of Edinburgh with fifty dragoons. Twelve days later a Scottish convention parliament (one assembled, owing to an abeyance of the Crown, without summons by a sovereign) proclaimed him 'fugitive and rebel' at the Mercat Cross – ironically, in King James's name. 'Bonnie Dundee' was a hero for Jacobites and a demon for Whigs, Macaulay giving him a 'seared conscience and adamantine heart'. Walter Scott, however, although he thought him cruel, treasured his sword as a holy relic because he glimpsed the spell that made men follow him.

Curiously, Dundee – James Grahame of Claverhouse – was a former Cornet of Horse in the Prince of Orange's Guards who had saved William's life in battle. But he had also been very useful to James when James was Lord High Commissioner of Scotland, enforcing his orders ruthlessly. Late in 1688, James made him deputy commander of all Scottish troops and a viscount.

Having accompanied the king on his last stroll down the Mall, during which he begged him not to leave, Dundee returned to Scotland. Here the Revolution had been more violent than in England, with mobs sacking Holyrood and lynching James's men. Going to Edinburgh for the convention parliament, he found himself threatened in the streets.

But despite his Popery, King James remained popular with Scots. As Commissioner from 1681–2, though he persecuted Cameronian fanatics he had taken a genuine interest in their country, planning a New Town for Edinburgh, while his presence at Holyrood flattered the ruling class. Instead of punitive expeditions, he had instituted a Commission for Securing the Peace of the Highlands that enlisted the chiefs and had considerable success.

When the Three Estates met on 14 March in the Great Hall of Parliament House, the Bishop of Edinburgh, Alexander Rose, opened the session with a prayer for God 'to have compassion on King James'. Yet although Whigs and Jacobites were equal in number, the Whigs secured the election of their leader, the Duke of Hamilton, as president, gaining control of the parliament. Dundee and the Earl of Balcarres tried to rally those loyal to the king, but their efforts were wrecked by a letter from James – countersigned by Melfort, formerly Secretary of State for Scotland. It ordered Parliament to assert James's rights against men who had brought about the blackest of usurpations, workers of iniquity, threatening those disinclined to return to their duty with the full rigour of the law. Even the faithful Lord Ailesbury thought the letter disastrous, commenting that the king cut his own throat by having Melfort countersign it, 'a person abominated in that kingdom.'[1]

After failing to persuade fellow Jacobites to call a rival parliament in James's name at Stirling, Viscount Dundee left Edinburgh.[2] Before leaving, in his gold-laced uniform he clambered up the Castle Rock to the castle's 'sallyport', to stiffen the nerve of the Duke of Gordon who held the castle for James. He told him, 'I go whither the shade of Montrose shall direct me.' He was referring to the Marquis of Montrose, the guerilla leader who forty years earlier had put the fear of God into Charles I's enemies.[3]

On 11 April 1689, backed by Scottish regiments from Holland and cheered by the mob who had sacked Holyrood, the Edinburgh convention proclaimed at the Mercat Cross that James had forfeited the throne by 'misconduct', and their sovereigns were now William and Mary. It enacted a Claim of Right – a Scots version of England's Bill of Rights. Yet the new regime was unpopular across wide areas of Scotland. James's cause seemed far from lost.

Scotland's first Jacobite rising

In March 1689, a Maclean had gone to Dublin, just after King James's arrival there, to tell him that if he sent a regiment from Ireland to Argyll, it would be joined by 4,000 Highlanders. The claim was justified since Sir Ewen Cameron of Lochiel was eager to rise, as were other chiefs. A veteran Cavalier who had played a key role in restoring Charles II, Lochiel was admired by his clansmen for having bitten the throat out of a Roundhead officer and killed the last wolf in Scotland. Macaulay calls him 'the Ulysses of the Highlands'.

Encouraged, James promoted Dundee to lieutenant-general, ordering him 'to command all such forces as can be raised', and promising to send Irish troops. On 13 April, two days after William and Mary were proclaimed at Edinburgh, Dundee raised King James's standard, he and his fifty dragoons having been joined by the Earl of Dunfermline with a handful of gentry. Then he rode for two months, looking for allies among the clans of the *Gàidhealtachd*, the Gaelic-speaking western Highlands and islands.

He had a hard journey, according to the *Grameid*, a Latin epic written by his standard bearer James Philip of Almerieclose that describes how day after day he rode along rough paths over high hills and barren moors, through forests and raging torrents, and through marshes that swallowed up horses. In this 'chaos of mountain, wood and sky', he and his men slept under the stars, half-starved, shivering with cold.

At Inverness he dissuaded MacDonald of Keppoch – 'Coll of the Cows' – from burning the town to the ground. (Macaulay calls Coll 'an excellent specimen of the genuine Highland Jacobite', adding that 'a Macdonald or a Macgregor in his tartan was to a citizen of Edinburgh or Glasgow what an Indian hunter in his war paint is to an inhabitant of Philadelphia or Boston.') However, Dundee knew how to deal with him and from Inverness sent out the fiery cross to every loyal Highlander. Then he rode on, extracting money, arms and provisions from Dunkeld and Perth.

'I have now received letters from Ireland by which I am sure nothing but want of fair wind can hinder the landing of a considerable force in this country, from thence, and that the King will be with us very soon', Dundee wrote to Ewen Macpherson of Cluny on 19 May.[4] Until the end, he believed James would come in person. So did the clansmen whom he reviewed at Glenroy six days later.

All summer, Dundee was pursued by General Hugh Mackay of Scourie, a veteran commander who had served abroad, mostly with the Scots Brigade in Holland. Each tried to outmanoeuvre the other, convinced that if he caught his enemy off balance, he would defeat him.

Able and courageous, Mackay was also a sanctimonious martinet who, although a Gaelic speaking Highlander, despised fellow Highlanders. In contrast, the Lowlander Dundee modelled himself on Montrose. He ate the same sparse rations as his men, dismounted to walk at their side and, fluent in Gaelic, cheered them on with jokes or quotations from their legends.

Mackay's troops, Lowlanders and English, were musketeers with 'plug' bayonets that screwed into the muzzle, although a few carried pikes – one was armed with a bow. Some were veterans from Scots regiments in Dutch service, but many were raw recruits. He had a hundred cavalry and three 'leather cannon' – light copper guns that generally blew up after firing a few rounds.

Before embarking on his Highland campaign, Mackay had captured Edinburgh Castle. Bombarded day and night, its garrison had taken refuge in the cellars. On 13 June the Duke of Gordon surrendered, short of food, water and ammunition.

All this time Dundee hoped that troops would arrive from Ireland, led by the king. 'Some of the French fleet hath been seen amongst the islands', he wrote in a letter of 23 June to the Highland chief McLeod of McLeod. 'The king . . . hath nothing to do but bring over his army, which many people fancy is already landed in the west. He will have little to oppose him there, and probably will march towards England.' James had promised 'not only to me, but to all that will join [him] such marks of favour as after ages shall see what honour and advantage there is in being loyal.'

Dundee gives a list of the clans who will rise. He includes the Breadalbane Campbells, but he had not yet got the measure of 'Pale John', their wily chief.[5]

Expecting an invasion from Ireland no less than did Dundee, the Edinburgh Parliament begged Mackay to return from the Highlands and save it. But James was held up by the Ulster settlers' stubborn resistance.

In a letter to Melfort dated 27 June, Dundee explained his tactics:

When I had a seen advantage, I endeavoured to profit on it, but, on the other hand, shunned to hazard anything, for fear of a ruffle; for the least of that would have discouraged all. I thought if I could gain time, and keep up a figure of a party without loss, it was my best [plan] till we got assistance, which the enemy got from England every day . . .

When we came first out, I had but fifty pounds of powder; more I could not get; all the great towns and sea-ports were in rebellion, and had seized the powder, and would sell none. But I had one

advantage, the Highlanders will not fire above once, and then take
to the broad-sword.

'The poor [Episcopalian] ministers are sorely oppressed', he adds. 'They
generally stand right.' Giving a list of loyal peers ready to rise when the king
arrives, he says 'Most of the gentry on this side the Forth, and many on the
other, will do so too. But they suffer mightily in the meantime.' He suggests
in the letter that James should land at Inverlochy with 6,000 foot and 800
horse, then march inland. He would bring his men to meet him, raising the
country as he went.[6]

Only a single regiment of poor quality, dismounted, Irish dragoons
arrived. Yet Dundee remained convinced that more were on their way.

Killiecrankie

What forced a confrontation with Mackay was the siege of Blair Atholl
Castle which, commanding a road used by the Highlanders for their raids,
had considerable strategic value. Occupied by Jacobites, it was invested by
Whig troops, but relieved by Dundee, who installed himself in the castle.

Learning that Mackay was approaching with 3,500 foot and a hundred
cavalry, Dundee decided to ambush him at the wooded pass of Killiecrankie.
He had 2,400 clansmen, forty cavalry, a few mounted gentlemen volunteers
and 500 Irish troops.

On 27 July he took up position on the side of a ridge north east of the
pass's exit, looking down on the path, protected by a screen of trees and
bushes, and a series of terraces. (Describing another battle in *Old Mortality*,
Sir Walter Scott compares Dundee to 'a hawk perched on a rock, and eyeing
the time to perch on its prey' – it was the same on this occasion.) When
enemy scouts reached the exit late in the afternoon, his men opened fire with
their few muskets.

In response, Mackay placed his men on a slope facing the Jacobites. To
exploit their superior firepower, they were in a long line three deep instead
of the usual six.[7] For the next few hours they exchanged shots with their
enemies, killing several. Shortly before 8 p.m., some redcoats ran forward to
flush a sniper's nest out of a bothy, then rejoined the line. By now the sun was
waning, no longer in the Highlanders' eyes.

Suddenly, led by the sixty-year-old Lochiel, the clansmen – Camerons,
MacDonalds and Macleans – flung off their plaids and charged downhill

roaring in Gaelic, partially shielded by irregular, sloping ground. Firing a single shot at the last moment, they dropped their guns and went in with the claymore.

Mackay's men fired two volleys but, spread out too thinly, frantically trying to reload or plug in bayonets, blinded by the sun and black-powder smoke, were knocked off their feet. On the right, the charge was slowed by dry-stone walls until Dundee and his troop of horse rode down to finish the job. The Whig cavalry had already bolted. Overwhelmed, the redcoats ran for their lives.

General Mackay somehow hacked a way through triumphant clansmen to rising ground at the side, where he rallied a few hundred troops whom he led as fast as he could into the mountains. He had lost half his army, 2,000 killed or wounded, besides 500 taken prisoner. The Highlanders were too busy looting to chase him. Marching night and day, he reached Stirling in safety, but many men threw away their weapons or deserted despite his threats to shoot them.

The Highlanders suffered 600 casualties. Worse still, their general was dead. Waving his plumed hat as he cheered on the clansmen, Dundee had received a musket shot in the stomach. Lifted down from the saddle, he asked 'How goes the day?' Told, 'Well for King James, but I am sorry for your Lordship', he muttered, 'If it goes well for him, it matters the less for me.'

He died in a few minutes. The fear he inspired is shown by the tale of his being slain by a silver bullet. Archibald Pitcairne (Edinburgh's leading physician) composed an elegiac Latin epitaph, translated by that staunch English Jacobite, John Dryden:

> O last and best of Scots! who didst maintain
> Thy Country's Freedom from a Foreign Reign[8]

Dunkeld and the Haugh of Cromdale

Dundee was irreplaceable yet had he lived it is unlikely he would have toppled the regime at Edinburgh, despite making large areas of Scotland ungovernable. Only if James had sent several thousand troops could Dundee have brought about a Restoration.

His successor was Colonel Alexander Cannon, an uninspiring Lowlander in late middle age from Galloway, who did not speak Gaelic. Lochiel was so insulted at not being given command that he took his Camerons home.

Even so, Highlanders flocked to join Cannon's army, doubling its numbers, and on 21 August he attacked the little Perthshire town of Dunkeld on the River Tay. He was driven off with heavy casualties by the Cameronian zealots defending it, who fought to the death from house to house in the streets around the cathedral, despite their leaders being killed and despite half the town being burned to the ground. The Jacobite army disintegrated, the clansmen trotted home with their booty, and Cannon and the Irish troops took refuge on Mull.

Early in 1690 Lochiel contacted James in Ireland, promising to raise the clans again. In response, the king sent Major-General Thomas Buchan of Auchmacoy, who marched into Strathspey with 800 Highlanders. However, on 1 May, 1,200 Whig cavalry under Sir Thomas Livingstone, garrison commander at Inverness, took them by surprise at the Haugh of Cromdale, killing or capturing 400 clansmen. The remainder bolted back to their mountains.

Buchan was then pursued by General Mackay who had rebuilt Fort William as a base in Cameron country. The Earl of Seaforth surrendered, depriving him of the Mackenzies – who could muster 4,000 men – while Lochiel unexpectedly took to his bed with a wound received in a duel. Worst of all, King James was defeated at the Boyne in July 1690.

Buchan hid in the wilds of Lochaber, but although the clansmen held out, they did little more than launch a few half-hearted raids. Finally, the government was approached by John Campbell, Lord Breadalbane, hitherto a Jacobite, who offered to buy off the clans if it gave him the money.

Keeping the cash for himself, 'Pale John' coaxed the chiefs into asking James for permission to make peace, which came in December 1691 after the Jacobites' defeat in Ireland. Buchan, Cannon and 150 other officers were allowed to go to France where, to avoid starvation, most joined a Scots company in a French regiment bound for the war in Spain, serving as private soldiers.

6

A Nation Once Again –
Jacobite Ireland, 1689–1690

*Traitors and enemies . . . offered your Imperial Crown to the
said Prince of Orange . . . which execrable act nothing can
equal but the barbarous murder of your royal father.*

The Irish Parliament's *Act of Recognition*

In March 1689, on the day his nephew and his daughter were crowned in
London, James landed at Kinsale on the southern coast of Ireland, intend-
ing to use the country as a springboard from which to reconquer his other
realms. He brought 2,500 French troops and two sons, James FitzJames, the
Duke of Berwick, and Henry FitzJames, the Grand Prior. Next day he was
greeted at Cork by Richard Talbot, Earl of Tyrconnell and Lord Deputy of
Ireland, who sat by his side during dinner – normally a monarch dined alone.
Then he created him a duke.

After a progress north – joyful despite being 'slobbered' by the kisses of
frenziedly loyal country women – James rode into Dublin on 24 March,
the Duke of Powis and the Earl of Granard riding at his left, the Duke of
Berwick and the Earl of Melfort at his right. Cheering streets were lined by
pipers and harpers playing 'When the King enjoys his Own again' while as
he approached the castle, forty maidens in white danced before his cavalcade,
strewing flowers. The Dubliners saw him as heir to the old High Kings of
Ireland because of the Stuarts' supposed descent from Fergus Mór, an ancient
Irish monarch.

For fifteen months there was a royal court at Dublin Castle. Macaulay
sneers that it was 'busied with dice and claret, love letters and challenges [by

duelists]', but he never has anything good to say of Irishmen. For Catholics, this was one of the happiest periods there had ever been in Dublin's history.

The king amused himself with operas and sermons, writing regularly to Queen Mary at St Germain, yet he was in an odd mood. Mistresses were a thing of the past. Warning against the 'forbidden love of Women', in the *Instructions* for his son that he wrote at this time, he says (in nostalgic tribute to Arabella Churchill and Catherine Sedley), 'Of all Vices, it is the most bewitching.' He adds how he himself is an example of what God does to those who succumb – 'I have paid dear for it.'[1]

Moreover, he was ill at ease among high-spirited Hibernians, especially Irish speakers. Later, he wrote of 'their natural hatred' for Englishmen, and the need to 'teach the Children of the old Natives English, [which] would by degrees weare out the Irish language'. He adds, 'Severall of the O's and Macks, who were forfited for Rebelling in King James the firsts time, and before . . . will allways be ready to rise in arms against the English.'[2]

Reassuringly, the Dublin court included Jacobites from his other lands. The lord chamberlain, the Duke of Powis, was a Welshman, while the secretary of state was the Scottish Earl of Melfort. There were other Scots, such as John Wauchope and his brother Francis from Midlothian, Thomas Buchan from Aberdeenshire and Thomas Maxwell who had married the handsome Jane, Duchess of Norfolk. Among many recusant Englishmen were Dominick Sheldon and William Dorrington.

Jacobite Ireland

At nearly three million people, Ireland's population was three times that of Scotland. (England's was five million.) Twenty per cent were Anglican English or Presbyterian Scots colonists, hated by the Catholic Irish, most of whom spoke a language closer to Latvian than English. Understandably, colonists were for William and natives for James.

Confiscation of Catholic estates by Elizabeth Tudor and Cromwell, and their purchase by Protestant settlers, had left barely a fifth of the land in Catholic hands, especially after the 1641 rebellion. There were numerous embittered descendants of the former ruling class, the 'aboriginal aristocracy' as Macaulay calls them. Some had joined foreign armies or turned to being farmers, others Franciscan friars whose revengeful preaching frightened 'heretics'. They hoped that a Catholic king would give them back their estates.

With nearly 60,000 inhabitants, Dublin was bigger than any city in James's domains other than London, prosperous from manufacturing wool, linen and even velvet and from selling wool and frieze to England and France. It had two cathedrals, well-laid-out streets, good bridges over the Liffey, fine houses with gardens, Trinity College, the King's Inns and the new hospital of Kilmainham for old soldiers.[3] Opposite Christchurch Cathedral stood the Tholsel, city hall and exchange, which had recently been rebuilt in an imposing Baroque style.

This was a rewardingly fertile country and in areas of good corn land, such as the Pale around Dublin and north Munster's 'Golden Vale', farming methods were advanced by the standards of the time. (Locals joked that the Vale was so lush that if you walked through a field there at harvest time your legs would be dripping with butter when you came out.) Besides the healthy woollen industry there was a busy trade with France, Spain and the Baltic, where Irish merchants were well-established. If much smaller than Dublin, the big ports – Waterford and Cork, Limerick and Galway – enjoyed a similar prosperity.

There was though a division between Gaelic Irish landowners and the Catholic 'Old English' landowners, who descended from medieval settlers. King James observed how 'Mack's and O's do not love the Leinster men, they (generally speaking) being of the old English families that first conquered that kingdom.'

He exaggerates, since they were linked by marriage and if Irish might not be the mother tongue of the Old English they spoke it as a second language. Some grander Gaels even took recusant wives from over the sea, like Tyrconnell's nephew, Sir Neil O'Neill of Slane's Castle, County Antrim, who married a daughter of Viscount Molyneux. (Descended from the kings of Tír Eoghain, he is the only chieftain known to have had himself painted in Irish dress – by John Michael Wright.)

Both groups were united by hatred of the Protestant colonists who had stolen their land. The Irish author of *A Light to the Blind*, a Jacobite account of the war, makes no distinction between Gael and Old English.[4]

James's first minister, Tyrconnell, was vain and arrogant yet also subtle and magnetic.[5] He had opened negotiations with William shortly after the Dutch invasion – reasonably enough, for if James had stayed in England as a puppet monarch he would have been doomed. The king's flight put new heart into the lord deputy, who had written to him in France, proposing he come to a realm still loyal.

'Tyrconnell's style was even-handed and impartial rather than triumphal-ist' is Professor R. E. Foster's verdict, 'he knew enough not to be as euphoric as some of his supporters.'[6] Yet while he hoped to create a Catholic Ireland linked to England only by the crown, Tyrconnell was a committed Jacobite who genuinely wished for a Restoration in all three realms. As a man from the Pale, that small, anglicised area consisting of the four counties around Dublin, his first loyalty was to his sovereign.

Even so, he loved his native land. Ever since becoming lord deputy in 1687, he had been replacing Protestant officers by Catholics, installing Catholic judges, ensuring that burgesses and aldermen were Catholics. 'He sometimes, indeed in his rants, talked with Norman haughtiness of the Celtic barbarians, but all his sympathies were really with the natives,' says Macaulay – for once, altogether accurate.

'He is not so clever as I would like, and doesn't care for troubling himself or hard work,' Louis XIV's ambassador in Ireland, the Comte d'Avaux, observed of Tyrconnell. 'But he achieves a lot because he acts in good faith, asks people for their opinion, and gives them work to do that suits them ...'[7] Berwick's recollection was 'a man with a very good mind, very obliging, if at the same time extraordinarily vain as well as extremely cunning.'[8]

A shrewd judge of men, Tyrconnell chose able advisers, generally lawyers. The cleverest was a barrister, Richard Nagle (from Monanimy Castle on Cork's Blackwater River), Speaker of the House of Commons, then a lord justice and finally a secretary of state, who became his political eyes and ears. Another was a Shropshire recusant, Francis Plowden, who also became a lord justice.

James's secretary of state, the Earl of Melfort, was lavish with unhelpful advice. The Comte d'Avaux thought him a ludicrous figure, trying to run a country of which he knew nothing without consulting its inhabitants, while Tyrconnell declared he would ruin Ireland. When Melfort claimed that the Duchess of Tyrconnell took bribes and slept with the French war minister, James sent him back to St Germain, fearing he would be murdered by Tyrconnel's henchmen. He left hastily under cover of darkness, replaced by Nagle.

On 7 May 1689 James called a parliament, known (since the nineteenth century) as the 'Patriot Parliament', that met at the King's Inns, then on the north bank of the Liffey, and sat until the end of July. The Commons numbered 230 MPs, only six of whom were Protestants and the first concern of the Catholic MPs was to recover their lost estates.

The thirty-five members of the Lords included five Protestant peers with four Protestant prelates and no Catholic bishops. The Protestant Earl of Granard from County Longford, seemed loyal enough to James despite his dislike for Tyrconnell. So did Bishop Dopping of Meath, who led what might be termed the opposition in the Upper House, if beginning to modify the passive obedience he had once preached with such conviction.

In royal robes and with a crown made by Dublin jewellers on his head, King James opened Parliament, stressing his wish for equality between Protestants and Catholics. He was no less sincere than he had been in England, but the Irish Commons would have none of it. Even so, despite considerable pressure, he refused to disestablish the Anglican Church in Ireland. (Nevertheless, Christ Church Cathedral was returned to Catholic worship, with a Catholic dean and chapter. Other churches, too, were taken back.)

James reminded his listeners of the injustice of the Act of Settlement that deprived so many Catholics of their lands. It was repealed, restoring estates to long dispossessed proprietors. An act of attainder declared over 2,500 Protestant landowners guilty of treason, a piece of revenge wanted by neither the king nor Tyrconnel.

Finding £20,000 granted by Parliament too little, James issued a proclamation doubling the value of money. Thwarted by merchants and shopkeepers who doubled their prices, he then had half-crowns and shillings struck in brass, copper and pewter, 'gun-money' that quickly lost its face value. Yet this did not affect his followers' optimism.

The Jacobite army of Ireland

James's army consisted of 35,000 Irish horse and foot, and the French infantry he brought with him. His heavy cavalry regiments were formed of gentlemen who provided their own horses and weapons, their job being to charge home and break up enemy formations. Riding cheap nags, his dragoons were mounted infantry who fought as scouts or skirmishers, dismounting to shoot, although occasionally charging like heavy cavalry.

Some of the infantry were armed with muskets, cumbersome matchlocks whose matches were not easy to keep alight under Irish rain. They fired a soft lead bullet weighing over an ounce. The majority of James's foot soldiers carried a 'rapparee', a pole tipped with a knife blade, and a big Irish dirk.

A surplus of officers helped to steady inexperienced rank and file. As the best Irish regiments had been trapped in England, most infantry were raw recruits – described by a modern Irish historian as 'peasant freebooters and cattle-drivers'.[9] Each regiment wore a red uniform with special facings and carried a regimental colour, marching to the music of drums and Irish bagpipes.

John Stevens was a captain in the Grand Prior's Regiment, named after its colonel Henry FitzJames – James's younger son and Grand Prior of the English Knights of Malta – but in reality commanded by a deputy. According to d'Avaux, the sixteen-year-old colonel was so far gone on brandy every morning that he could never mount a horse.

'Our men were newly brought from the mountains ... most of them had never fired a musket in their lives', writes Stevens. He says they would only obey officers who were relatives and reduced regiments to half size by desertion.[10] Unable to speak Irish, Stevens could not communicate with men who were better material than they looked. There were echoes of the old tribal relationship in the way they followed gentry from their area to whom they were intensely loyal. They would fight bravely, even magnificently, against opponents with better weapons.

James's greatest asset was his cavalry commanders – the Duke of Berwick, Patrick Sarsfield, Richard Hamilton, Neil O'Neill, Viscount Dungan and the Englishman Dominick Sheldon. The first two were outstanding.

Nineteen but already a veteran who had fought the Turks in Hungary, the Duke of Berwick was a born leader. In Ireland he became what Rupert of the Rhine had been to the Cavaliers, he and his Life Guards expert at 'scorched earth' tactics and isolating enemy garrisons.

From Lucan in County Dublin, half Old English, half Gael (his grandfather Rory O'More had led the Irish rising of 1641 in which Catholic gentry had attempted to seize control and force concessions for Catholics), Patrick Sarsfield had been fighting for James since the Battle of Sedgemoor and was among the few officers who had fought effectively during William's invasion of England. An amiable giant in his twenties, he was another born cavalry general whom even Williamites came to admire, not least because of his humane treatment of prisoners – in J. G. Simms's phrase, he was 'the Rommel of the Jacobite war'. Berwick called him 'Old Notorious'.[11]

There were also many Irish officers who had served in the armies of Europe or in their country's mid-century wars, with numerous English and Scots officers who had followed James overseas, but not one had commanded an army in the field. James himself had already shown his inadequacy as a soldier while, in Berwick's words, Tyrconnell 'was no military genius despite plenty of courage'.[12]

If James wanted to invade Scotland, he had to subdue Ulster – fast. His campaign began in mid March when Richard Hamilton routed a small force of Williamites at Dromore in County Down. But the northern settlers, fanatical Scots Presbyterians, were fighting for their lives.

A Jacobite army invested the port of Derry in northern Ulster on 18 April 1689, but without siege artillery it could only mount a blockade, and when the king came and ordered the citizens to surrender the garrison fired their cannon at him. Even so, he refused to take the advice of one of his staff, Count von Rosen from Latvia, that every Protestant in the area should be rounded up and left to starve in front of Derry, calling him 'a bloody Muscovite'. Despite near starvation, the arrival of siege guns and several assaults, the little city held out with great gallantry until English ships ran the blockade on 30 July.

On the same day as Derry's relief, Enniskillen settlers routed a Jacobite force at Newtownbutler in County Fermanagh, killing 2,000 men and capturing their commander, the short-sighted Viscount Mountcashel. With hindsight, we can see that these two reverses were the war's turning point.

A fortnight later, a Marshal of France, the Duke of Schomberg landed in Ulster with 10,000 troops. Among their regimental chaplains was a Cumberland parson, George Story, who kept a journal, later published as *A True and Impartial History of the Wars of Ireland*. To some extent this deserves its name, if written from a Williamite viewpoint.

Schomberg quickly invested Carrickfergus in County Antrim, on the north shore of Belfast Lough, whose garrison surrendered when its ammunition ran out. Although he rode through the streets pistol in hand to prevent a massacre, the Ulster Scots stripped women naked and made them run the gauntlet. Joined every day by Protestant settlers, Schomberg's army doubled. It looked as if the Jacobites would face a formidable offensive.

Discouraged by the relief of Derry and the rout at Newtownbutler, after losing Carrickfergus, d'Avaux told James that his only hope was to leave Dublin and fall back behind the River Shannon, which was the frontier of Connacht, Ireland's barren western province. The king refused – 'I am resolved not to be tamely walked out of Ireland, but to have one blow for it at least.'[13]

Yet he did nothing, staying away from his troops. Then Tyrconnell, who had been ill for most of the summer, rose from his sickbed and told him 'abandoning the army is to forfeit the crown'.[14] It made James confront the situation. A recent biographer, Pádraig Lenihan, believes that Tyrconnell not only saved the capital, but was responsible for the Jacobite army 'putting up a brave front' and inflicting 'the most severe defeat of the war on the Williamites with hardly a shot fired.'[15]

Schomberg began his march south on Dublin early in September – too late in the year, given the Irish climate. Because of poor staffwork and raids by Berwick's cavalry, his supplies ran out. When he reached Dundalk in County Louth which, as the crow flies, was less than fifty miles from the capital, he established a fortified camp for his troops, who were weak from lack of food – there were even rumours of cannibalism. Although impregnable, the site was flooded by incessant rain, his men did not build proper huts and there was the stench of disease in the waterlogged trenches.

James's advisers guessed that Schomberg's reluctance to fight was because his troops were sick. Accordingly, James led his army to Dundalk, showing considerable courage in trying to make the enemy give battle. In George Story's words, on 21 September, 'the enemy displayed their standard royal and all drew out, both horse and foot'.[16] But the marshal refused to leave his trenches.

'Pray take this perspective glass, and then give me your opinion,' he told a friend of Lord Ailesbury. 'That gentleman perceived King James with his blue ribbon riding about the ranks, and his army in all appearance numerous and in excellent order, also the troopers well-mounted. The Marshal went on, "Now, Mr Harbord, you see the reason I cannot quit my post ... so here I will rest and will surmount all difficulties. The great rains come in generally in this country about Bartholomew tide, and then the Irish army must of necessity go into quarters ..."'[17]

Schomberg's men were dying from dysentery or typhus. After James withdrew in November, beneath 'the great rains', the old marshal – nearly seventy-five – took what was left of his army to winter quarters further north. Had he fought and been beaten, he might have lost the war. Yet his retreat horrified William, already concerned about European allies who seemed on the verge of defeat.

In March 1690, in exchange for five Irish regiments sent to fight for France,

6,000 French infantry landed in County Cork led by the Comte de Lauzun, a clever, unkempt dwarf with a sharp tongue, who had endeared himself to James by organising the escape of the queen and Prince of Wales from England. No food had been provided for his men, but they managed to reach Dublin where James made him commander-in-chief despite his lack of military experience.

During the winter, which he spent at Dublin Castle, James was again in despair. Yet his position was far from hopeless. Sarsfield's cavalry had run William's supporters out of Galway and Sligo, so the king still ruled all Ireland except for Ulster. And he now had French regulars.

7

Disaster – the Battle of
the Boyne, 1 July 1690

That they [the Irish] were overcome is not so much to be
wondered at, as their holding out against the power and
wealth of England, and against all nations so long as they did.

> Anon, *A short and true Relation of Intrigues,*
> *transacted both at Home and Abroad, to restore*
> *the late King James,* 1694[1]

War broke out again in February 1690 when Schomberg burned Cavan and
then besieged Charlemont Fort in County Armagh, Ulster's last Jacobite
stronghold. The fort surrendered in May, after a spirited defence by the
eccentric Teague O'Regan, a bibulous hunchback who wore a fur muff. The
entire province of Ulster was now in Williamite hands.

William landed at Carrickfergus on 14 June. He had spared no expense
(as England would ruefully appreciate) on hiring the finest mercenaries in
Europe – Brandenburgers, Swiss, Danes and Huguenots, armed with the
new flintlock muskets – to reinforce his Dutch veterans and on buying the
best artillery. Joined by Protestant settlers, this massive war-machine grew to
27,000 infantry and 8,000 cavalry, with fifty guns.

Some recruits were of dubious value, however, refusing to obey orders,
such as the 'Enniskillen Dragoons' who were led by the fire-eating Colonel
Zachariah Tiffin. Half-naked, on shaggy little ponies, swords or pistols
hanging from their belts, they looked like Tartars.

William knew that if he conquered Ireland he could then use England's
resources to fight France. In contrast, Louis XIV sent insufficient men and
mediocre generals, an error that cost him not just the Irish war but the war in

Europe. Even so, William's expedition to Ireland was a gamble. As Tyrconnell wryly observed, a single French squadron could have destroyed his invasion fleet.

James marched his troops up to Dundalk, but fell back as William advanced, abandoning the pass at Moyra, north of Dundalk, where he might have inflicted fatal damage. His strategy, devised by Tyrconnell, Lauzun and Sarsfield – inspired by the sufferings of Schomberg's men – was to retreat slowly, avoiding battle even if it meant losing Dublin, and withdraw across the Shannon into the wastes of Connacht. This would wear out William's army in a fruitless pursuit over scorched earth.

But James disliked the idea of losing his one remaining capital, let alone of burning it as French advisers counselled, or of firing crops and farms. After sending his baggage and six of his twelve cannon to Dublin, at the last moment he changed his mind and decided to fight a totally unnecessary battle. In his memoirs he explains why. 'If he did not then he must lose all without a stroke, and be obliged to quit Dublin and all Munster, and retire behind the Shannon, and so be reduced to the Province of Connough [sic], where having no magazines [depots], he could not subsist very long, it being the worst corn country in Ireland. Besides, his men seem'd desirous to fight.'[2] As Burnet observes, his officers had the impression 'he was weary of the struggle, and even of life, and longed to see an end of it.'[3]

He concentrated 8,000 Irish and French foot with 5,000 Irish horse at Oldbridge, a hamlet on the border of Meath and Louth, on the south side of the Boyne. (Many of his soldiers wore slips of white paper in their hats, to avoid being mistaken for Williamites – the origin of the White Cockade.) He had only six cannon and his Irish infantry were armed mainly with half-pikes or scythes – those with matchlocks had just four rounds of ammunition – but his position seemed strong enough. On his right lay the well-garrisoned town of Drogheda, on his left an impassable bog, and in front, fortified by earthworks and farm buildings, a river that could only be crossed by a ford.

If James's artillerymen had few guns, they knew how to use them. On 30 June, reconnoitering from the far bank, William was hit on the right shoulder by a spent cannon ball that knocked him off his horse, but inflicted only bruises. In Dutch, he muttered, 'That was too close!' Another ball killed a trooper and two horses nearby. The Jacobites cheered so loudly that he rode through his army to show he was still alive.

The Battle of the Boyne

The battle was fought on 1 July, a fine, sunny day. King James watched from the hill of Donore above Oldbridge that gave him a bird's-eye view. Stevens says that on the morning of the battle many of James's infantry were drunk on brandy handed out by a staff error, incapable of fighting. However, the king's horse and French foot were a different matter.

William's tactics were a flanking attack followed by a frontal assault across the river. At 6 a.m., 10,000 men under Schomberg's son, Count Meinhardt, arrived at the ford at Rosnaree, two and a half miles west. Despite superior numbers, Meinhardt was held up for half an hour by 800 of Neil O'Neill's dragoons, who followed him devotedly. But when Sir Neil fell mortally wounded, by a bullet that smashed his thigh, the dragoons lost heart and the enemy reached the opposite bank.

Fearing they might roll up his flank and block his retreat along the Duleek Pass, James sent two-thirds of his army to Rosnaree, including the well-armed French infantry under the Comte de Lauzun, his best cavalry regiments and six cannon. The Williamites were then checked by an unexpected bog, but less than 5,000 infantry remained to defend the Oldbridge ford. The king had weakened his front, fatally.

William attacked at Oldbridge at 9 a.m., fifty cannon and howitzers shelling the opposite bank to destroy the earthworks. An hour later, three battalions of blue-coated Dutch Guards led by Count Solms waded through the Boyne, slamming volley after volley from flintlock muskets at short range into Tyrconnell's badly armed Irish infantry, who fired a single, ragged volley. Many Jacobite officers were killed. The men broke, but were rescued by the return of their cavalry from Rosnaree, with Richard Hamilton leading a charge that hurled the enemy into the river, save for a group who screwed in their plug bayonets and clung to a small strip of land.

Charging repeatedly – one charge led by Tyrconnell – it seemed the Irish cavalry might gain the upper hand. Marshal Schomberg, white hair waving in the wind, tried to rally a Huguenot regiment that had lost its officers, but was killed by a bullet in the neck. However, downstream to the east, the Duke of Württemberg launched a new flanking attack across another ford with the green-uniformed Danish Guards, while a detachment of William's horse struggled across still further down. James sent troops to deal with this fresh threat, again weakening his centre.

William then led his cavalry through the Boyne, nearly unhorsed when his mount's feet stuck in the mud. Charge and counter-charge ensued. By noon

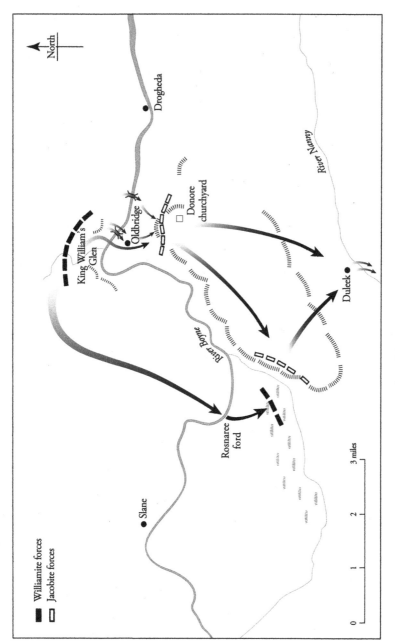

The Battle of the Boyne, 1 July 1690

North

Drogheda

River Nanny

Donore
churchyard

Oldbridge

King William's
Glen

River Boyne

Duleek

Rosnaree
ford

Slane

Williamite forces
Jacobite forces

0   1   2   3 miles

the Jacobite cavalry was decimated – the Duke of Berwick had charged ten times with his Life Guards, only sixteen of whom remained unwounded, he himself having his horse killed under him. Sarsfield's eight squadrons would have made all the difference, but James kept them back as a bodyguard.

Despite an asthma attack, William led a final onslaught across the river, his disciplined regiments advancing relentlessly. When Tyrconnell ordered what was left of his infantry at Oldbridge to withdraw, it ran. The Jacobite cavalry fought a brave rearguard action around the hill at Donore but were overwhelmed, many shot down in a narrow lane. The king and his bodyguard had already left for Dublin, thirty miles away.

Thanks to a fighting retreat by the remnants of their cavalry and the French regulars – in action for the first time that day – most of the Jacobite army escaped through the Pass of Duleek with only 1,500 casualties (less than William's 2,000 killed and wounded). The enemy's exhaustion, together with a deep bog beside the road, saved it from annihilation. However, many irreplaceable officers had been lost – O'Neill and Lord Dungan were dead, Hamilton had been taken prisoner.

There is a legend which preserves the bitterness felt by many that when James rode into Dublin Castle he was met by the Duchess of Tyrconnell, who had the same sharp tongue as her termagant sister, the future Duchess of Marlborough. He grumbled that his army had run away, to which she replied, 'I see your Majesty has won the race.' Three days later, he sailed for France.

As in England in 1688, James's nerve and judgement failed him utterly at the Boyne – before, during and after. Nothing better illustrates his failure to understand the Irish than his reaction to a single lost battle. He admits in his memoirs that he made a grave mistake, 'to abandon a cause which still had so much hope of life in it'.[4]

8

Defiance – the Siege of Limerick, August 1690

Limerick . . . last asylum of a Church and of a nation

Thomas Macaulay, *The History of England*

The country had been split into King James's Ireland west of the Shannon and King William's east of it. Limerick, 'Queen of the Shannon' and the the country's second largest city, became the new Stuart capital. The cry among Jacobites was, 'To Limerick! To Limerick!', which was crammed with refugees.

Stevens says he saw Tyrconnell en route for Limerick saluted by a guard of honour armed only with half-pikes. The lord deputy looked years older. Besides the shock of defeat, his horse had been killed under him at the Boyne and favourite kinsmen were dead. He had lost heart and, guessing that William wanted to end the war quickly, thought he might extract a reasonable settlement. The Restoration must come in another kingdom.

But when, supported by Lauzun, the lord deputy told the council at Limerick, 'All is lost', younger commanders, led by Sarsfield, planned a putsch – Tyrconnell and Lauzun were to be arrested, French regiments sent back to France and their muskets given to Irishmen. Warned, the lord deputy backed down, agreeing to fight on. His authority was badly damaged, however, and from now on many saw him as a defeatist, even as a secret traitor.

The first Siege of Athlone

Wide, fast flowing, with few crossings, the Shannon was a formidable barrier. Further upstream from Limerick, Lieutenant-General James Douglas arrived at Athlone on 17 July with 12,000 troops, intending to march over its bridge and down the far bank, which would let him attack Limerick while William did so from the other side of the river.

The city straddled the Shannon and its governor, Colonel Richard Grace (of Moyelly Castle in County Laois), had destroyed part of the bridge, to protect the western half of the city. The garrison was a mere 4,000 men yet when Grace – a septuagenarian who had served under Prince Rupert at Marston Moor during the Civil War in 1644 – was summoned to surrender, he fired a pistol over the messenger's head, swearing he would fight on in the besieged city until he had eaten his boots. Then he hung a red flag from the walls, in token that he refused to give, or accept, quarter.

Douglas shelled the city, but cannon responded defiantly from its medieval castle and he wasted his ammunition. Two days later, his men failed to ford the river, suffering heavy casualties. After a week, rumours that Sarsfield's much feared cavalry were approaching forced Douglas to beat a hasty retreat.

The first Siege of Limerick

Early in August, William set up camp with 25,000 troops at Caherconlish, seven miles south east of Limerick. Stevens thought the city defenceless, with 'an old stone wall made against bows and arrows' as sole protection.[1] Sneering that the wall would collapse if apples were thrown at it, Lauzun took the French regiments off to Galway, leaving behind his second-in-command, the Marquis de Boisseleau. Tyrconnell appointed Boisseleau as the city's governor before he, too, discreetly left for Galway.

Sarsfield was determined to hold Limerick. So was Boisseleau, a soldier who had experienced nine major sieges and served under the great French military engineer Vauban. On the banks of the Shannon, cut in two by a tributary (forming 'English Town' and 'Irish Town'), it was not easy to besiege despite its tumble-down walls. With 10,000 infantry inside and 3,500 cavalry led by Berwick operating outside, east of the river, they saw no reason for surrender. Under Boisseleau's guidance the citizens, who had a prophecy that the 'Saxons' would suffer a catastrophic defeat at Limerick, built trenches and mounted batteries.

Over confident, William arrived at Limerick on 9 August. Surrounding the city, his equally over confident men could hear the defenders talking in 'their damned Irish brogues' and yelled at them, 'Ye toads, are ye there? We'll be with you presently.' The entire Williamite army, from the commander down, was astonished to receive a refusal to surrender.

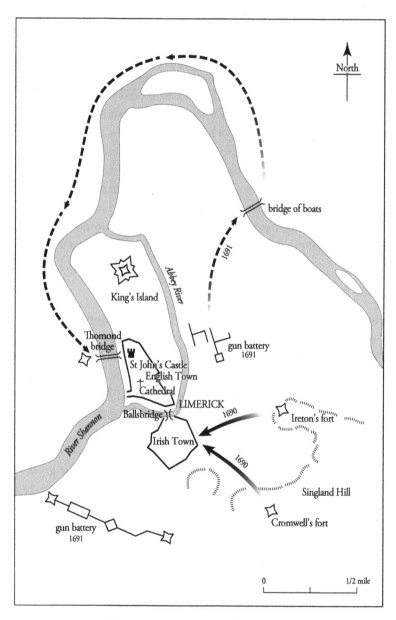

North

bridge of boats

1691

Abbey River

King's Island

gun battery
1691

Thomond
bridge

St John's Castle
English Town
Cathedral

LIMERICK

1690

Ireton's fort

Ballsbridge

Irish Town

River Shannon

1690

Singland Hill

gun battery
1691

Cromwell's fort

0   1/2 mile

The Sieges of Limerick, 1690–1

William immediately began a bombardment, but had only brought light field artillery while the garrison's own guns proved surprisingly effective. On 11 August he was forced to pull his cannon out of range, moving his tent after several people nearby were killed. However, a siege train bringing six 24-pounders and ammunition, with boats for a pontoon bridge, was on its way.

A deserter warned the garrison that the siege train was coming. Fording the Shannon, riding by night along mountain paths, hiding by day in ravines, Sarsfield led 500 cavalry to ambush it. At Ballyneety, fourteen miles from Limerick, on the night of 11 August, he blew up the siege guns with 120 barrels of gunpowder. Ironically, the Williamite password had been 'Sarsfield' and sentries who challenged the Irish horsemen, received the reply, 'Sarsfield is the word and Sarsfield is the man!' The explosion shook the ground like an earthquake, its flash seen for miles. 'As the smoke of a candle up into the sky', sang the poet Ó Bruadair.

Evading an attempt to cut off his retreat, Sarsfield returned to Limerick. The Williamites managed to repair six of the guns, but there were too few big horses to pull them into position and not enough powder.

Nine days later another siege train arrived, however, bringing six 24-pounders with ample ammunition. Red-hot shells, firebombs and grenades rained down on Limerick, setting houses alight. Sarsfield and Boisseleau asked the women to move to the Clare suburb on the far bank, but many refused, instead carrying ammunition to the troops. The defenders' cannon fired back, discharging a shot that 'would have struck His Majesty and [his] horse too, all to pieces, if his usual good angel had not defended him.'[2]

On 25 August heavy rain made it difficult for William's guns to fire, turning the ground under them into a quagmire. However, they had made a narrow breach. Anticipating further rain and aware his ammunition was running low, William decided to capture the counterscarp behind it, then enlarge the breach for assault on a wide front.

On 27 August a 'forlorn hope' of 500 grenadiers attacked at the head of 10,000 troops. Disobeying orders, a Danish regiment stormed through the breach, followed by other regiments, to find that Boisseleau had built an unexpected 'retirade', or angled trench, from behind which cannon mowed down the Williamites while women on the walls threw broken bottles, bricks and stones. Some soldiers penetrated into the narrow streets, only to be slaughtered.

At the same time, cannon blasted into the men on the counterscarp. At seven o'clock in the evening an entire Brandenburger regiment, which had captured a tower called the Black Battery used as an arsenal, was blown sky high when its powder magazine exploded – the Irish having detonated a mine beneath it. The few survivors 'looked like furies', says George Story. Then the Irish charged out, hurling the enemy off the counterscarp.

The engagement had lasted three hours. William offered to lead another assault in person, but after losing 3,000 men in an afternoon his officers refused. The bombardment recommenced next day, with little effect. William still wanted to attack, although by now the rain was falling in torrents – 'everybody began to dread the consequences of it', remembered Story.

The downpour was the last straw for William's demoralised troops. Badly fed, sleeping in wet, muddy fields, many of them sick, they felt dangerously cut off. Jacobite cavalry watched the roads, killing stragglers, and winter was not far away. On 30 August William angrily gave the order to withdraw along the waterlogged roads. He had lost twenty per cent of his army – 3,000 killed in action, 2,000 dead from disease – while only 400 defenders had fallen.

In the aftermath, Captain Stevens revised his opinion of Irish soldiers. He says that they 'rather starved than lived', but did not go over to an enemy who would pay and feed them well. 'We have already seen them defend an almost defenceless town against a victorious disciplined army and we shall see the following summer under all these hardships fight with the utmost bravery.'[3]

Even Macaulay praises the heroism of the defenders of Limerick. They made possible the Stuart Kingdom of Ireland's survival for another year.

Alarmed by news from other fronts, William hastily left Ireland. King Louis's navy had routed an Anglo-Dutch fleet at Beachy Head while his army had won a big victory over the Imperial forces. A French invasion of England, bringing King James with it, seemed inevitable. The Revolution was in danger.

Tyrconnell, too, left Ireland, sailing with Lauzun from Galway in September, to confer with James in France. Berwick was put in charge, advised by a council of twelve, but soon he was invalided to France, and Sarsfield took over.

9

The Last Sad Hour of Freedom's Dream, 1691

Forget not the field where they perish'd
The truest, the last of the brave.

Thomas Moore

Despite the odds, Catholic Irishmen remained committed to the Restoration. A much-quoted bard dubbed James *Seamas an Chaca* (James the Shit) because he abandoned them after the Boyne, yet for Catholics he continued to be the symbol of nationhood – their only hope of fair government. In his lament, 'The Shipwreck', Ó Bruadair calls him 'the Kind Hearted King'.

In France the Duke of Tyrconnell showed his old powers of persuasion, convincing everybody that victory was possible. King James made him a Knight of the Garter and Lord Lieutenant of Ireland, while King Louis promised guns and ammunition, with a better commander than Lauzun.

When Tyrconnell returned to Limerick in December 1690 he found Jacobite Ireland riven by faction. Historians argue about the rift – Gael versus Old English, or Irish Jacobite versus English Jacobite – but ultimately it was between those ready to negotiate and those wanting to fight on. Neither felt much confidence in a man who had counselled giving in after the Boyne.

Even so, the king's lord lieutenant still inspired respect among many, and Ó Bruadair was glad he was back, writing

Although the bull-flesh dastards had become
Distressful at the prowess of his card

> By Patrick, to the old coat I prefer
> Talbot's coming in the best of health.

'Bull-flesh dastards' refers of course to Tyrconnell's thick-necked enemies.[1]

The Williamites had continued the campaign despite autumn rain, with 5,000 troops under John Churchill, Earl of Marlborough landing at Cork harbour in September, joined by Dutch and Danish regiments from Limerick. Cork's city walls were ruinous, but the governor, Colonel Roger MacElligott, tried to hold out, ignoring Berwick's orders to retreat to Kinsale. After only three days the walls were breached, MacElligott surrendering on 28 September. The terms were broken shamefully – every Catholic in the city was jailed so their houses could be plundered, while some of the soldiers taken prisoner were murdered.

Marlborough then besieged Kinsale, defended by two massive forts in which the septuagenarian commander Sir Edward Scott had concentrated his 1,700 strong garrison. The arsenal of one fort exploded, the enemy storming in, while after the other had been bombarded for three days Scott asked for a parley. Marlborough gave good terms since he dared not prolong the siege into the winter rains, allowing 1,200 Jacobite troops to march off to Limerick.

The winter campaigns of 1690–1

Sarsfield, now Earl of Lucan, built entrenchments on each bank of every bridge or ford across the Shannon, stationing 2,000 cavalry at Athlone who were ready to ride to any threatened crossing at a moment's notice. He also established bases deep in enemy territory. The Irish idolised him:

> The chieftain to kindle the country is Patrick
> In bone-smashing slaughter the sturdiest hand[2]

The new enemy commander was another Dutchman, Baron de Ginkel, who had come to Ireland with Schomberg and had fought at the Boyne. Appointed commander-in-chief (William did not trust Englishmen), he spent the winter of 1690–1 trying, unsuccessfully, to establish bridgeheads on the far bank of the Shannon.

By now, the war was inflicting terrible misery, as if Cromwell had come again.

Children and women migrating in fear and dread
From Shannon to Leamhain [Limerick], bemoaning their misery,
Having nought between them and the rush of the bloody
    sword...[3]

Many men became rapparees, irregular soldiers armed with the half-pikes from which they took their name, killing and mutilating Williamite stragglers – dragging out their intestines. They raided enemy camps, stealing food and weapons, and devastated Protestant enclaves, torching houses, driving off livestock and firing hayricks. When pursued, they hid in long grass or underwater in rivers, or pretended to be farm workers. If caught, the Williamite militia (mainly Ulster Protestants) hanged them from the nearest tree, cutting off their heads for which there was a reward. Entire villages were burned down, their crops and livestock destroyed, for harbouring rapparees.

In their own way, the rapparees were patriots, as they demonstrated in welcoming Hugh Balldearg O'Donnell, a colonel in the Spanish army who claimed to be heir of the old kings of Tyrconnel. Since he had a red birthmark (*ball dearg* means red spot) and there was a prophecy that an O'Donnell with a mark like this would free Ireland, he was greeted joyfully. By the end of 1690 he had a rapparee army 8,000 strong.

On 9 May 1691 French men-of-war sailed into the Shannon with a new commander-in-chief who was received warmly, *Te Deum* being sung at Limerick Cathedral. He was the Marquis de Saint-Ruth, an Alsatian who could not speak English, let alone Irish. His manners did not help – Sarsfield's biographer calls him 'a vain, strutting and insufferably rude Frenchman'.[4] But he brought cannon and muskets, with several hundred English and Scots Jacobites, as well as many French officers.

At Limerick he found the best army the Jacobites ever put in the field, its men veterans if not professionals. The French had already delivered 8,000 muskets and 4,000 long pikes, while the winter had been spent recruiting and training. Theoretically, he was under the lord lieutenant's orders, although Sarsfield had become the real power.

Saint-Ruth came just in time. With an army bigger than William's the previous year and a massive artillery train, Ginkel, after capturing Sarsfield's forward base near Mullingar had chosen mid summer for his main attack, when Irish weather was comparatively free from rain. His strategy was simple – to smash his way over the Shannon and capture Limerick.

The second Siege of Athlone

Ginkel appeared before Athlone on 19 June with fourteen heavy cannon. Its fortifications had been improved since 1690, the garrison defending the east bank as well as the west. However, within days Ginkel had reduced the east to rubble, its garrison demolishing the bridge. But the defenders had killed 400 besiegers, wounding many others, and had won time for reinforcements to arrive.

'Ginkel deserves to be hanged for trying to take Athlone when I am here to defend it with such a big army', bragged Saint-Ruth. 'And I deserve to be hanged myself if I lose it!'

With three of the bridge's five arches still standing Ginkel had planks laid across the gaps for an assault. When they were in place, eleven defenders volunteered to throw them into the Shannon. They were mown down by grapeshot, but another eleven rushed forward and succeeded, although only two survived.

'The great and small shot never ceased firing', recalled Stevens, stationed near the bridge. 'That place was a mere hell on earth, for the place was very narrow which made the fire scorch, and so many cannon and mortars incessantly playing on it there seemed to be no chance of any man coming off alive.'[5] Story heard that Williamite artillery fired 12,000 cannon balls and 600 mortar-bombs, using fifty tons of gunpowder.

Yet Athlone held out. Ginkel contemplated abandoning the siege, and on the afternoon of Tuesday 30 July, Saint-Ruth gave a dinner for his officers to celebrate the Williamites' imminent withdrawal.

The morning had been very quiet. Then, 'In the afternoon on a sudden the whole camp was alarmed', Stevens recalled. 'We understood the town was taken, the enemy having entered both at the bridge and the ford without the least opposition made on our side.'[6] A Williamite general had found an unguarded ford the previous day. Seeing the Shannon unusually low, he offered a pardon to three Danish soldiers under sentence of death if they tested its depth. Wading shoulder deep, they crossed. Moreover, Ginkel knew that raw, newly recruited Irish troops were guarding the bridge, and he knew the time when they changed guard.

Sixty grenadiers struggled across the ford at the head of a mass of infantry, while Major-General Hugh Mackay (Dundee's old opponent at Killiecrankie) led a charge over the bridge, his men laying planks as they went. The inexperienced defenders fled. Rushing back from Saint-Ruth's dinner, the garrison's officers tried to rally them, but it was too late.

The Williamites captured Athlone within half an hour, losing only thirteen dead and thirty-five wounded, killing 500 of their enemies – Danish troops slaughtering many Jacobite soldiers whom they found hiding 'in dark corners'. Altogether, 1,200 defenders died during the siege. Among them, discovered dead beneath the rubble, was Colonel Richard Grace, in his eightieth year.

The city's fall was entirely due to Saint-Ruth's inadequate staff work. 'Thus the place was lost, against all expectation, through a ford, which might have been defended with a thousand firelocks by the help of a trench in the bank, maugre the whole army of the enemy.'[7] He had also omitted to build a line of defence behind the bridge.

Athlone's capture meant that Ginkel had crossed the Shannon.

The Battle of Aughrim

Most of the Jacobite army escaped, regrouping, after which Saint-Ruth marched it into Galway towards Ballinasloe. Remembering what had happened to Schomberg at Dundalk and William at Limerick, the Irish wanted to leave their infantry to defend Limerick and fight a cavalry war – wrecking Ginkel's supply lines, devastating Leinster if he invaded Connacht, striking at Dublin if he besieged Galway. But against Sarsfield's advice and Tyrconnell's express orders, Saint-Ruth, who had about 25,000 men, gave battle.[8]

He chose a position facing east on the road to Limerick, near the ruined castle of Aughrim, placing his infantry on a long ridge along Kilcommadon Hill, protected by a bog behind which was fencing and thick hedges. A stream would hamper any attack from his right. His left could only be reached over a narrow causeway across a bog – sixty yards long, with room for no more than two horsemen to ride abreast.

Ginkel's artillery opened fire on the afternoon of Sunday 12 July. He had 18,000 men, as usual better armed than their opponents. They included 6,000 heavy cavalry and dragoons, several squadrons of whom he sent to charge his enemy's right flank. Saint-Ruth moved troops from the left to strengthen it, leaving fewer to guard the causeway.

After the attack on the right flank ground to a halt, the Williamite infantry mounted a frontal attack, wading waist deep across the bog, but as soon as they reached dry ground Jacobite troops counter-attacked, driving them back through the morass. Triumphantly, Saint-Ruth shouted, '*La jour, c'est à nous, mes enfants!*' However, the enemy's second rank counter-attacked in turn, gaining a foothold on the far side of the bog.

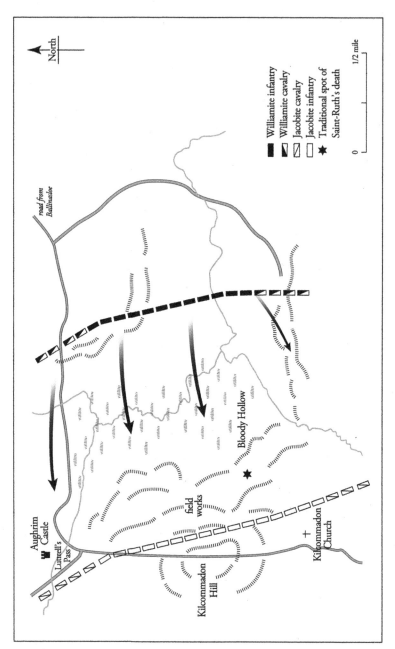

North

road from
Ballinasloe

Aughrim
Castle
Luttrell's
Pass

field
works

Bloody Hollow

Kilcommadon
Hill

Kilcommadon
Church

Williamite infantry
Williamite cavalry
Jacobite cavalry
Jacobite infantry
Traditional spot of
Saint-Ruth's death

0   1/2 mile

The Battle of Aughrim, 12 July 1691

Finally, at about sunset, Hugh Mackay's cavalry forced their way along the causeway on the left, laying hurdles over the bog. Sent to stop them with his dragoons, Dominick Sheldon lost his nerve and did not charge, while Brigadier Henry Luttrell, in command of a cavalry regiment, simply rode away. Undismayed, Saint-Ruth prepared to charge the Williamites himself, crying 'They are beaten!' – at which point a cannon ball took his head off.

The Irish horse's failure to hold the causeway panicked the Jacobite foot, who started to run. Sarsfield led several charges in a desperate attempt to save the situation but, after half an hour, the infantry on the Jacobite right broke too, the enemy storming the fencing behind the bog.

Terrible scenes ensued as the Williamites cut down the fleeing Jacobite infantry. Wounded soldiers and horses lay dying, some men begging to be killed, while the roads were blocked by camp followers, women and children, wailing and weeping. So much ground was covered with blood that it was hard to keep one's footing.[9] Ginkel's men, who had suffered 3,000 casualties, gave no quarter, slaughtering 7,000 Jacobites – among them nine colonels and two brigadiers. Many were cut down in a bog east of the battlefield, including eighty priests who had led charges brandishing crucifixes.

Nightfall and rain stopped further pursuit from *Eachroim an áir* – 'Aughrim of the Slaughter'. Next day, standing on top of Kilcommadon Hill, Story saw four miles of green turf and bog dotted by white objects that at a distance looked like grazing sheep: corpses stripped naked by Williamite camp followers. It is said that the dogs who ate them acquired such a taste for human flesh that it became dangerous for a man to visit Aughrim by himself.

Collecting what cavalry he could, Sarsfield rode to Limerick, the remnants of the infantry limping behind. Ten day later, Galway surrendered, its garrison allowed to march out to Limerick. Sligo yielded soon after, the governor Sir Teague O'Regan likewise taking his 600 men to Limerick. Hugh Balldearg O'Donnell, who had been plundering with his rapparees instead of fighting at Aughrim, was bought off by Ginkel with a pension of £500 a year.

Tyrconnell took command at Limerick, preparing for the inevitable siege and making every senior officer swear not to make terms for himself. Brigadier Luttrell declined, so the duke court-martialled him for secret communication with the enemy. Many believed Luttrell's only concern was securing his elder brother's estate, one of the finest in County Dublin.

In control again, Tyrconnell recovered his spirits. On 10 August the French officers gave a dinner for him at which he was full of laughter, drinking quantities of ratafia, brandy spiced with powdered apricot kernels. That night he suffered a massive stroke, dying four days later. His successors were a triumvirate of lawyers – Sir Richard Nagle with Lord Chancellor Fitton and Francis Plowden. General d'Usson took command of the army.

'If the Duke of Tyrconnell were then alive (I utter it with certainty) he would not hearken to any offer of surrender, because he expected to retrieve the country by spinning out the war', claimed the anonymous author of the Jacobite tract *A Light to the Blind*. 'He grounded his expectation upon the courage of the army made evident unto him by the Battle of Aughrim, and upon the reinforcement he was to receive out of France the following spring.'[10] Wishful thinking, but a tribute to Tyrconnell's powers of persuasion.

The second Siege of Limerick

Ginkel arrived on 30 August. The Jacobites were 17,000 strong but only 10,000 had weapons, the rest having lost them at Aughrim. The besiegers, who brought an artillery train, were supported by the guns of a naval squadron in the Shannon estuary. But the autumn rains were near, their communications were disrupted by rapparees and French warships were on their way.

Remembering what had happened to William, Ginkel was in a hurry, but although the walls were soon breached he decided the breach was too small. Shelling went on night and day. Tyrconnell's sister, Mary, whose husband Viscount Dillon had fallen at Aughrim, was killed in early September by 'the bursting of an explosive device' – a mortar bomb.

On 17 September, using a pontoon bridge, the Williamites crossed further along the Shannon in force, taking by surprise the Jacobite sentries who bolted back to Limerick. Five days later, Ginkel's guns breached the walls of a fort outside the city that guarded the Thomond Bridge into Clare. Panicking, a French officer raised the drawbridge, cutting off 600 Irish troops who were mown down.

The Thomond Bridge massacre broke the defenders' spirit. Senior Irish officers forced d'Usson to hand over command to Sarsfield, who on 23 September asked for a parley. Some of the younger officers broke their swords for shame – many ordinary soldiers threw away their muskets.

Ginkel was a subtle negotiator, reassuring and lavish with promises. He invited Sarsfield, whom he addressed by his Jacobite title, Earl of Lucan, and Major-General Wauchope to dine with him in his camp. They asked for the terms to be guaranteed by King William's lord justices at Dublin, who obligingly came to Limerick.

On 3 October 1691 the Treaty of Limerick was signed in a field outside the city. Its main clauses were that Catholics could practise their religion as freely as in Charles II's day and the Dublin Parliament would pass legislation to confirm this freedom; that everyone in Connacht and West Munster who had fought for James should keep their estates and follow their professions unmolested so long as they swore allegiance to William and Mary; and that soldiers and rapparees could go to France or join the English army.

On 5 October the garrison marched out with the honours of war, drums beating, 'colours flying and matches lighting', on to a parade ground. Of 14,000 troops more than 12,000, led by Sarsfield and Wauchope, opted for France and King James. Only seven of 1,400 soldiers of the King's Royal Irish Regiment of Foot Guards chose English service.

When the Jacobite leaders made peace at Limerick they had more in mind than their estates. Their first concern was to save their army for an invasion of England that would bring a Restoration in all three kingdoms – and at the time of signing France's navy ruled the waves. Ten days later, a French fleet arrived at Limerick.

Many thousands of civilians had been killed while over wide areas there was mass starvation, with whole towns and villages left in ruins. Often the town walls that survived were adorned with heads on spikes, including those of young boys. Men, women and children were to be seen by the roadside wolfing raw meat cut from the rotting carcase of a horse.

Defeat was followed by destruction of the Catholic ruling class, Gael and Old English in what Jacobites called the 'Irish Revolution'. More than a million acres of land was confiscated by King William, whose first priority was to reward his favourites. Bentinck received 150,000 acres and Keppel 100,000, while Meinhardt Schomberg became Duke of Leinster and Ginkel Earl of Athlone, both given vast estates taken from the old nobility. The Munster poet Aogán Ó Rathaille wrote a heartbroken lament for 'The ruin that befell the great families of Erin.'[11] Colonists poured in, English and Huguenots – unlovingly known as *Clann Ugha* by the natives.

Paradoxically, the Treaty of Limerick ensured Irish Jacobitism's survival because of the thousands who over the years joined the armies of France, Spain and other Catholic powers. At home in Ireland the Stuart cause endured for nearly a century, during which political poetry in Irish was

Jacobite poetry.[12] Ó Rathaille devised the *aisling* (reverie), a verse form with wild, mysterious imagery in which Erin (the personification of Ireland) is often a sad maiden or a poor old woman, while there are coded references to her saviours, the banished kings. James became 'a messianic figure in whom all the hopes of the defeated Irish Jacobites were invested', writes Éamonn Ó Ciardha. 'Moreover, their belief in his return provided a balm for the wounds received at the Boyne and Aughrim . . .'[13]

The French ships sailed back to France, taking with them the first of the Wild Geese – Irish soldiers in exile. In his own ancient, outcast language an unknown Irish poet wrote a valedictory farewell, '*Slán le Pádraig Sairséal*', in which he wishes Sarsfield good fortune on his journey, and hopes he will kindle King Louis's anger into flames, 'Though you leave sick Eire in tears . . .'[14]

10

Invading England?
1691–1696

My sight goes beyond
The depth of a pond . . .
Whereby I can tell
That all shall be well
When the King enjoys his Own again.

'When the King enjoys his Own again'

On 28 January 1691 Mr John Ashton, once clerk of the closet to Queen Mary (of Modena), stood beneath the gallows at Tyburn. Just before the hangman fastened the rope around his neck, he handed the sheriff a sheet of paper that would seriously embarrass the authorities.

In December 1690, English Jacobite leaders – Lords Clarendon, Dartmouth and Preston, the Bishop of Ely and Sir William Penn – had sent a joint letter to King James. Urging him to invade in the spring, they warned he must make it clear that his foreign troops were only coming to protect him and would soon be sent home – and that he left the terms of the Restoration to Parliament.

Ashton and a Major Elliott set off to deliver the letter, with details of the English fleet, but the smack taking them to France was intercepted at Tilbury. Both were condemned to death. However, only Ashton was hanged although he could have saved his life by betraying other conspirators.

The paper he gave to the sheriff explained why they wanted James back. Declaring that he died in the faith of the Church of England, Ashton stated that 'new methods' of government were making the nation poor and defenceless and putting the Church in danger. 'There seemed to me no way to prevent the impending evils, but the calling home [of] our injured sovereign.' He added, 'I am so far from repining at the loss of my life, that had I ten thousand, I should rather think myself obliged to sacrifice them all.'[1]

Printed, the paper circulated widely, causing such a stir that the authorities commissioned a pamphlet to refute it. Ashton was the first Jacobite martyr and James made his son a baronet.

There had already been an invasion scare. In June 1690, off Beachy Head, sixty-eight French ships of the line under the Comte de Tourville had routed an Anglo-Dutch fleet of fifty-six commanded by Admiral the Earl of Torrington. One English and six Dutch vessels were sunk, the rest fleeing up the Thames. The French did not lose a single ship.

'Most men were in fear the French would invade', said Torrington at his court martial, borne out by the diarist John Evelyn, who noted 'The whole Nation now exceedingly alarm'd by the French fleete braving our Coast even to the very Thames mouth.'[2] People near the sea hid their valuables. London panicked, the Kent militia camping on Blackheath, while Catholics and known Jacobites were imprisoned – including, for a second time, Samuel Pepys.

In July, Tourville landed a force at Torbay, sacking the little town of Teignmouth. James begged Louis to launch a full-scale invasion, but no troops were available.

In November 1690, a few months after leaving Ireland, James made the first of several annual retreats at La Trappe, the strictest monastery in France. His spiritual adviser was the 'Thundering Abbot', Armand de Rancé, founder of the Trappists, who was impressed by his piety. Privately, some Jacobites thought their king better suited to a cloister than a throne.

James believed it was his duty to recover his kingdoms, his mission to convert them to Catholicism – through toleration and example. At La Trappe, he startled the monks by holding his sword drawn while the Gospel was sung, to demonstrate that he was Defender of the Faith.[3] He prepared himself by hard exercise, hunting every day, and by prayer.

All at St Germain were cheered by the birth of a sister for the Prince of Wales on 18 June 1692. She was named Louisa Mary, Louisa after the king who had behaved so generously to her parents. Courtiers called her *La Consolatrice*.

In 1693, despite Lord Melfort's abysmal showing in Ireland, James appointed him secretary for all three kingdoms. A fanatical Catholic convert from

Calvinism, Melfort did not know the meaning of diplomacy, except in dealing with his employer and King Louis in which he showed himself a master of flattery. He led the 'Non-Compounder' exiles at St Germain, who insisted no mercy must be shown to men of the Revolution. In contrast, the 'Compounders' – most Jacobites in England, people like the late John Ashton – argued that a Restoration could only be achieved by compromise and pardon.

In the last months of 1691 Melfort warned the English Jacobites to be ready to take up arms. Louis XIV had decided to invade England as his navy controlled the Channel. Even if the invasion was opposed, the ensuing civil war might keep William out of Europe.

The invasion of 1692

Establishing himself at Nantes, James planned his homecoming. He would land at Glasgow with 25,000 infantry and 3,000 horse, then march into England where he expected to be joined by a host of North Country Jacobites. Waiting at their camp at the little port of Saint-Vaast-La Hougue (La Hogue) in the Cotentin Peninsula of Normandy, his 14,000 Irish soldiers were eager to avenge Aughrim. They had nearly starved when they arrived from Limerick, but were at last given pay, new uniforms and arms.

However, Louis's ships only had room for 8,000 troops, so James changed his plan. Instead, he would land in Kent and capture the entire English fleet in the Medway. He felt certain this would make such an impression that his supporters could take over London.

He issued a Declaration, drawn up by Melfort. While promising to end 'the illegal taxes lately imposed on the Nation' and bring in toleration 'of all opinions in matters of religion', he refused to admit he had made a single mistake. He also listed those he was going to punish – they included all lawyers and jurymen involved in trying Jacobites, even the Kentish fishermen who had arrested him. Magistrates who did not declare for him as soon as he landed would be guilty of treason.

The Declaration made such a bad impression that Queen Mary had it republished, with sarcastic comments. Most English Jacobites were horrified. Some circulated a false declaration that pretended to offer a pardon to all save four leading Whigs, guaranteed everybody lower taxes and promised to reinstate deprived bishops.

One should not exaggerate the number of English Jacobites; by now no more than one out of every six or seven landowners wanted the Stuarts back.[4]

Apart from the recusants' secret army, few Jacobites were prepared to rise for James. All they would do, sneered Daniel Defoe, was 'stay at home, and drink for him, swear for him, rail and snarl at those they dare not oppose'.[5]

Yet many who were in no sense Jacobites would not actively oppose a Restoration, a fact of which the government was neurotically aware as in 1690 when it panicked at the prospect of invasion. The militia was again called out and regular troops made ready to rush to wherever the armada landed.

Everyone knew how Charles II had been restored under less favourable circumstances. Leading politicians took out insurance policies, assuring James of their loyalty in verbal messages taken to St Germain by reliable agents. Early in 1691 Marlborough (that 'wise, brave, wicked man' as Macaulay calls him), who had betrayed James so spectacularly, contacted St Germain, begging for forgiveness.

Never bothered by scruple, Marlborough supplied details of all English troop movements, warning when prominent Jacobites were in danger of discovery. Gullible as always, James became convinced of his sincerity. During 1692 Marlborough was arrested and sent to the Tower for treason, but was released after letters that involved him in plotting William and Mary's overthrow were shown to be forgeries.

Two more pillars of the Williamite regime who made overtures were Lord Shrewsbury and Sydney Godolphin. The former, until recently Secretary for the Southern Department, was genuinely confused, while Godolphin, First Lord of the Treasury, had once been Mary of Modena's seemingly devoted chamberlain. Like Marlborough, neither wanted a Restoration, but both thought it possible.

Throughout May 1692, French and Irish troops at La Hogue waited to board the transports. James would be assisted by Marshal de Bellefonds and by General d'Usson. All that remained was for Admiral Tourville to defeat William's navy.

But on 29 May Tourville's forty-four ships of the line were routed off Barfleur by eighty-two Anglo-Dutch vessels. (Their commander, Admiral Edward Russell, had recently been in touch with St Germain in case the invasion succeeded.) During a five day battle the Williamite allies drove damaged French warships on to the beach at La Hogue, landing shore parties to burn them. Watching from the fort at Saint Vaast, James – despite being nearly mown down by gunfire – could not help cheering on the boarders, shouting, 'None but my brave English could do so brave an action!'

For the moment, the French navy's defeat ended any invasion plans. James was undismayed, knowing that the new regime in England was growing unpopular. In 1689 the Bill of Rights had placed the monarch under the nation's control, but as William and Mary's reign went by it did not look like this. If most Englishmen welcomed the outcome of the Irish war, they were horrified by its expense and increasingly shocked by the cost of William's Continental wars, especially when he suffered major defeats.

In August 1692, five British regiments were wiped out by the French at Steenkirk in the southern Netherlands – General Mackay of Killiecrankie fame being among the dead. The gentry grumbled at financing such campaigns with a new land tax at four shillings in the pound. Small squires were particularly angry, recalling that King James, who believed in taxing luxuries instead, 'would not have laid one farthing on land'.[6] They resented the power of the new 'monied interest', the City bankers and financiers, whom they identified with Whiggery.

The Earl of Ailesbury came up with a new plan. As James had not been replaced as Lord High Admiral, Britain's navy was commanded by three men – Admirals Killigrew, Delaval and Shovel. Ailesbury's plan was for the entire navy to put far out into the Atlantic under false sealed orders, which would let the French rush the king and his army over to England. Killigrew and Delaval agreed to co-operate, and to make Shovel act with them.

In April 1693 Ailesbury visited St Germain secretly, as 'Mr Allen', having paid the notorious 'Farmer Hunt' of Romney Marsh £10 to spirit him across the Channel in a smuggler's boat. (Hunt made £3,000 a year from smuggling Jacobites until he was kidnapped and taken to France in 1696, to stop him talking.) When the earl arrived, he entered James's presence in a sedan-chair, concealing his identity from the court.

He found the king unaltered but thought Mary of Modena had aged. They welcomed him warmly, presenting him to the little Prince of Wales, although James was 'a little stunned' when the earl expressed less than enthusiasm for his Declaration. Unwillingly, Ailesbury discussed his plan with Melfort, the Earl of Middleton – newly appointed joint secretary of state, before taking over completely in May – and Lord Caryll.

He was then given an audience at Versailles by King Louis, who rejected the scheme – the admirals could not be trusted. He smiled when the earl said that while many Englishmen were loyal to James they hated the French and would never let them restore him. 'I see you are a plain speaker and no flatterer', Louis replied, 'and there is great reason in what you have said.'[7]

'I resolved that I would enter no more into what might bring me to my last end – and for nothing', Ailesbury wrote afterwards.[8] Unfortunately, the Prince of Wales told everybody that he had met the biggest man he had ever seen and all St Germain guessed it was the earl, who was exceptionally tall.

Even the Williamite spy John Macky described Lord Middleton, James's new secretary of state, a cynical Scot with a dry sense of humour, as 'one of the pleasantest companions in the world', who possessed 'a great deal of wit mixed with a very sound judgement'. On his advice, shortly after Ailesbury's visit, James issued another 'Declaration to all his most Loving Subjects'.

It delighted Compounders. He promised pardons for everyone and 'impartial liberty of conscience' for Parliament, besides reassuring Anglicans – 'we will protect the Church of England'. He was encouraged in May 1694 when Marlborough sent him details of an English plan to capture Brest.

When the childless Duke of Modena died in 1694 his sister Queen Mary should have succeeded him, but James refused to let her claim the beautiful little duchy. He also declined to become a candidate for the crown of Poland despite strong French encouragement – still convinced that his destiny was to save his three kingdoms from Protestantism.

The Nine Years War between France and the League of Augsburg was going badly for Louis, who was by now running short of money. In 1695, after losing Namur in Wallonia, he again considered restoring James. It would knock out William, the soul of the Grand Alliance. A fresh plan emerged. English Jacobites would seize a bridgehead on the Kent coast so that James could bring troops over in fast, shallow-draughted transports – during winter, to catch William's fleet off guard. Then they would march on London, most of William's British army being in Flanders. The port's capture was to be organised by an experienced officer, Brigadier-General Sir George Barclay.

In February 1696 James ordered Barclay to go to England and take command, sending Berwick to persuade the Jacobite magnates to rise. He himself went to Calais, ready to cross the Channel.

However, Berwick hastily returned, having left his London lodgings two hours before Williamite 'messengers' (agents) came for him. The plan had been betrayed. London was in an uproar, the militia were called up everywhere, Admiral Russell was assembling the fleet to patrol the coast, and two regiments were being brought home urgently.

What had gone wrong?

11

Murder Dutch Billy?
1695–1696

The Indictment first charges him with Compassing and Designing to depose the King, and put him to Death. The Second Charge is, For inciting the French King to send an Army of Soldiers to invade this Kingdom, and make a miserable Slaughter . . .

Bill of Attainder against Sir John Fenwick,
November 1696

The death of Mary II, 'Goneril', from smallpox on 28 December 1694 was welcomed with joy by Jacobites, who at Bristol rang the church bells and sang 'When the King enjoys his Own again' in the streets. But thousands filed past her embalmed body as it lay in state in Whitehall, the warm-hearted Ailesbury referring to her as 'that incomparable Queen' despite his principles. We are moved to this day by Purcell's music for her funeral.

William was grief stricken. As her passing deprived him of most of his dynastic fig leaf, he doubled the Dutch Guard at Whitehall. At St Germain King James forbade his court to wear mourning for the 'Princess of Orange' and expressed regret that she had condemned herself to eternal damnation.

Moreover, there was growing dissatisfaction in England. In June 1693 a largely British army had been routed by French forces at Landen in present-day Belgium (Sarsfield was killed there, fighting for France, his last words being, 'Oh, that this were for Ireland!'). There was further resentment at British blood being shed in a foreign cause, while despite their defeat at La Hogue the previous year, the French navy was causing serious damage to British merchant shipping.

Privateers operating from St Malo took over 1,200 British vessels in the nine years after 1688, some skippers profiting so much that they built châteaux known as '*malouinières*', so called for their proximity to the port. A year after La Hogue, French warships intercepted the 'Turkey fleet' of 400 English merchantmen off southern Portugal, sinking or capturing ninety-two with cargoes worth over a million pounds – 'the greatest blow was ever given the Citty since the Fire'.[1]

William's need of money to pay for his wars hurt everybody, not just landowners or City magnates. Customs duties rose in 1690 and went on rising. Although the National Debt was contained by founding the Bank of England in 1694, there was no relaxation in land tax, while the next year a window tax hurt all save the poorest. In 1696 recoinage unbalanced the currency. Such burdens had been unknown since Cromwell, and the English knew they were being taxed to defend their foreign king's homeland.

Although anxious to avoid involvement, Ailesbury was still eager to hear of any invasion plans. He describes a series of dinners in London with committed Jacobites where 'because I would not enter into their vain schemes, they grew jealous of me, and swore they did not know what to make of me'. One London house where he dined in 1695 was Sir John Fenwick's.

A former MP who had served under William in Flanders as a colonel of foot, Fenwick hated the king and queen with a bitterness that verged on mania. In 1691 he had accosted Queen Mary in Kensington Gardens and, instead of bowing, cocked his hat in her face. William never forgave the impertinence. Early in 1695, after a drunken party at a Drury Lane tavern Fenwick and his friends blew trumpets in the street outside, forcing anyone they met to drink King James's health.

A leader in the invasion plot, Fenwick had been given a secret commission as major-general, writing to St Germain that all over England men were ready to rise, and that the king would be greeted by 4,000 horse when he landed. In reality Sir John was a boastful windbag – no such force existed.

At one dinner, the company discussed what jobs they would take after the Restoration, Fenwick said he wanted to be Governor of the Isle of Wight. Laughing, Ailesbury declared, 'Give me a place that requires no attendance at Court but that brings a great income – and all transacted by secretaries and clerks, as, for example, Auditor of the Exchequer!'

In May 1695 Ailesbury gave a dinner at Mrs Mountjoy's Tavern in St James's where his guests included Fenwick, Sir John Friend, Sir William Parkyns,

Captain George Porter and Robert Charnock. Its object was to find a job for Charnock – a Catholic priest, ex-fellow of Magdalen College, Oxford, and 'poor Grumbling Jacobite'. Ailesbury did not know that Charnock, who held a secret commission from James as captain, was a key player in the invasion plot and had recruited Parkyns and Porter.

A rich City merchant knighted by Charles II, Parkyns had amassed an arsenal at his country house. Sir John Friend, a wealthy brewer, was equally uncompromising. Captain Porter was an ex-cavalry officer, murderer, suspected highwayman and debauched 'man of pleasure', who in the summer of 1695 had been arrested at one of the Drury Lane taverns for drinking King James's health.

Unaware of what dangerous company he was keeping, Ailesbury went to yet another Jacobite dinner at the King's Head, Leadenhall Street, which he feared was a brothel. This too was attended by Charnock and also by Cardonell Goodman (otherwise known as 'Scum Goodman'), a professional actor, pimp and poisoner, so poor that occasionally he shared a shirt, and whose sole claim to respectability lay in having been briefly a Page of the Backstairs to Charles II.

Furthermore, Ailesbury's hardline Jacobite acquaintances included Peter Cook, noisily indiscreet but trusted because his uncle, Colonel Cook, had been a family friend, and William Berkenhead who was one of King James's few formidable agents, expert at spiriting men in and out of the country. On one visit, he alarmed the earl by bringing 'Farmer Hunt', the Romney Marsh smuggler.

Sir George Barclay, who had been among Dundee's most trusted officers and fought at Killiecrankie, arrived from St Germain in January 1696. He found that despite Fenwick's bluster there were no troops other than a few determined supporters assembled by Charnock. Using Covent Garden as his headquarters, Barclay began recruiting Jacobites, hoping to raise 2,000 horse.

A few days later, the Duke of Berwick (like Barclay, smuggled over by 'Farmer Hunt') made a brief visit. Heavily disguised, he was warmly received by Jacobite magnates, who gave a masquerade for him to meet supporters. Their names are unknown, but they represented southern England's recusants. While swearing undying loyalty to his father, they refused to risk their necks unless a French army landed.

However, capturing a port and holding it long enough for James to arrive would not be easy, while even if the French transports evaded William's warships they might be scattered by a winter storm. Barclay preferred

Charnock's suggestion, to 'kidnap' William – in other words, to kill him. Untruthfully, Barclay insisted that James had authorised assassination.

Barclay and Charnock's friends, about forty in all, adopted a plot drawn up by George Porter. Every Saturday William hunted in Richmond Park, which involved a journey from Kensington through open country down the Middlesex bank of the Thames to Turnham Green, where he was ferried over to Surrey. The plan was to ambush his coach in the dusk as it returned from Turnham Green along a narrow, muddy lane when he was alone save for a handful of guards – Barclay, assisted by eight picked men, would shoot or sabre him. The date chosen was 15 February or, if William did not hunt on that day, 22 February.

On 13 February Porter tried to recruit Thomas Prendergast, an Irish Jacobite. Next day, horrified at the idea of murder in cold blood and certain that James would never have countenanced it, Prendergast went to William Bentinck, Lord Portland, warning him the king must not hunt, but refusing to name any conspirators. William was sceptical until another informant appeared with a similar story and a list of names. The king announced he was ill and would not hunt on Saturday 15 February, which did not alarm the plotters.

When William did not hunt for a second Saturday, they grew terrified, with good reason. Most were captured on Sunday 23 February but Barclay, who was the real brains behind the plot, escaped to France (where a shocked King James refused to receive him). Next day, William informed Parliament that a conspiracy to assassinate him had been discovered. In all, 300 Jacobites were arrested including seven peers, among them Lord Ailesbury.

Porter, whom Ailesbury calls 'that monster of a man', turned King's Evidence, receiving a pardon and a cash payment for testifying against his fellow conspirators – even against his own servant. Seven were executed while five spent decades in Newgate without trial, the last dying in 1736. After a year in the Tower, Ailesbury was released. Everybody knew he was too decent to be involved in such a business.

Charnock's *Letter to a Friend Written Shortly Before His Execution*, argued that he had tried 'to rid the World of a Publick Enemy who has kindled a War all over Europe', calling William 'a common Usurper' and an 'unjust ravisher'. From the scaffold, on 18 March 1696, he claimed that King James had known nothing of the plot. Sir John Friend and Sir William Parkyns suffered the same fate on 3 April, Friend declaring 'it is altogether new and unintelligible to me that the King's subjects can depose or dethrone him on any account' while Parkyn insisted he had done his duty 'as a subject and an Englishman'.[2]

The nonjuror priest and polemicist Jeremy Collier, who accompanied them to Tyburn, laid his hands on their heads before they were turned off the scaffold ladder, absolving them.

For months Sir John Fenwick, who had been against assassination, evaded capture, to be caught in June while trying to escape across the Channel. Only two men would testify against Fenwick, Porter and 'Scum' Goodman, who had also turned King's Evidence. Porter betrayed a plot to bribe him into leaving the country, but Goodman went to France in return for £500 a year, depriving the prosecution of a vital witness.

Among others, Fenwick accused Shrewsbury and Godolphin of being Jacobites, which made Godolphin resign as First Lord of the Treasury. William, who realised their contact with St Germain was mere insurance, did not worry, yet many important men were nervous of what Sir John might reveal.

Lack of a witness other than Porter meant that a trial could not find Fenwick guilty. The authorities resorted to a bill of attainder which, after angry debates in both Houses of Parliament, was passed in December 1696. Many peers and MPs thought it amounted to murder, a violation of all laws of evidence, but William gave his assent. Instead of being hanged, drawn and quartered, Fenwick was beheaded on Tower Hill. 'My religion taught me loyalty, which I bless God is untainted', he declared from the scaffold. 'And I have ever endeavoured in the station wherein I have been placed to support the crown of England in the true and lineal course of descent, without interruption.'[3]

Whig MPs exploited the situation, introducing an 'Instrument of Association' that bound those who signed it to defend King William, 'our rightful and lawful sovereign' against all enemies. Nearly ninety Tory MPs refused to sign. An Act of Parliament obliged all office holders to sign, which resulted in the dismissal of over eighty magistrates and a hundred deputy lieutenants.

The 'Assassination Plot' did Jacobitism a lot of harm. John Evelyn commented in his diary, 'tho' many did formerly pity K. James's Condition, this designe of Assassination, & bringing over a French Army, did much to alienate many of his Friends, & was like to produce a more perfect estab-lishment of K. William.'[4] Berwick's brief visit had given the impression that the plotters were acting on James's orders. However, we have Ailesbury's testimony that, 'By indirect ways I knew for certain that King James detested that action.'

12

'King William's Ill Years' – Scotland, 1694–1702

And the Lord hardened the heart of Pharaoh, and he
hearkened not . . . For now I will stretch out my hand,
that now I may smite thee and thy people with pestilence

Book of Exodus, ix:13–15

In Scotland, Dundee's war was followed by a decade of famine, plague and financial ruin that Jacobites claimed was God's punishment for the Revolution. They likened William to Pharoah. The comparison did not seem far-fetched to a people who lived by the Bible.

In August 1691 the government proclaimed that clan chiefs who swore allegiance to King William before a magistrate by New Year's Day 1692 would receive a full pardon. Otherwise, 'letters of fire and sword' would be issued against them. MacDonald of Glencoe failed to swear in time, which was the pretext for the mass murder of his clan in February 1692. Everyone knew that William had signed an 'Instrument' stating it would be 'a proper vindication of the publick justice to extirpate that nest of thieves' and the Scots blamed him for the crime.[1] What shocked them most was its having been done 'under trust', violating the laws of hospitality, the troops who perpetrated the massacre having been given shelter and entertainment by the MacDonalds for a fortnight.

In September 1692 a pamphlet appeared, *Great Britain's Just Complaint*, deploring 'so barbarous a murther' that 'put Glencou [sic] and all the males of his clan under seventy to death'. It blamed crimes like this on the Revolution. There was no excuse for deposing James – 'The Catholicks of Great Britain are not one in a hundred; they have neither Health, Heart nor Hands enough to force a National Conversion.' The author praised James warmly, quoting the note he had left at Rochester.[2]

The pamphlet made the Scots Parliament demand an enquiry into who was responsible for Glencoe. This reported that Scotland's secretary of state, Sir John Dalrymple, later Earl of Stair, had set the massacre in motion. He was dismissed, perhaps partly because of his family background. (His mother, 'The Witch of Endor', was credited with casting spells on enemies and changing into a cat; his sister had stabbed her husband to death on their wedding night; his brother had been poisoned; and one of his sons had killed another son.) Stair lived out the rest of his life in fear, his house ringed by bodyguards while when he died it was rumoured he had hanged himself. But the Scots still blamed King William.

Not only in Scotland but in the other kingdoms, Jacobites highlighted the scandal. At Dublin, then at London, Charles Leslie, a former Church of Ireland priest, published *Gallienus Redivivus: or Murther will Out*, gleefully comparing William to an insecure and horribly cruel Roman Emperor who had persecuted Christians.

The author of *Great Britain's Just Complaint* was an Ayrshire laird, Sir James Montgomerie of Skelmorlie ('a man of considerable abilities, but of loose temper, insatiable cupidity, and implacable malevolence' says Macaulay), who had welcomed the Revolution. Furious at not being appointed Scottish secretary of state, he founded 'the Club', a group of MPs who wrecked the regime's business at Parliament House, refusing supplies and attacking government spokesmen.

When William refused to read his grievances, Montgomerie 'fell a treating with King James's party in England'[3], claiming he knew how to persuade the Scots Parliament to accept a Restoration. In the event, his ally Lord Ross betrayed the 'Montgomerie Plot', which amounted to little more than boasting. Sir James was arrested, but escaped to France.

Under the new regime Scotland's Parliament was freer of royal control, owing to the abolition of a parliamentary committee known as 'The Lords of the Articles' that had previously directed all its business. However, the Whig government was hamstrung by faction and strapped for cash – Scottish annual revenue amounted to a fortnight's English revenue, while the English pound was worth 12 pounds Scots.

The Highland War of 1689–91 had virtually bankrupted Scotland, which now relied on English money to stay solvent. This was not always easy to extract from London. Unlike his Stuart predecessors, William left Scottish politics to magnates who squabbled with each other for precedence, making firm rule an impossibility.

Montgomerie's 'Club' survived his disappearance, changing into a party known as the 'Cavaliers' – Jacobites. In an attempt to control them, in 1693 William appointed the immensely rich James Douglas, Duke of Queensberry, as Lord High Treasurer, then Lord Privy Seal and finally Lord High Commissioner or viceroy. But Queensberry failed to cow his opponents. And, as David Hume later observed, 'We never had any Tories in Scotland', only Jacobites.[4]

The situation was made more difficult by a deep division among Scotland's Protestants. When the Dutch armada had been blown off course in 1688, the Scots bishops wrote to James, expressing their hope that the king 'might have the necks of all his enemies'.

After the Revolution, so Burnet tells us, Episcopal churchmen 'finding themselves under a cloud, had no refuge but to shelter themselves under the Earl [sic] of Dundee', adding that throughout Scotland's south western counties bands of Presbyterians 'broke in upon the Episcopal clergy with great insolence and much cruelty. They carried them about the parishes in a mock procession; they tore their gowns, and drove them from their churches and houses.'[5] The mobs chose Christmas for their 'rabbling' as it was a prelatical feast day.

Between a third and a half of Scots were Episcopalians, concentrated mainly in the central and eastern Lowlands, with others as far north as Aberdeen. There were also many in the Highlands whose population was five times larger than today. They were served by fourteen bishops and a thousand priests, two thirds of whom were evicted from their livings. (A hundred years later there would be only four Episcopalian bishops and fifty priests.)

The two forms of Protestantism repelled each other. Presbyterians thought Episcopalian worship diabolically 'Popish' while, immune to the steely logic of Calvin's *Institutes*, Episcopalians ridiculed the Kirk's long sermons and metric psalms which, they claimed, were sung 'out of tune, more like people in the agony of death howling for pain, than praising God with a Cheerful spirit'.[6] Both denominations firmly believed the other was going to hell en bloc.

William saw danger in giving Presbyterians exclusive authority, but in June 1690 the Scottish Parliament made Presbyterianism the official religion. The restored Kirk took Godly delight in harrying 'Prelatists', who were deprived of all say in the Church's government and subjected to the same persecution as Catholics. As William feared, Episcopalianism became a Jacobite faith.

William's regime was vulnerable in other ways, too. With a population as small as a million, despite its fine universities and thriving intellectual life, seventeenth-century Scotland was one of Europe's poorest countries, some areas scarcely better off than Iceland. Even at this date it had not recovered from the Covenanting wars and the Cromwellian occupation.

Most of Edinburgh's 50,000 citizens (compared to London's half-million) were crammed into tenements, often ten or fifteen stories high – 'wynds' and 'closes', that were devastated by a terrible fire in 1700. They contrasted oddly with stately public buildings like the Baroque Parliament House, while in Daniel Defoe's opinion the main thoroughfare, the Royal Mile, was 'the most spacious, the longest, and best inhabited street in Europe'.[7]

Apart from the ports of Leith, Montrose and Aberdeen, commerce was on a very small scale, dwindling rather than increasing, except for the export of coal, wool and linen, and a certain amount of grain. There was almost no mercantile shipping along most of the west coast.

The exception was Glasgow, the kingdom's most prosperous city, which carried on a lucrative contraband trade with North America, bringing back coffee, sugar and tobacco that it sold even in the Highlands. Defoe thought Glasgow's four main streets 'the finest for breadth and the finest built that I have ever seen in one city together',[8] while in 1735, the road builder Edmund Burt commented in his *Letters from a Gentleman in the North of Scotland* that it was 'the prettiest and most uniform town that I ever saw'.[9]

Outside the cities and scattered little towns – whose population was falling – people lived in rough cabins while, save for a few wealthy magnates (and the endeavours of James Smith of Whitehill and Sir William Bruce), the lairds still inhabited gaunt towers or turreted mansions designed for defence. Most men were cottars with minute holdings and short leases that prevented such refinements as efficient drainage. Even on the best Lowland soil where holdings were larger, farming remained primitive, with oats and kale the main crops. Improving landlords who enclosed land were only just emerging.

On their rain-sodden mountains the Gaelic-speaking Highlanders, who formed a third of the population, scratched a bare subsistence with wooden 'foot-ploughs' from thin, stony soil and during the harsh, snowy winters had little to eat – when their oatmeal ran out, they bled a cow, boiling the blood into cakes.

'This [winter] is a bad season with them', Burt tells us. 'They have no diversions to amuse them, but sit brooding in the smoke over the fire till their legs and thighs are scorched to an extraordinary degree; and many have sore eyes, and some are quite blind.'[10] Cattle rearing and droving, their one profitable activity, made life a bit better for a few. Some chiefs were entrepreneurial, selling timber from their forests on a commercial scale, but this did not benefit many of the clansmen.

Burt observes that while the gentry (by which he meant the *fine* or clan elite) were as big as Lowlanders, ordinary Highlanders were small from 'being starved in the womb, and never afterwards well fed'. He says the gentry were 'a handsome people, but the commonalty much otherwise; one would hardly think, by their faces, they were of the same country, which plainly proceeds from their bad food, smoke at home, and sun, wind, and rain abroad'.[11]

What shocked Burt most was 'the despotic power of the chiefs', their power of pit and gallows, which was to condemn women to drown and men to hang. (Minor sentences were equally barbaric – in 1700, for consorting with an outlaw, a woman at Grantown was stripped to the waist, given thirty lashes and had an ear cut off, before being banished.)[12] Yet Burt was impressed by the clansmen's loyalty to their chief, even if the chief saw them as chattels whom he sometimes sold in the West Indies as indentured labour – white slaves.

Everybody, Lowlanders and Highlanders, rich and poor, dreaded a bad harvest. During William's reign, due to unusually cold winters accompanied by gales and flooding, two harvests failed completely and others were bad. In consequence, oatmeal, which formed the staple diet, was in short supply, as were peas and beans, while livestock died in large numbers from lack of fodder. 'God helpe the poor people', wrote an eyewitness in 1696, 'for I never did sie such outcryes for want of meall'.[13] Another said he saw death in the faces of the poor. Men and women begged from door to door, some dropping dead in the streets from hunger. In 1699, food riots broke out.

This was not the only disaster. Merchants lost what little trade they had with France and Holland because of the Nine Years War and French privateers. What industry there was collapsed while flooding wrecked the coal mines. Roads were not maintained and houses fell into disrepair

Plague followed famine, killer diseases such as smallpox, typhus or dysentery. There were so many corpses that they had to be buried en masse in pits or burned. Thousands of starving Scots fled abroad, to beg in England or Ulster, or join the armies of Sweden, Germany or Russia. Nearly a fifth of the country's population died from hunger and disease or was lost to emigration.

The Darien fiasco

In 1695 Sir William Paterson persuaded the Scots Parliament to pass an Act creating the Scottish Darien Trading Company, which was given a monopoly of Scottish trade with the Far East. The company decided to concentrate instead on South America and establish a colony in Panama. A founder of the Bank of England, Paterson's antecedents were impeccable and his alluringly advertised scheme inspired an orgy of speculation that anticipated England's South Sea Bubble. Eager to escape from the horrors at home, Scots flocked to join the settlement.

In 1698 ten ships landed in Panama, bringing Paterson and 1,200 eager colonists. However, most of New Edinburgh's inhabitants quickly succumbed to yellow fever or malaria, including Paterson's wife and child. The survivors lived in dread of the Spaniards while King William forebade English colonists to trade with them. In 1700, Spanish troops evicted the diseased remnant, who sailed back in two ships. When they returned, riots broke out at the news. The scheme used up half of Scotland's scant liquid capital, ruining many investors. King William was blamed, although the Scots could scarcely expect him to approve the seizure of territory that belonged to Spain, his ally.

Looking back, James VII's reign seemed an era of milk and honey compared to 'King William's Ill Years', as Jacobites called them. The Darien Company's failure discredited the Whig regime at Edinburgh even further.

Every Sunday, Episcopalian clergy prayed for the exiled royal family, teaching that loyalty to it was indispensable for salvation, ascribing the country's miseries to God's displeasure. A flavour of their sermons can be gleaned from the future Primus, Thomas Rattray of Craighall, in which he denounced 'the Execrable usurper, and the Banishment of the righteous Heir'.[14]

They had reason for bitterness, as the normally partisan Macaulay admits: 'Manses had been sacked; churches shut up; prayer books burned; sacred garments torn; congregations dispersed by violence; priests hustled, pilloried, driven forth with their wives and babes, to beg or die of hunger.'

Even Presbyterians who took comfort in their Kirk's triumph could not forget how King William put Holland before England – and England before

Scotland. He ignored the northern kingdom save when it threatened his security. 'My Lord, I only wish it was a hundred thousand miles off and that you was King of it!' he told the Duke of Hamilton.

The Scots hearkened to the diatribes of the 'Cavaliers' against an inefficient government directed from London. They were infuriated in 1701 when the English Parliament passed an Act of Settlement deciding the succession to the throne in all three kingdoms without consulting the Scottish Parliament. According to Scots Law, the Act could not apply to Scotland.

13

Waiting for 'the gentleman in black velvet'

Then fears avaunt, upon the hill
My hope shall cast her anchor still
Until I see some peaceful dove
Bring home the branch I dearly love

'When the King enjoys his Own again'

Because of the war France was starving. Some Frenchmen thought that King James must be the cause, stoning guards on duty outside St Germain. However, in 1696 James saw new hope when the Duke of Savoy abandoned the Grand Alliance, making a separate peace with Louis XIV.

But when a congress to end the Nine Years War met at Ryswick near the Hague in May 1697, it rejected James's request to send an envoy and his protest that any treaty made without him would be invalid. At the treaty signed in September, besides surrendering most of his conquests, Louis recognised William as King of Great Britain, agreeing not to help his enemies – directly or indirectly. It was the worst blow that James had suffered since 1688.

England rejoiced at the peace, church bells pealing. Throughout the country there were bonfires, banquets and processions with banners bearing the words, 'God bless King William!' Everyone hoped for less taxation, yet it was a distinctly fragile peace.

Louis told James that although he acknowledged William III, France would guarantee the Prince of Wales's succession. William offered to adopt the boy as his son, but James declined – it meant his abdication – while he did not want the child to grow up a Protestant. William also tried to buy off James with a promise, never fulfilled, to pay the £50,000 dowry granted by Parliament a decade before to Mary of Modena.

James was deeply concerned for his Irish soldiers, who had fought for him since 1689. Five regiments of infantry and one of cavalry were kept as part of France's military establishment, but many men found themselves without employment. When he protested to Louis, some officers were allowed to form a unit in the French army, serving as privates. Reduced to beggary, others became highwaymen.

A final blow came in 1698 – the news that his Palace of Whitehall had been burned to the ground.

Life at St Germain

James stayed at St Germain, still treated as a king by Louis. The atmosphere was dismal, Lord Middleton described the palace as 'the dreadfullest place in France next to the Bastille'. A host of Jacobite refugees, English, Scots and Irish, added to the gloom. James did what he could for men who had ruined themselves in his cause, but he did not have enough funds – the queen having already sold her diamonds to help them.

He grew steadily more devout and made further retreats at La Trappe, edifying Abbot Rancé by his acceptance of God's will.[1] Worldly observers, among them Louis, saw this as crippling fatalism. Had they known of it, they would also have deplored his interest in Jansenism with its Calvinist stress on predestination and belief that most people go to hell – a heresy detested by Louis.

Annually, he touched for the King's Evil (scrofula, or swollen lymph glands), laying hands on the head of the sufferer whom he presented with a silver-gilt touch-piece bearing an image of the Archangel Michael. Those afflicted came from miles around. Among them were recusants from England, such as the daughter of Sir Nicholas Shireburne of Stonyhurst in 1698.[2]

The Prince of Wales's household was staffed by English recusants, but in 1696 he was given a Scottish 'governor', the Earl (later Duke) of Perth, who was Melfort's elder brother and like him a fervent Catholic convert. Perth's job was to oversee a rigid programme of education devised by the king. He appointed as tutor Dr John Betham from Warwickshire, who had been a chaplain at Whitehall.

The boy was very aware of what should have been his inheritance. When he was eleven some Scots told him that if he went to their country he would immediately be acclaimed as the rightful heir. He was so thrilled that his guards had to be increased to stop him from running away to Scotland.

The last years of William III

William's new popularity did not last. He had less control over Parliament, which annulled the grants of confiscated Irish estates to his Dutch favourites, selling them to pay for his wars. Led by an eloquent young Oxford don called Francis Atterbury, Convocation (the clergy's 'parliament') was up in arms against concessions to Dissenters and if most were not yet Jacobites these turbulent priests regretted the Revolution. The king was even blamed for the harsh winters and bad harvests of the late 1690s.

Another European conflict was feared at any moment. A grandson of Louis XIV, Philip of Anjou, was expected to claim the Spanish throne when the moribund Carlos II died, which could mean an attempt to unite France and Spain. Yet Parliament insisted on cutting the army to 7,000 men – even William's Dutch Blue Guards were sent back to Holland. For a moment, he considered abdication.

The main aim of Tory MPs, now in a majority, was reducing taxation. However, a gaffe by Lord Melfort changed their minds. Although no longer secretary of state, early in 1701 he wrote to his brother, Lord Perth, assuring him that Louis XIV had every intention of restoring James. Sent via London by mistake and intercepted, it caused uproar, Parliament voting to re-equip the fleet.

One policy on which William and most of his subjects agreed was that a Protestant must succeed him on the throne. Princess Anne, who was next in line, had a son William, Duke of Gloucester, but he was sickly and might die prematurely like her other children.

As early as 1689 King William had tried unsuccessfully to insert a clause in the Declaration of Right giving the succession to the dowager Electress of Hanover, the aged Princess Sophia (a granddaughter of James I) should Anne die childless. There were many closer heirs with a far better claim in blood as descendants of Charles I, but they were all Catholics and although a Lutheran Sophia was at least a Protestant.

There was more to William's choice than religion. As a nonjuror later pointed out, 'how much it is in the Interest of the States of Holland to have a friend of theirs upon the Throne of Great Britain'. Hanover was near Holland and a useful ally if joined with Britain.[3]

When Gloucester died in 1700, a decision became unavoidable. Next year a bill was introduced in the Commons to make Anne heir presumptive and settle the succession on Sophia – and to exclude not only James's son the Prince of Wales but all Catholic claimants. The bill had a difficult passage.

The prince's heir was his first cousin Anne, Duchess of Savoy (daughter of James II's sister Henrietta, Duchess of Orleans), and her husband's envoy went before Parliament to protest at setting aside their son's claim – there were rumours that the duke promised to bring him up as an Anglican.

Few in England had ever heard of the Hanoverian Welph ('Whelp' in Scots), little princelings who were in no sense a great German ruling family like Bavaria's Wittelsbach or Saxony's Wettin, let alone Habsburgs. Resentful at the way William had used English resources to aid Holland, many feared a Hanoverian king would do the same for Hanover. The Commons passed the bill by a single vote. 'Old Sophy' was pessimistic, commenting that Parliament might change its mind.

Death of James II

Although wearing spectacles to read, James lived his usual life until 1699, dividing his time between hunting and prayer – besides teaching his son how to shoot and fence. 'He himself seemed to be the least concerned in all his misfortunes.'[4] Yet he never abandoned hope of a Restoration, keeping in touch with well-affected noblemen and even planning a Jacobite takeover of the Darien colony until it collapsed. He also commissioned 7,000 medals with the Prince of Wales's head, for distribution across the Channel.

In March 1701 he was struck down by a stroke, but recovered sufficiently to resume his hunting. Early in September, however, he suffered another, a brain haemorrhage which finally killed him on 17 September. The Prince of Wales wept when he saw his father lying ashen-faced and bearded on a bed drenched in blood, begging him never to change his religion. Louis XIV visited the dying man three times, promising he would recognise his son as King of England.

Whatever Parliament decreed, James remained King of Great Britain and Ireland for legitimists until the day he died. So did his son. Aware that it meant war with Williamite England, Louis XIV sent heralds to St Germain, to proclaim the twelve-year-old 'King James III' at the palace gates – in Latin, French and English. A long reign had begun, if one without crown or kingdom.

After regal funeral ceremonies, the old king's coffin was taken to Paris, to the English Benedictine priory in the rue St Jacques. Here it lay on a catafalque in the chapel of St Edmund, awaiting burial at Westminster.

William's response to James III's succession was an Act of Parliament in March 1702, attainting both him and 'his pretended mother', making them liable to the death penalty. It also included a compulsory oath of abjuration for office holders – 'I do believe in my Conscience That the Person . . . taking upon himself the Stile and Title of King of England by the Name of King James the Third hath not any Right or Title whatsoever to the Crown of this Realm.'[5]

Some anonymous lines on the oath written a few years later reveal what Jacobites thought of those who took it.

> Our Fathers took Oaths, as their Wives,
> To Have and to Hold for the Term of their Lives;
> But we take the Oaths, like a Whore for our Ease
> And a Whore and a Rogue may part when they please.[6]

Death of William III

On 21 February 1702, William's horse stumbled on a molehill in Richmond Park, throwing him and breaking his collarbone. Pneumonia set in and he died on 8 March, the day after signing the Abjuration Act, so weak that he used a stamp. He was fifty-one years old. Jacobites drank to 'the little gentleman in black velvet', recalling how his horse, Sorrel, had been confiscated from Sir John Fenwick.

One of the ablest men who ever ruled Britain, he had been amazingly successful in retaining the throne while despite, the wars, his reign had brought prosperity. Yet no king was ever less mourned.

PART TWO

James III – A Second Restoration?

14

Queen Anne, 1702

When Royal Anne became our queen, the Church of
   England's glory,
Another face of things was seen, and I became a Tory...

'The Vicar of Bray'

In March 1712 a small boy from Lichfield went to St James's Palace to be cured of the King's Evil. Seated on a throne, a portly lady in black, hooded and glittering with diamonds, laid her hands on his head, then hung a gold medallion around his neck – a touch-piece he wore for the rest of his life.[1] The lady was Queen Anne and the boy Samuel Johnson, who never ceased to venerate the House of Stuart.

Obese, purple-faced, rheumy-eyed, a martyr to gout, almost continually ill, Anne was unjustly nicknamed 'Brandy Nan' because of a supposed fondness for spirits. Her sole graces were a beautiful voice and innate dignity. Muddle-headed, demoralised by her last surviving child's recent death, lacking in self-confidence, with an amiable, useless drunk of a husband who died halfway through her reign, she was dominated by women favourites – first the vixenish Sarah Churchill, Duchess of Marlborough, then the sly Mrs Masham.

Despite eighteen pregnancies, Anne saw herself as another Elizabeth, never missing a cabinet meeting, determined to defend the Crown's prerogative. The new Virgin Queen's only political talent was an ability to conceal her real opinions. Although one of nature's Tories, on Sarah Churchill's insistence she ruled at first through Whigs led by Godolphin and Marlborough.

By now Jacobites were a mere three per cent of England's population, although this was going to change. However, they were convinced that when Anne died a Restoration was inevitable. A rumour circulated that James had attended her coronation in disguise and that she had kissed him during the ceremony.

In reality, she believed the warming-pan story that James was not her brother but a changeling – otherwise she would be a usurper. With surprising cunning, she never said whom she wanted to succeed her, not even when dying. Her refusal to commit herself ensured that English Jacobites did not cause trouble during her reign.

James III's court in exile

Now that James II had left the scene and Mary of Modena, acting on behalf of her thirteen-year-old son, was regent, more realism prevailed at St Germain. Mary's role as a canny politician is under-appreciated because she spent so much time preparing for the next world with the Nuns of Chaillot. However, she never let Louis XIV forget his promise to restore her son, charming everybody at the French court who might be useful, making friends with Louis's morganatic wife Madame de Maintenon. A shrewd judge of men, until James moved his court to Bar in 1713 she employed a network of spies.[2]

Wisely, she kept the Earl of Middleton as secretary of state, a man who invariably urged moderation. However, he damaged his standing with many Jacobites when, hitherto a staunch Protestant, he turned Catholic and his explanation, that in a dream the late king had commanded him to convert, satisfied few Anglicans. In 1702 he would resign as secretary, but be persuaded to change his mind.

In November 1701 Lord Belhaven, a Scots patriot rather than a Jacobite, arrived at St Germain. He had fought for William at Killiecrankie, but strongly opposed the Act of Settlement. In his view, the union of the two crowns had ruined Scotland. Restoring James VIII as King of Scots was the one chance of avoiding the still greater calamity of a union of the two Parliaments – of England taking over his country.

He claimed to represent many Scottish noblemen, including the Duke of Hamilton, who were ready to rise for James if he became a Protestant. When Queen Mary refused, Belhaven suggested that a rising might still be possible if the King promised never to interfere in matters of religion, and went to Scotland in person to lead his followers. Although the offer was declined, it seemed a good omen.

Another was a visit by a High Churchman, Dr Leybourne, who came in February 1702. He wanted pledges that his Church would be free from royal interference, with bishops chosen by a committee of prelates instead of the king, while to win over parsons no tithes must be paid to the Crown. Laws against Catholics should be moderated by Parliament. Mary agreed to all this.[3]

One of the regent's first real trials was Simon Lovat. The ruthless young chief of the Frasers, deservedly known in the Highlands as *An Sionnach* (the Fox), had become a Jacobite to secure the Lovat peerage. However, this title was disputed by Lord John Murray, the Earl of Tullibardine, whose sister Amelia was the previous Lord Lovat's widow. Failing to marry her daughter, Simon abducted Amelia herself and despite her screams had a marriage service performed by a drunken parson, after which he raped her – his ghillies having ripped open the lady's dress with their dirks during the 'wedding'. Eventually, Amelia was rescued by Tullibardine.

In 1702, escaping from 'letters of fire and sword' Lovat fled to France, where he produced a plan that he explained to Queen Mary and King Louis – a French expeditionary force would land on the east coast of Scotland and a smaller force in the west, then, gathering strength as they went, they would march on Edinburgh. With considerable reservations, Mary sent him back to Scotland to obtain guarantees of support.

As soon as Lovat returned to Scotland he contacted James Douglas, the Duke of Queensberry. Despite realising at once that his 'plot' was a pack of lies, the wily duke told Lovat to implicate every gentleman who opposed union with England. Lockhart of Carnwath calls this a 'hellish conspiracy', adding 'there was not one unbyassed person that did not see it was all trick and villainy'.[4] Lovat returned to France with a glib explanation, but Mary had seen through him and he went to the Bastille.

The regent had bigger fish to fry than Lovat. The looming Union between England and Scotland would rally vast numbers of Scots to the Stuart cause and strengthen the likelihood of a Restoration in all three realms.

Queen Anne's golden reign – in England

Meanwhile, the reign of Queen Anne was turning out to be a minor golden age for her English subjects, who prospered despite cruel taxes to pay for the War of the Spanish Succession that broke out just after she came to the throne, following the death of Charles II of Spain. The country took pride in Marlborough's military victories (at Blenheim, Ramillies, Oudenarde and Malplaquet) while fine writers emerged including the essayists Joseph

Addison and Jonathan Swift, and the poet Alexander Pope (a covert Jacobite). Tories in particular loved Anne for being a Stuart, who was more devoutly Anglican than any monarch since her grandfather Charles I, the Martyr.

However, whether her reign was quite so golden for her Scottish subjects is still a matter for heated discussion.

Ever since 1689 England had been planning to impose Union, and the queen and her Whig ministers believed that if they ruled Scotland from Westminster they would be better able to overcome any Jacobite challenge. What they did not grasp was how much this would anger a large section of the Scottish people.

15

'A parcel of rogues in a nation' – the Union, 1707

Fareweel to a' our Scottish fame,
  Fareweel our ancient glory;
Fareweel e'en to the Scottish name ...

'Such a Parcel of Rogues in a Nation'[1]

On 6 May 1703, after the first election since 1689, the 'Riding' of the 227 members of the Scots Parliament wound its way down Edinburgh's Royal Mile from Holyrood to Parliament House. First came burgh members in their finest clothes and carrying swords, two by two on foot, then shire members similarly clad, two by two but on horseback, then peers ('lords of parliament') who were mounted and followed by glittering retinues. Last came the high commissioner, the Duke of Queensberry, with the Honours (crown jewels) of Scotland – crown, sceptre and Sword of State.

As high commissioner, Queensberry asked parliament to vote for further money for the war. However, while he could count on the Court party, most of whom enjoyed places of profit under the Crown or pensions, or were officers in the army or navy and would not risk losing their commissions, the election had returned a majority of less biddable members.

In terms of the major Scottish political parties, the 'Cavaliers' as Episcopalians, were Tories, while if the 'squadron volante' were Presbyterian and Whiggish minded, they were at the same time pragmatic independents who could suddenly switch loyalties – hence their name of 'light cavalry'. There were also the ducal parties. 'Argathelians' were Whigs like their leader the Duke of Argyll, those of the Duke of Hamilton followed his opportunist line, and the Duke of Atholl's men were Presbyterians and stiff nationalists.

The one formidable duke other than Queensberry was Argyll, who was still in his early twenties. Chief of the Campbells, one of the most powerful of the clans and known as the 'Children of the Mist', as such he was hated by rival chiefs. He was also half English, educated at Eton and already one of Marlborough's veteran colonels. He disliked both Queensbery and the squadrone, perhaps because they were too Scottish for him. Iron-willed but charming and persuasive – there is an attractive portrait of him in Walter Scott's *The Heart of the Midlothian* – Argyll wanted Union.

The squadrone and many ducal MPs shared the Cavaliers' resentment at England for dictating Scottish policy. Queensberry lost control. A bland piece of legislation designed to preserve the status quo, an Act anent Peace and War, was transformed into a law by the Scottish Parliament making it illegal for England to decide whether or not Scotland should go to war.

Remembering Cromwell's occupation less than fifty years before, the opposition rejected any idea of closer links with England, Fletcher of Saltoun warning them that already they seemed more like a conquered province than an independent people. An Act of Security was passed, stipulating that the Scots Parliament must decide who should follow Anne as sovereign, although he or she must belong to the ancient royal line and no Catholic.

The Earl of Marchmont – a former high commissioner, and an unreconstructed Williamite Whig mockingly referred to as 'Jack Presbyter's darling' – introduced a bill that would give the succession to the Hanoverians. It was thrown out by a majority of fifty-seven. Some members demanded that Marchmont should be imprisoned in Edinburgh Castle (the Scots version of commitment to the Tower for treason) and his bill be burned by the public hangman.

A Jacobite crowed

> Old Scotland is at last grown wise,
> And England shall bully no more ...[2]

He crowed too soon.

Meanwhile, at St Germain, James III and VIII was now a tall, thin, swarthy, youth who save for a great hook nose looked not unlike his uncle Charles II. His health was poor – a consumptive and a depressive, he suffered from bouts of malaria. His best qualities were amiability, 'sad lucidity', patience and moderation.[3] Kind-hearted, he always showed compassion for anyone who suffered in his cause. If he lacked charisma, he inspired affection and loyalty.

Had he renounced Catholicism, he would have been welcomed home. But while his great-grandfather Henri IV had said Paris was worth a Mass and had converted, never for a moment did James think London worth the Prayer Book. On the other hand, he inherited his father's toleration, seeing himself as born to reign over a Protestant country – converting only by good example.

Close friends with the Bourbon princes, he enjoyed French court life, hunting and dancing. His chief ally was his sister the Princess Royal, Louisa Mary. Tall, stately and high spirited, she was strikingly good looking, with her mother's dark Italian eyes. Among those considered as husbands for her were the Duc de Berry, Louis XIV's grandson, and Sweden's warrior king, Charles XII.

Across the Channel, with increasing alarm Whigs watched the maturing of the youth whom they called 'the Pretender'.

England decides on annexation

The Scottish political nation had signed its own death warrant with the Act of Security, which alarmed the London government so much that for a moment it considered military occupation. Its first retaliatory shot was the Aliens' Act of February 1705 – unless the Scots accepted the Hanoverian succession by 25 December they would be treated as foreigners and there would be an embargo on their paltry imports. However, it was never put into practice.

Godolphin and Marlborough decided the only sure way of taming the Scots was annexation. Accordingly, in July 1706 Westminster passed a preliminary Act for Union with Scotland. Queensberry, once again Keeper of the Privy Seal of Scotland, and his lieutenant John Erskine, Earl of Mar, set about creating a majority. They were helped by the idea of Union being welcomed by a fair number of the Scottish political class, men like Argyll, who while genuinely patriotic, believed it would be their country's economic salvation. It would also – in Whig theory at least – stop a Popish Pretender from ever becoming King of Scots.

The clinching inducement was that the Scots would share England's prosperity, free to trade anywhere within a new United Kingdom and her plantations overseas. Among the keenest supporters were forward-looking merchants – characterised by men such as the Glaswegian bailie, Nicol Jarvie, in Walter Scott's *Rob Roy* who wants to drain Loch Lomond, 'giving to plough and harrow many a hundred, ay, many a thousand acres'.

But if all classes are taken into account, especially the less privileged, then the majority saw the Union as a shabby conspiracy to deny the Scottish people control of their own destiny. Fletcher of Saltoun claimed that the Edinburgh mob was the true spirit of the country, and undoubtedly most ordinary men and women wanted to remain Scots, not to become 'North British'. Many were infuriated by so blatant a denial of their nationhood.[4]

At Edinburgh, pro-Union members were threatened with lynching as they pushed their way through angry crowds to Parliament House, which had to be ringed by troops. A rumour that the Honours of Scotland would be melted down and sold caused outrage. At one point the Lord Provost's mansion was stormed by a mob – the writer, and spy, Daniel Defoe feared that the entire capital would erupt in armed rebellion.

Elsewhere the Lord Provost of Glasgow, an outspoken Unionist, had to hide under a bed to avoid being murdered by his fellow citizens, and in the Highlands the aged poet Iain Lom (a Keppoch MacDonald who had fought for Dundee at Killiecrankie) wrote *Oran an Aghaidh an Aonaidh*, a 'song against the impertinence of Union'. In Perthshire, despite owing his dukedom to Queen Anne, the Duke of Atholl held a rally of 6,000 clansmen to express disapproval.[5]

At first, Presbyterians were fiercely opposed. They did not trust Queensberry, whom they rightly suspected of Episcopalian leanings, and feared they might fall under Anglican (in their eyes, quasi-Popish) dominance. But when a separate act was passed to ensure the Kirk's future as Scotland's established Church, they ceased to object. Some ministers became keen supporters.[6]

As the most authoritative study of the campaign for Union tells us, 'There were moments through to the end of November [1706] and perhaps even later when the court seemed on the verge of succumbing to the weight of popular opposition, but by resorting to the use of troops, and with the application of the full force of the law outside Parliament, they kept the upper hand.'[7]

Opposition at Parliament House was divided and unable to agree on tactics. The Duke of Hamilton (after the Hanoverians, the senior Protestant heir to the Scots throne) to whom its members looked for leadership proved a broken reed, despite having seemingly favoured the Cavaliers and although his spirited old mother, Duchess Anne – hotly against the Union – tried to put backbone into him. Self-interested and vacillating, on the day the crucial vote took place he hid in his Holyrood apartment, pleading toothache.

The end of Scotland as a political nation

The Duke of Queensberry and his allies made a solemn entry into Edinburgh for the Treaty of Union's enactment, in a procession of twenty carriages, each drawn by six horses. On 16 January 1707 the Treaty was ratified by Parliament, cunningly managed by Queensberry who had won over the squadrone volante. In favour were 110 members, with 67 against. The vote might have been closer, but many opposition members stayed away in despair. Then the duke touched the document with the royal sceptre, in token of Her Majesty's approval.

The sheer number of troops ringing Parliament House, who had their work cut out to save it from being stormed, is revealing. (Other troops were quartered all over Edinburgh, with two further regiments at Leith and Musselburgh.) There was anger throughout Scotland. Had the country been polled, it would have overwhelmingly rejected the Treaty.

There were sweeteners. The Presbyterian Kirk remained the established Church, the Scottish legal system with its partially Roman law was left intact (Parliament House becoming the seat of its senior courts), universities and burghs kept their ancient privileges. Scottish merchants could now trade freely with the plantations while most of the Darien shareholders got their money back. Two earls became dukes, several commoners were ennobled, lucrative sinecures were bestowed and high officials received arrears of pay.

There was also a small amount of direct bribery from a secret political fund, although it scarcely affected the outcome. Peers who were undecided, such as the Earl of Balcarres and Lord Elibank, were paid respectively £500 and £50 to make up their minds. For eleven guineas Lord Banff, a cash-strapped Catholic nobleman, not only voted for the Union but turned Protestant into the bargain.

Basically, the terms were that instead of 155 Scottish MPs at Edinburgh, 45 would sit at London (Cornwall had 44) with 513 English MPs in the House of Commons, while the 160 Scottish peers would elect a mere 16 of their number to sit with 180 English peers in the Lords. From then on the Act of Settlement applied to Scotland, with the Hanoverians as heirs to the Kingdom of Scots.

Opponents never stood a chance against the propaganda that Daniel Defoe orchestrated in a pamphlet war, hammering out a message that only in a Union could the Scots hope to achieve England's prosperity. (Looking back, one observer thought that had people recognised Defoe's gang and guessed what they were up to, they would have been torn limb from limb.) Yet even without propaganda the Union bill would have been passed because a majority of the Scottish ruling class supported it, if with regret. 'Now there's ane end of ane old sang', was the sad comment of the Earl of Seafield, last Lord Chancellor of Scotland, although a convinced Unionist.

Queensberry was warmly congratulated by Queen Anne, who created him Duke of Dover in the English peerage, but his enjoyment was marred by what opponents of the Union saw as divine retribution. Shortly after it came into force, Queensberry's promising ten-year-old son and heir, the Earl of Drumlanrig, was found in the kitchens at Queensberry House eating a scullion whom he had roasted alive on a spit. Instead of being counselled, the young lord was disinherited.

English customs and excise were introduced, replacing easy-going Scots tariffs. Officials arrived from England, who according to George Lockhart were 'scum and canalia'. They 'treated the natives with all the contempt, and executed the laws with all the rigour imaginable'.[8] There were riots throughout the kingdom. Two lines in verses later polished up by Robert Burns recapture the resentment at becoming a mere English province:

> We're bought and sold for English gold:
> Such a parcel of rogues in a nation.[9]

This was the view of countless Scotsmen – and Scotswomen.

Resentment turned into rejection of Queen Anne whom, so a mournful Jacobite ditty claimed, had ordered the Honours of Scotland to be made into dildoes. George Lockhart recalled how 'People of all Ranks and Perswasions . . . were daily more and more perswaded that nothing but the Restoration of the Royal Family, and that by the means of Scotsmen, could restore them to their Rights.' He continued, 'so likewise was there an universal Expectation of the King's coming over to them'.

'Nay, the Presbyterians and Cameronians were willing to pass over the objection of his being papist', adds Lockhart. '"For", said they (according to their predestinating principles), "God may convert him, or he may have Protestant children, but the Union can never be good."[10] He also says that Presbyterian ministers lost influence over their flocks if they were thought to support the Union.

All this was grist for the Jacobite mill.

16

The 'enterprise of Scotland', 1708

Take heed, Queen Anne, Queen Anne,
Take heed, Queen Anne, my dow.

Anon, *Queen Anne; or, the Auld Grey Mare*[1]

Far from ending the Jacobite threat in Scotland, the Whigs had created a political void for King James's followers to fill. While conceding the Union had 'genuinely principled support among some sections of Scots society', the modern historian Daniel Szechi is right in stressing that it alienated people of all classes – what he calls 'febrile, potentially violent opposition' lay very close to the surface.[2]

No doubt the economic benefits would one day be huge, overseas trade profiting almost at once. However, these gains were not immediately apparent to most Scots, who were unable to peer into the future. Some industries collapsed in the face of English competition while everybody resented the painful hike in taxes and bullying new tax inspectors.

Soon, many who had supported the Union in 1701 saw it as no better than thralldom. Among them were the Earls of Mar and Seafield, formerly among its greatest advocates.

Colonel Hooke's mission

Although Louis XIV had bribed members of the Scottish Parliament to vote against the Union, which he believed would strengthen England, from the beginning he realised it would bring an increase in the number of Scots who supported James. As early as 1705, hoping to weaken the Allies' threat to northern France, he sent an agent to sound out the Scottish ruling class and learn whether they might rise for James.

Colonel Nathaniel Hooke was an Irish adventurer who, after attending the universities of Dublin, Glasgow and Cambridge without gaining a degree, had been Monmouth's agent in London during the duke's rebellion. Pardoned by James II, he had become a Catholic, a knight of Malta and a devoted Jacobite, joining Dundee in 1689, fighting at the Boyne and then with the Irish Brigade in Spain.

When he arrived in 1705 the Scots did not trust him. Nor did they trust Louis XIV, Lockhart suspecting that the Colonel had been 'palmed on the Court of St Germains, being pitched on by the French King as one that would follow his Directions ... to raise a Civil War' rather than to restore James. This was too cynical – Louis genuinely wanted a Restoration. However, Hooke was eventually able to report that seven Scottish peers of Parliament (the Cavalier party's leaders) had formed what they called a 'Juncto', and had told him that twenty-six other peers, whom they named, would be ready to 'come out'.

Two years later, Hooke made a second visit, disguised as a cattle-drover called 'Mr Hickey'. He found solid evidence that the Union had aroused 'great discontent and hearty dislike'. Forgetting that the Highland chiefs who possessed their own private armies were the key to a successful rising, he concentrated on the magnates and richer gentry of the Lowlands.

However, it was impossible to obtain promises of support from such wily noblemen as the Duke of Hamilton, who was 'perhaps a little too Cautious or rather Timorous'. With no doubt a certain exaggeration, the duke's chamberlain claimed his master was 'breathing with the utmost difficulty, having suffered twenty-nine fits of the fever', which was why Hooke could not see him. (In the end, he realised Hamilton was useless.) Other magnates were equally coy, while a double agent assured Hooke, untruthfully, that even the fanatical Cameronian Covenanters would rise for James.

On the other hand, the Catholic Duke of Gordon could bring 2,500 men to the field and his fiercely Jacobite Duchess, who was a daughter of the Duke of Norfolk, wanted him to come out. However, a realist, Gordon told Hooke that the Scots detested Catholics and would never follow a Popish leader. He must find a Protestant to head the rising.

Despite so much discouragement, the colonel brought back a 'memorial' that earned him a Jacobite peerage ('Baron Hooke of Castle Hooke') and a French pension, for it persuaded King Louis to launch *l'entreprise d'Ecosse*, a full-scale invasion. Signed by six Scots peers and four powerful lairds, the memorial promised 30,000 armed men if France would send 18,000 troops, a good general and weaponry. It also asked for cash to finance the campaign, explaining,

> With respect to money, the state of this nation is very deplorable
> ... the English have employed all sorts of artifices to draw it out of the
> kingdom, the expedition of Darien has cost large sums: our merchants
> have exported a good deal: we have had five years of famine, during
> which we were obliged to send our money into England and Ireland
> to purchase provisions; and the constant residence of our Peers and
> Nobility at London has drained us of the rest.

Even so, the memorial insisted, 'The whole nation will rise upon the arrival of its King: he will become master of Scotland without any opposition, and the present government will be entirely abolished.'[3] This was no exaggeration. An Episcopalian laird, Lockhart was on bad terms with his Presbyterian tenants, but they assured him they were ready to fight for the Cause. The memorial was borne out by a double agent, John Ogilvie, who warned the Edinburgh regime that in the event of invasion James would receive massive support – from the government's own army.

King Louis's navy assembled thirty ships big enough to transport 5,000 troops under 200 veteran Irish officers – another 200 were waiting to follow. The invasion fleet's admiral was the Comte de Forbin with General the Comte de Gacé (a future Marshal of France) as commander-in-chief. 'The best I can wish you is that I hope I never see you again', Louis told James. The departure was delayed by James falling ill with measles, at first mistaken for smallpox, but at last the fleet sailed from Dunkirk on 17 March 1708, intending to land near Edinburgh.

In London, Anne and her government were deeply alarmed while there was panic in the City with a run on the Bank of England and a stock market crash. Whig Scotland was woefully unprepared. When he arrived there, the Earl of Leven, an experienced soldier whom Godolphin hastily appointed Keeper of Edinburgh Castle, sent word that he had only 2,500 inferior troops who were poorly armed and unreliable, divided between Edinburgh and Fort William. If James landed, he would have no option but to retreat to Berwick.

However, Forbin was terrified of Admiral Sir George Byng, who was chasing him with six men-of-war from the Royal Navy. His own ships' cannon had been removed, to lighten them for carrying troops, so they were in no condition to fight a sea battle. Apart from saving his fleet, he saw his duty as ensuring that James did not come to any harm.

Through poor seamanship, he missed the mouth of the Firth of Forth, giving Byng almost time to catch up, and when he did enter it he signalled to the wrong bank, failing to contact Jacobites who were waiting on the other side. Then he fled north before Byng. After two more days, ignoring the king's frantic entreaties to be put ashore, he returned to Dunkirk.

Never given another command, in retirement he wrote a bland, self-exculpatory account of the voyage in which he claims, unconvincingly, that he had always doubted the invasion's viability. 'Knowing the situation in Scotland, I realized there was no hope of success.'[4]

Whatever Forbin says, there had been every chance of success. Edinburgh Castle was defenceless, its cannon without ammunition. 'It must be confest, never was nation in such a condition to be invaded and there is no doubt, but had the French landed their forces, and got their stores of arms and ammunition on shore, as they might easily have done if they had not overshot their port, they would with very little opposition been masters of the whole country', admitted even Defoe.[5]

In the aftermath, only a small band of lairds who had assembled at Brig o'Turk near Stirling were arrested. Charged with high treason, they were all acquitted, the only evidence being that they had drunk James's health. Asked to testify against John Stirling of Keir, his steward swore he remembered nothing. 'I ken fine what ye mean', he answered when afterwards Keir teased him about his loss of memory. 'But I thocht it was far safer to trust my immortal soul to the mercy o' Heaven than your Honour's body to thae damned Whigs.'[6]

'It is too Melancholy a Subject to insist upon the Grief this disasterous Expedition rais'd in the Hearts of all True Scots Men', lamented Lockhart of Carnwath. 'The Reader may easily conceive it was very great, since thereon depended the Nation's Freedom from Oppression and Slavery.' He adds that Sterling Castle and Edinburgh Castle, with every other prison in Edinburgh, were 'crammed full of Nobility and Gentry'.[7]

Later that year Parliament extended the Treason Act to Scotland, despite strong opposition from every Scottish peer and MP. Hitherto, Scotsmen found guilty of treason had been spared the obscene penalty of being hanged, drawn like a chicken and quartered.

What the leaders of Scotland's Jacobites had wanted was as much revolution as Restoration, something far more radical than the English 'Revolution' of 1688, an 'economically viable and independent Scotland with a constitution that would have turned it, in effect, into a noble republic with a largely ceremonial monarchy'. (It anticipated what Disraeli called the 'Venetian oligarchy', later developed by full-blown English Whiggery.) They had also hoped to end 'England's domination of her sister kingdoms'. They had dreamed, too, of trading freely with France's new possessions overseas.[8]

Always objective, Mary of Modena told Colonel Hooke in 1707, 'it would be better to be King of Scotland alone than to remain without a kingdom'.[9] Yet how long James would have remained King of Scots is questionable. Instead of rejoining his army overseas Marlborough stayed at home until the crisis was over, and by early summer 1708 England had 20,000 infantry and 3,000 cavalry available – all regulars.[10] It seems unlikely that the Scots could have produced a commander to defeat Europe's finest soldier.

Never a man to fret over what might have been, at the end of April James sent a message to his Scottish supporters, saying how much he regretted any trouble they were suffering as a result of the expedition's failure, but that he would come again with money and weapons, and raise the Highlanders. He ordered dies to be made for gold and silver coins bearing his name and image.

17

'Fire smothered under flax' – Ireland, 1708

They bribed the flock, they bribed the son,
  To sell the priest and rob the sire;
Their dogs were taught alike to run
  Upon the scent of wolf and friar . . .

Thomas Osborne Davis, The Penal Days

Although English Jacobites remained supine, an intoxicating belief in Scotland's ability to recover her independence by bringing back her ancient line of kings spread across the Irish Sea. Some Irishmen thought that a Stuart Restoration might be feasible in their own country.

Until recently, Irish historians believed that Jacobitism died after James II fled from the Boyne, with the sieges of Limerick and 'Aughrim of the Slaughter' as postscripts. However, by using Irish language sources a modern scholar, the late Breandán Ó Buachalla, showed how loyalty to the House of Stuart survived in Ireland for most of the eighteenth century.

When the abjuration oath was introduced by the English in March 1702, the poet Aogan Ó Rathaille lamented, 'It is foul and evil, it is treason in that wicked race, to brandish audacious perjuries that the children of James have no hereditary claim to the noble crown of the three kingdoms.'[1] In their archaic Carolingian script, Gaelic poets wrote longingly of the Blackbird, the Merchant or the Phoenix , among the many secret names for James III that were instantly recognisable by Irish speaking Jacobites.

The Penal Laws

In 1703 the lands confiscated from Ireland's Jacobite gentry had finally been sold at London, the English Parliament forbidding Catholics from purchasing more than two acres. Next year, the Parliament at Dublin passed an 'Act for the Prevention of the Further Growth of Popery', the first stage in draconian legislation known as the Penal Laws.[2]

These included dividing a dead Catholic's estate between his children and barring Catholics from public office or the professions, forbidding Catholic gentlemen to carry swords, and ordering them to sell a horse for five pounds to any Protestant who fancied it. Marriage between Catholics and Protestants became illegal. The aim was to force Catholic landowners to emigrate or convert.

Furthermore, 'Discoverers' were employed, paid to catch and prosecute anyone trying to evade the laws. They were also known as 'priest hunters' since they pursued Catholic bishops, monks, friars and Jesuits, who were banished – subject to the death penalty on return. Any priest who became a Protestant was to be paid £40. Catholic schools were outlawed. However, an imaginative proposal to castrate all Popish clergy did not reach the statute books.

The Catholic plot of 1708

Understandably resentful, the Catholic gentry had been so encouraged by the Scottish expedition that they plotted a rising of their own. Ironically, the man they wanted to lead them was a Protestant nobleman from County Longford, Arthur Forbes, second Earl of Granard, who despised the new Ascendancy, the economic and political domination of Ireland by a new, arriviste, Protestant elite. Few details survive, but we do know that Dublin Castle reacted swiftly, arresting forty prominent Catholic peers, gentry and clergy, who were held in prison without charge, and seizing the horses of other potential leaders.

In some areas of Connacht and west Munster, soldiers forced Catholic gentlemen to take the oath of abjuration, imprisoning anyone who dared to refuse. The Protestant Archbishop of Dublin, Dr William King (who has been described as Ireland's Bishop Burnet), reported of his co-religionists at the capital, 'People here are almost frightened out of their wits with the fear of an invasion.'[3]

Wide areas of Ireland were impossible to police, however, with no roads and no markets, where no English was spoken, dangerous to garrison or patrol since raparees still operated. One or two old-style Irish chieftains had survived, and in south west Munster the O'Sullivan Beare and the O'Donoghue of the Glens were a constant headache for the government.

In their wild fastnesses these two chieftains defiantly sheltered hunted priests or rapparees on the run. Renowned for savagery, the O'Donoghue, who amiably told a quaking magistrate he would have his throat out the next time he met him, could muster 500 devoted followers at his home in Glenfesk, among the hills of County Kerry.

There was, however, another side to Domhnall O'Donoghue Mór. A lover of the old ways and the old tongue, he always had a welcome at Glenfesk for Munster's wandering Gaelic bards, who sang his praises. When he presented a badly needed pair of new shoes to poor Aogán Ó Rathaille who had been reduced to digging potatoes, the poet thanked him in the only way he could, writing

> A chief of the sun-bright race of the Fianna of Failbhe,
> Of the nobles of Cashel, who were manly and hospitable;
> He it was who bestowed on me those splendid shoes.
> Though he has been some time dwelling with the English,
> He learned from them nor churlishness, nor ill-humour ...[4]

The Irish language and Jacobitism went hand in hand.

There was also considerable Ascendancy alarm at the activities of French privateers, who regularly boarded and plundered Irish merchant shipping, on the western and southern coasts of Ireland. Many of these 'French' pirate vessels were in fact owned by exiled Irish Jacobites.

Another worry for Dublin Castle was the recruiting, despite heavy penalties, of young men for the regiments of the Irish Brigade, that group of Irish exiles serving in the French army whose existence was an uncomfortable reminder of support for James III. Sometimes they left Ireland on board the privateers, one day they might return – under arms.

In spring 1708, Queen Mary, believing her son's Scottish expedition was bound to succeed, sent Ambrose O'Conor, a Dominican friar, to gauge the extent of support in Ireland, just as Hooke had done in Scotland, so that the conflict could be widened. Despite the failure of *l'entreprise d'Ecosse*, he went ahead with his mission. Although the authorities nearly caught Friar Ambrose for whom, dead or alive they offered a large reward, he returned safely to St Germain after contacting Jacobite leaders.

He brought back encouraging news. The Earls of Antrim and Fingall, together with the Catholic bishops, had assured him that if just a few troops bringing arms and ammunition were to arrive, Ireland would rise for James. In five south western counties alone he could count on at least 20,000 men – 'all the true Irish throughout the whole kingdom were ready to hazard their lives to serve the King'.[5]

However, when a French transport carrying Jacobite troops to Scotland was intercepted in March, Irish officers on board were sent to Newgate in irons, to await trial for treason. During their imprisonment splendid meals and fine wines were sent to them every day by anonymous sympathisers, and they were never tried. In retaliation, the French put in irons two Huguenot officers in the British service whom they had captured, threatening to execute them if the Irishmen were hanged and promising to do the same to every other prisoner of war. Discreetly, Britain repatriated the Irish officers and their men to France.

Found on board another French vessel, Captain Peter Drake of Drakerath, County Meath, was tried for treason. In his memoirs he recalls how an English judge indignantly told him, 'good subjects should chuse rather to lie down in a ditch, and starve, than take up arms against their lawful Prince'. To which Drake replied with brutal logic, 'If that doctrine had been preached and adhered to at the Revolution, I should not now be hampered.'

Although condemned to death, he too was sent back to France for fear of what might happen to Huguenot officers captured by the French.[6]

Outwardly, the Ascendancy displayed boundless self-confidence, building magnificent Palladian mansions that they filled with fine furniture, silver plate and family portraits. Inwardly, they lived in constant dread of tenants and neighbours whose language they did not understand, in fear of men whose lands they had stolen. They were haunted by the spectre of a Restoration that might cost them their estates and their houses – and their lives.

Surprisingly, there was an Irish Protestant Jacobitism, much in evidence within Trinity College, Dublin, where High Church dons and undergraduates had no estates or grand houses to forfeit. Their uproarious celebrations on 10 June, James's birthday (known as White Rose Day), sometimes ended in rioting, with shouts of 'King James!' For many years this Jacobite interest also included great Protestant landowners, such as the Earls of Granard and of Antrim, whose families had held their lands for so long that there was no risk of losing them under a Restoration.

In September 1705, not quite three years before Friar Ambrose O'Conor's mission, a very great Jacobite lady overseas, the Countess of Erroll (wife to the High Constable of Scotland), described Ireland as 'fire smothered under flax', which remained the case for years to come. Had they known Lady Erroll's opinion, the Ascendancy as a whole would have agreed with her.[7]

18

Stuart or Hanover?

Too long he's been excluded,
Too long we've been deluded.

Anon, 'Let our Great James come over'

The Bell Tavern in King Street was within strolling distance of the Palace of Westminster and from the early years of Anne's reign High Tory MPs who belonged to the Country Party – the landed interest – had met there to drink vast quantities of October ale (so called from being brewed in that month). Although a portrait of the Queen hung in the room where they gathered, many toasts were drunk to 'The King over the Water', a name now used by Jacobites when drinking James III's health as they passed their tankards over a decanter, a finger bowl or a glass filled with water.

Backwoodsmen of the sort caricatured by Joseph Addison in *The Tory Foxhunter*, they were High Churchmen who detested the 'Rump' (the Whig party), 'Low Churchmen' (Latitudinarians) and Dissenters. They wanted to purge Parliament by impeaching half a dozen Whig MPs – 'get off five or six heads', as Jonathan Swift put it – and opposed not only taxes for wars abroad but a standing army in time of peace.[1] In 1709 the political wind began to blow their way.

On Guy Fawkes Day, Dr Henry Sacheverell of Magdalen College, Oxford, gave a sermon at St Paul's Cathedral on 'The Perils of False Brethren' which attacked the Toleration Act, Low Churchmen and Dissenters, claiming the Church of England was in mortal danger. Although he ranted, he had a point. Since the Toleration Act of 1691 over 2,500 Dissenting chapels had been licensed and everywhere parsons were dismayed by the numbers who attended them instead of worshipping at the parish church.

Printed as a pamphlet, the sermon sold 100,000 copies. In a second sermon, Sacheverell belittled the Revolution, extolling passive obedience and referring to the Whig leader Godolphin as 'Volpone' – the sly villain of Ben Jonson's comedy. Every High Churchman applauded him. There were roars of approval at the Bell Tavern, his health drunk in bumper after bumper.

The doctor was impeached for criticising 'her Majesty and her government' and tried at Westminster Hall, with General Stanhope insisting that the sermons favoured 'a prince on the other side of the water'.[2] Although she disapproved of him, the queen attended his trial, her sedan chair greeted by a pro-Sacheverell crowd with shouts of 'God bless your Majesty and the Church'. Mobs destroyed Dissenter meeting houses and did their best to set fire to the London residence of the Low Church Bishop of Salisbury, the aged Gilbert Burnet.

Found guilty, the doctor was forbidden to preach for three years, his sermons being burned by the common hangman, but it was a Pyrrhic victory for the government. Rewarded by an admirer with a rich living on the Welsh Border, Sacheverell's coach was cheered all the way to Shropshire. What upset the Whigs was his attack on the Revolution, which they saw as a message of support for the Restoration. They were quite right – soon after, he wrote to King James, offering his services.

Dr Sacheverell's friends were not confined to the Bell Tavern or the Country Party, but to be found in large numbers among the London mob and in the applauding crowds along the Great West Road – especially at Bath and Bristol.

James III's baptism of fire 1709–10

In November 1709 Archbishop Fénélon of Cambray, a cleric of a very different sort from Rancé or the Jansenists, met King James and was struck by his good sense and amiability. Soon a close friend, Fénélon gave him his own conviction that every man has an overriding duty to care for his neighbour. He may also have instilled Quietism – abandonment to God's will to the point of never asking his help – which encouraged a mood akin to fatalism.

Notwithstanding Quietism, to gain combat experience the king served with the French army as the Chevalier de St George in the Maison du Roy (Louis XIV's household brigade) and fought against Marlborough. He saw action at Oudenarde in 1708, admirably cool under fire, according to Berwick – he laughed when he saw Georg August of Hanover, the Elector's son, have his horse shot under him. Afterwards, Marlborough openly expressed pleasure at hearing such a good account of James. But it was in September 1709 during the murderous bloodbath at Malplaquet, Marlborough's last great victory over the French, that he really distinguished himself, charging twelve times with the Maison du Roy and being wounded. At one point he fought on foot at the head of the French grenadiers. Afterwards, English soldiers drank his health, Marlborough warmly praising his gallantry.

The war became unpopular in England, despite the Duke of Marlborough's victories and Whig attempts to turn him into a national hero. Many resented his rewards, such as Blenheim Palace, and his thriftiness – at Bath he went on foot in the worst weather rather than pay 6d for a sedan chair. People wanted an end to spiralling war taxation, besides being shocked by the casualties. Queen Anne wailed, 'Will this bloodshed never stop?'

She had transferred her affections from the Duchess of Marlborough to the ingratiating Abigail Masham, a distressed gentlewoman who had joined the royal household as a 'dresser' – a lady's maid. The duchess responded to the takeover by hinting at lesbianism. Unruffled, Mrs Masham, a Tory (and secret Jacobite) undermined Anne's confidence in Godolphin, securing his dismissal in August 1710.

At a general election in October the Tories won a big majority, partly because of Sacheverell's trial but mainly from anger at never ending war and heavy taxes. They immediately formed a government. The Bell Tavern circle increased to over 150 MPs, naming itself the October Club in honour of the new ministry and its favourite beverage. It included a hundred known Jacobites, the most extreme of whom were nicknamed 'Tantivies'.

Written early in the next reign, Addison's *The Tory Foxhunter* preserves the way they thought. Addison (a Whig) makes his anti-hero, who is a country bumpkin squire and a Tantivy, say there has been no good weather since the Revolution and calls the Whigs 'factious sons of whores'. His opinion of the Hanoverians is 'these foreigners will never be loved in England, sir; they have not that wit and good breeding that we have'. He adds, 'I and my father before me have always been for passive obedience.'

The Tantivies had better arguments than Addison cared to mention. One was that it would be humiliating for England to become an appendage of a petty German state such as Hanover. The Tories feared the tail might wag the dog, embroiling England in European wars.

The men who led the Tories, Robert Harley and Henry St John, had little in common with Tantivies, however. Their first act was to issue a beautifully written party newspaper, emulating *The Review* (edited by Defoe) that had been so useful to Whigs. *The Examiner*'s editor was Jonathan Swift, its contributors the day's finest writers. But it catered for moderate Tories rather than Jacobites.

A former Whig who had served under Godolphin, the smooth, subtle Harley, now Chancellor of the Exchequer, possessed a well-merited reputation for double-dealing. Completely without scruple, he cultivated the middle way to secure power and left his ministers' salaries in arrears to control them. He was also Mrs Masham's cousin, which put him in the Queen's good books. His weakness was alcohol – at home, after consuming bottle after bottle he once asked a friend why was the House sitting so late.

Still more treacherous, St John was a mixture of debauchery and brilliant intellect, who boasted of 'drinking like a fish and —— like a stoat'. On one occasion he ran naked through St James's Park when crazed with drink and on another penned a letter on 'the finest desk in the universe, Black Betty's black arse' – Betty being the pretty black barmaid at the King's Coffee House. (Although, remarkably, he combined misogyny with womanising.) Yet he was gifted with a supreme dialectic, able to out-argue everybody even if he might not convince them, while in later life he impressed Voltaire by his erudition. His essay *Patriot King* was admired by Edmund Burke, Benjamin Disraeli and G. K. Chesterton for its statement of Tory doctrine

Although the pair loudly trumpeted the slogans of Church and Monarchy their sole aim was to stay in power. For all their cleverness, they let a situation develop that in the end meant their one chance of doing so lay in a Stuart Restoration – a fact of political life they failed to grasp until fatally outmanoeuvred by the Whigs.

Lord Middleton did not hope for much from them. 'It is the life of a dog to be always hunting on a cold scent', he wrote sadly in autumn 1710. 'Sometimes as on enchanted ground we have a view, but when we draw near, it vanishes.'[3] He was quite right. Soon the October Club were cursing Harley for his lack of commitment.

Harley regained popularity, however, when a would-be assassin failed to kill him with a penknife, and in May 1711 a horrified Queen Anne created him Earl of Oxford, besides appointing him Lord High Treasurer – her first minister. He had already opened secret negotiations with James, spreading rumours that he was working for a Restoration, if at first only to ensure the support of Jacobite MPs. So did St John, now Viscount Bolingbroke. At this stage, convinced of the impossibility of a Restoration without James turning Protestant, both men were confident he would prefer the Crown to the Mass.

The king had no option other than take their approaches at face value. He made it clear that he did not mind letting his half-sister occupy his throne for the rest of her life so long as he inherited it. He could scarcely do otherwise. He also stressed that he would protect the Church of England and the constitution.

Like most Jacobites, James mistakenly believed that Anne wanted him to follow her. On 2 May 1711 he sent her a letter that must have been the product of a great deal of thought and Middleton's advice. Blaming 'the enemies of our family, and of the monarchy' for keeping them apart, he expressed 'the natural affection I bear you, and that the king our father had for you till his last breath', and pleaded with the queen to bequeath him the throne.

'In the meantime, I assure you, Madam, and am ready to give all the security that can be desired, that it is my unalterable resolution to make the law of the land the rule of my government, to preserve every man's right, liberty and property equally with the rights of the crown; and to secure and maintain those of the Church of England, in all their just rights and privileges as by law established; and to grant such a toleration to dissenters as the Parliament shall think fit.'[4]

He never received a reply.

At this time James suffered two personal sorrows. In April 1711, he lost a valuable friend when the Dauphin Louis died of smallpox. A heavy, dull man, who loathed books and whose favourite occupation was exterminating wolves, he had nonetheless been devoted to his young English cousin. Had he lived, he would certainly have done his best to secure a Restoration.

In April 1712 both James and his sister also caught smallpox. He recovered, but Louisa Maria did not and was buried near her father at St Edmund's Chapel in Paris, the king was devastated. 'She was by all who knew her admired as a most extraordinary person in all respects', wrote old Bishop Burnet, who adds that by her death, James 'lost a great deal of strength'.

Scottish resentment

The Scots were growing angrier by the day with the Union. In 1711 Scottish peers were formally forbidden to sit in the House of Lords by virtue of hereditary right, which made their peerages inferior to those of England. In

1712, despite promises to the Kirk, High Churchmen secured an act that gave toleration to Episcopalians, allowed patrons to appoint clergy to livings and brought back 'Popish' holidays.

On 10 June 1712, White Rose Day, there were riots all over Edinburgh, men and women falling on their knees to drink the health of James VIII. A huge bonfire was lit on top of Arthur's Seat and a mob stormed up to royal Holyrood singing the Jacobite anthem 'When the King enjoys his Own again'. There were similar riots at Leith. A ballad declared,

> Of all the days of all the year,
> The Tenth of June I love most dear
> When our white roses will appear
> For the sake of Jamie the Rover ...[5]

Scenes like this would never have occurred before the Union.

In 1713 Scottish malt became liable to the tax levied in England, forcing up the price of beer, which particularly hurt Lowlanders who drank small beer in place of water. (A bushel of Scots barley rendered far less barley than a bushel of the superior English barley but was taxed at the same rate.) A ballad, 'The Curses', complained of the 'everlasting slavery' imposed by the Union. It ends,

> And curs'd be every whining Whig,
> For they have damned the nation.[6]

For some time the 'Lutheran Dame', Sophia, Electress-Dowager of Hanover, had been attending Church of England services celebrated at her son's court by a parson whom she had specially imported – in preparation for the day when she should ascend the British throne.

However, alarmed by reports of the October Club's noisy optimism, Sophia began to fear that Anne and her Tory government might change their minds, a fear fuelled by the queen's coldness. Despite creating Sophia's son Georg Ludwig, Duke of Cambridge, Anne was irritated by his requests to take his seat in the Lords and for his son to visit England. She made it clear that neither would be welcome on British soil.

'My experience of the Earl of Clarendon's capacity determined me to send him to your court', said a letter from Anne introducing the envoy who brought this message to Hanover – mischievously drafted by Bolingbroke.

Considered the most stupid nobleman in the whole roll of English peers, Clarendon's one claim to 'capacity' was to have dressed in women's clothes when governor of New York, to represent the queen more fully.[7] It is unlikely that the Hanoverians appreciated Bolingbroke's humour.

They were equally worried by England's new foreign policy. The Tories had been elected to end the war, and in September 1711 England signed the Treaty of Utrecht with France, the British army's numbers dropping from 75,000 to 8,000, which meant abandoning their European allies, including Hanover. Baron von Schutz, the Hanoverian envoy at London, confided to a friend that a miracle was needed for his prince to inherit the throne.

Although the Whigs, who had been the war party, could not reverse the peace process, they did their best to ingratiate themselves with Old Sophy and Georg Ludwig. In any case, men of 'revolution principles' would never countenance the return of James II's son. In 1712 Marlborough and his friends sent a message to Georg Ludwig, begging him to invade England. They had certain knowledge, they said, that in less than two months the Prince of Wales would announce his conversion to Protestantism and cross the Channel.

While the Hanoverians declined Marlborough's invitation, they began to see Whigs as their only friends in Britain and Tories as deadly enemies. It made no difference that plenty of Tory MPs were committed to the Protestant Succession.

In contrast to the Whigs, the Tories were divided. While most Tantivies were hardline Jacobites, the rest of the party found difficulty in committing themselves. Robert Harley, Lord Oxford, who had no long-term strategy, tried to use James to win votes in the election of May 1713, asking him to tell Jacobites to vote for the Tories – as they would have done in any case.

So ill throughout the first six months of 1713 that she had to be carried everywhere in a sedan chair, the queen fell dangerously ill again at Christmas. Although she recovered, Oxford understood that her days were numbered. His preferred successor was a Protestant James and in January 1714 he sent a message to the king, telling him he must join the Church of England if he hoped to be restored.

The following month Bolingbroke, who had fallen out with Oxford and hoped to take over the Tory party, sent James a similar message – he must convert to Anglicanism. He added soothingly (no doubt with the king's uncle Charles II in mind) that he might of course stay Catholic in his soul if outwardly a Protestant. He also told him not to worry should Georg Ludwig succeed Anne on the throne as he would be sent home in under a year – no German could ever understand English politics.

In March, King James rejected Bolingbroke's advice, in an open letter designed to reach as wide a circulation as possible. Promising to support the Anglican Church in every way, he also made it clear that he would never convert. 'Plain dealing is best in all things, especially in matters of religion, and . . . I am resolved never to dissemble.'[8] Oxford and Bolingbroke, neither of whom cared much for plain dealing, must have groaned when they read this.

In June, Oxford abandoned even the pretence of negotiating with James, the government proposing that anyone who captured him if he arrived in Britain uninvited should receive a reward of £5,000, which next day was increased by the House of Commons. Jacobite MPs retaliated by blocking supply bills.

Privately, Bolingbroke assured them he was doing his best to ensure a Restoration – he may even have been sincere. It meant purging central and local government, and the army, but he could not do this while Lord Oxford remained chief minister. However, Oxford refused to resign although near to collapse under the strain and going drunk to audiences with the queen, whom he treated with a scandalous lack of respect.

Tory MPs did not mince words when referring to the Elector, like old Sir William Whitelock who had sat in the Protectorate Parliament and dressed in the style of the 1660s. 'If ever he comes to the throne, which I hope he never will', he told the Commons, Georg would prefer 'his German interests and dominions to the interest and honour of Britain', just as William had put first those of Holland.[9]

James leaves France

The Treaty of Utrecht stipulated that James must leave French soil, so he took refuge in the Duchy of Lorraine, an independent state that was not too far from the North Sea and a ship to his kingdoms. In February 1713, he wrote a careful letter to Louis XIV, thanking him for 'the asylum which you have been pleased to grant me, almost ever since I was born'. He begged Louis to continue supporting him and his mother, 'the only person who is left of all those who were most dear to me'. He also promised he would be a faithful ally, 'if ever I shall see myself restored to my dominions'.[10]

In 1711 his visitors had included Dr Charles Leslie, who published a description. Remarking on his expression, 'always chearful but seldom merry, thoughtful but not dejected', Leslie noted he 'spends much time in his closet [and] writes much, which no man does better or more succinctly'. Above all, 'He will press no man's conscience, and he may reasonably expect that his own should not be pressed.'[11]

James established his court at Bar-le-Duc where he did little more than hunt, his social life consisting of rare visits to Duke Leopold's court at Lunéville. When the British government protested at his being allowed to live in the duchy, Leopold wrote to Queen Anne that he could not refuse shelter to a man who had committed no crime other than being the last male Stuart.

On Christmas Eve 1713, Lord Middleton resigned as secretary of state, worn down by the slanders of fellow exiles. The English and Irish disliked him because he was a Scot while the Scots accused him of supporting the Union. His undistinguished successor was Sir Thomas Higgons, a Protestant who had been accused (unjustly) of involvement in the plot to assassinate William III.

The death of Queen Anne

On 27 July 1714 Anne dismissed Lord Oxford from his post as lord treasurer and, although a very sick woman, insisted on presiding over the cabinet meetings to choose his successor until she suffered a stroke. On 1 August she died, aged only forty-nine. A royal doctor wrote, 'I believe sleep was never more welcome to a weary traveller than death was to her.'

High Tory pamphleteers jeered it was fitting that the queen's statue, erected outside St Paul's Cathedral just before she died, should show her 'with her rump to the church, gazing longingly into a wineshop'.[12] Yet she was remembered with affection by the English, if not by the Scots.

The day after Anne died, Bolingbroke told the French ambassador that within another six weeks all army officers who supported Hanover would be cashiered. However, when barely conscious, the queen had acted on the Privy Council's advice, appointing the Whig Duke of Shrewsbury lord treasurer. He replaced Bolingbroke with General Stanhope.

19

The Illustrious House of
Hanover, 1714

The illustrious House of Hanover and Protestant succession
    To these I do allegiance swear – while they can hold possession.
For in my faith and loyalty I never more will falter,
    And George my lawful king shall be – until the times do alter.

'The Vicar of Bray'

Informed opinion knew that the Act of Settlement, passed by only one vote, was far from insuperable. Only 150 years earlier a similar act barring Elizabeth Tudor from the succession because she was a bastard had been set aside and even hardline Whigs thought there might be a Restoration. This can be seen from the Edinburgh MP Lockhart of Carnwath's account of his conversation with a leading Whig in August 1713, after the dissolution of Queen Anne's last Parliament.

> I met General Stanhope walking all alone and very humdrum in Westminster Hall ... 'Well', said he, 'tis no jest, you'll get your Pretender, and you'll repent it, I dare answer for it, e'er long!'. And with that he went off in a prodigious fury.
>
> That the Queen did of a long time design her brother's restoration, I do not in the least question [adds the deluded Lockhart]. But [she] was prevaild with to postpone and delay it, partly by her own timorous nature, partly by the divisions and discord of her Ministry, and partly by the tricks, intrigues and pretences of the Lord Oxford. [But] it pleased God by the queen's death to blast all our hopes and expectations.[1]

Lockhart's delusion was that of most Jacobites, which explains why they were caught without a plan to thwart a Hanoverian takeover. In Bolingbroke's words, 'As to what might happen afterwards, on the death of the Queen, to speak truly, none of us had any settled resolution.'[2]

Charles Talbot, Duke of Shrewsbury, the new Whig lord treasurer, whose unreliable backbone was stiffened by two other Whig dukes, Argyll and Somerset, implemented the Act of Settlement as fast as he could. The Privy Council decreed the accession of Georg Ludwig, swiftly proclaimed King 'George' by the heralds and formally invited to England. (Old Sophy having died in June.) Ports were closed, a watch kept for suspicious arrivals and troops were ordered to London.

The knowledge that he had lost the game turned Bolingbroke into a full-blooded Jacobite. On 19 August 1714 he wrote to James, 'Things are hastening to that point, that either you, Sir, as the head of the Tories, must save the Church and Constitution of England, or both must be inevitably lost for ever.'[3]

It was too late to stop Georg Ludwig. On 8 September 1714 the fifty-four-year-old Elector, with his thirty-year-old son Georg August, two mistresses and a pair of Turkish slaves, accompanied by ninety courtiers and servants, landed at Greenwich. Advised by his envoy Baron von Bothmer, on 27 September George appointed a Whig ministry headed by the Earl of Halifax, but in practice run by Lord Townshend as Secretary of State for the Northern Department and General Stanhope as Secretary of State for the Southern.

When he heard of Anne's death James rushed to Paris, where he arrived in disguise on 10 August, hoping to obtain help from King Louis. But the French foreign secretary, the Marquis de Torcy, told him to go back to Lorraine – neither troops nor arms were available. As Berwick recalled, James received no news whatever from England, 'where everything was turned upside down and from where no information came about where he could land in safety'.

On 15 September a proclamation was issued at London, promising £100,000 to anyone who captured the Pretender if he attempted to land, so that he could be tried for high treason.

On 29 October 1714 the Elector of Hanover, fifty-eighth in line of succession to the throne (which meant that there were fifty-seven men, women and children alive with a better claim in blood, barred because they were Catholics), went to Westminster for his coronation. Many peers stayed away. Nearly ninety, Archbishop Tennison, quaveringly declaimed, 'Sirs, I here present to you your undoubted king', and told all those present to do homage. Pointing to all the troops in the abbey, James II's ancient mistress, the Countess of Dorchester (Catherine Sedley), whispered to a neighbour, 'Does the old fool think anyone would say no?'

A week after George's crowning, James issued a protest: 'We have beheld a Foreign Family, Aliens to our Country, distant in Blood and strangers even to our Language, ascend the throne.' It made little difference.[4]

George I

Georg Ludwig had very moderate abilities other than a certain, dogged determination. His worst faults were avarice and a vindictive streak. He disliked public life, homesick for the flat landscape of Hanover where he would return for long periods. In manner he was boorish, speaking little, never returning a bow. His English was inadequate, so he communicated with his minsters in French or dog Latin.

'His views and affections were singly confined to the narrow compass of the Electorate', recalled the Earl of Chesterfield, who knew George well, having married one of his bastard daughters. 'England was too big for him.' Whigs carefully referred to the 'Illustrious House of Hanover' because that was precisely what it was not. The electorate had only recently been established, in 1692, for the Dukes of Brunswick-Lüneburg. With reason, the Scots called him 'the wee German Lairdie'.

Unable to grasp that not all Tories were Jacobites, despite the speaker Sir Thomas Hanmer and a small group of Tory MPs (known as 'Whimsicals') being anti-Stuart, George excluded the Tories from government. Choosing only Whigs for his ministers, he rarely attended cabinet meetings and left them a much freer hand, unable to see the dangers of a single-party state.

Unlike William and Mary, he lacked a dynastic fig leaf and was king purely by Act of Parliament. There was a widespread feeling among the English, then the most xenophobic people in Europe, that a German sovereign could not be the real thing. His refusal to touch for the King's Evil confirmed High Churchmen in their suspicion that he remained a Lutheran. (In fact, neither Georg Ludwig nor his son took much interest in religion, except as a ritual prop for monarchy.)

John Miller, in his history *The Stuarts*, defines the allure of the King over the Water: 'For some, the exiled Stuarts became the epitome of ultimate justice and of lost monarchical ideals and values. Much of Jacobite writing, indeed, was pervaded by a sense of loss, of a vanished royalist, chivalric and even magical past that could be restored only by the special providence of God.'[5]

This had been the instinct of many Tories as Anne's reign grew to a close. Only James could fill the void. They wanted him as king for the same reason they supported Anne – from the old line of monarchs, he stood for the old ways. The sole obstacle was his Catholicism, but he might produce Protestant heirs.

His other asset lay in being 'the only born English-man now left of the Royall family', as he called himself in a handbill of August 1714, which gave him an almost Arthurian appeal, even for those at the bottom of a rigidly hierarchical society. Criminals about to hang pledged their loyalty to him just before being turned off the gallows – rejecting the law that condemned them.

Jacobite politicians might have been caught off balance, but pamphleteers swung quickly into action and saw an easy target. Heavily middle-aged, short and fat, with pendulous cheeks and bulging eyes, George was distinctly un-Arthurian, especially his image on coins of the realm – his wife had exclaimed 'Pig Snout!' on first seeing his miniature – that contrasted poorly with James's profile on widely circulating medals. His new subjects named him the 'Hanover Rat' or 'Turnip', claiming he had been hoeing turnips when told of Queen Anne's death.

Frequently burned in effigy during 1714–15, he was often given a cuck-old's horns because of a rumour that he had had Count Königsmarck, the lover of his wife Sofia Dorothea, murdered and buried under the floor of the Leineschlosse, a Hanoverian palace. She was under permanent house arrest, which seemed to confirm the tale. (In fact, in August 2016 the count's skeleton was found beneath the Leineschlosse.) His son's alleged bastardy became the Jacobite response to the Whigs' warming-pan story about James.

The two German concubines who accompanied him everywhere did not enhance his image. The tall, thin Melusine von der Schulenburg (Duchess of Kendal) and the enormously stout Sophia von Kielmansegg (created Countess of Darlington) became standing jokes, known as the 'Goose and the Elephant'. One ballad refers obscenely to 'Geordie's grace riding on a goosie' while another, 'The Bed Tester's Plot', pictures the fat little king and the Elephant copulating on a bed that gives way beneath their weight, with George bellowing, 'A Jacobite Plot!'[6]

On his coronation day and for the rest of October 1714, riots broke out in thirty towns in southern and western England, and in the midlands. Ostensibly rioting against Dissenters, among other slogans, mobs were heard to yell, 'Damn all foreigners!', 'No Hanover!' and 'Kill the old rogue!' A ballad jeered

> Here he hath brought the dear Illustrious House of Hanover,
> That is, Himself, a close-stool & a louse;
> Two Turks, three whores & half a doz'n Nurses,
> Five hundred Germans all with empty purses.[7]

Yet for all the abuse, he was determined to keep the kingdoms he had won like some prize in a lottery. He was also what is nowadays called a survivor.

A well-organised rising in the weeks after George's arrival would have sent him back to Germany. But the Jacobites lost their chance through a lack of forward planning. Some unknown Tantivy bard wrote sadly at the end of 1714:

> Farewell old year, for Thou to us did bring
> Strange changes in our State, a stranger King;
> Farewell old year, for thou with Broomstick hard
> Hast drove poor Tory from St James's Yard;
> Farewell old year, old Monarch, and old Tory,
> Farewell old England, Thou hast lost thy glory.[8]

Yet there were Tories who thought it still possible to bring in James III. However daunting the odds, it was the nature of a Jacobite to believe in the Restoration's inevitability.

20

'Now or Never!' 1715

I think it is now more than ever, 'Now or Never!'

James III, August 1715[1]

Britain became the Whigs' Promised Land. Lord lieutenants were replaced, government posts and sinecures snatched back from Tories and given to Whigs. Tory officers were purged, Marlborough reinstated as captain general – which despite his parsimony did not stop him from sending £4,000 (£300,000 in today's money) to James, just in case a Restoration happened after all.

At a general election early in 1715, despite fewer votes, the Whigs strengthened their hold by a big majority in the Commons, having bribed electors in carefully targeted constituencies. George had already created a dozen new peerages to ensure the Lords were under Whig control.

Bolingbroke and the Jacobite court

One March evening, warned by Marlborough that his arrest was imminent, Bolingbroke went to his usual box at Drury Lane theatre. Then he slipped out, put on a black wig and rode through the night to Dover from where a boat took him across the Channel. When he reached France, James made him an earl and secretary of state. So gifted a statesman seemed a godsend.

Unfortunately, he spent most of his time at Paris, enslaved by an old flame, Claudine de Tencin, a libidinous ex-nun with literary pretensions and a most unsavoury reputation. Among her other lovers was the Duc d'Orléans's henchman, the Abbé Guillaume Dubois (described by Saint-Simon as 'a little, pitiful, wizened, herring-gutted man, in a flaxen wig, with a weasel's face'), who arranged orgies for his patron. What made Claudine's affair with Dubois dangerous was that he regularly sold information to foreign powers.

Worse still, the hard-drinking Bolingbroke made close friends with George's ambassador, the Earl of Stair (son of 'Glencoe' Stair, named for his part in the 1695 massacre) whom he contacted as soon as he arrived in Paris – odd behaviour for a Jacobite secretary of state. When drunk he blurted out secrets to Stair, while he also blabbed them out in bed with Claudine. This meant that the Whig government nearly always knew in advance the outline of every Jacobite plan.

In any case, Bolingbroke liked neither King James nor his court. He fumed at the way the king would not let him dictate proclamations and was irritated by his refusing a suggestion that he marry the Regent's daughter. He was baffled by James's tolerant brand of Catholicism, declaring his new employer had 'all the superstition of a Capuchin, but . . . absolutely forbids all discourse concerning religion'. If the king was so moderate, why couldn't he convert?[2]

'Here, I found a multitude at work', Bolingbroke wrote scornfully of the Jacobite court after abandoning the Cause. 'Care and hope sat on every busy Irish face. No sex was excluded from this ministry. Fanny Oglethorpe, whom you may remember from England, has a corner in it, and Olive Trant is the great wheel of the machine.'[3]

Fanny Oglethorpe, later the Marquise des Marches, brought up at St Germain with the king, belonged to an English Jacobite family who had gone into exile at the Revolution, but then returned to their Surrey estate at Godalming. Staying in Paris, she helped the Cause for many years as agent and courier, as did her sister Eleanor, Marquise de Mézieres.

Olive Trant, daughter of a dispossessed Kerry landowner and a famous beauty, was known as 'the Sybil of the Bois de Boulogne' where her lover, Orléans, kept her in a little house belonging to 'an ancient gentlewoman'. Bolingbroke, who pretended to be shocked by her reputation, called her 'the great wheel' because as a fervent Jacobite she coaxed Orléans into meeting both himself and the Duke of Ormonde, even if nothing came of their meeting. Sardonically, King James referred to Olive as 'the Young Nymph', although she was thirty and in modern terms a high-class escort.

Looking back, Bolingbroke sneered at how James's court was elated by news of riots and 'every meeting-house demolished'. Each Jacobite courtier thought 'the Restoration, which he took for granted, would be brought about within a very few weeks'.[4] Even so, Bolingbroke congratulated himself on having left England where in April the new ministry began legal proceedings against him, and against Oxford and Ormonde, for their role in the Treaty of Utrecht. All were impeached in June.

The virtual proscription of the Tory party, whose members had expected to be treated by King George as they were by William III, turned more and more Tories into Jacobites – in Bolingbroke's words, 'The violence of the Whigs forced them into the arms of the pretender.'[5] Fearful for Anglicanism's future in the hands of a Lutheran Defender of the Faith, they were at last ready to take armed action and in February 1715 the French ambassador reported that England appeared to be on the verge of civil war.[6]

They were encouraged by further anti-Hanoverian riots. On 8 May 1715 a group of horsemen proclaimed 'King James III' at Manchester. On Royal Oak Day (29 May), a London mob broke the windows of any house not lit up in celebration, including the Lord Mayor's, howling 'High Church and Ormonde!' besides burning a portrait of William III. At Oxford there was prolonged street fighting between Jacobites and Whigs, with shouts of 'James III, true King!' and 'No usurpers!' At Bristol a crowd sang 'When the King enjoys his Own again'.

From White Rose Day (10 June) to August there were similar riots in towns in Somerset, the Midlands and the North Country. They were put down with some brutality by troops under the new Riot Act that came into force in August – a crowd of more than twelve persons had to disperse on pain of death within an hour of it being read. The army was increased to 15,000 men in England and 12,000 in Ireland, a treaty with Holland ensuring the services, if needed, of 6,000 Dutch troops.

Jacobite numbers and strategy

Berwick, who was not prone to self-deception, believed there would be more than adequate support for a rising, convinced that five in every six Englishmen wanted a Restoration. Modern historians query his estimate, yet Bolingbroke agreed with him.

'I went about a month after the Queen's death, as soon as the seals were taken from me, into the country; and whilst I continued there I felt the general disposition to Jacobitism increase daily among people of all ranks', he says in his letter to Sir William Wyndham of 1717.[7] He is borne out by the Prussian envoy who reported in spring 1715 that James's cause had gained more support during the last eight months than in the last four years of Anne's reign when the country was ruled by Tories.

There was also a new song:

> Now Britain may rejoice and sing
>   'Tis now a happy nation,
> Governed by a German thing,
>   Our sovereign by creation.
>
> And whensoe'er this sovereign fails,
>   And pops into the dark, sir,
> O then we have a Prince of Wales,
>   The brat of Koenigsmark, sir,
>
> Our king, he has a cuckold's luck,
>   His praises we will sing, sir,
> Far from a petty German duke,
>   He's now become a king, sir ...[8]

A three-pronged strategy emerged, sound enough on paper. The Duke of Ormonde, James's principal agent in England, would lead a rising in the West Country, aided by Tory officers who had recently been purged. Lord Lansdowne, second in command, had collected an arsenal at Bath that included not just muskets and broadswords but cannon. They intended to seize Bristol and Plymouth.

James was to join them with 2,000 troops whom he would bring from Le Havre on board a dozen ships laden with arms and ammunition supplied by Louis, even though France, exhausted by war, was close to bankruptcy. He expected solid support – not just in the West Country, but in Wales and on the Welsh Border, and also in Worcestershire, Staffordshire and Derbyshire. Two lesser risings were planned, in the North Country and in the Highlands. A commission was drawn up for Lord Granard to lead another rising in Ireland.

The obvious man to lead the main operation was James Butler, Duke of Ormonde, an Irish Protestant who was the richest landowner in his own country (where he had twice been lord lieutenant), besides owning big estates in England. Until sacked by George, he was Marlborough's successor as 'generalissimo' of the British army. Reputedly the best-bred man of his age, he was much liked, especially by the military, and for the last three months had enjoyed a high profile, his health drunk with James's during demonstrations.

Sadly, however, as Berwick comments in his memoirs, Ormonde 'had few of the talents needed for such an enterprise, and very little knowledge of the art of war'.[9] Even so, he and his lieutenants, Sir William Wyndham in Somerset and Sir Richard Vyvyan in Cornwall, would be advised by some good officers.

The West Country rising never took place. Impeached on 17 June, the duke moved from Ormonde House in St James's Square to his mansion at Richmond near London, intending to go down to Devon and seize ports to use as bridgeheads. But on 21 July, warned that troops were coming to arrest him, Ormonde fled to Sussex, to the recusant Gage family at Firle who smuggled him over to Calais. The rising had lost its leader.

His place was taken by Lord Lansdowne, who had been Tory secretary of war and was at least a West Countryman if no soldier. He had every intention of carrying out Ormonde's plan – a rising centred on Bath that would break out simultaneously at other places in the West. His strategy remained the duke's, its primary objectives Bristol and Plymouth whose possession would enable Jacobite forces to join him from France.

For a moment the government panicked, believing the entire West Country was about to rise. On the night Ormonde fled, unsure of the army's loyalty, it drew up plans for evacuating George to Holland should King James's standard be unfurled anywhere in England.

On the day the rising was due to break out, Jacobite gentlemen who had assembled outside Bath, ostensibly for a race meeting, hastily went home when a message came from Sir William Wyndham that all was discovered. The government's tardy reaction shows it had only just been warned – perhaps by Bolingbroke's drunken indiscretions. By late September, Lansdowne and other peers, with nine MPs including Wyndham and Vyvyan, were in the Tower.

Another indication of how seriously King George's government took the threat was its speed in sending troops to Bath and Bristol. At Oxford, town and gown attempted to recruit a Jacobite regiment, proclaiming James III on 27 October, but cavalry swiftly rode in to cow them.

Ormonde sailed from St Malo with twenty officers at the end of October, expecting to be greeted by a Jacobite army – James had already been proclaimed at St Columb. However, when he landed in Cornwall there was no one to meet him and he returned to France. His plans had been betrayed down to the last detail by his secretary, Colonel MacLean.

King James wrote,

> I must confess my affairs have a very melancholy prospect, every post almost brings some ill news or other, all hopes of the least foreign help are extinguished, instead of gaining new friends, we apprehend a powerfull enemy, and all our endeavours and pains are in a manner lost, and 'tis all rowing against the tide. Yet so far from discouraging me ... it doth but confirm me in my opinion of a present undertaking, for I cannot but see that affairs grow dayly worse and worse by delays.[10]

Moreover, the death of Louis XIV on 1 September was disastrous, Bolingbroke commenting 'My hopes sunk as he declined and died when he expired.'[11] Louis XV was only five years old and sickly while France's regent, the Duc d'Orléans, was no friend to the Stuarts. If the boy king died and Orléans took his place, Philip of Spain would challenge his claim to the throne, so he wanted to avoid war with Britain. He forbade the fleet at Le Havre to sail but, with what Bolingbroke calls his 'double trimming character', pretended to be well-disposed towards James.

Berwick's desertion

Scotland and Northern England had risen, and James had intended to appoint as commander-in-chief there his half-brother the Duke of Berwick, famous as a soldier throughout Europe. After he defeated the English at Almanza in 1707, winning Valencia for the Bourbons, Louis XIV created him Duke of FitzJames while Philip V of Spain made him Duke of Liria.

James told Bolingbroke he found his brother 'incommunicable and incomprehensible', even suspecting he had turned Orléans against him. Nevertheless, on 13 October he sent Berwick a commission as captain-general. But the duke had become a naturalised Frenchman, settling in France with his wife's family and did not wish to lose his home. Three weeks later he replied that he could not leave France without the regent's permission. For once the king lost his temper, writing that never again would he ask favours from 'a disobedient subject and bastard'.

The Jacobite rising in the West Country never even got off the ground. Its failure should be blamed on Ormonde's loss of nerve rather than Bolingbroke's loose talk. Had the duke gone to Bath instead of fleeing to France, he would have found huge support.

Now, all depended on 'sideshows' in Scotland and Northumberland – originally intended as mere diversions.

21

The Fifteen

There'll never be peace till Jamie comes hame.
The church is in ruins, the state is in jars,
Delusions, oppressions, and murderous wars;
We darena weel say't, but we ken wha's to blame;
There'll never be peace till Jamie comes hame.

Anon, 'There'll never be peace till Jamie comes hame'[1]

On 1 August 1715, which was the anniversary of George's accession, John Erskine, 23rd Earl of Mar, attended a royal levée at St James's Palace. A handsome man if on the plump side, formerly Tory secretary of state for Scotland, arrogant but charming when he wished, he was instantly recognisable from the dark green sash of a Knight of the Thistle, and from a slight hump and a nervous tic that earned him the nickname 'Bobbing John' – later attributed to his habit of changing sides.

When George arrived in England, Mar had sent him a grovelling letter pledging loyalty, followed by a letter of allegiance that he signed jointly with twelve Highland chiefs. His estates were encumbered with debt and only ministerial office and its perquisites could save him from ruin – the government owed him £7,000 in arrears. Moreover, he needed vast sums to satisfy his passion for architecture, and build the great houses and gardens, even cities, that he designed in his leisure moments. (He was an admirer of the architect James Gibbs.) But he had been too much of a Tory for the king, who acknowledged his letter by an order to return his seals of office.

George Lockhart had written in 1708, 'surely the Consideration of Scotland's present Circumstances must be grievous to any that will take but a short view of the State from which that Kingdom is fallen, and what it was before

England Usurped such a Dominion over it'.[2] By 1713 no less an observer than Defoe admitted that 'not one Man in Fifteen' would now vote for the Union.

The imposition of the Malt Tax, given the shaky state of Scotland's economy had been the last straw. In 1713 a Bill to repeal the Union, proposed by Lockhart in the Commons and moved by Scotland's repentant former lord chancellor Seafield in the Upper House, supported even by the Duke of Argyll and his brother Lord Ilay, had come close to success.

Resentful Scots sang ballads such as 'O whurry, Whigs awa, man!' that referred to their new ruler in less than affectionate terms.

> We then sought out a German thing
>   Call'd George, and brought him here, man;
> And for this beggar cuckold king
>   Sore taxes we maun bear, man . . .[3]

Some taxes had risen five-fold since the Union, levied by inspectors who shocked devout churchgoers by paying them visits on the Sabbath. Scottish industries such as shoe, candle and paper making were collapsing. So was the manufacture of linen and wool while everybody in Scotland resented the malt tax. On King George's official birthday in 1715, a tax inspector at Crieff had his ears cut off for drinking the health of the 'German thing'.

In autumn 1714, after the order to return his seals of office, Mar had revived the agitation to dissolve the Union (for which he had so vigorously campaigned in 1707 as Queensberry's right-hand man), presenting a petition for its dissolution. Advised by his ministers, the king saw opposition to the Union as trying to stir up trouble and rejected it.

At the birthday levée of 1715 the earl boldly confronted George, telling him to dissolve the Union and replace it by a federal system – if he did so, Mar had 16,000 Highlanders who would crush any rising led by the Pretender. When this was translated into German the king turned his back. The earl saw he had no political future under the Hanoverians. He also feared impeachment for his part in the peace of Utrecht.

Since 1710 he had been in touch with James, committing himself to nothing, although early in 1715 he had sent as insurance the exiled court a plan for a rising accompanied by an invasion. He now realised that his only hope of prospering lay in a Stuart Restoration. That evening, 1 August, accompanied by Major-General George Hamilton and Colonel John Hay of the Foot Guards, he left London in disguise, on board a coal barge bound for Newcastle where they found a boat that took them on to Crail in the East Neuk of Fife.

Although, according to the Master of Sinclair, Mar's only credentials were a miniature of James that he kept pulling out of his pocket and kissing, he summoned Jacobite leaders to a meeting at Braemar for a supposed deer hunt. He explained that while in Queen Anne's reign he had been largely responsible for joining England and Scotland, his eyes were opened and he saw he had made a terrible mistake. He would do everything he could to end a Union that turned the Scots into slaves of the English and begged his hearers to take up arms for King James VIII, who 'had the only undoubted Right to the Crown'.

On 6 September 1715, with barely a hundred men, the earl raised the standard of James VIII and III, one side of which bore the cross of St Andrew and the other the thistle with the words 'No Union'. The gold ball on the top fell off – just as it had from the standard of James's grandfather Charles I when he raised it at Nottingham in 1642. Ignoring the omen, Mar and his troops placed the white cockade in their bonnets, its first appearance in Scotland.

Three days later, Mar issued a declaration in which he appealed to Scots patriotism. He would 'endeavour the restoring not only of our rightful and native King, but also our Country to its ancient free and independent Constitution under him whose ancestors have reigned over us for so many generations'.

A well-conceived attempt to seize Edinburgh Castle failed on 19 September. Two soldiers in the garrison had been bribed to let down grapnels to which a storming party of forty would fasten ropes and scale the rock. However, having stopped to drink at a tavern, they arrived after the garrison had been alerted by an indiscreet plotter's Whig sister-in-law. Although only a few were caught, most were arrested on suspicion. Among them were Lockhart of Carnwath and half a dozen peers.

Mar used fair means and foul to gather an army, promising everyone that King James or Berwick would come at any moment to lead them. 'Particularly let my own tenants in Kildrummy know, that if they come not forth with their best arms, I will send a party to burn what they shall miss taking from them', he wrote to his Aberdeenshire bailie, 'Black Jock' Forbes, 'And they may believe this only a threat but, by all that's sacred, I'll put it into execution.'[4]

Overall, his army grew to 20,000 men, Highlanders and Lowlanders, which was remarkable for so sparsely populated a country, even if half went home before hostilities began. Seventy per cent were Highlanders, from twenty-six clans. Some must have been forced to come out like Mar's tenants, but most were eager to fight for King James.

A Whig 'Act for Encouraging Loyalty in Scotland' ordered sixty peers and lairds to surrender themselves at Edinburgh on pain of forfeiting their estates, but had little effect. In the Highlands, Silias (Julia) MacDonald of Keppoch – sister to Coll MacDonald, known as 'Coll of the Cows' – wrote a rousing Gaelic song in which she begs the Scots to rise before the 'Sasunnaich' cut their throats in the same way that they have already plundered them.

Some of the clansmen who joined Mar were Killiecrankie veterans, like old Coll. No less formidable were the Captain of Clanranald, Cameron the Younger of Lochiel, and Alexander MacDonald of Glengarry – 'the Black Glengarry' of whom the Master of Sinclair observed, 'it's hard to say whither he has more of the bear, the lyon, or the fox in him'.[5] The eighteen-year-old Earl of Strathmore was a natural leader who, says Sinclair, 'had the most good qualities, and feuest vices, of any younge man I ever saw'.[6] Others were half-hearted, including Rob Roy MacGregor and Sinclair himself.

Over eighty, too frail to come in person, that most calculating of all Scots noblemen John Campbell, the Earl of Breadalbane, who had persuaded the chieftains to end the Highland War in 1691, sent 300 of his Campbell clansmen. Twenty years before, 'Pale John' had been described as 'cunning as a fox, wiser than a serpent, slippery as an eel'.[7] The chances of success must have seemed very promising indeed to persuade someone quite so shrewd to commit himself.

The army might have been even larger had not Mar antagonised the Duke of Atholl who could raise 6,000 armed men. As it was, three of Atholl's sons came out, including his heir the Marquis of Tullibardine, and Lord George Murray (of whom more will be heard). For 'the Hanoverian regime on top of the last years of Anne constituted a very grave temptation to a patriotic Scottish gentleman to seek redress of grievance by the sword'.[8]

As well as insisting that a Restoration would end the Union, Mar announced that London was planning heavy new taxes on livestock, flour, malt and salt. He disarmed fears of James's Catholicism, promising that 'in due Time, good examples and Conversation with our learned Divines, will remove these Prejudices, which we know Education in a Popish Country has not rivetted in his discerning Mind'.[9]

King James II and VII and Mary of Modena in exile in 1694, with the Prince of Wales and the Princess Royal. Inept and heavy handed yet well-meaning, the king had been driven out for a policy of tolerance, not intolerance – and, above all, for being a Catholic. By Pierre Mignard. (Royal Collection Trust/ © Her Majesty Queen Elizabeth II 2019)

An Irish chieftain in traditional dress, Sir Neil O' Neill of Shane's Castle, Co. Antrim, descended from the Kings of Tír Eoghain. Over seventy, fighting at the head of the regiment of dragoons he had raised for King James, he was mortally wounded during the Battle of the Boyne. By Joseph Michael Wright. (Art Collection 2/Alamy Stock Photo)

James III and VIII in middle age. A stronger and abler man than is generally appreciated but who lacked dynamism. Had he given up his Catholicism he would almost certainly have regained the three crowns for the Stuarts. By Louis Gabriel Blanchet. (© National Portrait Gallery, London)

The charming, cultivated and two-faced Duke of Mar, 'Bobbing John', who raised Scotland for James VIII, turned Jacobite victory into defeat at Sheriffmuir, became James's secretary of state and ended as a double agent in Hanoverian pay. Artist unknown.
(Geneva/photograph @ Grégory Maillot)

James III and VIII marries Princess Clementina Sobieska, the granddaughter of King John III of Poland, at Montefiascone in September 1719. The king wears a purple coat in mourning for his mother, Mary of Modena. By Agostino Masucci. (National Galleries Scotland)

What Charles Edward Stuart really looked like during the 1740s:

(Above) Propaganda medallion in bronze of *c.*1745–50. By Thomas Pingo. (© National Portrait Gallery, London)

(Right) Gilt plaster portrait bust of 1746, thought by Charles himself to be the best likeness of him. By Jean Baptiste Lemoyne. (Royal Collection Trust/© Her Majesty Queen Elizabeth II 2019)

An Incident in the Rebellion of 1745, by David Morier. Contrary to popular belief, the only Highlanders who fought like this were the clan gentry – most of Prince Charles's troops were armed with muskets and bayonets. (GL Archive/Alamy Stock Photo)

The last male Stuart:

As Duke of York in 1746–7 (formerly thought to be a portrait of his brother). By Maurice Quentin de La Tour. (National Galleries of Scotland)

As Henry IX in 1788 – 'King . . . not by Men's desire but by the will of God'. By Gioacchino Hamerani. (© National Portrait Gallery, London)

On 14 September Colonel John Hay of Cromlix captured Perth, which gave Mar control of Scotland's east coast north of the Tay. On 2 October the Master of Sinclair raided the little port of Burntisland in Fife, opposite Leith across the Firth, boarding two ships in the harbour and seizing 300 muskets with 300 pounds of powder that were on their way to the Whig Earl of Sutherland. Soon after, Mar's troops overran the entire Kingdom of Fife.

The rising in Northumberland

In Northumberland, on 6 October Mr Thomas Forster, MP, and the Earl of Derwentwater proclaimed James III at Waterfall Hill on the moors north of Hexham, collecting sixty armed horsemen who included the recusant Lord Widdrington. Among them were three Irish Jacobites – Colonel Oxburgh, once an officer of James II, and two brothers called Wogan – who had been riding from manor house to manor house since June, whipping up support. Everybody believed the king would soon arrive with a large force of regulars, landing either in Northumberland or Scotland.

Tom Forster was a High Church Tory, who afterwards claimed he had been 'Blustered into the Business' by Tantivies but 'would never again believe a Drunken Tory'.[10] He was also short of money. However, he enjoyed a certain respect as the Bishop of Durham's nephew. We know what he looked like – thirty-five, medium height, plump, round shouldered, with a long nose and grey-eyes, speaking in a Geordie dialect.

Ten years younger, strikingly handsome, with big estates and a young wife and child, the recusant Lord Derwentwater, who was liked by everybody because of his affability, had much to lose. His maternal grandparents had been Charles II and Moll Flanders, and he joined the rising from genuine affection for his cousin King James with whom he had been brought up at St Germain.

Knowing it would play into Whig hands if a Catholic led the rising, Derwentwater acted as second-in-command to Forster, who despite a complete lack of military background called himself 'General'. Yet the fact that so many Catholics supported King James deterred men who might otherwise have risen. As Daniel Szechi stresses, in 1715 Catholic Jacobites rose by the hundred whereas Protestant Jacobites only rose in dozens.[11]

The Cause was seriously hampered by England's fear of Popery. Referring to 'the horrid plot' early in September 1715, the Derbyshire squire Francis Sitwell of Renishaw wrote sardonically, 'The true and most genuine sons of the Church, it seems, are discovered to be deeply engaged in ... bringing in those who are worse than heathen and infidels' – by which he meant Catholics. Unfortunately for King James, too many Englishmen thought like Sitwell.[12]

As it was, the recusant squires of lonely manors in the wildernesses of Northumberland, North Yorkshire and Lancashire (Beaumonts, Charltons, Claverings, Erringtons, Gascoignes, Riddells, Shuttleworths, Swinburnes, Thorntons and many others) who armed their servants with any weapons they could lay hands on, were fighting for James III and equality before the law, not to destroy Anglicanism. If some rose because their estates were encumbered and they faced ruin – war taxation had been the last straw – their loyalty to the House of Stuart was genuine enough.

The Northumbrian rising had an early, short-lived success when Mr Lancelot Errington and his nephew (both Catholics) captured Lindisfarne Castle on Holy Island, overpowering its garrison. They were not reinforced however and it was soon retaken by troops from Berwick. Forster had planned to seize Newcastle as the mayor was a Jacobite and many 'keelmen' (dockers or bargees) were nonjurors who supported King James. However, the Whigs kept control of the city.

Growing to 400 men in five troops, the little army wandered through Northumberland, sheltered by sympathetic squires with whom the leaders caroused while waiting for James's arrival. Women carried messages, two Swinburne girls known as the 'Capheaton Gallopers' bringing muskets and pistols that had been hidden in the curtains of their father's house.

Eventually, heartening news came from across the border. On 12 October Viscount Kenmure had declared for the king in Dumfrieshire and was riding to join them with 200 Scots horsemen who included the Earls of Nithsdale and Carnwath. A detachment from Mar's army under Brigadier William Mackintosh of Borlum was coming too – over a thousand Highlanders accompanied by another small force of cavalry.

One of the few heroes of the Fifteen, as the rising became known, 'Old Borlum' would have made an infinitely better commander than Mar. He was described a few months later (in a warrant for his arrest) as 'A tall, raw-boned man, about 60 Years of age, fair Complexioned, Beetle-browed, Grey Eyed, speaks broad Scotch.' He was also a fine soldier. Crossing the Firth of Forth in fishing boats, he had hoped to take Edinburgh but, failing, decided to link up with Forster.

On 22 October the troops of Forster, Kenmure and Old Borlum met at Kelso in Roxburghshire where the Teviot flows into the Tweed. Together, they amounted to 600 horsemen and 1,400 foot. Next day, a Sunday, they went to church at Kelso's Great Kirk, many standing outside. Forster's chaplain, Mr Robert Patten, preached the sermon. Perpetual Curate of Allendale, nicknamed 'Creeping Bob', he had recruited a band of Newcastle keelmen whom he brought with him. His text encapsulated what Jacobitism was all about: 'The right of the first-born is his'.[13]

22

The Battles of Sheriffmuir
and Preston, 1715

Now is the Time for all good men to show their zeal for his
Majesty's service . . . and the relief of our Native Country from
oppression and a foreign yoke.

Mar's Declaration, September 1715

After waiting in vain at Perth for James or Berwick, Mar marched south,
intending to join Forster in Lancashire. He had 10,000 foot and 800 horse
but many of the former lacked firearms while his cavalry consisted of 'gentlemen volunteers' who had mounted their servants and given them swords.

Whig Britain's saviour was John Campbell, Duke of Argyll, whose
family had been sworn enemies of the Stuarts for generations. A veteran of
Malplaquet, where he had distinguished himself by his bravery, his clansmen
called him 'Red John of the Battles'. Waiting at Dunblane to intercept Mar,
with only 2,200 infantry and 960 dragoons, he was seriously outnumbered.
Yet in September he had warned London that without reinforcements
Scotland must fall to the Jacobites and England would be under grave threat.

Mar's army grew all the time, unlike Argyll's, but he had no idea of how
to lead it. 'The many gallant gentlemen who had rallied to Mar's standard
rallied, in the last analysis, to a self-centred, monstrously incompetent
poltroon', writes a historian of the Fifteen.[1] This is a little unfair. Even if no
soldier, he had raised Scotland for King James, entirely on his own initiative.

Sheriffmuir, 13 November 1715

The two armies met on 12 November at Sheriffmuir, moorland near Dunblane
and six miles north of Stirling, both having slept on the frozen ground. 'We

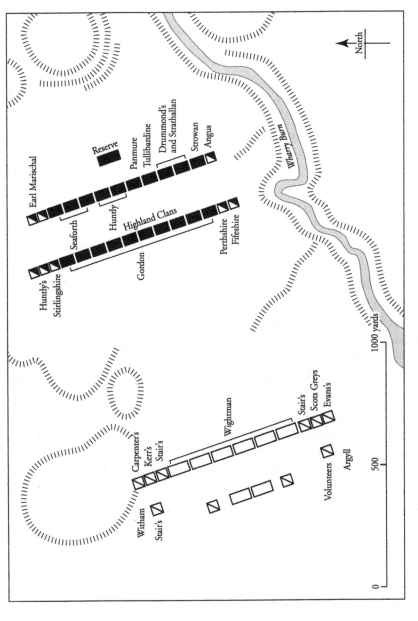

North

Earl Marischal
Reserve
Panmure
Tullibardine
Drummond's
and Strathallan
Strowan
Angus

Seaforth
Huntly
Highland Clans

Huntly's
Stirlingshire
Gordon
Perthshire
Fifeshire

Wharry Burn

Witham
Stair's
Carpenter's
Kerr's
Stair's
Wightman
Stair's
Scots Greys
Evans's
Volunteers
Argyll

0   500   1000 yards

The Battle of Sheriffmuir, 13 November 1715

had resolved to fight', recalled the usually cynical Master of Sinclair, 'and no man, who had a drope of Scots blood in him, but must [have] been elevated to see the cheerfullness of his countriemen on that occasion; and for my oun part, in spite of my reason, I made no manner of doubt of gaineing the victorie.'[2]

The battle opened at noon the next day, Mar commanding his right wing, which consisted entirely of clansmen. When their opponents, regular soldiers, fired a single volley, the Highlanders threw themselves flat on their bellies and were unscathed, save for Ailean Dearg of Clanranald, who was leading them on horseback and fell mortally wounded. The captain's death 'struck a Damp' upon their spirits, 'as they had a Respect for that Gentleman that fell little short of Adoration'. (Although some thought Red Allan had been shot in the back.)

However, Clanranald's second-in-command, the Black Glengarry, yelled 'Revenge! Revenge! Today for revenge and tomorrow for mourning!', and charged forward, waving his bonnet. He 'so animated the Men, that they followed him like Furies close up to the Muzells of the Muskets, push'd by the Bayonets with their Targets, and with their broad Swords spread nothing but Death and Terror'. The enemy's left flank disintegrated, their commander, General Whetham fleeing at full gallop to Stirling where he announced, 'all was lost'.[3]

Attacked from the rear, despite their ring-bayonets Argyll's centre nearly gave way, too, before the broadswords – 'this savage Way of Fighting, against which all the Rules of War had made no Provision' – but the imperturbable General Wightman kept his head, moving his battered troops to the right and joining forces with the duke. He recalled that the Jacobites 'might have entirely destroyed my Body of Foot'.[4]

At the east of the moor, Mar's left flank under General George Hamilton, had not yet formed up. Seeing they were without cavalry, Argyll sent his dragoons over an 'impassable' bog that had frozen solid during the night. Riding in close formation, knee to knee, they crashed into their opponents who broke, running back to the River Allen two miles to their rear. Seizing the colours, young Lord Strathmore rallied a handful of men and tried to make a stand, but was shot in the stomach, captured and then murdered in cold blood. Yet if some drowned in the River Alloa, few were killed because Argyll's horse were hampered by boggy ground that had not frozen.

Each army had destroyed the other's left wing, but with so few troops Argyll could not afford such heavy losses. Forming up his exhausted men behind dry-stone walls, he and General Wightman awaited an attack that must inevitably overwhelm them. Looking down from the hill of Kippendavie, Mar could see how few they were. With his superior numbers, all he had to do was hammer away, inflicting as many casualties as possible, and the enemy army would bleed to death. Yet after half an hour he gave orders to retreat, turning victory into defeat. As he rode away, Glenbuchat sighed, 'Oh for an hour of Dundee!'

By his own account, Argyll suffered over 500 casualties, with 133 of his troops taken prisoner, while about the same number of Mar's men had been killed or captured. Both sides claimed a victory, Sileas MacDonald writing *Là Sliabh an t-Siorrain* – 'To the Army of the Earl of Mar' or 'Song on the Battle of Sheriffmuir' – in which she exults over the plunder the clansmen are going to win in London.

However, a pawky Lallans ballad gives us the best idea what actually happened:

> We baith did fight, and baith were beat,
> And baith did run awa . . .

But by withdrawing when they could have won, the Jacobites lost the war.

Next morning, Argyll marched his men back on to the battlefield to rescue his wounded, finding nobody to oppose him. It need not have been like this. General Hamilton told Mar that in view of the duke's inferior forces he should fight him once a week until he won. But the earl merely stayed at Perth, many of his men drifting away.

Argyll was fully aware of how lucky he had been. Over a week later, he wrote to Lord Townshend, Secretary for the Northern Department, that the 'Rebels' are 'ten times more formidable than our friends in England ever believed'. He adds, 'there is nobody here think[s] it will ever chance that three thousand men will get the better of 9,000 of the Rebels again'.[5]

Bobbing John disagreed. Expecting the Duke of Berwick to come and take over from him, bringing a fleet from Le Havre with regular troops, he had not bothered to capture Stirling and invade the central Lowlands. Now, besides realising Berwick would never arrive, he learned that the fleet had been prevented from sailing. Secretly, he sent Colonel Lawrence, a Whig prisoner, to Argyll to obtain terms.

He also tried to stop James from coming to Scotland. 'This, Sir, is a melancholy account', he wrote early in December, 'but unless your Majesty have Troops with you, which I'm afraid you have not, I see not how we can Oppose [the enemy].' Reassuringly, he ended 'If it do not please God to bless your Kingdoms at this time with your being settled on your Throne I make no doubt of it's doing so at another time.'[6]

No answer came from Argyll. But the king was already on his way.

Preston, 13 November

On the same day as Sheriffmuir, Forster's Jacobites fought another battle, in England. They had crossed the border into Cumberland, with 1,400 men, half horse and half foot. Near Penrith they were intercepted by the county militia, 10,000 strong but ploughboys and shepherds who took one look at the Highlanders and fled. The 'victory' enabled them to capture many much needed horses besides arms and ammunition.

At Kendal, Peter Clarke, an attorney's clerk who wrote a journal of the next fortnight, watched them enter the town on 5 November. 'It rained very hard this day, and had for several days before, so that the horse and the footmen did not draw their swords, nor shew their collours, neither did any drums beat,' he remembered. 'Onely six highland bagpipes played.'

An hour before, he had seen Old Borlum precede them: 'Brigadeer Mackintoss and his man came both a horseback, having both plads on, their targets hanging on their backs, either of them a sord by his side, as also either a gun and a case of pistols. The said Brigadeer looked with a grim countenance.'

The Jacobite army marched to the market cross, to read a proclamation that began, 'Whereas George Elector of Brunswick has usurped and taken upon him the stile of the king of these realms' and declared that James III had 'imedietly after his said fathers decease became our only and lawful liege'. Clarke was so impressed that he joined them.[7]

Forster and Borlum found a warm welcome with many more recruits in Lancashire, England's most Catholic county. Unusually, in some places one in four of its population was Catholic, especially in the south and west and along the Ribble Valley, recusant gentry owning a third of all tenant farm land.[8] There were also plenty of nonjurors and High Churchmen, especially at Manchester, while in other Lancashire towns many who were neither nonjurors nor Catholics remained loyal to the Stuarts. 'King George is no more fit to wear the Crown than my Dogg', a Liverpool baker had declared at the end of August.

The Jacobite army reached Preston on Wednesday 9 November. Near the mouth of the Ribble, with 3,000 inhabitants who included many Catholics, it was a handsome town, without factories but with many attorneys, and known as 'Proud Preston' according to Daniel Defoe who visited it not long after. Clarke tells us the ladies there were 'so very beautyfull and so richly atired that the gentlemen soldiers from Wednesday to Saturday minded nothing but courting and feasting'.

Here the army was joined by 1,200 Catholic gentlemen with their Catholic servants and tenants, as well as many Catholic farm labourers, so that it grew to about 2,500. However, the new recruits were poorly armed, some with rusty swords but no muskets, others with muskets or fowling pieces but no swords, some with pitchforks. In contrast to the Scots, most of whom wore Highland dress, the English were in everyday clothes, with white cockades in their hats.

Borlum was appalled at seeing such a rabble. 'Look ye there Forster, are yon fellows the men ye intend to fight [General] Wills with?' he exclaimed, watching them from a window. 'Good faith, sir, an' ye had ten thousand of them, I'd fight them all with a thousand of his dragoons.'[9]

There were few Protestant recruits although the area was so full of High Churchmen. 'Indeed, that Party, who never are right Hearty for the Cause, 'till they are Mellow, as they call it, over a Bottle or two, began now to shew us their Blind-side', the Jacobite chaplain Mr Patten recalled contemptuously, 'and that is their just Character, that they do not care for venturing their Carcases any farther than the Tavern.'[10]

Riots were so frequent in Lancashire that the government had stationed troops in the county under Major-General Charles Wills who hastened to Preston with six regiments of dragoons and one of foot. Lieutenant-General George Carpenter was also on his way with three more regiments of cavalry. All units were under strength, together amounting to 2,500 men at most, the majority newly enlisted and half-trained, while both generals were second rate. Nor did they have cannon. However, they had some excellent junior officers.

When Forster learned they were coming he drank so much that he had to be put to bed. He left the defence to Borlum, who established his headquarters in the parish church and erected four barricades, strengthened by trenches. This enabled the defenders to move men quickly from one point to another – which ever happened to be under most pressure from attackers.

One barricade was manned by Lord Kenmure with his friends, another by Lord Charles Murray with the Atholl men, a third by Borlum with his Highlanders and the fourth by Lord Derwentwater with the Northumberland contingent. Patten acted as Derwentwater's aide-de-camp. He records how the earl 'signally behav'd, having stript into his Waistcoat, and encouraged the Men by giving them Money to cast up Trenches, and animating them to a vigorous Defence'.

Wills launched an attack as soon as he arrived on Saturday, sending his regiment of foot and dismounted dragoons to storm the barricade at the eastern end of Preston. He thought the Highlanders who defended it would run for their lives when his regulars appeared. Instead, 'so terrible a Fire was made upon them, as well from the Barricado as from the Houses on both sides, that they were obliged to retreat back to the Entrance of the Town'. They had lost 120 men killed or wounded in just ten minutes.

Some of Wills's troops though did reach the town centre, behind the barricades, but made little progress. Fighting continued until dark, the defenders inflicting further casualties in small, fiercely fought engagements. However, the attackers captured two tall houses overlooking the town and were able to shoot from their windows. Shortly before midnight, Lord Charles Murray visited Forster to ask him to launch a full-scale counter-attack as the Jacobites' ammunition was running short. He found the general 'lying in his naked bed, with a sack posset and some confections by him'.[11]

During the night Wills's men continued sniping from the windows of the two houses, their aim helped by fires breaking out. Many local Jacobites, especially labourers, took advantage of the darkness to desert. Far from encouraging his troops, General Forster stayed in bed, clutching his bottle.

Next morning, Wills's men charged a barricade, again without success. But just before 10 a.m., General Carpenter arrived, blocking every exit. Forster's nerve broke altogether as did Lord Widdrington's. Normally civilians, they were shocked by the bloodshed – 276 enemy soldiers had been killed or wounded although the defenders had suffered comparatively few casualties. Secretly, Forster sent Colonel Oxburgh to General Wills to negotiate a surrender. Concealing his astonishment, Wills agreed to spare their lives but no more. Cravenly, Forster accepted his terms.

'The Highlanders were for sallying out upon the King's Forces, and dying, as they call'd it, like Men of Honour with their Swords in their hands,' Patten tells us, but obeyed when their chiefs told them to lay down their arms. Lord Derwentwater, who also wanted to fight his way out, was overruled. A Scots gentleman tried to shoot Forster, but Patten struck up the pistol 'so that the bullet went through the Wainscot'. During the surrender Derwentwater and Colonel Mackintosh of Mackintosh acted as hostages.

The government captured 1,400 Jacobites. Besides the leaders, they included the Earls of Carnwath, Nithsdale and Wintoun, Lords Kenmure and Nairn, and Lord Charles Murray, with many North Country Catholic squires. Until orders came from London, peers were confined in the town's best inns, officers and gentry in lesser hostelries, while rank and file were shut in the parish church, living on bread and water.

Under anybody else than Forster they would have won — their opponents had suffered ten times more casualties. 'The accolade for worst commander on the government side during the rebellion has undoubtedly to go to a professional army officer: Major-General Charles Wills', Szechi believes. '. . . if the Jacobites had responded as aggressively to his botched attacks at Preston as some of them were clamouring to do, he might have gained the distinction of being the architect of a truly catastrophic defeat.'[12]

In the far north of Scotland there was another disaster for King James on the same day as Sheriffmuir and Preston — the surrender of Inverness to Whig forces.

Captured by Old Borlum two months before, the little Highland town had become the focus of a complex if largely bloodless struggle between the Catholic and Jacobite Earl of Seaforth, head of Clan Mackenzie, and the Earl of Sutherland who supported Hanover. Sutherland was joined by Clan Fraser under Lord Lovat, until recently a Jacobite, whose skilful planning resulted in the capture of Inverness on 13 November.

The loss of Inverness was serious enough for the Jacobites, but the desertion of so shrewd a politician as Lovat was ominous — clearly, he believed James VIII's cause had little future. No less disheartening, early in December Argyll was reinforced by Dutch and Swiss infantry who were accompanied by English cavalry.

At least one historian, John Baynes, a professional soldier who had an eye for strategy, believes the Fifteen very nearly succeeded. 'There can be no doubt that at one point in October 1715 only slightly different conduct on the part of the Jacobites could well have led to victory,' he writes. 'A little more sense of urgency, a little more daring, and the Stuarts might have regained their throne.'[13]

The regime that panicked when Ormonde fled from Richmond did not deserve to win. Had Ormonde raised the king's standard at Bath, had Berwick led at Sheriffmuir, had Forster kept his nerve at Preston or had Orléans let the Franco-Irish force sail, there would have been a very different outcome.

23

King James VIII
in Scotland, 1716

Come we next to the Time of the Ch[evalier]'s Arrival. At
the first news wherof, it is impossible to express the Joy and
Vigour of our Men. Now we hop'd the Day was come when
we should live more like Soldiers and should be led on to
Face our Enemies . . .

Anon, *A True Account of the Proceedings at Perth*[1]

Reaching a port had meant a perilous journey in disguise for James, hunted
by Whig agents who planned to murder him. Yet 'I never knew any to
have better temper, be more familiar and good, always pleased and in good
humour, notwithstanding all the crosses and accidents that happened during
his journey; never the least disquieted but with the greatest courage and
firmness resolved to go through what he had designed on', recalled Captain
O'Flannagan who accompanied him to St Malo.[2]

Having arrived at St Malo early in November, gales prevented him from
sailing. Dressed as a deck hand, he finally embarked on 27 December from
Dunkirk on a small sloop lent by an Irish merchant that after six stormy days,
narrowly evading enemy patrols, landed him at the little fishing harbour
of Peterhead in Aberdeenshire. His only companions were Captain Allan
Cameron (Younger of Lochiel's brother) and two servants.

From Peterhead, James wrote to Bolingbroke, 'I am at last, thank God, in
my ancient kingdom', adding hopefully, 'I find things in a prosperous way.'[3]
Exhausted by his voyage across the North Sea, he fell ill while travelling to
Perth of an 'aguish Distemper' (influenza) on Christmas Eve at Mar's castle
of Fetteresso, where he lay in bed for five days. Recovering, he resumed his

journey, en route staying at Glamis Castle, the late Lord Strathmore's home, and touching for the King's Evil.

What we know of his time in Scotland comes largely from *A True Account of the Proceedings at Perth* by a 'rebel', published in 1716. The author was a Whig agent (possibly Daniel Defoe), who used eyewitness information obtained from spies. His method was to neutralise rather than attack and, mixing truth with fiction, this vivid narrative subtly denigrates the king and his followers.

Leaving Glamis, 'on Friday, about Eleven o'Clock in the Morning, he made his publick Entry on Horseback into Dundee, with a Retinue of about 300 Men on Horseback, having the Earl of Mar on his Right, and the Earl Marischal on his Left', says the *True Account*. 'His Friends desiring it, he continued about an Hour on Horseback in the Market-Place, the People kissing his Hand all the while.'

When he reached Perth, where his little army (which was down to 5,000) was waiting for him, he made a ceremonial entry and reviewed the troops, before establishing his headquarters at Scone Palace two miles away – 'Our Court at Scone'. Here he spent Hogmanay. A proclamation announced that he would be crowned on 23 January on the hill at Scone, the traditional crowning place of the kings of Scots. There was no regalia, so Jacobite ladies offered their jewellery to make a crown. But the coronation never took place.

The notables with James included the the Marquis of Drummond (the Duke of Perth's son) and William Keith, Earl Marischal of Scotland. Another was the Earl of Panmure, who had proclaimed James VIII at the Mercat Cross of Brechin. There was also the royal vice-chamberlain, Lieutenant-General Dominick Sheldon, a veteran from the Irish war who had arrived with fifty Irish officers – regulars in the French army.

James was charmed by Mar. 'I never met with a more able nor more reasonable man, nor more truly disinterested and affectionate to me', he wrote to Bolingbroke. 'It is wonderful how he has managed matters here, and with what dexterity he hath, till now, managed all parties, and kept life on so many sinking spirits.'[4]

Momentarily reinvigorated, his army was cast down on learning that the king had not brought troops. His council were scarcely encouraged when he told them it was no new thing for him to be unfortunate. He upset Protestants by refusing to attend an Episcopalian *Te Deum* at St John's Kirk and insisting that a Catholic chaplain say grace at his meals. However, he compensated by his warm welcome for Episcopalian clergymen.

A spy who watched James wrote or supplied material for a vicious little piece of journalism, *A Hue and Cry after the Pretender*, printed in February 1716: 'And now, lest any of you shou'd mistake him, remember, he is a tall, slim, black, yellow, brown, sallow, heavy, dull, good-for-nothing fellow.' He 'never laughs till he gets drunk', which is nonsense – if he liked his wine, he was never known to drink to excess.[5] However, another smear, that he spurned the advances of two Highland whores 'nicely washed, but venal', rings true.

Jacobite morale was high, despite the Duke of Argyll having gathered a large army. 'Never Men appear'd better disposed for Action than ours of the Clans', says *A True Account of the Proceedings at Perth*. 'The Gentlemen embrac'd one another upon the News, drank to the good Day, and prepar'd as Men that resolved with Chearfulness to behave themselves as Scots Gentlemen ... our Pipers played incessantly and we shook Hands with one another like Men invited to a Feast rather than call'd to a Battle.'[6]

There were however few grounds for optimism. The winter was unusually harsh, even for the Highlands, while fuel at Perth was in short supply, both wood and coal. Snow made roads impassable so no reinforcements came from the clans. The 'Grand Council' directing military operations was a talking shop that did nothing but argue. Worst of all, the army was paralysed by lack of a command structure, Generals Hamilton and Gordon of Auchintoul vying for control.

The only action taken to hinder an enemy advance on Perth was to destroy houses where they might shelter from the cold, with all food supplies and forage. Reluctantly, James signed a 'Burning Order', and MacDonalds led by the new Captain of Clanranald burned the town of Auchterarder to the ground, stealing everything portable. Its people were left to freeze or starve to death. Lord George Murray's Atholl men did the same at the village of Dunning, torching cabins, lofts, corn yards, barns and stables with blazing straw. In the height of winter its inhabitants were driven into the snowy fields, cripples who did not get out fast enough being smothered in the flames.

Other places suffered too, including the market town of Crieff. James tried to help the survivors, but the burnings induced 'ane utter abhorrence of a popish Pretender' in many minds. Apart from those in Ireland, they were among the most shameful atrocities ever committed by Jacobites, if not by Hanoverians.

Meanwhile, an enemy force 3,000 strong, half Dutch, half Swiss, under

Argyll and General Cadogan, supported by portable huts and coal carts, was pushing its way towards Perth through snowdrifts as high as a horse's belly, making local villagers clear a road. The news divided the Council at Perth. Should it order a retreat? Or turn the city, fortified with redoubts and a trench, into a Scottish Limerick?

Listing strong points on which to base the defence and mount cannon, explaining how defending cavalry might make use of the frozen River Tay, a French engineer officer advised them to stay in the town, where they could inflict maximum casualties on an enemy who lacked siege artillery. Because of frozen ground, he could not mine or, unable to make breaches, mount storming parties. His men would not survive sleeping in the snow for more than a few nights. (Argyll himself was fearful this might happen.)

'I am perswaded there is not a Man in the Troops I have the Honour to be at [the] Head of but had rather Fight and be Kill'd than turn their Backs and Escape,' declared one Highland officer. 'I do not see the least Reason for Retreating.' Yet despite angry protests by other Highlanders and the Irish officers, who all wanted to stay and fight, the council lost its nerve, convinced that the enemy army was twice its size. It decided to retreat north east and join forces with the Marquess of Huntley. What made up the council's mind were rumours of a plot by unnamed chieftains to surrender the king.

'I am in despair at finding myself compelled to withdraw from Perth without a fight', James told Berwick's son, the Duke of Liria, 'but to offer battle would be to expose brave men to utter ruin, since the enemy is twice as strong as we are.' He still thought his troops might defeat Argyll if they succeeded in joining Huntley's army.[7] For a last time he wrote to Berwick, begging him to come and take command.

Throwing their cannon and heavy baggage into the river, on 30 January 1716 the Jacobite army marched off through the snowy wastes across the Tay, which had frozen hard enough to bear horse and man. Next day, Argyll rode into Perth with an advance party of dragoons, joined that evening by the rest of his troops. Within forty-eight hours, the Jacobites, by now only 4,000, reached Montrose and Brechin, which if indefensible provided shelter. It was thought, mistakenly, that for the moment the enemy would rest content with capturing Perth.

James's advisers warned him his situation was desperate – his army had failed to win at Sheriffmuir, the English rising had been crushed, there was no sign of reinforcements from France. They insisted that he owed it to his Scots supporters to leave – 'by retiring beyond Sea, to preserve himself for a better Occasion of asserting his own Right and restoring them to their ancient Liberties'.[8]

Still hoping to join forces with Huntley, the king refused to accept this assessment, until enemy troops were just three miles away. The only chance of an effective stand would have been in the mountains, but snow put this out of the question.

His advisers explained that his presence was the sole reason for the enemy's perseverance – 'they would pursue him, even with the Hazard of their whole Army, his Person being the chief Object of their Pursuit, as his Destruction was the only thing that could secure their Usurpation'.[9] They made it clear his departure was the sole hope of saving their own lives as the enemy would not be so eager to hunt them down in such terrible weather, and they might obtain terms. James saw that if he stayed he would destroy men who had already sacrificed everything for him. With deep reluctance, he agreed to leave Scotland. 'And I daresay no Consent he ever gave was so uneasy to him as this.'

The end of the Fifteen

Providentially, a French ship lay at anchor in Montrose harbour, the *Marie Thérèse* of St Malo. A small vessel of about ninety tons, she could carry only a few passengers. Among those whom the king asked to accompany him on his second voyage into exile were the Duke of Mar, the Marquess of Drummond, the Earl Marischal and General Sheldon.

He appointed General Alexander Gordon of Auchintoul commander-in-chief of what remained of his army, with power to negotiate a surrender. He also left money for the villagers around Perth who had been burned out by his troops and a letter for Argyll (never sent in the flurry of departure) asking him to see they received it.

The letter began: 'It was with the view of delivering this my Kingdom from the hardships it lies under and restoring to its former happiness and independency that brought me into this country: and all hopes of effecting that at this time being taken from me I have been reduced much against my inclination, but by a cruel necessity to leave the Kingdom with as many of my faithful subjects as were desirous to follow me or I was able to carry with me.' It concluded, 'I must earnestly request of you to do at least all in your power to save your country from utter ruin.'[10]

Orders were given to abandon Montrose and march to Aberdeen, the enemy having come even closer. To avoid disheartening the men, horses were tethered outside the house at which James lodged, as if he were going with them. Then, like his father at Rochester, he left by a back door and stole down to the harbour.

On 5 February he was rowed out to the *Marie Thérèse,* anchored a mile offshore. He postponed putting to sea as long as he could, hoping to be joined by the Earl Marischal and other officers whose lives were particularly at risk, but eventually gave up. Setting sail at 2.15 a.m., the darkness helped the little ship evade nine enemy men-of-war patrolling the area. Going up to Norway then back through the North Sea along the Dutch coast, after a surprisingly uneventful voyage, she landed the king at Waldam, a small port near Calais.

When the Black Glengarry learned James had left, he broke his sword in the market place at Montrose, swearing he would never fight for him again. Even so, the Jacobite army held together. After reaching Aberdeen it marched westward through Strathspey and Strathdon into Badenoch. It never surrendered, the foot soldiers hiding in the snowy mountains, those with horses riding off to find boats that would take them abroad.

One group went to the Orkneys where they were rescued by French frigates. Some reached France by way of Sweden. Others, including several clan chieftains, were hunted through the hills by Argyll's troops, but escaped via Skye or Lewis. Boarding a barely seaworthy ship in foul weather, the Master of Sinclair recalled being 'indifferent to which course they'd steer, provided they went any way where I could hope to get out of that hell'.[11]

The Fifteen ended in disaster: aborted in the West Country, crushed in Lancashire, broken in Scotland. Yet the Jacobite plan had been sound enough. As the historian Bruce Lenman stresses, 'George I and the establishment of a rabidly partisan minority ascendancy in Whig hands [had] alienated so large a proportion of the English political nation as to render the whole British political fabric susceptible to revolution.'[12] Nor had the Scots forgiven the rape of their nationhood. The Fifteen showed the strength of loyalty to the old dynasty; all it lacked was the right commander.

In *The Four Georges* William Makepeace Thackeray, in counter-factual vein, imagines an alternative scenario:

> Edinburgh Castle, and town, and all Scotland were King James's. The north of England rises, and marches over Barnet Heath upon London. Wyndham is up in Somersetshire; Packington in

Worcestershire; and Vyvyan in Cornwall. The Elector of Hanover, and his hideous mistresses, pack up the plate, and perhaps the crown jewels in London, and are off *via* Harwich and Helvoetsluys, for dear old Deutschland. The king – God save him! – lands at Dover, with tumultuous applause; shouting multitudes, roaring cannon, the Duke of Marlborough weeping tears of joy, and all the bishops kneeling in the mud.

24

Hanover's Reckoning, 1716

Remember that I lay down my life for asserting the right of my only lawful sovereign, King James the Third.

'Mad Jack' Hall of Otterburn[1]

James and his supporters, English, Scottish and Irish, believed that while they might have lost battles they had not lost the war. James's aura as rightful king in exile remained undiminished. Everybody was ready to try again. 'Whatever may now be our Fate, we still have one solid Ground of Comfort, that the Chevalier hath (as we hope) got safe out of the Reach of his Enemies' wrote an anonymous Jacobite officer who had been with him, possibly Mar himself. 'For in the Safety of his Person lies all our Hopes of Relief.'[2]

James was far from despairing. Like all Jacobites he believed that nine-tenths of the three kingdoms' population wanted him to come home, a belief strengthened by the warmth of his welcome in Scotland. He *knew* he was king and was still convinced that one day he would regain his inheritance.

James's return to France

As soon as the king reached France, he went to see Queen Mary at St Germain, visiting her secretly, as he knew George would demand his expulsion from French soil. His first action was to sack Bolingbroke, whom he replaced by Mar. Blaming him for failing to send arms to Scotland, the king says his removal had 'long been foreseen' and he had always had 'a very bad opinion both of the discretion and integrity of Lord Bolingbroke'.[3]

In a letter of 3 March 1716, Bolingbroke's highly amused ambassador friend Lord Stair explained why 'poor Harry' was sacked: 'He had a mistress here at Paris [Claudine]; and got drunk now and then; and he spent the money upon his mistress that he should have bought powder with, and neglected buying and sending the powder and arms, and never went near the Queen [Mary]; and in one word told Lord Stair all their [Jacobite] designs.'[4]

There were other reasons, too. He was rumoured to have made fun of James when drinking with Stair. He was also suspected of being in touch with Marlborough, although by then the duke was sinking into senility.

Berwick thought it a mistake to dismiss someone so able, but Bolingbroke was incapable of loyalty. Already discouraged by Louis XIV's death, having assured the French that Ormonde could raise 20,000 men in the West Country he had been shamed by the duke arriving in Paris as a penniless refugee. He would have gone over to George sooner or later, as he did in 1717. Ten years later, he bought his pardon with a backhander to George's mistress, the Goose.

The Duke of Lorraine no longer dared to shelter James, so, on the advice of the queen, who was supported by Mar and Ormonde, the king moved his court to Avignon. In a letter to the duke thanking him for his hospitality, James wrote 'Our poor Scots have escaped into the hills – a death by slow fire: God knows how they will exist, and what manner of terms they may obtain, resourceless as they are. I have sent them two ships in the hope of saving some of them.'[5]

Shaken by so much support for their enemy, George and the Whigs set about punishing those involved in the rising. They wanted revenge as well as security, but found difficulty in enforcing the law.

Important prisoners taken at Preston were brought to London on led horses, their arms tied behind their backs. The peers were tried and condemned early in 1716. The Earl of Derwentwater and Lord Kenmure, who both pleaded guilty, died on Tower Hill on 24 February, despite Derwentwater's wife having knelt at George's feet and begged for mercy.

In black, a gold crucifix at his neck, Derwentwater went first. He had been promised a reprieve if he would turn Protestant and recognise George as king. On the scaffold he told the crowd, 'Some means have been offered me for saving my life, which I look upon as inconsistent with honour and conscience, and therefore I have rejected them.' He also said that he regretted having pleaded guilty at his trial because James III was the true sovereign and that 'him I had an inclination to serve from my infancy, and was moved thereto by a natural love I had to his person, knowing him to be capable of making his people happy ... I only wish now, that the laying down [of] my life might contribute to the service of my King and Country, and the re-establishment of the ancient and fundamental Constitution of these Kingdoms.'[6] The axe took his head off with a single blow.

Kenmure suffered next, behaving with equal dignity, but saying little. However, he expressed regret at having pleaded guilty and, as an Episcopalian, prayed for King James. This time the operation needed two blows.

The dignified deaths of these peers, particularly that of the handsome young Derwentwater – despite his Catholicism – aroused widespread pity. Ballads were written in their honour, notably 'Derwentwater's Farewell' and 'Kenmure's on and awa' Willie'. In his farewell letter to the Duke of Lorraine, James wrote, 'You will have been touched by the death of poor Lord Derwentwater: he died as a true Christian hero.'[7]

But there were also escapes. Lord Nithsdale, another Catholic, who had proclaimed James VIII at Dumfries and had been captured at Preston, was due to suffer with Derwentwater and Kenmure. However, his wife (the Duke of Powis's daughter, Lady Winifrid Herbert) was unusually resourceful. After George refused to reprieve him, having dragged her along the floor as he walked away when she clung to his coat-tails after flinging herself at his feet – she changed her tactics.

Visiting her husband at the Tower on the night before the execution, Lady Nithsdale framed his face with false curls, rouged and powdered it, dressed him in a cloak and hood, and then led him out, pretending he was her maid. Disguised as a footman, he hid at the Venetian embassy before leaving for France with the ambassador, who was unaware of his presence. During the voyage, he heard the ship's captain say 'the wind could not have served better if his passengers had been flying for their lives'. His wife joined him later.[8]

On learning of Nithsdale's escape, George flew into a frenzy, shouting that traitors were at work, and sent messengers to the Tower with instructions to see other prisoners were strictly guarded. But he soon had further provocation.

On 11 April, Tom Forster, wearing a nightgown over his clothes, was visited in his cell by the governor of Newgate, Mr Pitt, and the pair 'discussed' a bottle of wine. Leaving his guest for a moment, to go to the privy, he vanished – only his nightgown was found. No one knew how he escaped, but probably he used skeleton keys. Within twenty-four hours the 'General' was in France.

Early in May there was another sensational escape. On the day before they were to be tried, having got rid of their manacles, Old Borlum, with his son and a dozen friends, rushed the guards in Newgate's exercise yard and broke out. Unfamiliar with London, eight were recaptured, but Borlum got clean away.

Among those who escaped with Borlum was a seventeen-year-old Irishman, Charles Wogan, who had been captured at Preston. Later, he recalled the experience in a memoir he wrote for the Queen of France. Hiding in what he called 'the thick forest of the city of London', hunted by messengers (police), at one point he was 'driven to take refuge, at noon-day, upon the roof of the house where he lodged, by the fury of his pursuers and a huge crowd'. Somehow, despite £500 being offered for his recapture, he too got clean away.[9]

'They are very sever after Forster and McIntosh's breaking out of this, with some others that went away', wrote a Highland officer. 'We are all in irons and closs prison in our rooms, but very hearty. The [gaol] fever again is begun, which make[s] us all afrayd.'[10]

In the summer, the next to suffer in London were hanged, drawn and quartered as commoners. All died bravely during what Daniel Szechi calls 'The Jacobite Theatre of Death', each reaffirming from the scaffold their loyalty to James as their 'true and rightful sovereign'.[11] Colonel Oxburgh, a Catholic, refuted the myth that the 'Papists' had planned to re-establish their Church. 'If King James had been a Protestant, I should think myself oblig'd to pay him the same duty.'

William Paul was a Derbyshire vicar who had taken the oaths of allegiance and abjuration during Anne's reign despite being a product of St John's College, Cambridge, and a convinced Jacobite. Joining Forster's army at Preston, he had several times read prayers in church for King James, escaping before the surrender. He thought he would be safe in London but, sauntering in St James's Park as a layman in expensive clothes and a gold-laced hat, he was recognised and arrested by a Derbyshire Justice of the Peace.

Dressed in black, Mr Paul went to Tyburn as a parson, declaring he belonged to the true, nonjuring Church of England. When he denounced the Elector of Hanover, the sheriff stopped him from saying more. However, his speech was printed. It claimed the Revolution had let in atheism and that the nation could never be happy until James was restored. 'I wish I had Quarters enough to send to every Parish in the Kingdom, to testify that a Clergyman of the Church of England was martyr'd for being Loyal to his King.'[12]

Such gallant deaths and such loyalty to James made a strong impression. So did the butchery. On the day after Oxburgh's execution a jury refused to convict two Lancashire gentlemen, Edward Tildesley and Richard Towneley, despite damning evidence and the judge's fury. A Highland officer who was being taken to his trial with Derwentwater's brother found their coach surrounded by a huge crowd. 'All the ladyes and mob cryed and weepd, and cryed that the Almighty would preserve us against all our enimies.' On the way back to Newgate thousands followed them, 'and all for Derwentwater's brother.'[13]

To some extent this was from Jacobite solidarity as well as pity. Large amounts of food, clothing and money were donated to the prisoners by sympathisers. Mr Towneley, held in London's Marshalsea Prison, was sent £2,000 by Lancashire friends.[14]

It dawned on the Whigs that, for all their king's warm approval, the executions in London were not endearing the Illustrious House of Hanover to its new subjects. No more peers suffered. But it was too late for the government to regret having singled out Lancashire for punishment.

Provincial reprisals

The first Jacobite captives to die in the north were four former serving officers of George's army, who were shot at Preston for desertion on 2 December. A special court arrived at Liverpool in mid January, sentencing thirty-four more prisoners to die less comfortably. The first five suffered a modified version of the tradtional penalty for high treason at Preston on 28 January. A Leeds schoolmaster, John Lucas, who was an eyewitness, describes what this meant:

> When they were hung for so long that they were concluded dead, they were cut down, then stripped, laid on their backs, and their privy members being cut off were thrown into a great fire made there for the purpose, then they were turned upon their faces and their heads being chopped off, they were turned over again and their bellies ripped open to their hearts, their bowels, their livers and lastly their hearts thrown into the fire, then their arms, legs & thighs were chopped off, which with the trunks of their bodies and their heads were putt into coffins.[15]

Each operation's edifying climax came when the executioner shouted 'Behold the heart of a traitor!' and held up a lump of bleeding offal that he then threw into the fire. Generally butchers or slaughterhouse men were employed for such work.

Most victims were spared disembowelment alive. But a Catholic gentleman, Richard Shuttleworth of Turnover Hall near Garstang in Lancashire, had the distinction of having his head stuck on a pole on top of Preston Town Hall. No doubt this was because he had been accused of saying 'He hoped to see the streets running with Hereticks' blood as fast as if it had rained for four days.'[16]

Another twenty-nine were hanged but not quartered during February at Preston, Wigan, Manchester, Garstang, Lancaster and Liverpool. Two were beheaded after death. One was 'Old Mr Chorley' of Chorley who had his head 'set up' on a pole at Preston, to accompany Shuttleworth's. The other was the blacksmith Tom Syddall, whose head was fixed to the market cross at Manchester where he had led the rioting. Like their comrades in London, all told the crowds around the scaffold that they were dying for James III. At the end of February an order arrived to reduce the number of hangings.

The alternative though was not much better, the vast majority of northern captives being held in insanitary prisons where large numbers, weakened by starvation, perished from gaol fever (typhus) or the cold of a harsh winter. Those at Chester Castle died 'in droves like rotten sheep', with four or five thrown into the moat every night – their only grave.[17] Yet many remained defiant, never drinking a glass of beer, or even water, without a 'God bless King James III'.[18] About a thousand who petitioned the Crown for pardon were sentenced to transportation to the Americas or the West Indies.

This meant a hellish voyage manacled in irons in a ship's hold, before being sold as an indentured servant for seven years. In the West Indies purchasers literally worked them to death on the plantations, although they fared better in America. Some escaped en route at Cork, bribing the skipper to put them ashore, while a few had their indentures bought when they arrived by friends who had been told they were coming. One group overpowered the crew of the vessel transporting them, then sailed her to France.

Seen as hardline Jacobites, no group suffered more than the recusants, twenty-one Catholic estates in Lancashire and twenty-one in Northumberland being confiscated while Catholic manor houses and farms were plundered.[19] Whig ministers shared the loot, creating a new Whig ascendancy in northern England. Although the government abandoned as unworkable its plans for confiscating two-thirds of every Catholic estate, it doubled the land tax for recusant squires.

A new act made it legal for any two Justices of the Peace to order a Catholic to take the oath of abjuration – refusal meant prison and swingeing fines. Many were only saved from ruin by the connivance of Protestant neighbours who secretly shared their loyalty to King James, like Squire Inglewood in Scott's *Rob Roy*. However, in 1717, Rome gave them permission to take the oath.

High Churchmen were also attacked by Hanoverian supporters. In 1717, the English actor–manager Colley Cibber put on *The Nonjuror* at Drury Lane, a clumsy adaptation of Molière's *Tartuffe* that replaces the arch-hypocrite of the title by a clergyman spy in James's pay. Even so, the Jacobites won the propaganda war, a flood of pamphlets turning every execution into a martyrdom.

The reckoning in Scotland

Matters were different in Scotland, where there was sympathy for men who had fought for Scottish independence, and lawyers were loath to ask for the recently introduced English sentence of hanging and disembowelment. Archibald Burnett of Carlops was an exception, suffering the full penalty. Conscious when the executioner ripped him open, he is recorded as scream-ing horribly, which cannot have impressed spectators with the benefits of Union.

The Duke of Argyll wanted to amnesty his prisoners-of-war, but George ordered him to treat them as rebels. He was so angered by the duke's attitude that in the summer of 1716 he dismissed from all government posts the commander who, single-handed, had saved the Scottish crown for Hanover.

Eighty gentlemen prisoners were marched from Edinburgh to Carlisle so that they could be tried by English judges, but their Scottish lawyers proved more than a match for the system. Apart from Burnett, the only Scots who suffered the death penalty or transportation were those who had fallen into English hands at Preston.

The Commission for Forfeited Estates that decimated northern England's recusants could not cope with the Scots. Every Scottish lawyer, from judges to Writers to the Signet, impeded prosecutions with a fog of legal stratagems and costs. The Commissioners may well have quoted an old Parliament House proverb, "'Hame's hame,' as the Devil said when he found himself at the Court of Session.'

One rash attempt to investigate a Highland estate resulted in the

Commission's officials being killed, wounded or else fleeing. Some Jacobite lairds lost their lands in law but went on enjoying most, if not all, of the income.

In 1716 Parliament passed the Septennial Act which decreed that future general elections should be held every seven years instead of every three. The official object was to reduce election expenses, but the real aim was to prolong the Whig majority in the House of Commons until 1722, and in the long term lessen the influence of comparatively few voters. A Peerage Bill was introduced in 1719 to restrict the creation of new peers and give ministers control of the House of Lords. This, however, was rejected by the Commons.

The Whig programme was a denial of 'revolution principles', more arbitrary than anything attempted by James II. Judge Jeffreys's Bloody Assizes may have been on a par with reprisals after the Fifteen, but James had never contemplated imposing such savage laws as the Smuggling Act or the Black Act that made poachers liable to the death penalty.

In July, George returned to Hanover for six month's holiday, although he had enough imagination to realise his throne was still in danger and that one day he might have to go home for good. There were too many Tories like Addison's Foxhunter who, referring to his new German ruler's use of mercenaries, asked, 'But is it not strange that we should be making war upon Church of England men with Dutch and Swiss soldiers, men of anti-monarchical principles?'

While making the Whigs still more odious to Tories and High Churchmen, the crisis forged an even closer bond between the Hanoverians and the party who saved them. The consequences of defeat terrified English Jacobites, especially Catholics, who from now on declined to rise without the support of regular troops. With hindsight, we can see that a Restoration would never again be quite so nearly within King James's grasp.

25

Swedes and Russians,
1716–1718

Here's a health to the valiant Swede,
He's not a king that man hath made;
May no oppressors him invade.

Anon, 'Here's a health to the valiant Swede'[1]

George I is best remembered for the 'Water Music' composed by Handel for his famous trip down the Thames in 1717, music exuding serenity that the king had played three times. Yet there was nothing serene about his reign, not even in Germany where his policy made dangerous enemies. The Jacobites offered them a means of eliminating him.

Early in April 1716 King James arrived at Avignon in Provence, the capital of the Comtat Venaissin and technically in papal territory. The Hôtel de la Serre, which housed the commander of the Pontifical Guard, became his official residence and where he established his court. Lent was not yet over, so he attended the Lenten services punctiliously. His courtiers followed him to Avignon, notably Mar, the new secretary of state, and the Duke of Ormonde.

The court soon grew to 500 people, counting servants, swollen by starving, ragged refugees, English, Scots and Irish, who included peers and clan chieftains. From inadequate resources James and Queen Mary did their best to help them in a graded system of pensions – peers received 200 livres a month, chieftains 150, ex-lieutenants 30 and the few rank and file who had reached France 10. It was barely enough to support life and rather than starve a number of officers, some not even Irish, joined the Irish Brigade to serve as privates.[2]

James liked Avignon, whose inhabitants were flattered by his presence. But in September he was struck down by an anal fistula and underwent an agonising operation. His recovery took three months, confining him to bed.

The Regent Orléans' conviction that France would do better to ally with Hanoverian England was disastrous for James. Yet other powers might be willing to help.

In the same way that William III had used British resources to further Dutch interests, as predicted George employed them to benefit Hanover. However, his designs on Swedish territory in Germany gave James a new ally and if Sweden's Baltic empire was on the verge of collapse in the Great Northern War her warrior king, Charles XII, was still a formidable enemy.

Until recently, because of her conquests, Sweden had been the third largest state in Europe, but after a catastrophic defeat by Russia at Poltava in 1709 she lost Livonia and Estonia. Forfeiting their revenues was a severe blow to King Charles, who had been fighting to save the Swedish empire since he was eighteen. He was desperate to recover Bremen and Verden, two former Swedish duchies at the mouth of the Weser and the Elbe that levied valuable tolls on shipping from inland Germany.

Exploiting Charles's weakness, George had sent his tiny Hanoverian army to occupy both towns, then tried to buy them at a fraction of their value. Charles refused to sell, so in 1715 George entered the Great Northern War against Sweden, joining Russia, Saxony-Poland, Denmark and Prussia. In flagrant breach of the Act of Settlement that bound him to avoid embroiling Britain in foreign wars, he secretly ordered the Royal Navy to harass Swedish shipping.

Having failed to raise a million riksdalers to finance the Swedish war effort, in 1716 Baron von Görtz, who was King Charles's most trusted adviser, decided to play the Jacobite card after Tory MPs contacted the Swedish ambassador at London, Count Gyllenborg. Görtz, a huge, bullying man with an enamelled glass eye that struck fear into beholders, decided that an alliance with James could be of the utmost value. Usefully, Gyllenborg's English wife happened to be a fervent Jacobite.

Gyllenborg asked advice from Lord Oxford, still in the Tower from having been impeached, who put him in touch with Bishop Atterbury, James's new agent in England. Together, Gyllenborg and Atterbury produced a plan of which the king at Avignon warmly approved. The man they chose to organise it was a protégé of Oxford, Charles Caesar, a High Churchman, Tory MP and former member of the October Club, who had been treasurer of the navy under Queen Anne.[3]

The Gyllenborg Plot

The plan was simple. After the Jacobites had sent money to Stockholm to finance the expedition, 10,000 Swedish regulars would land in April 1717 in Northern England where James's followers would join them. It meant that the Restoration was to be the work of a Protestant war hero and Protestant troops. (Usefully, over a thousand Scots were serving in the Swedish army, many as officers.)

Support for the project was so enthusiastic that Caesar quickly raised £18,000 of the £60,000 stipulated. Much of this was collected from the Catholic gentry by Thomas Southcott, a monk of St Edmund's Chapel in Paris who was known as 'Mr Scravenmor' or 'the man in black'. (In England Catholic priests wore brown, to avoid detection.) Quite apart from loyalty to the King over the Water, recusant squires saw the invasion as their only hope of escaping the double land tax.

Throughout, Gyllenborg was in touch with Count Sparre, Sweden's envoy at Paris. Sparre however fell ill and, his judgement weakened by sickness, to save expense sent letters through the ordinary post instead of by special courier, relying on cypher to disguise their contents. Intercepted, the Whig government's highly efficient decipherer at the Secret Office, the Reverend Edward Willes, broke the Swedish code and warned his employers of the plot.

In October 1716 Lord Townshend informed General Stanhope that a letter from Gyllenborg 'confirms all we have ever suspected ... his saying money will not be wanting to complete his scheme, shows plainly that he has had large offers from the [Jacobite] party, and that they are determined to try once more their fortune if the King of Sweden will assist them with troops'. He adds, 'Count Gyllenborg has passed most of this summer with Caesar, a creature of Lord Oxford's in Hertfordshire.'

Once Parliament's authority to act had been obtained, Stanhope, the Whig ministry's most ruthless member, moved quickly. Ignoring diplomatic immunity, in February 1717 the Swedish embassy at London was ringed by troops, General George Wade forcing his way in to arrest Gyllenborg and seize his papers. Stanhope also persuaded the Dutch to expel Baron von Görtz. Wild rumours circulated, the indefatigable Daniel Defoe publishing a pamphlet – *What if the Swedes should Come?*

Among those arrested were Caesar, Lord Lansdowne, Sir Jacob Banks (a naturalised Swede with a distinguished career in the Royal Navy) and Colonel Hay, who was the brother of Mar's henchman. Nothing was found in Gyllenborg's papers that could be used as grounds for legal action against them. Only Hay was brought to trial, but although condemned to death on other charges, he escaped and made his way to Avignon.

Lord Oxford was so impressed by Caesar's determination to carry on that he sent a message to Avignon asking for a portrait of James to be sent to him in token of appreciation – 'there are few in England so useful in the King's affairs; he spares neither money nor pains . . .'[4] Caesar's wife was delighted when James's picture arrived, showing it to everybody.

After the uproar died down and Gyllenborg was released, Caesar advised him that Sweden should launch the invasion in autumn 1717, during the Parliamentary recess and when the fleet would be laid up. He had high hopes of disaffection to George among both officers and men in the British army, especially among half-pay officers who had been 'turned out' – purged – by the Whigs because they were Tories.

Charles XII never committed himself to the Gyllenborg Plot, but was well aware of it. If he could make peace on other fronts, a Jacobite Restoration offered him his best chance of recovering Bremen and Verden. During an exploratory conference it looked as though he might be able to make peace and help James.

There was even a possibility Russia might join. Görtz and the Russian envoy at the conference, Count Osterman, agreed that should Britain try to interfere with Charles's recovery of the two cities, then Sweden and Russia would invade England.[5] But they were to be overtaken by events.

In his letter to Gyllenborg, Caesar mentioned the recent Act of Grace. This new Act freed prisoners who had been taken during the Fifteen, including about 200 of those captured at Preston and all still held in Scotland, while it pardoned three peers and forty-three gentlemen under sentence of death. But the act excluded many people from pardon and did not restore confiscated estates, omissions that in Caesar's opinon disgusted even Whigs.

Death of Charles XII and the end of the Swedish plan

The Jacobites still hoped Sweden would help as Charles had not forgiven his ambassador's arrest. However, in December 1718, while besieging the fortress of Frederiksten in Norway he was killed by a stray missile. Some suspected murder, perhaps by the aide-de-camp of his brother-in-law Prince Frederick. His death remains a mystery.

Sweden was exhausted. In 1721, at the Treaty of Nystad, her new rulers, Charles's sister Queen Ulrika Eleanora and her husband King Frederick, made peace, surrendering Bremen and Verden to Hanover. The sinister Baron von Görtz was beheaded, but Gyllenborg secured a leading role in the regime that now governed Sweden. Even so, the Jacobites still hoped the Swedes might rescue them – if supported by another great power.

Had King Charles's men landed, British regulars would have had a shock, never having faced Swedish troops, who before the advent of Frederick the Great's Prussians were considered the most formidable in Europe. There was no command for 'retreat' in Swedish military manuals, while Swedish cavalry and infantry were both famous for their devastating charge.

Since 1716 a ballad had been sung about the Swedish plan. (Caesar's sense of security left a lot to be desired.) The same ballad mentions Russia and Peter the Great:

> Here's a health to the mysterious Czar
> I hope he'll send us help from afar,
> To end the work begun by Mar.[6]

Under Peter, Russia had emerged as a great European power. English, Scots and Irish Jacobites joined the Russian navy and army in such large numbers, especially after the Fifteen, that they became a worry for the Whig regime in London. The most influential Jacobite émigré in Russia was a kinsman of Mar who had become the Tsar's doctor, Robert Erskine ('Araskin'). His loyalty to the Stuarts was shared by his fellow exile, Admiral Thomas Gordon.[7]

The Tsar met other Jacobites on a tour of Europe from February to October 1717, during which he spent several months at Copenhagen and The Hague. Dr Erskine was in attendance throughout. What made the situation explosive was that the Whig government knew Count Gyllenborg had arranged to meet Erskine in Holland, but was prevented by his arrest. Already alarmed by the presence of Russian troops in Mecklenburg on the Hanoverian border, George saw that Tsar Peter was not only planning to switch sides and join Sweden, but offering to help Charles recover Bremen and Verden. Admiral Norris and twelve British men-of-war were sent to the Baltic.

The Tsar decided the Jacobites could be useful, especially when they said they could help him negotiate with Sweden. In summer 1717 Ormonde, accompanied by George Jerningham, Charles Wogan and Colonel Daniel O'Brian (King James's agent at Paris), went to Danzig, hoping to meet both Charles XII and Tsar Peter. When Ormonde arrived at Mitau (Jelgava) in Latvia, he received a letter from Dr Erskine.

The doctor told him he had spoken to the Tsar about his mission, and that Peter suggested trying France if Sweden procrastinated any further. Erskine also guaranteed that in the event of the Swedes making peace with Peter, he would send 20,000 troops to occupy Rostock, Mecklenburg's principal city. This would force George to hurry back to Hanover.

Besides expressing a hope that the invasion to restore King James would take place before winter, the Tsar offered him his ten-year-old daughter, Grand Duchess Anna Petrovna, in marriage.[8] However, the offer depended on James's successful restoration by the Swedes. In any case, from James's point of view she was not only too young but belonged to the Orthodox Church.

Nothing concrete came of these negotiations between Tsar Peter and the court of James III. Even so, eager to weaken Hanover, Peter might well have supported a Swedish or Franco-Irish expedition with money or men, or with both. As will be seen, long after Charles XII's death (and also that of Dr Erskine in the same year), Peter maintained friendly relations with James.

The two episodes, Swedish and Russian, show that even without French support James remained an important player on the European stage. Meanwhile, another great power had come to his assistance.

26

The Nineteen

All of a sudden wee received the joyfull news of
the King of Spain's having declared for
our King.

George Lockhart of Carnwath[1]

Unlike the Fifteen or the Forty-Five, the Nineteen was a small affair, over
very quickly. Even so, the story deserves to be told.

After the War of the Spanish Succession, Spain re-emerged as a European
power, despite a Bourbon king who was on the brink of insanity. A depressive, Philip V slept throughout the day and only rose at nightfall, to confess
his sins three times before dawn – guilt ridden by the thought of men
having died to put him on his throne. Eventually, the famous Italian castrato
Farinelli came to sooth his nerves by singing to him every night, but this did
not happen until years later.

Philip's queen, Elizabeth Farnese, had fallen under the sway of Cardinal
Giulio Alberoni, an Italian adventurer to whose machinations she owed her
marriage. Spain's real ruler, prime minister since 1715 after (partially) restoring his adopted country's finances, Alberoni hoped to recover Spain's lost
territories in Italy. As a first step, Spanish troops reconquered first Sardinia
and then Sicily the following year in July 1718.

Alarmed by the prospect of a major new conflict, Britain hastily joined
France, the Empire and the Dutch Republic to form the Quadruple Alliance.
In August, without any warning, the Royal Navy blew a Spanish fleet out
of the water off Cape Passaro in Sicily. Britain then declared war on Spain,
followed by France after the discovery of a plot to murder Orléans and
replace him as regent by King Philip – little Louis XV's uncle.

Spain allies with James III

Alberoni had been cultivating James for some time, paying him a small pension. Now he decided to throw Spain's resources behind him in a bid to overthrow George and knock Britain out of the Alliance. An armada carrying 6,000 troops under the Duke of Ormonde, who had been made a Spanish general, would invade the West Country. A smaller force under the Earl Marischal would land in Scotland and raise the clans.

Ormonde had several meetings with Alberoni, which he reported in a letter to James at the end of December. The cardinal had asked him to implore Charles XII to invade Britain before spring. Accordingly, the duke had sent his Irish aide-de-camp, George Bagenal, to Sweden – 'his Instructions are to tell the King that no money will be given by the King of Spain unless he consents to make an Attempt on England by the time proposed'. Bagenal was to say that 'two Thousand men to Scotland with five Thousand Arms' would be sufficient.

> Alberoni seem'd very uneasy at your situation in Italy. [Ormonde continues] He fears that your person is not in Safety, considering the late inhuman Proceedings against the Princess [see Chapter 27]. He thinks Rome the worst place for you to be in, because of the Emperor's Spys and the Difficulty you will have of getting privately from thence ... it is my humble opinion that you ought to come to Spain with all expedition, that you may be out of the Emperor's power; and your presence is necessary here, Either to embark with the Troops, if you can arrive in time, or to follow as soon as possible.[2]

At the end of 1718, Alberoni invited James to Spain. Pretending he would travel overland, the king ordered the Duke of Perth to impersonate him and go north where, mistaken for James, Perth was arrested as soon as he entered the Duchy of Milan – Imperial territory. Meanwhile, the king sailed secretly from Nettuno, a small port near Anzio. News of his departure got out and he was pursued by two British warships.

Blown off course, he was forced to land in France, hiding for three days at Marseilles in the house of his ship's skipper. He then had to put in at Villefranche and spend twenty-four hours there, having fallen ill with 'a Fever' and needing to be bled. Another storm blew him into the islands off Hyères, where 'he was compelled to share the accommodation of a Miserable Inn with a crowd of dirty Wretches, and though he was suffering from sea-sickness, to dance with the Landlady, it being Carnival time,'[3] Alberoni informed Ormonde.

Landing at Roses, in Catalonia, in March 1719, James made a state entry into Madrid in Philip's own coach, greeted with royal honours as ruler of Great Britain and Ireland. The Spanish king and queen presented him with 25,000 gold pistoles and a service of silver plate, as well as the palace of Buen Retiro for his residence. During his stay, they dined with him every day.

However, intending to join his troops in England, after only a week he left Madrid for Corunna. Here he received dismal news.

Ormonde had waited at Corunna to go on board his armada of twenty-seven vessels, which sailed from Cádiz early in March 1719. He intended to land near Bristol where there were many Jacobites. The Whig government knew his plans, so British fleets were sent to patrol the Bay of Biscay and off the Lizard to intercept his armada, while four regiments were brought back from Ireland and concentrated at Bristol.

However, the armada never reached Corunna. On leaving Cádiz it ran into gales that lasted for three weeks, exhausting its provisions. Then, off Cape Finisterre towards one o'clock in the morning of 29 March, it was struck by a storm that continued for forty-eight hours. Some ships were dismasted, others threw cannon and horses overboard to stay afloat. Eventually, they limped into the nearest Galician ports, the soldiers on the transports having gone without food or water for four days.

The Earl Marischal's expedition

George Keith was the tenth and last Earl Marischal. His family had been custodians of the Honours of Scotland since 1458, successfully hiding them during the Cromwellian occupation. Despite serving under Marlborough in Flanders, he had always been a Jacobite and fought for James in 1715, after which he lost his Aberdeenshire estates. An intellectual, in old age he became a friend of Rousseau, who – of all people – found 'something strange and wayward in his turn of mind'.

In mid March, Lord Marischal and his two frigates set sail from 'Port Passage' (Pasajes) on the Guipúzkoan coast. On board were 300 Spanish regulars from the regiment of Galicia in white uniforms with yellow facings, among whom were several Irish officers. Due to the Basque sailors' fine seamanship, the vessels weathered the storms, landing on Lewis where he billeted his men at Stornoway.

Here he was joined by his brother, James Keith, with the Marquess of Tullibardine, the Earl of Seaforth, Lord George Murray (a former subaltern in Queen Anne's army) and other gentlemen, who arrived from France in a tiny 'barque' of twenty-five tons, having sailed through an enemy fleet at night. Tullibardine produced a commission from James, appointing him commander-in-chief. Marischal accepted it, but insisted he was in command of the ships.

The expedition sailed to the mainland, landing at Loch Alsh in Kintail, Seaforth's country, on 13 April, where the troops built a rough barracks. Instead of attacking isolated enemy garrisons, they waited for news of Ormonde's landing. Tullibardine and Seaforth, who had both advised staying on Lewis until they received definite information of the landing having taken place, began to lose their nerve. To show there could be no going back, Lord Marischal sent home the Spanish frigates.

Tullibardine wrote to the clan chieftains, asking them to rise. Only about 1,500 clansmen responded to the summons, mainly Seaforth's Mackenzies and their MacRae allies, with some Mackinnons and a party of MacGregors who included Rob Roy. Cameron of Lochiel and MacDonald of Clanranald came too, but with disappointingly few followers. All were well-armed, however, since the frigates had brought 2,000 muskets and ammunition.

The beautiful little castle of Eilean Donan, seemingly impregnable on its tidal island, was occupied for use as a headquarters and arsenal. When three enemy warships appeared on 9 May, it was evacuated, leaving Captain Stapleton, an Irish officer in the Spanish service, and forty Spaniards as garrison. After two days of bombardment from the sea, Eilean Donan was stormed by a landing party. Over 340 barrels of gunpowder and fifty of musket shot were found inside the castle, the powder being used to blow it up. The prisoners were sent to Edinburgh.

By June, Marischal and Tullibardine knew that Ormonde's armada would never come. Even so, they decided to attack Inverness, which was about sixty miles away, approaching it by way of Glenmoriston and the Great Glen. They then learned that Major-General Wightman, the Hanoverian commander-in-chief in Scotland and a veteran of Sheriffmuir, had left Inverness on 5 June and was marching to meet them, on the same road.

Wightman brought with him the Inverness garrison, which consisted of 850 foot, 120 dragoons and 150 pro-Hanoverian Highlanders – Mackays and Munroes. He also had four Coehorn mortars. Easily portable (each one could be carried by four men) and throwing an explosive shell with a time-fuse in a high-arching trajectory, these were alarmingly effective – the target could see the shell coming towards him.

The Jacobite army numbered 250 Spaniards and about 1,800 Highlanders, heartened by the last minute arrival of another small party of Lochiel's Camerons. On the night of 9 June, the clansmen took up a defensive position south of the little River Shiel on high ground at each side of Glenshiel, at the foot of the mountain Sgùrr na Ciste Duibhe. The Spaniards occupied the centre of the glen. Not far from Loch Duich, this was ringed by other spectacular mountains.

'Our right was cover'd by a rivulet which was difficult to pass, and our left by a ravine, and in the front the ground was so rugged and deep that it was impossible to come at us', James Keith recalled.[4] The Jacobites strengthened the position with trenches and a barricade of stones on the pass through the glen. A tiny handful of cavalry was placed on moorland. 'Their Dispositions for Defence were extraordinary, with the Advantages of Rocks, Mountains and Intrenchments,' Wightman later reported in a dispatch.[5]

On Sunday 10 June, between five and six o'clock in the evening, Wightman opened the battle, attacking the Jacobite right wing under Lord George Murray with a barrage from his mortars, supplemented by grenades. (His troops included 150 grenadiers.) Then he sent his infantry forward, firing by volleys. Murray, who was wounded, hastily withdrew.

Next, Wightman attacked the Jacobite left under Lord Seaforth. On a hill-side and protected by rocks, the Highlanders there were harder to dislodge, but eventually they fled into the mountains, carrying Seaforth who had been bady wounded in the arm.

Finally, at about 9 p.m., pausing from time to time to fire at their pursuers, the white-coated Spanish regulars under Tullibardine in the centre also retreated into the mountains.

The clansmen immediately made for home so that next morning the Spaniards were the only troops that remained. Tullibardine wanted to take them through the Highlands and gather fresh support, but the other leaders disagreed. They also declined a gallant offer by Don Nicolas Bolano, who commanded the Spaniards, to attack the enemy, advising him to surrender.

Hanoverian casualties were twenty-one killed and 121 wounded, the Jacobites having lost a hundred dead and many more wounded. Ironically the day on which the battle was fought was White Rose Day, King James's birthday. Lords Marischal, Tullibardine, Seaforth and George Murray escaped through the mountains to the Western Isles and, when pursuit slackened, to France.

'I am taking a tour through all the difficult passes of Seaforth's country, to terrify the rebels by burning the houses of the guilty, and preserving those of the honest,' General Wightman reported a week later to his commanding officer, Lord Carpenter.[6] It is unlikely the 'tour' had much effect, except to strengthen the Mackenzies' loyalty to King James.

At the end of April 1719 British warships appeared before Corunna, so James moved inland to the little town of Lugo where, hoping to hear from Lord Marischal, he waited until the end of June. Learning of the disaster at Glenshiel, he went to Vinaròs in Catalonia, from where in August he took ship for Leghorn (Livorno) aboard a comfortable galley supplied by Alberoni, his court accompanying him on another. He needed to return urgently to Italy for his impending marriage to Clementina Sobieska, the granddaughter of King John III Sobieski of Poland.

After Spanish defeats on all fronts, the cardinal's position became untenable. In December he was banished from Spain, who made peace with her enemies. Nonetheless, Philip V and Elizabeth Farnese always remained well-disposed towards James, even if they could not help him.

Had the Marischal's expedition been successful, there would have been a rising in Ireland. There had been rumblings during the Fifteen involving the Earl of Granard, the Bishop of Derry and Viscount Ikerrin, with an unusually violent riot in Dublin and mud thrown at King Billy's statue, but they came to nothing.[7] Officers from the Irish Brigade had gone to Scotland in January 1716, too late to be of any use.

In spring 1716 Captain Richard Bourke had informed Bolingbroke, still James's secretary of state, that a rising was feasible in Connacht and later that year another Irishman advised Mar to send Ormonde with 3,000 troops to Ireland 'for the King there has six to one for him.' In 1718 a Fr. Calanan had visited James to tell him 'want of a diversion in Ireland much contributed towards the ill success of the King's affairs in Scotland' during the Fifteen.

In 1719 Dublin Castle feared Ormonde's armada was destined for Ireland rather than England. Panic set in when it learned that 'Sarsfield, otherwise called Earl of Lucan, and several officers . . . had held conferences with divers Papists of distinction, with design to foment a rebellion in favour of the Pretender.'[8] A reward of £1,000 was offfered for each of them, dead or alive.

Lucan was the son of the great Patrick Sarsfield who had fought for James's father in England and Ireland, and had led the Wild Geese to France.

All we know of his plans is that sometime in March he arrived in Connacht with Irish officers from the Spanish army, intending to organise risings throughout Ireland that would distract the regime when Ormonde landed in England. After Ormonde's armada failed to materialise, he left for Flanders in a ship from Kilcolgan in County Galway – dying not long after.[9]

In 1720 the authorities arrested James Cotter, a flamboyant Irish-speaking Catholic landowner in County Cork who tied white roses on his foxhounds and was an obvious leader should there be a rising. The charge, clearly false, was the rape of his mistress Elizabeth Squibb. Found guilty, despite Miss Squibb and the jury pleading for mercy he was hanged at Cork – brought forward in the knowledge that a stay of execution was on its way.

Cotter's legal murder caused riots all over Ireland, a dozen Munster poets keening for his death. Brazenly, Dublin Castle insisted on his sons being brought up as Protestants.[10] So flagrant an abuse of the law reveals the depth of the Ascendancy's insecurity and its neurotic dread of invasion.

27

A Prince of Wales Is Born, 1720

The Chevalier de St George, being the only Male Descendant of his Family, had often been solicited by his Friends to change his Condition, in order to revive their Hopes, by raising up an Heir.

Sir Charles Wogan, *Female Fortitude*, 1722[1]

Georg August, Hanoverian Prince of Wales, learned to speak English albeit with a strong accent, a modest achievement that irritated his father. The prince had always resented his mother's imprisonment, but the rift between father and son grew worse when the king insisted on making his lord chamberlain godfather to Georg August's son and Georg August promptly challenging the lord chamberlain to a duel. From then on, the prince deliberately opposed his parent's policies in England and in Germany.

'The tyranny of the father, and the behaviour of the son in this affair, has opened the eyes of many, that everybody thought would blindly support the interest of that family', Charles Caesar commented in a letter of December 1717 to the Duke of Mar. 'They do not now scruple to own that this family cannot be suffered to continue here.'[2]

Yet the simple fact that Georg August existed meant that the Hanoverians had an heir, while the childless James III had only Italian cousins to inherit his claims. King George used every trick he knew to stop James from marrying and fathering a child who would carry on the Stuart dynasty.

Even before the Nineteen, George had insisted on James leaving Avignon, even if it was papal territory – he wanted him on the far side of the Alps. In February 1717, James set out for the Papal States, the only country that would give him refuge, travelling as the 'Marquis de Cavallone' but with seventy courtiers. He found himself unwelcome at Turin despite Queen Anna Maria being his heir presumptive, as her husband Victor Amadeus (Duke of Savoy and King of Sicily) was George's ally. He received a kinder reception at Modena from another kinsman, Duke Rinaldo.

When he arrived at Rome in May, Pope Clement XI (Giovanni Albani) greeted him as a martyr for the faith, giving him the beautiful hilltop palace of Urbino and a pension of 12,000 scudi. However, he did not enjoy life in the remote Marche region, feeling cut off from the world during an unusually harsh winter. 'The want of [congenial society over a bottle of Burgundy] makes us very dull here', he wrote on 1 January to Sir John Erskine of Alva, who had once been a boon companion. 'I am weary of the country I am in. I am now writing to you in the middle of hills, frost and snow, and not like to see the ground these two months.'[3]

To some extent Mar, who had accompanied James, whiled away the time with music parties in his rooms – he played a harpsichord, Earl Marischal the flute and the Earl of Panmure the violin. Yet even Mar admitted the boredom was such that he feared he would 'die of the spleen'.

James went back to Rome early in summer 1718 but had difficulty in finding a home. He also seemed unable to find a queen. Among others, he proposed to Maria d'Este, the Duke of Modena's eldest daughter, which delighted Queen Mary, but the duke forebade the marriage. James contemplated taking a wife that was not even royal – Maria Vittoria di Caprara of Bologna, heiress to a great fortune, with whom he appears to have been genuinely in love

No doubt King George was encouraged by Queen Mary's death in May 1718 and James's shortage of funds. The regent of France stopped paying the late queen's pension, rendering many of her courtiers destitute. James was deeply upset at being unable to help them but was himself in financial straits.

However, in March 1718, George had been thunderstruck to learn that James had at last found a bride, of impeccably royal blood as well as great wealth. James was betrothed to the sixteen-year-old Princess Maria Clementina Sobieska. Her father had been a candidate for the Polish throne as the son of King John III Sobieski (who saved Vienna from the Turks), while her mother, Countess Palatine Elizabeth of Neuburg, was an aunt of the Emperor and the Spanish queen. Among Europe's richest heiresses, small, slightly built but shapely, with large blue eyes and long, light brown hair reaching nearly to her feet, Clementina appeared to be cheerful and intelligent.

George asked the Emperor, his ally, to stop the marriage. In October, when Clementina was travelling from her home Ohlau (Oława) in Silesia to

Italy with her mother for the wedding, on Charles VI's orders the pair were arrested at Innsbruck by the governor, General Heister, who imprisoned them in Schloss Ambras, a castle just outside the city.

James was so discouraged that he again contemplated marrying Maria Vittoria di Caprara. In any case, as has been seen, he was away in Spain, hoping to join the Duke of Ormonde's expedition to England.

A 'Gentleman of Ireland', as he called himself, Captain Wogan from Kildare, who had escaped from Newgate in 1716, came to Clementina's rescue. After serving in Dillon's Regiment of the Irish Brigade he entered James's household at Rome and accompanied Ormonde on his mission to Russia. En route, he saw the princess and, when he returned, suggested to James that she would make a suitable consort. He then delivered the king's proposal to her father. Clementina was thrilled, having as a little girl often played at being Queen of England.

Ignoring the risk of being hanged by the emperor or sent to England for a more painful death, Wogan secured a warrant (*plein pouvoir*) from Clementina's father, Prince Sobieski, telling her to co-operate, after which he wrote to the princess for her permission to organise an escape. Then he went to Dillon's Regiment, quartered near Strasbourg, and enlisted the help of three brother officers.

One was his uncle, Major Richard Gaydon, while the other two were his cousins, Captain John Misset and the handsome Captain Luke O'Toole who spoke German fluently. Although heavily pregnant, Misset's wife was enlisted since the princess had asked for a lady to be in the party and young Mrs Misset had 'a sprightly Turn of Wit and a Conversation so engaging as could not fail to make her an acceptable Companion'. She in turn brought her youthful maid, Jenny. Wogan also took a Florentine named Michele Vozzi, a valet of King James who had helped Lord Nithsdale escape from the Tower.

Imperial passports were procured at Rome for the 'Comte and Comtesse de Cernes' (Major Gaydon and Mrs Misset) who were supposedly making a pilgrimage to Loretto. The rest pretended to be their household. A carriage drawn by six horses was bought, with spare parts in case of a breakdown. They set out from Strasbourg on 16 April 1719, Wogan rode in the carriage with Jenny and 'Cernes', he as the 'Countess's' brother, she as her sister. Misset, O'Toole and Vozzi rode beside the vehicle, as armed outriders.

It took them a week to reach Innsbruck. Here, through her mother's gentleman usher, they told Clementina she must keep to her bed for two days as if seriously ill and then in a hooded riding habit, escorted by her Polish page Konski, go out into the street where Wogan would be waiting. Jenny would impersonate the princess, staying in her bed with the curtains drawn to delay pursuit for as long as possible. Clementina must leave a letter of apology to her mother, giving the impression that she had taken no part in the escape.

Understandably, Jenny baulked at her role, even when begged by O'Toole with whom she had fallen in love. She only agreed after being given an expensive damask dress and money in gold, with a promise of more to come. Wearing the riding habit, she entered the castle shortly after midnight on 27 April, the page persuading the porter to admit her.

Putting on the hooded habit, Princess Clementina slipped into the street with Konski at 1 a.m., carrying her jewels in a small parcel. They found themselves in a blizzard that kept everybody indoors – without a sentry-box, the solitary sentry outside had taken refuge in a tavern – except for Wogan, who emerged from the shadows and took her to his inn where Mrs Misset produced dry clothes.

By 2 a.m. the party had left Innsbruck, bound for Italy. There was a momentary panic when Clementina found she had left her jewels at the inn, but O'Toole rode back and retrieved them – lifting the door off its hinges to avoid waking those inside.

Although they had too big a start to be overtaken by cavalry, they feared a fast courier might be sent with orders for local governors to arrest them. Just before arriving at Trent, the courier in question entered an inn where they had stopped. Realising who he was, Misset and O'Toole drank him into a stupor, lacing his wine with brandy, then tore up his dispatches.

It was an uncomfortable journey. They could not find fresh horses at the posting stations and the carriage axle broke, replaced with an axle from a farm cart which in turn broke. However, they bought a 'calash', a dogcart with room for two. Leaving some of the party to bring the carriage when its axle had been mended, Clementina and Mrs Misset in the calash with Wogan and Misset walking behind, crossed the Imperial frontier into Venetian territory early on Sunday 30 April. They woke the princess, to sing a *Te Deum*.

Rejoined by the others, on 2 May they reached Bologna in the Papal States where they were welcomed by the Cardinal Legate. On 15 May, Clementina finally entered Rome.

Throughout, she had impressed her rescuers by her courage, gaiety and disregard for comfort, not even complaining when the parcel with her jewels was lost. Wogan later wrote that she showed 'such a Greatness of Soul, such a Steadiness in one who had not yet accomplished the Age of seventeen, that all Europe must admire it'. Yet there were disturbing signs. She had fainted too easily and eaten too little – only two eggs on the first day of her escape as it was a Friday.

The Pope, who had always liked James and wanted a Catholic heir to the British throne, was in ecstasy. He sent the carriage of his brother, Cardinal Albani, to meet the princess outside Rome and take her to the Ursuline convent of Santa Cecilia in Via Nomentana (now Accademia Musicale di Santa Cecilia) with his own niece as lady-in-waiting. Here Clementina remained under the name of 'Madame de St George' until James returned from Spain, despite asking to join him there, and celebrated her seventeenth birthday on 2 June.

Pope Clement created Wogan and his friends Roman senators while King James gave Wogan a baronetcy, knighting the other three. Jenny, thrown into a dungeon by General Heister, was eventually freed by the princess's mother who sent her to her daughter in Rome. Later, Mrs Misset was appointed governess to James and Clementina's first child, the infant Prince Charles.

George was so angry that, on his instructions, when Wogan was at Genoa soon after, the British envoy unsuccessfully demanded his arrest on a false charge of murdering Imperial couriers. George also sent a paranoiac letter to Emperor Charles VI, complaining of 'dangerous consequences' – England or Scotland might burst into flames at any moment.

Marriage of King James and Princess Clementina

Following the Nineteen, James returned to Italy at the end of August 1719 and on 1 September arrived at the little city of Montefiascone near Viterbo. Two days later he and Clementina were married here by the bishop, with Sir Charles Wogan among the witnesses. A painting of the ceremony by Agostino Masucci shows a radiant Clementina and a careworn James, who looks older than he was. Although he wrote to Ormonde of his delight with his queen, he was worried about money since her dowry had not yet materialised. Nor did he have a home. For two months the couple were forced to stay in the bishop's palace at Montefiascone.

In November, however, Pope Clement gave the king a suitably impressive residence in Rome, Palazzo del Re in Piazza dei Santi Apostoli, and as a country retreat Palazzo Savelli at Albano on the Appian Way – near Castel Gandolfo.

James quickly established a small but dignified court of over a hundred persons, subsidised by a papal pension increased to 80,000 scudi. It became one of Rome's most important musical centres with concerts once or twice a week by famous instrumentalists and a weekly ball during the pre-Lent carnival and on royal birthdays.[4] As there was no British embassy, it attracted rich men from all three realms who were on the Grand Tour, a secret staircase enabling them to make discreet visits after dark.

The birth of Charles, Prince of Wales, at Palazzo del Re in December 1720 put new heart into Jacobites everywhere – instead of a single Stuart Pretender there was a dynasty in waiting. In Rome, Fort Sant'Angelo's cannon fired salvoes in salute while the *Te Deum* was sung by the English, Scots and Irish Colleges. All over France exiles rejoiced, the community at St Germain paying for a huge bonfire despite their poverty. Not only was it a blow for the Hanoverians, but James was taken more seriously by European powers.

An ode sent to Palazzo del Re by a humble supporter in England declared

> Lett German Mungrills now give place
> To Sobyesky's Royal Race.[5]

There was a new Jacobite toast – 'The King, the Queen, the Prince!'

Yet James was worried about his future at Rome. When Clement XI died in March 1721 he summoned the king to his deathbed, telling the cardinals who came to see him die that James must be allowed to keep the Palazzo del Re and the Palazzo Savelli, with his pension, until he regained his kingdoms.

The new pontiff, Innocent XIII (Michaelangelo dei Conti), continued to recognise James as king, letting him keep his palaces and paying his pension, but treated him with noticeable coldness. Perhaps he was irritated by his repeated attempts to borrow money. This was needed urgently, to finance a rising in England that was led by another prelate – who belonged to another Church.

28

South Sea Foulness

I am almost persuaded, the King being this time abroad, that could the Pretender have then landed at the Tower, he might have rode to St James's with very few hands held up against him.

Arthur Onslow, MP[1]

The King's Theatre, Haymarket, built in bright red brick and white stone in Queen Anne's day but since renamed, still looked brand new in 1721. One December evening, escorted by a troop of Horse Guards in cuirasses and three-cornered hats, a line of carriages drew up outside, from the first of which alighted a tubby little man of about sixty, with two remarkably ugly women in late middle age, one tall and thin, and the other enormously fat. It was George with his concubines.

They had come to hear Mr Handel's latest opera *Floridante* whose melifluous arias told how Elmira, heiress of Persia, won back her throne from a usurper, Oronte. Elmira was sung by Anastasia Robinson, famous for an exceptionally sweet contralto voice, Oronte by the basso Giuseppe Maria Boschi.

When the usurper was led off in chains and the rightful sovereign crowned, the entire theatre clapped wildly – deliberately insulting George.

The South Sea Bubble

The South Sea Company had made George more disliked than ever. Founded to reduce the National Debt by selling African slaves to Spain's American colonies, George had been 'Governor' (chairman) since 1718 when it became a company with multiple schemes for liquidating the entire Debt.

In 1720, giving free stock to peers and MPs the bankers who ran it persuaded Parliament to ban rival ventures. Shares soared in an orgy of speculation.

Late that summer the share price fell from £1,000 to £150, ruining thousands of investors who included some very distinguished people indeed, the Duke of Wharton losing £120,000 and Sir Isaac Newton £20,000. Another heavy loser was Olive Trant – Orléans's former mistress but by now respectable, having married the dim-witted Prince de la Tour d'Auvergne.

The king himself had acquired £50,000 worth of free stock with £30,000 for his mistresses, for which he paid nothing, selling at the top of the market just before the Bubble burst and moving the money to Hanover via a Dutch bank. England took a poor view of this 'insider trading', but there was no proof as Robert Knight, the company cashier, had fled abroad with the ledger recording payments. George signed a warrant for Knight's extradition, secretly ordering his murder.

When an MP suggested that 'bankers' should be thrown into the Thames in sacks filled with snakes, he meant ministers who had made obscene profits, and by implication George and his mistresses. 'We are ruined by Trulls, nay, what is more, by old, ugly Trulls.' Booed while driving through London, one of them screamed from her carriage window, 'Goot people, why do you abuse us? We come for all your goots', to which a voice yelled back, 'Damn ye, and for all our chattels too!'[2]

Even before the Bubble, the way the government handed out sinecures and pensions to 'placemen' (peers and MPs or their friends) had shocked Tories. Dr Johnson's definition in his dictionary of a pension tells us how they saw it: 'pay given to a state hireling for treason to his country'. The Bubble shook England's entire financial structure and the nation wanted those responsible to be punished. Earl Stanhope broke under the strain, dying of a stroke, while another minister committed suicide.

The Jacobite response

George's involvement in the Bubble gave the Jacobites fresh hope. It was hard to refute their claim that such disgraceful behaviour was only to be expected from a man who had stolen a throne.

In October 1720 King James issued a declaration. The calamity brought about 'by the avarice of a few miscreants' he wrote, increased his impatience to come home and 'have an opportunity to show Ourselves the Father of our People'. He hoped 'such a Restoration may be effected as was that of our royal uncle King Charles the 2nd, without the least bloodshed ... that trade may flourish again, credit and public faith [be] restored, and honest industry encouraged'. He ended, 'our ambition is not so much to wear the crown of our ancestors, as to show that we deserve it'.[3]

Among those seen as responsible for the Bubble was the Earl of Sunderland (son of James II's minster), who was First Lord of the Treasury. To add to his troubles, he had quarrelled with the Prince of Wales and dreaded the prospect of a George II. He believed instead that a carefully managed election might return a Tory majority and bring back the exiled royal family, ensuring his political survival.

Then he had doubts, deciding it might be easier to restore James at George's death. His attitude to the Stuart cause was purely opportunistic, however, and he never contacted James. In any case, his role in the Bubble forced him to resign in April 1721, to be replaced by Robert Walpole.

Sunderland died a year later. While he lived, he had headed off attempts to investigate Jacobite activity – it is significant that so shrewd a politician thought, if only briefly, that a Restoration might be achieved by constitutional means.

Meanwhile, James named a Council of Regency. It included the Earl of Oxford (now a physical and mental wreck), the Earl of Strafford, Earl Gower, and Lord North and Grey, with two Anglo-Irishmen – the Earl of Arran (Ormonde's brother) and the Earl of Orrery. Each was a Tory in Dr Johnson's sense, 'one who adheres to the ancient constitution of the state, and the apostolical hierarchy of the Church of England'. They saw George as a threat to both.

There was also a committee of exiles in Paris – Lord Mar, Count Dillon and Lord Lansdowne. 'I was born and bred a servant of your family', Lansdowne had written to King James in April 1720. 'My affection for it began with my life and shall end with it.' Many others felt the same.[4]

Discouragingly the regent, Orléans, wanted good relations with George while the new secretary for foreign affairs, Claudine de Tencin's lover, Dubois – recently made a cardinal – was suspected of taking Hanoverian bribes. (He had recently spent two years in London as French ambassador.) Even so, the committee thought Dubois could be kept quiet by the Controller General of Finances, John Law, who was a staunch Jacobite.

The Jacobite leader in England was Dr Francis Atterbury. Born in 1663, a scholar and man of letters who had translated Dryden's *Absalom and Achitophel* into Latin hexameters, as well as writing an elegant preface for a new edition of Edmund Waller's verse, he corresponded regularly with Alexander Pope and Jonathan Swift.

Despite his hot-temper and vanity, he was a hero to High Churchmen, as a leader in the tradition of Sancroft who wanted Anglicanism to regain the position it had enjoyed in the golden days before 1689, a champion of Convocation, a preacher of scholarly but heart-warming sermons that were a tonic after the coldly rational discourses of John Tillotson's disciples.[5] His views suited Queen Anne's Tory government so well that he was made Bishop of Rochester and Dean of Westminster, with a palace at Bromley and a house adjoining Parliament.

While abominating 'Popery', Atterbury saw James's faith as an asset – a restored Stuart would never dare to meddle with the Anglican Church, leaving it free to rebuild its pre-Revolution dominance. Robert Walpole wrote that when Anne died, the bishop had offered to go to Charing Cross in his robes to proclaim James as King and finding nobody to support him had shouted, 'There is the best cause in England lost for lack of spirit!'[6] If perhaps untrue, the story is certainly in character.

Despite swearing allegiance and (as Dean of Westminster) carrying the crown at George's coronation, Atterbury published an anonymous pamphlet in January 1715 savaging the king for being a foreigner who did not speak English and a Lutheran who endangered Anglicanism. Just what, it asked, had happened to George's wife and her lover?[7] He led Tory peers in attacking the regime's policies, organising opposition to the Septennial Act in 1716 – the year he became King James's 'Resident in England'.

In spring 1717 Benjamin Hoadly, Bishop of Bangor, preached a sermon before George, arguing that 'apostolical hierarchy' had no basis in scripture, which meant the Church should be governed by Parliament. Convocation prepared to denounce him as an enemy to the English Church's doctrine and authority, but was instead prorogued by the Archbishop of Canterbury, acting on the government's instructions, never to meet again until Queen Victoria's reign.

The 'Bangor Controversy' had confirmed Atterbury in his long-held opinion that the only way to save the Church was to restore the Stuarts. When the South Sea Bubble burst, he decided it was time to act.

29

The Atterbury Plot, 1721–1722

> Sir, the time has now come when with very little assistance
> from your friends abroad, your way to your friends at home is
> become safe and easy.
>
> Bishop Atterbury to James III, 22 April 1721

In his invitation to James, the bishop added, 'Your friends are in good earnest interesting themselves for that purpose. They will never despair but must always think this the most promising juncture that ever offered itself.'[1] In the month when Robert Walpole replaced Sunderland as First Lord of the Treasury this was somewhat optimistic.

Admittedly, the French ambassador Philippe Destouches believed the entire country wanted a free Parliament, presumably to evict George. And Atterbury could call on veteran commanders: in Spain the Duke of Ormonde, in France Count Dillon, and in Britain Lord North and Grey, who had fought in Marlborough's campaigns and had lost a hand at the Battle of Blenheim (later replaced by a hook), after which he became a lieutenant-general. When governor of Portsmouth North's garrison drank King James's health so often that George had him dismissed.

Among other allies was the young Duke, formerly Marquess, of Wharton. On the Grand Tour he had met James who made him Duke of Northumberland, an honour that King George countered by making him Duke of Wharton. His Jacobitism was soon reinforced, however, by loans from Jacobite bankers. A fluent orator and a graceful writer, his political (and financial) worth was reduced by wild dissipation that would turn him into a tragi-comic figure.

For his legal adviser, North employed a sharp young barrister, Christopher Layer, who besides owning an estate in Norfolk worth £800 a year had a healthy practice at the bar, with several other peers among his clients. If reputed to cut corners in business matters, Layer believed totally in the Stuart cause. His encyclopaedic knowledge of potential supporters shows that he was more than a mere enthusiast.

A plan began to take shape. During the Fifteen, suspecting Jacobite sympathies, the Whig government had ordered Colonel Sir Henry Goring, a Sussex baronet from a famous Cavalier family and a former MP, to sell his commission and leave the army. Their suspicions were justified. In March 1721 he wrote to Ormonde stating that all England, Whigs as well as Tories, wanted to be rid of the Hanover family – if the duke invaded with 1,000 soldiers and 10,000 swords and muskets, 'it is a safe gain'.[2]

Moreover, in May 1721 he informed Ormonde that Spain was willing to lend Irish troops and might supply money and arms. He had meetings with Dillon and with Mar, who called him 'a worthy, frank fellow'. Sussex smugglers ran wool over to France, bringing back brandy in spite of revenue men, and Goring claimed he could enlist a gang called the Waltham Blacks: 'I once saw two Hundred and upwards of these Blacks in a Body within half a mile of my own house [Highden, near Steyning]: they had been running of Brandy, there was 24 Customs House officers following them who they abus'd heartily & carried off their Cargo. I am told there is not less than a thousand of them & indeed I believe ... they have now taken Loyalty into their heads.'[3]

All sorts of schemes were suggested, the Duke of Wharton offering to bribe Thames watermen to capture the powder magazine at Greenwich. Another suggestion was to enlist the 'Minters'. These were victims of the Bubble who, to avoid death by starvation or gaol fever in a debtors' prison, lived in a rundown area of Southwark known as the 'Mint', that provided immunity from arrest.

In addition, there were plans for risings in Scotland and Ireland – to be co-ordinated by Count Dillon, who alerted officers of the Irish Brigade.

In spring 1721 Layer went to Rome to see James, bringing a list of men of substance likely to join a rising. He took with him John Plunkett, a Dubliner known as 'the Jesuit', who had been secretary to the Imperial ambassador at London. Not only was Layer given three audiences at Palazzo del Re and presented to Queen Clementina, but the royal couple offered to be godparents to his baby when it was born. Dazzled, he returned to England with dreams of becoming lord chancellor.

A letter supposedly written by the Duke of Marlborough's grandson, the Marquess of Blandford, and published anonymously in May that year, gives us some idea of what captivated Layer. In March, the writer met the king by chance – strolling in the Ludovisi gardens. He saw a man 'easily distinguished from the rest by his star and garter, as well as by an air of greatness' and 'a very graceful countenance'. He was invited to a concert at Palazzo del Re by the young queen whose 'wit, vivacity and mildness of temper are painted in her looks', and to dinner. The king dined on roast beef and Devonshire Pie (layers of mutton and apple), washed down by English ale. However, at the dessert he 'drank of champagne very heartily'.

James told his guest he 'bemoaned the misfortune of England groaning under a load of debts ... to support foreign interests' and deplored the way the nation was run by 'a new set of people' bent on enriching themselves. He said that in religion 'it should never be my business to study how to become an Apostle, but how to become a good king to all my people, which shall be found true, if ever it please God to restore me'. The writer was edified to learn he could hear the Church of England's Easter Sunday service at Palazzo del Re, celebrated by two resident Anglican chaplains, Messers Berkeley and Cooper.[4]

The letter was written or edited by a skilled propagandist who conjured up 'a vision of a little bit of jolly Old England tucked away in Baroque Rome'. The chaplains, mentioned to show James's sympathy for Anglicanism, were in fact Episcopalians, their names anglicised from Barclay and Coupar.[5]

Jacobite propaganda increased. A medal circulated widely in 1721, bearing a fine profile of the King over the Water with the inscription *Salus Unica*, 'The Only Salvation'. Its other side shows the White Horse of Hanover trampling on the Lion and the Unicorn in the presence of a grieving Britannia, while three little figures run off to Germany with bags of plunder – George and his ladies.

In 1722, *Female Fortitude* appeared, a racy narrative of how Wogan had rescued James's bride from a usurper's machinations which, claimed the anonymous publisher, possessed 'all the entertaining Variety of a Novel'. Besides glamorising Queen Clementina, it reminded the world that there was a Stuart Prince of Wales.

Atterbury was behind another pamphlet, one that charged George of having been up to his neck in South Sea 'foulness', bestowing peerages on men from the gutter, bribing voters and treating barbarously those who had surrendered in 1715. Spending seven months a year in Hanover, he was using English troops to increase his German domains.[6]

Another pamphlet, *The Advantages that have Accru'd to England, in the Succession of the Illustrious House of Hanover*, accused George of robbing England's coffers and making her fight Hanover's wars. He was illegitimate, it claimed, his mother (Old Sophy) having been been 'very amorously inclined' due to heavy drinking, especially 'her own Health in a Bumper'. As for his wife, 'this young Lady's appetites were too violent to be confin'd to one Man' – Prince Georg August's birth must be looked into. Moreover, the king slept with the sister of one of his mistresses. 'Nor did the King's two Daughters by these two Ladies go without their Turns in his Majesty's Seraglio.'

If most of this was mere mud slinging, the author (Matthias Earbery) was reasonable enough in claiming that 'false fear of Popery here among the great, vulgar and small' had enabled 'the Establishment of a Foreign Family on this Throne'.[7] Brought to his attention and translated by some zealous courtier, the pamphlet infuriated George.

The final plan was timed for the general election of March–May 1722, when the army was banned by law from all constituencies. In London, troops led by Tory officers of the First Foot Guards whom Lord North had recruited would seize the Tower, the Mint and the Bank, with the Hanover family and their ministers. After arms from secret depots had been handed out, a rising would take over the main streets, setting up barricades.

Similars risings were to break out in selected constituencies, rallying points for Jacobite lords and gentry all over the country, who would march on the capital as soon as it was under control. At the same time, a task force of Irish troops from France would sail up the Thames to London in a small brig with King James and the Duke of Ormonde, who would then be joined by the Waltham Blacks under Goring.[8] To help with the London coup Layer, using taverns as recruiting bases, had enlisted other ranks, including eight sergeants in the Guards and sixty men who mounted guard at the Tower.[9]

James tried to enlist Russian help and, angered by the Royal Navy's presence in the Baltic, Tsar Peter gave his envoys a sympathetic hearing. At a meeting with Prince Ivan Dolgoruky in March or early April 1722, Count Dillon proposed a joint invasion of England by Russia and Sweden in support of the imminent rising. Although Dolgoruky told him the Tsar would never act without the Swedes, he did not hide Peter's hostility to George, implying that he would welcome his overthrow.

Nevertheless, King James made plans to go to Genoa on a Swedish ship, as did Ormonde. Two more vessels, including one of forty guns, were waiting at Genoa to take them to France for the crossing to England. Unfortunately, not enough money had been raised to buy arms for the coup in London and at the last moment the rising was postponed. Atterbury grabbed 'Harry' Goring by the scruff of the neck and shook him, shouting, 'This is rocking the cradle!'[10]

The bishop hoped to try again when George left for his annual German holiday, but he forgot that John Law's ruin (eighteen months previously from the collapse of his Compagnie des Indes, France's South Sea Bubble) had deprived them of the one man who could control the maniacally venal Cardinal Dubois. On 20 April, after Atterbury asked for 4,000 Irish troops, Dubois, no doubt richly rewarded, warned London that George was in danger. He confirmed Mar's discreet hints to Lord Stair. At the same time the Post Office was intercepting letters in cypher that referred to a plot.

Walpole reacted swiftly, stationing troops in Hyde Park, more to frighten the public than as a precaution, while hunting down plotters. One of these was George Kelly, a nonjuring cleric from Roscommon who in 1718, after preaching a fiery sermon at Dublin on the need for a Restoration, had fled to Paris where he made money speculating on John Law's financial scheme. Moving to London, he had become Atterbury's henchman. An experienced secret agent, he always carried a sword, which was unusual for a man of the cloth.

At dawn on 21 May three 'messengers' (government agents) burst into Kelly's lodgings in Westminster. Seizing his sword and papers, the messengers left them on a window seat to make a thorough search. 'Their negligence gave Kelly an opportunity of recovering his sword, which he drew, and swore he would run through the first man that disturb'd him in what he was doing; which was burning his papers in a candle with his left hand, whilst he held the drawn sword in the other. When the papers were burnt, he surrender'd himself.'[11]

However, he would not talk, so Walpole discovered little until a young Irish nonjuror, Philip Neynoe, who had been employed by Kelly to copy letters, tried to sell the government some fairly harmless information and then, panicking, fled to France. Arrested in August, he broke under interrogation, revealing that Atterbury, North, Goring and Orrery were the leaders, then drowned in a bid to escape by jumping into the Thames – depriving Walpole of his key witness.

In July 1722, wearing a false beard, Viscount Falkland – posing as 'Mr

Skinner' – was sent to London by King James to learn what was happening. He found the plotters in a panic. (James was so impressed by Falkland's daring that he made him an earl.) Atterbury, North and Orrery were arrested in August, Goring fled across the Channel on his yacht, and the historian Thomas Carte, who edited the Jacobite *Freeholder's Journal*, was hidden by friends despite £1,000 being offered for his capture. Many others, however, were held in prison without being brought to trial. In October, Parliament suspended habeas corpus for a year, increasing the army to 18,000 men.

On 20 September, the day after he was arrested as North's agent, Christopher Layer escaped from the messenger's house down a rope of blankets, hoping to find refuge with the Minters in Southwark, but was recaptured and taken to the Tower. On King George's express orders, he was put into such heavy chains – 'like an Algerine captive' – that he could barely stand, and which left open sores on his wrists and ankles.

On 21 October 1722 Layer was charged with high treason at the King's Bench. The prosecution described how the 'popish bigoted Pretender' and his wife were godparents to Layer's daughter, with Lord North and the Duchess of Ormonde as proxies at her christening in a Chelsea china shop. He and North had drunk a toast in the Green Man at Leytonstone to 'The King, the Queen, the Prince'.

Layer made a spirited defence, wrecked by Mrs Mason, a brothelkeeper, who handed in a copy of the 'scheme' he had hidden at her bawdy house the day before his arrest. (Although it did not include the list of supporters.) The attorney general movingly conjured up 'what a scene of misery would have opened!' had the plot succeeded. 'All your estates and properties must have been at the will of a provoked and exasperated usurper; liberty must have given way to slavery and the best of religions to Popery and superstition.'[12]

On 27 November, Layer was found guilty. Walpole delayed his execution, hoping he would turn King's Evidence, but he refused to betray North and Atterbury. On the scaffold, in May 1723, he declared that if he himself would soon be happy, 'this nation can never be so, nor even easy, until their lawful king is placed on the throne'. (When his skull fell from Temple Bar, it was acquired as a holy relic by a nonjuring bishop, Richard Rawlinson.) King James gave Mrs Layer, who had been reduced to beggary, £100 a year for life.

No proof that would stand up in court could be found against Kelly or John Plunkett, 'the Jesuit' (whom George wrongly believed to have written

The Illustrious House of Hanover). Walpole resorted to a Bill of Pains and Penalties, but the pair gave away nothing during questioning at the Bar of both Houses of Parliament. Forged letters were produced while the 'bawd' Mrs Mason was called as a witness, all to no effect.

A little spaniel with a broken leg called Harlequin, sent by Mar to Kelly as a present for Mrs Atterbury, was cited to prove Kelly's links with Rome, but he insisted he had bought the dog as a gift for his landlady. (Later King James said he could not read Kelly's examination without laughing.)

The Bill of Pains and Penalties was passed in May 1723, sentencing Kelly to imprisonment in the Tower. A similar bill was passed against Plunkett, who was also sent back the Tower, to be put in irons – on George's orders – where he died in 1738. Yet Walpole had failed to find the evidence needed to destroy Atterbury, even if Mr Willes, the decipherer, produced a little from intercepted letters (for which he was made a Canon of Westminster.)

Confinement could not break Atterbury, who knocked down the Tower's governor for impertinence. In April 1723 the Commons passed another Bill of Pains and Penalties, and on 6 May he went on trial before the Lords. The only evidence was Neynoe's unsigned testimony so forged letters planted in a close-stool were produced, Harlequin featuring again. 'One intercepted dog might be as useful as ten intercepted letters', joked Atterbury who demolished the prosecution with a superb speech. Even Whig peers spoke in his defence, but after discreet bribery the bill passed on 15 May, condemning Atterbury to lose his bishopric and deanery, and go into perpetual exile.

Leaving the Tower on a man-of-war, as he sailed away England's last great priest–politician was cheered by crowds who lined the banks of the Thames. Declining James's invitation to be his secretary of state at Rome, he became his envoy in France.

No one would testify against a man so popular and well-liked as Lord North while Lord Orrery, who had been only marginally involved, was protected by powerful friends. After a few months, both were released. North went to Spain where he became a general. Orrery stayed in England to carry on the struggle.

The plot was 'the most fortunate and the greatest circumstance of Mr Walpole's life', recalled Mr Arthur Onslow, Speaker of the House of Commons. 'It fixed him with the King, and united for a time the whole body of Whigs to him, and gave him the universal credit of an able and vigilant Minister.'[13] George recognised that without Walpole he might lose his throne.

It had been more formidable than the Fifteen because it could call on professional generals instead of amateurs and because they targeted London. 'Scotland and Ireland signify not the fifth wheel of a coach of your Majesty's affairs', an Irish Jacobite had written to King James. 'Old England is to pay the piper, and for God's sake dance to the Bishop of Rochester's tune.' [14] North and Layer's success in recruiting rank-and-file soldiers shows the depth of hostility towards George.

Without Cardinal Dubois's betrayal, and to a lesser extent the Duke of Mar's, the story of *Floridante* might have been repeated in England.

PART THREE

Whig Tyranny

30

'A more dismal aspect?'

If we look into the state of the King's affairs, they appear with
a more dismal aspect than ever I knew them.

George Lockhart of Carnwath in 1728, *Memoirs*

So many plots had failed that it looked as if Jacobitism was finished. The
Hanoverians were entrenched, and the French no longer interested.

In 1725 another rise in the malt tax caused riots in Glasgow, the mob
yelling 'Up with Seaforth!' (a leader in the Nineteen) and growing so
violent that General Wade needed a thousand troops to disperse them. The
authorities were right to suspect that a plot was brewing. Bishop Atterbury
had persuaded a group of exiled Scottish chieftains led by Lord Seaforth to
plan a rising and in 1726 Lady Seaforth wrote to Buchan of Auchmacoy in
Aberdeenshire asking him to join. However, the scheme collapsed when
Seaforth was given back his estates.

Peter the Great died the same year. Jacobites went on pleading their
case at the Russian court until the 1750s and often received a sympathetic
hearing, but his successors lacked his visceral dislike of Hanover. Also in
1726, Atterbury's hopes of another Spanish expedition fell through. As a
last resort, he wrote to Walpole, pointing out that George I must soon die
and that his son was the prime minister's deadly enemy – it would be in Sir
Robert's interest to work for a Restoration. He never received an answer.[1]

The second Hanoverian

George I died in June 1727. When Georg August of Hanover and Caroline
of Brandenburg-Ansbach were crowned King and Queen of Great Britain
in October, Handel's stately anthems gave an impression of age-old tenure

of the throne. Their subjects were not deceived. 'The world is come to a fine pass indeed, if we are all fools except a parcel of Round-heads and Hanover rats,' Squire Western grumbled in Henry Fielding's *Tom Jones*, published twenty years later. 'Pox! I hope the times are coming when we shall all make fools of them, and every man *shall have his own again*.' (Western is quoting the Jacobite anthem.)

Over thirty before he came to England, an irritable, red-faced, over-dressed little man who spoke English with a thick German accent, exclaiming 'Dat is one big lie!' when informed of his father's death, George II was just as foreign. He much preferred Hanover to England, spending 1729–31 there and paying many further visits. His irritability worsened with age and tormenting piles. As he expressed contempt by turning his back and flicking his coat-tails, he was called 'Rump' – 'Rumper' also being slang for a Whig. A philistine who loathed the arts and literature, cursing his queen whenever he found her with a book, he became a figure of fun, his blowsy mistresses making him still more ridiculous.

The balladeers laughed:

> You may strut dapper George, but 'twill all be in vain;
> We know 'tis Queen Caroline, not you, that reign –
> You govern no more than Don Philip of Spain.
> Then if you would have us fall down and adore you,
> Lock up your fat spouse, as your dad did before you.[2]

The diarist Lord Hervey, who knew the new king well, says 'I do not believe there ever lived a man to whose temper benevolence was so absolute a stranger.'[3]

Had George been altogether like this, he could never have kept the throne, but he possessed at least some virtues, such as physical courage. A few of his subjects even admired him. 'When will England ever have a better prince?', observed John Wesley. However, Wesley had not met his king.

When George I had died in June, James had gone to Lorraine. (If Dr Johnson can be believed, there was a rumour that he wanted James to succeed him.) The Lochiel brothers reported there was no chance of Scotland rising while Catholic Ireland remained prostrate and Jacobite England supine. Walpole then bullied Duke Leopold into expelling his guest. By January 1728 James was back in Rome.

Tory MPs were split between Stuart supporters and 'Hanover Tories'. 'The Jacobite party had fallen so low, from the indolence of some, the defection of others, and the despair of all, that in reality it consisted of only a few veterans,' wrote Hervey, who adds that a few other MPs called themselves Jacobites, although their loyalty to James was 'quite worn out'.[4] (However, he says elsewhere that Jacobites were strong enough outside Parliament.)

Lockhart, still James's agent in Scotland, ended his memoirs by declaring 'no party is acting for his interests, no projects formed', that the cause 'must daylie languish and in process of time be tottally forgot. In which melancholy situation of the Kings affairs I leave them in the year 1728'.[5] Shortly after writing this, Lockhart's papers fell into the hands of the authorities and he fled to France. Allowed to return home, three years later he was killed in a duel.

In Lord Hervey's view, owing to 'revolution principles', 'religious reverence to God's anointed' had been replaced by the doctrine of 'a king being made for the people and not the people for the king'. No one should be surprised, he declared, that divine right had lost ground when it had been in the interest of three successive sovereigns to get rid of it. 'The clergy, who had been paid for preaching it up, were now paid for preaching it down.'[6]

The High Churchmen who had been Jacobitism's mainstay were fading away in a new intellectual climate ushered in by the philosopher John Locke and Archbishop Tillotson. Locke's *Reasonableness of Christianity* (1695) discounted dogma, revelation, miracles and liturgy, stressing individual reason. Tillotson held similar opinions, preaching a rational, 'Latitudinarian' Gospel of moral rectitude that had no time for 'enthusiasm', let alone divine right.

'Walpole's Pope', Edmund Gibson, the Bishop of London, helped him find servile prelates to vote with the government in the Lords. Eager for fatter rent rolls and bigger palaces, they were typified by the Low Church clergyman Benjamin Hoadly who toadied to the prime minister, cringing his way from one bishopric to another. (Predictably, he preached that Jacobitism meant political slavery.) No wonder, thought Hervey, that 'the inferior clergy, whose appetite for preferment was not less than their cormorant superiors, should after seventeen years' Whig adminstration slacken their efforts to promote a common desperate cause'.[7]

General Wade's Highland roads

In 1726, General Wade began to link Fort William, Fort George and Fort

Augustus by 'military roads' from the Lowlands. Edmund Burt tells us they replaced 'The old ways (for roads I shall not call them) that consisted chiefly of stony moors, bogs, rugged rapid falls, declivities of hills, entangling woods, and giddy precipices . . . a dreadful catalogue.' Wade's assistants were Major William Caulfield as inspector general and Burt (author of the *Letters*) as chief surveyor. Over the next decade, employing 500 soldiers they built 240 miles of military roads with forty bridges.

As far as possible the new roads, which were sixteen feet wide, went on straight lines. Over bogs, causeways of stone or timber had first to be built, drained by trenches at the side, while gunpowder was used to blast a way through rock. Where a road climbed a mountain such as Corrieyairack (2,500 feet above sea level) buttressed traverses about seventy or eighty yards long zigzagged up it.

Burt was especially proud of the bridges that 'prevent the dangers of the terrible fords'. The longest, the first over the Tay, was 370 feet long with five arches. After Wade was moved to other duties in 1740 Caulfield took over, constructing a further 900 roads and 600 bridges.

The chiefs resented the new roads, complaining their territory was no longer safe from invasion. Some grumbled that 'bridges, in particular, will render the ordinary people effeminate, and less fit to pass the waters in other places where there are none'.[8] What they did not say was that the roads weakened their power to menace the government.

The benevolent face of Scots Whiggery, Duncan Forbes of Culloden, a devout Presbyterian who, as a Highlander himself, understood clansmen, was another threat. In the Fifteen he and his brother-in-law Rose of Kilravock had raised a force that captured Inverness for King George. Afterwards, his appeals for clemency had given rise to unfounded suspicions of his being a Jacobite.

As Lord Advocate, then as Lord President of the Court of Session, Forbes worked hard at reconciling his countrymen to the Hanoverians, famous for his hospitality at Culloden House, whose doors were always open to strangers. When a guest arrived, Burt recalls nostalgically, he had to 'crack a nut' – drink a pint of champagne from a coconut. After this, claret flowed, the iron-headed host constantly proposing toasts. Most guests were eventually taken off to bed, in chairs with rings into which carrying poles were inserted.

From 1730 onwards Forbes helped General Wade and the Duke of Argyll to raise independent militia companies from among the Highlanders that were commanded by clan gentry. They did so from Presbyterian clans who (in theory) could be relied on to fight the Jacobites – Campbells, Frasers, Grants and Munros. Some like the Black Watch later became famous regiments.

Even so, regardless of appearances, the Honest Cause, as Jacobitism now called itself, still had plenty of life left, in England, Scotland and Ireland.

31

The Royal Oak Tree

Jacobitism is now every day trying all arts to spread itself, and everyday gaining ground in the nation.

Lord Hervey, 1733[1]

Despite the sad closure in recent years of so many fine old public houses, The Royal Oak is still a familiar sign – representing the tree in which Charles II found safety after his defeat by Cromwell, under whose regime the oak had been a symbol of hope for Cavaliers.It remained one for Jacobites, who drank the toast '*Revirescit!*' – meaning the oak tree will grow again.

Lockhart was too despondent. His objectivity, even his veracity, has been questioned by at least one modern historian.[2] We know he was writing under great pressure in his private life which may have clouded his judgement. For, although there were reasons for discouragement, loyalty to King James survived strongly in all three kingdoms.

One reason for optimism was the sheer uselessness of the Hanoverian Prince of Wales, Frederick (or simply 'Fred'), who was generally regarded as a bad joke. His father openly referred to him as a 'rascally puppy', even saying that he feared he might sell the crown to James. But there were other reasons too.

In England, the Stuarts' most loyal followers were to be found among university men and parsons. At Oxford, until the late 1750s, rioting undergraduates sang 'When the King enjoys his Own again' on Royal Oak Day and White Rose Day. 'In troubled times the High Street at Oxford was lined with bayonets', says Macaulay, adding that colleges were regularly searched by messengers looking for fugitives. 'Grave doctors were in the habit of talking very Ciceronian treason in the theatre; and the undergraduates drank bumpers to Jacobite toasts, and chanted Jacobite airs. Of four successive

Chancellors of the University one had notoriously been in the Pretender's service; the other three were fully believed to be in secret correspondence with the exiled family.'[3]

Many a parson remained a Stuart loyalist, passing the port over a finger bowl at his snug Georgian rectory, having been appointed to the living by the local Tory squire – no danger to the Whig regime, but a reminder that an alternative existed. Like Walter Scott's Dr Grumball in *Redgauntlet*, clerics of this sort detested 'the blasphemous, atheistical, and anarchical tenets of Locke and other deluders of the public mind', which they associated with Whigs and Hanoverians. So did the chaplains of great nonjuring landowners like the Duke of Beaufort, who ensured that their employers' children grew up Jacobites.[4]

Understandably, Catholics still hoped for a Restoration. Since 1688 the Penal Laws had grown steadily more severe so that it remained their only hope of a better life. As a Catholic in the first half of the eighteenth century, Alexander Pope, who was widely acknowledged to be the greatest poet of the age, possessed 'fewer rights than a South African black at the height of apartheid'.[5] He never declared for the King over the Water, yet his friendship with Atterbury, Cornbury and the Carylls shows where his loyalties lay.

The four Catholic bishops (vicars apostolic) told their dwindling flock not to support the Cause – every confiscated estate meant the loss of a Mass centre. However, Benedictine monks, Dominican friars and Jesuits, who were not subject to their control, stayed staunchly Jacobite.

Whatever Hervey says, a third of Tory MPs showed pro-Stuart sympathies throughout the period from 1715 to 1754, which made the Jacobites the largest pressure group in the party.[6] They included men of outstanding quality.

William Shippen, son of a High Church rector, was a barrister who believed James could be restored by constitutional means. He came to prominence in the Commons in 1717 when he said the King's Speech was more suited 'for the Meridian of Germany than for Great Britain', calling George 'a Stranger to our Language and Constitution'. The House sent him to the Tower. Yet even Walpole respected his bluff integrity. Pope was among his admirers, writing

> I love to pour out all myself, as plain
> As honest Shippen, or downright Montaigne.

For over twenty years he was a bulwark of Jacobite opposition in Parliament.

Although hampered by a stammer Sir John Hynde Cotton, a Cambridgeshire baronet, was among the House's best speakers, delivering short, hard hitting speeches full of malicious wit. A giant, as fat as he was tall, he boasted of drinking six bottles of wine a day with no ill consequences. A 'rank' Jacobite who never ceased to hope for a second Restoration, to show his admiration for the Highlanders he ordered a suit of tartan with skintight trews that set off his generous figure. Adding insult to injury, he accepted a well-paid appointment in the household of the 'Elector', which he held for two years without ever once voting with the government.

Another prominent MP, Sir Watkin Williams-Wynn, a baronet with estates in five Welsh counties, had founded a club for North Wales's Jacobite gentry, the Cycle of the White Rose, in 1710 when he was eighteen. Entering Parliament as MP for Denbighshire in 1716, he held the seat nearly all his life. Far from feigning 'revolution principles', he publicly burned portraits of the 'Hanover Rat' during the Atterbury Plot and ten years later when a Whig mob tried to stop the election of the Jacobite Sir Robert Grosvenor he routed them with 900 miners. Walpole made the Denbighshire sheriff rig the election of 1741 against him, but Williams-Wynn quickly regained the seat and the sheriff went to prison.

The youngest of these hardline MPs was Lord Charles Noel Somerset, born in 1709, the Duke of Beaufort's brother and heir, who had inherited all his family's Plantagenet contempt for the usurping dynasty. Described by Walpole as 'A most determined and unwavering Jacobite', eventually he became leader of the Jacobite Tories in the Commons.

Jacobitism did not depend on a presence in Parliament but 'often centred on personal pursuits, especially intellectual interests, such as antiquarianism or writing poetry'.[7] Others preserved it by collecting portraits, prints and medallions of the exiled family which they displayed to the faithful, commissioning plate, glass and china with Stuart symbols such as roses or oak trees. Recusant wives and mothers who kept their men loyal to Rome were unswerving in fidelity to the Catholic king.

Social life played an important role, especially dining clubs. At Oxford there was the High Borlase, at Cambridge the Family. There were similar societies all over England (often called Church-and-King clubs) while in North Wales Jacobitism centred around the Cycle Club of the White Rose and in South Wales around the Sea Serjeants. Everywhere the same toasts were drunk – 'The King over the Water!', 'Down with the Rump!' or 'Our

Old Friend!' There was also a London club, the Cocoa Tree in Pall Mall, with a secret underground passage for members on the run that led to a Picadilly tavern.

Survival of Jacobitism in Scotland and Ireland

For all the efforts of Duncan Forbes, Scots remained angry at the takeover of 1707, whose effects seemed far from beneficial. In 1720 a Jacobite, Robert Freebairn, published a pamphlet at Perth – *The Miserable State of Scotland*. 'Before the Union we had no taxes but were laid on by our own Parliaments, and those verie easy, and spent within our own Country', he complained. 'Now we have not only the Cess and Land tax, and Customs conform to the English Book of Rates, near the triple what we formerly pay'd, and Excise most rigorously exacted by a Parcel of Strangers sent down to us from England, but also the Malt-Tax, the Salt-Tax, the Leather-Tax, the Taxes upon Candles, Soap, Starch...'[8]

Sometimes there were food riots, while customs officers often met with armed resistance, even losing their lives. 'The inhabitants complain loudly that the English, since the union, have enhanced the rates of everything by giving extravagant prices', noted Burt during the 1730s.[9]

There was even deeper reason to stay loyal to the old dynasty because of a belief, especially in the *Gàidhealtachd*, that the Stuarts descended from Celtic Kings who had ruled since the dawn of history. Literate clan gentry read Blind Harry's *Wallace*, a regularly reprinted medieval life of the patriot hero William Wallace, which had the same impact then as the film *Braveheart* would have in the twentieth century. (It was just as popular with Lowlanders.)

At Dublin a mob annually celebrated White Rose Day on St Stephen's Green before picking fights with any Whigs available, while there was still a 'disaffected' element at Trinity College. Catholics stayed as loyal as ever, priests throughout Ireland asking their congregations to pray for 'the king for whom we yearn' (Ó Rathaille's phrase).[10] In 1729, Sir Charles Wogan wrote to James with a plan for a rising led by officers from the Irish Brigade – the clergy would ensure that their parishioners fought for him.

Another area in which the Honest Cause flourished from about 1716 onwards was freemasonry, although of its nature restricted to a small elite. English lodges at Paris, Avignon and Rome are known to have been Jacobite, and for a short time the exiled Earl of Derwentwater was their Grand Master. They lobbeyed Louis XV to abandon the foreign policy of his chief minister, Cardinal André-Hercule de Fleury, and restore King James, but were then taken over by Hanoverian agents.

Seeing this as a threat, James asked the new Pope, Clement XII, who took office in 1730, to intervene. Already irritated by the Roman lodge's admission of Protestant Jacobites, in 1738 the Pope issued the bull *In Eminenti Apostolatus*, which banned Catholics from becoming masons. This did not stop non-Catholic Jacobites from joining the lodges, but their importance is problematical because so little evidence survives.

A myth developed – later encouraged by the Prince of Wales, Charles, although never a mason himself – that the head of the House of Stuart was hereditary Grand Master of all Masons throughout the world.

Behind George II stood his prime minister, Robert Walpole. A hard-drinking Norfolk country gentleman who opened his gamekeeper's letters before all other correspondence and sometimes hunted five days a week, he looked like Squire Western in *Tom Jones*. In reality he was a political genius. King James never had a more dangerous enemy.

Ironically, while Sir Robert saved the Hanoverians, he also gave vigorous new life to Jacobitism.

32

The Private Life of
King James III and VIII

If I be waspish, best beware my sting.

Shakespeare, *The Taming of the Shrew*

The atmosphere at Palazzo del Re was poisoned by suspicion, every courtier distrusting the other, all fearful of double agents.[1] James was betrayed by his two most talented secretaries of state, Bolingbroke and Mar. He also had to cope with an unhappy wife, who if not exactly a shrew made his life a misery.

The Whig government spent huge sums on espionage. During the 1690s the poet Matthew Prior, who was secretary to Britain's ambassador at Paris, had run a highly efficient spy ring that ferreted out St Germain's secrets. In 1705 Mary of Modena told Colonel Hooke she was 'sure enough' there were 'traitors' at her court.[2] Between 1719 and 1731 Baron Philipp von Stosch (alias 'Wharton'), who outwardly followed the professions of bisexual pimp and shady antique dealer, operated another sophisticated network at Rome.

In 1739, Stosch was followed by Sir Horace Mann, Walpole's friend and British resident at Florence, whose agents kept Palazzo del Re under close surveillance, even recruiting a member of the Curia, Cardinal Alessandro Albani. Letters to and from courtiers at the Jacobite court were routinely intercepted, copies being sent back to London – if in code, they were decyphered by a team of well-paid cryptographers.

Communities of Jacobite exiles elsewhere, such as those in Paris or Aix-la-Chapelle, were full of spies. Not even their leaders could be trusted. Mar seemed unshakeably loyal, drawing up plans for a federation between England, Scotland, Ireland and France. (He also designed wonderful cities, palaces and gardens, even a new Town for Edinburgh.) In fact, he was a double agent, but the king was reassured by Bobbing John's easy charm.

Mar had led the Fifteen from motives of pure self-interest and in exile, desperate for money, concentrated on securing a pardon. He lived a shabby existence in France, tradesmen and even his servants insulting him because he did not pay them, his wife going mad from worry and having to be confined. In 1721 Lord Stair (still George's ambassador at Paris) provided £1,000 to settle his debts, offering a pension of £3,500 which Mar persuaded James to let him accept. In return the duke warned Stair of the Atterbury Plot, sending letters to conspirators that were designed to make them incriminate themselves.

Finding damning correspondence that proved Mar's guilt beyond doubt, Bishop Atterbury accused him of betrayal. Reluctantly, James sent John Hay of Cromlix to Paris to investigate. The duke tried to cover his tracks, presenting the regent, Orléans, with a plan for a French invasion of England – shipping troops over the Channel on fishing boats – but Hay's findings forced James to act. He dismissed his secretary of state in December 1723.

Despite failing to secure a pardon or recover his estates, and although his pension was never paid, Mar obliged Walpole's government in small ways until his death at Aix in 1732. His career was just one example of how the Jacobite cause was undermined by treachery.

Walpole replaced Mar's services by those of Charles Caesar, who had been such a Jacobite rock during the Swedish Plot and one of Atterbury's successors as James's agent in England. But after losing large sums in the South Sea Bubble, only immunity as an MP stood between him and a debtor's prison. When he spent lavishly on the election of 1729, Shippen, the Jacobite leader in the House of Commons, realised that he had become one of Walpole's pensioners.

Caesar's fellow agent, Lord Orrery, also supplied Walpole with information until he died in 1731. Even Ormonde was not entirely reliable. It was reported in 1737 that the duke 'had a favourite Lady at Avignon, who got all his Secrets out of him and revealed them'.[3]

James was distracted by the 'Great Domestic War' – driven nearly mad is a better description. It was largely his own fault.[4] Queen Clementina looked delightful, but possessed an uncontrollable temper, the girl who had seemed so light-hearted revealing herself as a depressive prone to mood swings made more extreme by her husband's lack of understanding.

The side effects of the premature birth of her second son Henry, Duke of York, on 6 March 1725 – no doubt including post-natal depression – further harmed her equilibrium. She took a fierce dislike to John Hay of Cromlix, whom her husband had appointed as the new secretary of state. Secretly created Earl of Inverness in 1718, Hay asserted himself, using his title openly. A difficult man if impeccably loyal to James, he brusquely ignored Clementina's wishes. Even worse, the king made Inverness's wife her lady-in-waiting, who treated her with barely concealed impertinence.

At the same time James appointed Lady Inverness's brother James Murray, Earl of Dunbar, as Prince Charles's governor. With astonishing rudeness, Dunbar would not let Clementina see the child unless he himself was present.[5] She became hysterically angry when he suggested her sons should be brought up at the Spanish court, nor was she placated when the king rejected the proposal.

From now on Clementina made a point of being violently unpleasant to Dunbar and to Inverness and his wife. Meanwhile her companion, Mrs Sheldon, was not only rude to King James, but convinced the queen that he intended to bring up Charles as a Protestant, distorting James's wish for his sons to be given a knowledge of Anglicanism and how it differed from Catholicism. (Dunbar and the Invernesses were all Protestants.) Clementina then accused James of sleeping with Lady Inverness, a rumour probably invented by Mar that spread all over Rome.

Early in November 1725 she threatened that if James did not sack her three bugbears she would enter a convent. He refused, insisting that her accusations were groundless, and dismissed Mrs Sheldon. In a letter to the queen he complained that she was being manipulated by his enemies and it would damage his reputation badly if she left him for a convent. He begged her to submit, in which case he would forgive her everything.

In a second letter, he rebuked her for believing everything unkind said about him, defended the Invernesses against her 'unjust and extravagant notions' and insisted he had every right to sack Mrs Sheldon whom he had long found unsatisfactory. But he also told Clementina that he had always loved her and wanted to please her in every way.

At the end of November, escorted by Mrs Sheldon and the Countess of Southesk, Clementina left the Palazzo del Re for the Santa Cecilia convent in Via Nomentana, where she had stayed after her arrival in Rome six years before. Mrs Sheldon, who was Mar's sister-in-law, kept him informed so that he could pass on the latest details to London. Luridly embellished, the story spread throughout the European courts.

The day after her flight, a prelate called on James with a letter from the

Pope, Benedict XIII, who was an unworldly Dominican friar. The letter stated that His Holiness would never permit the Stuart princes to be brought up as Protestants or let the king keep Lady Inverness as a concubine. In a rare fit of rage, James sent a furious reply. The princes' education was his own affair, he said, while he could not believe a message about concubinage was meant for him – in future anyone who brought such an insult would be thrown out of the window.

The queen found an adviser in the wily Cardinal Alberoni, banished from Spain and drawing a pension from Walpole, who told her the surest way of winning papal support was to insist that James really did mean to bring up their sons as Protestants. Pope Benedict believed her, sending three cardinals to Palazzo del Re to threaten that his pension would be stopped. Prompted by Alberoni, who still had influence with Elizabeth Farnese, Philip V forbade James to visit Spain without his consort.

Alberoni then spread a story that Inverness and his wife were Whig spies. When Lady Inverness had visited England on family business in 1724, she had been arrested as a Jacobite agent and sent to Newgate where a senior Whig minister, Lord Townshend, interrogated her. Eventually she was pardoned, on condition she never returned to Great Britain.

Stuart supporters at home and abroad, who all lived in a climate of feverish paranoia, suspected she had been released to 'turn' her husband and persuade him to play Lord Mar's role. Even Bishop Atterbury at Paris, with memories of Mar's betrayal, believed the story. However, King James dismissed it as nonsense invented by Whig enemies. Nevertheless, the accusation damaged Inverness's reputation badly.[6]

Clementina stayed in the convent for eighteen months. From April 1726 James allowed the princes to visit her and slowly yielded, replacing Dunbar by Sir John Graeme as Charles's governor in April 1727. Shortly after, the Duke of Liria (Berwick's son) negotiated a reconciliation. The king asked Inverness to resign, creating him a duke. Dunbar became secretary of state.

Inverness and his duchess moved to Pisa, then to Avignon which had a large Jacobite community. In 1731 he was received into the Roman Church and the dying Atterbury believed he was a Whig spy who had turned Catholic to discredit the king with Protestants. Ironically, some Jacobites suspected Atterbury himself of taking Whig bribes.

More or less forced out by Pope Benedict, Queen Clementina left Santa Cecilia in June, but the royal couple were not reunited until January 1728, at Bologna where the court was spending a few months. Even then, there was bickering over how much to pay Mrs Sheldon who was pensioned off into a convent. Marital relations were briefly resumed, with a false pregnancy reported at the beginning of 1729.

After that, the marriage was over, if not to outward appearances since the couple were often together, despite claims by historians that James preferred to live at Albano and leave Clementina at Palazzo del Re. She would always put on a front for the sake of her children.

She turned to religion, finding a spiritual adviser in Fra Leonardo da Porto Maurizzio (later canonised), a Franciscan who encouraged asceticism. This included rigorous fasting, in which as an anorexic she found a fatal attraction. Piety turned into religious mania, wrecking an already frail physique. Visions of the next world left no time for a husband.

The papal pension

Whenever a new Pope was elected James feared he might withdraw financial support. Clementina's father was reputedly worth 25 million scudi and owned a fabulous collection of jewels (he gave Wogan a snuffbox made from a single huge turquoise) but little of this reached James. Nor was it impossible that the Royal Navy might bombard the Papal States' main port, Civitá Vecchia, to make the pontiff evict him.

In the mid 1720s, Benedict XIII refused to pay James's debts, forcing him to reduce the royal household, while France and Spain stopped their pensions. For economy, he moved his court to Bologna, then to Lorraine and Avignon, before returning to Rome in 1729. When St John Nepomuk was canonised at St Peter's in March that year, James sat on a throne next to Pope Benedict.

From Clement XII, who was elected in 1730, the popes were more generous, while French and Spanish subsidies were resumed. When Queen Clementina's father died in 1737, he left half his huge fortune in trust to his Stuart grandsons, appointing James as trustee.[7]

Despite his financial worries James lived at the Palazzo del Re in splendour, giving lavish receptions and going to the opera in a gilded coach escorted by running footmen in red. He lived on the *piano nobile*, in whose state rooms he received cardinals and envoys of Catholic powers. His servants dressed in the livery worn at James II's Whitehall, his dining table was laden with gold and silver plate. Papal guards stood on duty outside. To 'contemporaries the

Palazzo del Re in Rome, like the Château de St Germain in France, housed an impressive royal court whose occupants were expected, sooner or later, to return in triumph to the British Isles'.[8]

The death of Queen Clementina

An asthmatic who suffered from the wet Italian winter, weakened by spiritual exercises that deprived her of nourishment and sleep, Queen Clementina died of tuberculosis at Palazzo del Re on 18 January 1735, only thirty-two years old. Wilful and hysterical, she had nonetheless inspired deep affection. James, who watched by her bed throughout her last illness, collapsed with grief.

Clement XII accorded Clementina the obsequies of a reigning sovereign's consort. At the funeral mass in Santi Apostoli, the parish church of Palazzo del Re, her body, dressed in royal robes, was attended by thirty-two cardinals, after which it was taken to St Peter's for burial in the crypt under the north aisle. Later, Pope Benedict XIV (an admirer of her confessor Fra Leonardo) commissioned a superb monument in the basilica by the sculptor Pietro Bracci with a mosaic portrait of the queen.

Her heart was interred separately, at Santi Apostoli, enshrined on a pier in the right-hand nave. For the rest of his life, when he was in Rome, James went to pray there every morning.

33

The Honest Cause

For the times will not mend
Till the King enjoys his own again.
    Yes, this I can tell
    That all will be well
When the King enjoys his Own again.

'When the King enjoys his Own again'

A bisexual exotic with a 'coffin-face' painted white, a silk eyepatch and a ghastly, toothless smile, Lord Hervey was caricatured as 'Lord Fanny' by Alexander Pope, who wrote of him that he 'Now trips a Lady, and now struts a Lord'. More to the point, Hervey was Queen Caroline's platonic gigolo, knew all the parliamentary gossip and was exceptionally well-connected – he was even said to have slept with Frederick, Prince of Wales. His memoirs, spiteful but often very funny, give us fascinating glimpses of Whig paranoia in the 1730s. While dismissing Jacobites as a spent force in Parliament, he shows a fear he cannot conceal whenever pro-Stuart riots break out in the streets.

Anger at Walpolean corruption compensated for any waning of belief in High Church and divine right. Since the Restoration, patronage had passed from the Crown to the chief minister who had hundreds of 'places' at his disposal – official posts with fat salaries, many of them sinecures. Inevitably, a one-party state exploited the situation. There was always a market for votes at the Treasury, MPs being openly rewarded with bank notes for voting the right way.

Under Walpole's rule, known as the 'Robinocracy', Whigs dominated every level of society. Only Whigs were created peers or baronets, only Whigs received the Garter or the Bath, only Whigs became bishops or deans although most clergy were Tories, and only Whigs were appointed to Crown livings. Only Whig lawyers became judges or King's Counsel, Whig squires replaced Tory magnates as Justices of the Peace. Senior rank in the army, and to some extent the navy, was monopolised by Whigs, blighting the careers of Tory younger sons. In the City, Whigs alone became directors of the Bank of England or masters of the great livery companies, or secured government contracts.

Walpole profited more than anyone, replacing his manor at Houghton with a palace adorned by a collection of paintings by great masters that was famous throughout Europe. He appointed his son, Horace, Usher of the Exchequer for life, a sinecure worth £3,000 a year, giving other valuable posts to political allies. Britain's first prime minister became known as 'the fount of corruption' and in *The Beggars' Opera* (1728) John Gay gave the highwayman Captain Macheath distinctly Walpolean traits that were immediately recognised by theatre-goers.

Macaulay argues that in Walpole's day 'the country could only be governed by corruption', the sole means of controlling Parliament.[1] This did not stop people from resenting it, and they began to reconsider the Stuarts.[2]

In January 1731 Henry Hyde, Viscount Cornbury arrived in Rome on the Grand Tour. Twenty years old, just down from Christchurch, scholarly and fastidious, he dabbled in literature, corresponding with Alexander Pope. At Oxford he had been a friend of William Murray (destined to be among the century's greatest lawyers) who in 1725 had assured King James of his own loyalty.

Cornbury was a protégé of Bolingbroke, by now realising he would never win George II's favour, who gave him a letter for James as son and heir of the king's cousin, the Earl of Clarendon. Invited to Palazzo del Re after dark, he was charmed by the royal couple. James appointed him a lord of the bedchamber while he discussed a Restoration with William Murray's brother, the Earl of Dunbar, the king's current secretary of state.

Shortly after this visit, Baron von Pollnitz observed the royal family closely. He thought the king 'a mere Skeleton' if like the portraits of his father 'only his Aspect is something more melancholy', and suspected he led a dull life save for going to the opera every day during carnival. Although a sincere Catholic, James was no 'Bigot' and his sons were being educated by Protestants – on Sundays a Church of England clergyman preached at the Palazzo del Re's Protestant chapel.

Pollnitz raved about Queen Clementina, who ate by herself at a little table (no doubt fasting) while the two princes sat at the high table with their father. He thought her 'a Princess who deserves in reality to be a Queen; and tho' not a sparkling Beauty, it may be said that her Person is infinitely charming'. (Unlike Queen Caroline, whom Walpole chivalrously called a 'fat old bitch'.) Clementina was friendly, compassionate and 'with a wonderfully quick Comprehension, an admirable Memory', speaking five languages like a native.

'I own to you, that of all the Princesses I have ever had the Honour to approach, I don't know one more deserving of the Veneration of the Public.' Were it not for his respect for the royal couple at London, 'I could wish to see her wear the Crown of the three Kingdoms'.[3]

Returning to his beautiful house, Cornbury Park, Lord Cornbury entered Parliament in the Tory interest as Member for Oxford University nearby, a constituency that swarmed with Stuart supporters. His visit to Rome had not gone unnoticed and Walpole tried, unsuccessfully, to buy his loyalty with a place worth £400 a year.

His first move was to enlist support from Whigs as well as Tories, promising offices and titles in the event of a Restoration. He elicited a cautious response from William Pulteney who, encouraged by Prince Frederick, led the self-styled 'Patriot Whigs' in opposing Walpole.

He then approached the French ambassador in London, the Comte de Chavigny, who responded warmly since France had been angered by Walpole's disregard for French interests when Britain signed a treaty with the Habsburg Emperor in 1731. British diplomacy failed to grasp the significance of the 'Family Alliance' between Bourbon France and Bourbon Spain, both of whose rulers were hereditary enemies of the Habsburgs.

Chavigny told Cornbury whom to contact in France. Accordingly, his secret envoy, Captain Hardy (cashiered from the Royal Navy for Jacobite sympathies) visited the French foreign secretary Germain-Louis Chauvelin, Marquis de Grosbois, who was the all powerful Cardinal Fleury's right hand man, and broached the possibility of a French invasion. Chauvelin reacted with enthusiasm.

A proclamation to the British people was prepared for King James's approval. Its main points were pledges to end Britain's involvement in German affairs and clean up parliamentary corruption, with guarantees for the Anglican Church, City privileges and a free Parliament. The scheme ground to a halt because of its leading supporters' reluctance to identify themselves to the French.

Chavigny consulted Bolingbroke, who assured him it was essential for Britain's well-being to repatriate the Hanoverians. Bolingbroke then sent an agent to Colonel Daniel O'Brien, King James's envoy to France, proposing the king should abdicate in favour of the Prince of Wales, who must be brought up as a Protestant. The French pointed out that James was unlikely to agree. In any case, like most people they did not trust Bolingbroke.

The scheme revived during the fury aroused by the Excise Bill of 1733, an attempt by Walpole to woo the country gentry by abolishing the land tax, whose revenue would be replaced by higher duties on wine, beer, candles and tobacco. The row lasted from March until May, causing almost as much indignation as the South Sea Bubble. Whig MPs joined Tories in opposing the Bill. Walpole backed down and withdrew it.

'For a fortnight after the Excise Bill was dropped all the newspapers were filled with nothing but accounts from every great town in England of rejoicing, burning effigies, letters of thanks from the constituents of those who had voted against the Bill to their representatives', Hervey tells us. 'This joy was carried so far as Oxford, that for three nights together, round the bonfires made there, the healths of Ormond, Bolingbroke and James the Third were publicly drank.'[4]

Walpole rallied the Whigs with a speech in which he accused opposition MPs of 'every day and every hour consulting with Jacobites, taking directions from Jacobites and promoting Jacobite measures'. He asked, 'What must become of this Government and this [Hanover] Family?'[5]

During the furore, James asked Cornbury to go to Paris and see what he could do. Received by Louis XV as well as Chauvelin, he showed them a plan for seizing London. Despite similarities to the Atterbury Plot, this must have been drawn up by France's new ambassador to London, the Marquis de Canillac, who was a soldier. It had the support of prominent Tories, including Sir William Wyndham who now led the Jacobite MPs.

The plan was for a French expedition to land on the south coast, making George's generals move the army from the capital to confront it, which would enable supporters to take over London. The Hanover family were to be unharmed, but sent home. At Paris, Chauvelin strongly approved and told Colonel O'Brien, who in June 1733 sent a hopeful report to Rome. James ordered the Earl Marischal to be ready to go to France.

When Cornbury told the French that 14,000 troops were needed, James hastened to explain that 5,000 would be quite enough, but Cardinal Fleury, who although eighty-two years old still ran France, took fright. Louis XV was already at war, fighting the Habsburgs in an attempt to restore his father-in-law Stanisław Leszczyński to the Polish throne – a risky adventure such as Cornbury's might unbalance the entire French budget. In November 1733 Fleury ordered Louis's council to reject the proposal.

The Marquis de Canillac was abruptly recalled in 1735, Walpole, having protested at his activities after intercepting his dispatches. Walpole also interviewed Colonel William Cecil, who had succeeded the Earl of Orrery as James's main agent in England, pretending to ask his advice – neatly branding him a double agent. The Jacobite leaders panicked, Bolingbroke left for another French holiday. Two years later, Cardinal Fleury dismissed Chauvelin, which ended any lingering hopes of an invasion.[6]

Cornbury was left in peace as there was no firm evidence against him. Alarmed by the inability of English Jacobites to keep secrets, he severed communications with them and stopped writing to King James. He continued to be MP for Oxford University, but avoided future schemes for a Restoration. Even so, in 1746 Jacobites on the run found shelter at Cornbury Park.[7]

There had never been much chance of a French invasion as France's army and navy were so committed elsewhere.[8] Yet the 'Cornbury Plot' did at least prove to French observers that there was still plenty of life in the Stuart cause. It also showed Jacobites that the accord between France and Hanoverian England had broken down.

Jacobite riots in the 1730s

'During this summer a licentious, riotous, seditious and almost ungovernable spirit in the people showed itself in many tumults and disorders, in different shapes, and in several parts of the kingdom', Hervey recorded in 1736, singling out a riot by Spitalfield weavers against competition from Irish workers that lasted for days. They 'began with railings against Irishmen, but came in twenty-four hours to cursing of Germans, reviling the King and the Queen, and huzzaing for James III'. Troops had to be sent in.[9]

Hervey was no less alarmed by 'an insurrection' at Edinburgh. Captain John Porteous, commander of the Town Guard, had been sentenced to death for firing on protesters at a hanging, and when reprieved by Queen Caroline (regent during George's absence in Hanover), was dragged out of the Tolbooth gaol and lynched. Throughout the incident the crowd yelled insults at their new royal family, Hervey later commenting it was a good thing that the queen had not been told half of what they said about her.

To everybody's surprise, in 1737 Walpole watered down a bill to punish those involved, revealing how fearful he was of rebellion in Scotland. He had heard of mysterious, clearly well-educated men having organised the riots and, although he had no proof, suspected they were Jacobites.

If mistaken, he was correct in recognising just how much the Scots disliked Hanoverians. He had only to listen to the balladeers:

> Our Darien can witness bear,
>   And so can our Glencoe, Sir.
> Our South Sea it can make appear
>   What to our kings we owe, Sir.
> We have been murder'd, starv'd and robbed
>   By those your Kings and knav'ry
> And all our treasure is stock-jobb'd
>   While we groan under slav'ry.[10]

Walpole was less concerned about Ireland whose Jacobite leaders were serving in armies abroad. Yet he realised the threat they posed, 'With the landing of a sizeable and well-armed contingent of the Irish Brigade, Irish Jacobites would almost certainly have provided a more formidable threat than their Scottish and English contemporaries.'[11]

Nearer home, the prime minister was undeceived when in 1738 Jacobite MPs led by Lord Charles Somerset proposed a smaller standing army on the grounds that the Cause no longer had many followers. Walpole told the House,

> No man of common prudence will profess himself openly a Jacobite; by so doing he not only may injure his private fortune, but he must render himself less able to do any effectual service to the cause he has embraced. Your right Jacobite, Sir, disguises his true sentiments, he roars out for Revolution principles . . .
>
> These are the men we have most reason to be afraid of: they are, I am afraid, more numerous than most gentlemen imagine. I am not ashamed to say I am in fear of the Pretender.[12]

PART FOUR

A King in Waiting

34

The Forty-Four?

Britons, now retrieve your glory,
   And your ancient rights maintain;
Drive th'usurping race before you,
   And restore a Stuart's reign.

Anon, 'Britons, now retrieve your glory'[1]

When Augustus II of Poland died in 1733 Queen Clementina's father, Prince Sobieski, begged James to become a candidate for the Polish throne, assuring him he stood an excellent chance of being elected. George's government was so alarmed that it ordered the British minister at Warsaw to do everything he could to prevent the election of the Pretender and his children.

James though was not interested in any crown other than that of Great Britain, but, when declining, said how sorry he was the Duke of York was not yet old enough to be a candidate. After all, through his mother, the boy had Sobieski blood and was descended from one of Poland's greatest kings

Everywhere, with Charles, Prince of Wales in mind, Jacobites were drinking the oak-tree toast, '*Revirescit!*' And there was good reason for their optimism.

In summer 1734, when the thirteen-year-old Charles was on board a Spanish man-of-war shelling Gaeta – a Neapolitan fortress occupied by Imperial troops – a gust of wind blew his gold-laced hat into the sea. The crew wanted to fish it out, but he stopped them, shouting 'Let my hat swim all the way to England and say, "I'm coming!"' His host, Charles VII of Naples, threw his own hat in the sea and amid the cheering promised to go with him.

The prince had been invited to the Siege of Gaeta by Charles, Philip of Spain's younger son and only four years his senior, who had just taken the throne of Naples from the Habsburgs. George was infuriated when he heard of the invitation, but Walpole stopped him from turning the affair into a full-scale diplomatic incident.

Charles and his brother Henry had been brought up in Rome, with English as their first language. They had fond parents, if James was melancholy and withdrawn, Clementina neurotic and fussy. All we know of the boys' attitude towards their governor James Murray, Earl of Dunbar, is that he was told to make them into good Englishmen and good Scots – and presumably into good Irishmen as well.

Their tutor was Sir Thomas Sheridan from Sligo, educated at Trinity College, Dublin, but a convert to Catholicism, who had fought at the Boyne in his youth. His mother was rumoured to be a bastard daughter of James II. Better at endearing himself than imparting knowledge, he provided a very mediocre education. A Protestant chaplain, Dr Wagstaff, also gave the boys instruction.

To amuse them, they were made 'Knights of Toboso', a mock order of chivalry resembling a Masonic lodge that had been founded by Jacobite exiles. The first grand master was Lord Marischal with Bishop Atterbury as 'grand prelate', its membership stretching from Rome to Paris, Madrid and St Petersburg. Their toast was 'A merry meeting on the green', meaning the Restoration. But the young princes had all the amusement they wanted – dancing, theatre, opera and, above all, hunting.[2]

Charles became a fine horseman, while he spent days shooting in the lonely Campagna, where he went barefoot and slept rough. He was keenest on learning how to be a soldier. When at Gaeta, although so young he impressed everybody by his courage.

In January 1735 he wept so much at Queen Clementina's death that the court feared for his life. He inherited her Polish good looks and charm, her moodiness and self-will. In 1737, calling himself the 'Count of Albany' he toured the courts of northern Italy with Lord Dunbar – received so warmly at Venice and Genoa that George II protested. George would have been still more alarmed had he heard how Charles wore Highland dress during the Roman carnival of 1741.

The Associators, 1738

Late in 1737 John Gordon of Glenbuchat, a 'bonnet-laird' from Aberdeenshire, presented himself at Palazzo del Re. En route, he had approached

Cardinal Fleury at Paris with proposals for a French invasion and a Scots rising that, as usual, were rejected. A veteran of Killiecrankie (when a boy of fourteen) and of Sheriffmuir, Glenbuchat, who had recently sold his tower house by the River Don to devote himself to the Cause, he invited the king to come to Scotland and raise his standard.

The Duke of Gordon's factor and father-in-law to three Highland chieftains, Glenbuchat was influential. James sent him home with a commission as Major-General, accompanied by Captain Hay of Drumelzie and a young Mr Murray (later Murray of Broughton), a Peeblesshire baronet's son who would act as co-ordinator. They gathered a like-minded group – the Duke of Perth, Cameron of Lochiel, the Earl of Traquair, Lord Lovat and MacGregor of Balhaldie.

They met regularly in Edinburgh at the Buck Club, a tavern near Parliament Close. However, the 'Associators' as they called themselves, were scarcely united. Murray described Balhaldie (chief of the MacGregors), who was their secretary at Paris, as an overbearing bully – 'master of as much bad French as to procure himself a whore and a dinner'.[3]

Their emergence as a political grouping is unsurprising. The Scottish face of Walpolean corruption was the Duke of Argyll and his brother the Earl of Ilay who together ran the country, with heavy bribery at elections for both MPs and representative peers.[4] Lord Milton, the Lord Justice Clerk, dispensed patronage for them, bestowing government 'places' and sinecures, choosing sheriffs. His appointments were excellent, but this did not lessen resentment. At a humbler level, the customs service was a byeword for venality and theft. The regime provoked the same support for a Restoration that it did in England.

In October 1739, Britain declared the 'War of Jenkins' Ear' on Spain, in essence a dispute over slave trading. This was when Walpole famously snarled, 'They now ring the bells but soon they will wring their hands.' Britain then became embroiled in the War of the Austrian Succession that broke out shortly after, allying with the Empire and Holland against Spain, France and Prussia.

Once again, the Stuarts were useful to France. They acquired a military leader, Lieutenant-General the Earl of Barrymore, a sprightly septuagenarian Irish peer who was MP for Wigan. Although he had last held command in Queen Anne's army, his soldierly qualifications impressed English Jacobites, even if until now he had been an enemy to Walpole rather than a

Restorationist. In May 1740 he went to Paris, trying in vain to persuade the regent, old Fleury, to send an invasion force.

The Tories had long hoped their exclusion from government would end when Walpole fell, as William Pulteney's 'Patriot Whigs' shared their detestation of the prime minister and were supported by George's heir, Prince Frederick, who hated anyone favoured by his father. An election in summer 1741 left Walpole with a bare majority – in September, King James told Jacobite MPs to vote with Pulteney and bring him down.

However, when Walpole resigned in February 1742, Pultney and his men joined a new Whig ministry without Tories. They had hoped for a 'Broad Bottom' government that lived up to its name (inspired by the Tory MP Sir John Hynde Cotton's physique) and contained Tories, but George II refused to countenance it.

'We are kept out of all public employment of power and profit, and live like aliens and pilgrims in the land of our nativity,' wrote a Whig who, posing as an anonymous Tory, was trying to persuade MPs to abandon Jacobitism. He continued: 'No quality, no fortune, no eloquence, no learning, no wisdom, no probity is of any use to any man of our unfortunate denomination, ecclesiastick or layman, lawyer or soldier, peer or commoner, for obtaining the most deserved advancement in his profession, or any favour of the Crown.'

The writer implies the situation is due to Hanoverian sovereigns who think every Tory a Jacobite – 'the bare merit of hating us, and everything we love and hold sacred, daily advances dunces in the law and church, cowards in our fleets and armies, republicans in the King's house, and idiots everwhere'.[5]

It was Hanoverian rejection, rather than love of divine right, that turned Tories into Jacobites. Nor were they a small minority. Had the number of votes cast at general elections decided membership of the House of Commons, Tory MPs would have been in a majority ever since 1714 – which meant that over half the country was disenfranchised by the House of Hanover.[6]

In 1980, the historian Bruce Lenman wrote of the 'massive apathy of the British peoples towards their arrogant, unrepresentative and appallingly incompetent government' in the first half of the eighteenth century.[7] Since then, research has shown that they were far from apathetic. It has been estimated that during the 1740s a quarter of English and Welsh landowners were

Jacobites,[8] and there must have been others who were better at covering their tracks. Fifty years ago, Sir Lewis Namier pointed out that almost no Tory family papers survive from the era of the first two Hanoverians – destroyed for fear of incrimination.[9]

Between 1741 and 1745 well over a third of the 150 Tory MPs supported James, secretly or openly, and were actively involved in working for a Restoration. A substantial proportion of London's business magnates (including six lord mayors between 1740 and 1753) held Jacobite views. City men like this accepted the need for drastic measures to free England from the Hanoverian one-party state, although most of them had no wish to be involved in the process.

Jacobitism called itself the Honest Cause, reasonably enough. Whatever Macaulay says about corruption being the only way Walpole could govern, men generally resent corrupt government, especially if they are excluded from it, and eighteenth century English and Scots were no exception. They also disliked the continuation of Walpole's regime by successors who were just as venal. Since no electoral remedy existed, the only solution was bringing back the Stuarts.

The new Jacobites

The leaders of the reinvigorated Tory party were the third Duke of Beaufort, the Earls of Westmoreland and Barrymore, Watkin Williams-Wynn and John Hynde Cotton, Robert Abdy – an Essex baronet and MP – and Dr William King, an Oxford don. Henry Somerset, the Duke of Beaufort, was their chief in the House of Commons.

In Parliament they attacked the use of British troops to further King George's German interests, in breach of the Act of Succession by which he reigned. Williams-Wynn and Hynde Cotton told the House in December 1742 that England had become a Hanoverian province while Sir John St Aubyn argued that George wanted to rule England the way he ruled Hanover. A Welsh baronet, Sir John Philipps, claimed the Exchequer was being charged nearly £400,000 to hire Hanoverian troops that cost King George only £100,000.

From a Whig family Philipps, of Picton Castle in Pembrokeshire and MP for Carmarthen, who had become a Jacobite when an Oxford undergraduate, played the role in South Wales that Williams-Wynn did in the north and was president of a Pembrokeshire group of Jacobites known as the Sea Serjeants.

Another new Jacobite MP was Sir Francis Dashwood of West Wycombe, founder of the Hell Fire Club, whose conversion to the Honest Cause in 1739 came after a meeting with Charles while on the Grand Tour. He wrote to a friend, 'I am at one with this gallant Prince; he has all the gifts of a true leader.'

In 1744, when a French invasion seemed imminent and a loyal address to George II was proposed, Dashwood strongly objected. In his speech, he referred to 'a weak, avaricious and narrow minded Prince on the throne [George], a great part of the nation proscribed and forced into disaffection, the daily encroachments made upon the constitution – no wonder there was an unwillingness in the people to support the Government'. Outraged, a Whig MP accused him of delivering an oration with 'the most of a Jacobite tendency of any speech ever pronounced in Parliament'. Later, Dashwood defined his political aims as introducing those cherished planks of the Cause in its new form – annual or triennial general elections, a national militia instead of an army and a purge of placemen.[10]

Early in 1742 Lord Barrymore saw promising prospects when the government announced it would send an army to Europe, leaving England largely without troops. As a young officer who had witnessed William III's invasion, he proposed another on the same lines, nearer London – a landing on the coast of Sussex, Kent or Essex, by 10,000 French regulars. However, he then presented the Duke of Argyll with two letters from King James, one hoping the duke (named in cypher) would live up to what had been said of him and the other a circular in which James asked supporters to rise.

Argyll panicked, sending the letters to King George. No action was taken against Barrymore, but he fled to his Irish estates where he lurked before returning to London at the end of the year.[11]

In January 1743 Cardinal Fleury died. Soon after, Lord Sempill, who was James's agent at Paris, delivered a letter to the French foreign minister, Amelot de Chaillou. Its signatories were Henry Somerset, Duke of Beaufort, and John Boyle, Earl of Orrery, as well as three baronets – Sir John Hynde Cotton, Sir Watkin Williams-Wynn and Sir Robert Abdy. They begged Louis XV to invade England so they could restore King James.

However, at the Battle of Dettingen (at Karlstein am Main, Germany) in June 1743 British, Hanoverian and Hessian troops nominally commanded by George II routed France's army, forcing it to withdraw across the Rhine. The Whigs praised George's behaviour to the skies, and he has gone down in history as 'the last British King to be present at a battle'. Embarrassingly, Tories pointed out that instead of a British officer's red sash he had worn a yellow, Imperial sash throughout, which implied that he thought of himself as a German.

The defeat helped the French ministers make up their minds. If they were to stop the enemy advancing into northern France, they must cause trouble for the British elsewhere. In August, James Butler, an Irishman who was Louis XV's Master of the Horse, arrived in London. Ostensibly here to buy English thoroughbreds, his true mission was gauging support for a Restoration. The Jacobites gave him lists of landowners and City of London grandees likely to welcome James III home, if not necessarily prepared to fight.

France's ministers decided that a Stuart Restoration was a sound investment – Austria would lose an ally, Spain an enemy. When in September 1743, led by the Duke of Beaufort, England's Jacobite leaders again asked the French to restore James they responded positively, and in November began preparations for an invasion, to some extent based on Barrymore's plan of the previous year.

The invasion of 1744

In February 1744, 10,000 French troops – two cavalry regiments and twenty infantry battalions – were to land in Essex near Maldon on the Blackwater Estuary. Among them was to be a new regiment of 650 Scots raised by Lord Lewis Drummond, the Royal Ecossais. The expedition's commander would be Marshal Saxe (Count Maurice of Saxony), who was Europe's greatest soldier. He would bring arms for James's supporters, led by Lord Barrymore.

Saxe's orders stated that Louis XV no longer recognised the Elector of Hanover as King of Great Britain and wished to restore the lawful sovereign. The invasion would be accompanied by the aged Duke of Ormonde who prepared a manifesto, promising that the French troops would be sent home as soon as they had done their job – besides stressing that Marshal Saxe was a Protestant.

At the last moment, responding to a request by the Jacobite leaders, a new plan was adopted – to sail up the Thames and disembark at Blackwall. Saxe's troops assembled at Dunkirk, ready to board the transports. (To avoid alerting spies, the Irish Brigade played no part in the operation.) The French navy under Admiral de Roquefeuil was waiting to sail out from Brest to distract

Admiral Sir John Norris's Channel Fleet from intercepting the transports. Commanded by Chef-d'Escadre Jean de Barrailh, these would then be guided by two Jacobite smugglers who knew the Thames and its tides.

Prince Charles had left Palazzo del Re for France shortly after Christmas, saying goodbye to a father whom he would never see again. Like James he was tall, but otherwise bore no resemblance to the Stuarts. Strongly built, he had reddish fair hair and probably took after his Sobieski ancestors in appearance – during the forthcoming campaign at least one observer thought he looked Polish. More important, he possessed a magnetic personality.

Travelling under many disguises, Charles arrived at Gravelines near Dunkirk in mid February, intending to cross to England after the invasion, where he would rule as regent, advised by a council headed by the Duke of Beaufort. The council drew up a declaration for the king, who was to follow later.

James promised to stop 'the treasures of the nation [being] applied to satiate private avarice and lavished for the support of German dominions'. He adds, 'Bribery and corruption have been openly and universally practised' – there will be no corruption in the free Parliament he is going to call. He explains why he is using French troops – to expel 'those shoals of foreign mercenaries, with which the Elector fills the kingdom whenever he thinks himself in danger'.[12] A separate declaration for Scotland denounces the Union and building 'forts and citadels' to cow Highlanders.

On 14 February 1744 the Whig government learned of the invasion from a spy in the French foreign office, de Bussy (code named '101'). There were only 10,000 troops in England so frantic messages for reinforcements were sent to Flanders and Ireland. Habeas corpus was again suspended while Barrymore, whom some called the 'Pretender's General', was arrested along with other suspects.

Among them, now over eighty, was bumbling old Colonel Cecil, who had no inkling of what was afoot but was sent to the Tower anyway. Captains O'Brien and O'Hara with other visiting officers from the Irish Brigade, were also taken into custody. They had been spying on British troop movements. No one appeared in court – there was too little evidence

On 15 February Marshal Saxe complained he would have been in England already but for de Barrailh's absence at sea, hunting for prizes. Then the gentleman who was bringing pilots for the invasion fleet failed to arrive on time. Finally, on 22 February the troops at Dunkirk boarded the transports.

Two days later, Roquefeuil's fifteen men-of-war anchored off Dungeness, ready to confront Norris's slightly larger fleet.

Heavy rain set in, followed by a ferocious gale that lasted for days. Roquefeuil reached Brest in safety but several of his warships lost their masts as did even more of Norris's. Many French transports were blown ashore at Dunkirk, their rigging in tatters, while vital supplies of food and munitions were ruined. On 28 February the French government called off the invasion.

Again, the Hanoverians had the devil's own luck. Ten thousand French veterans under Marshal Saxe would not have been easy to defeat, and an early French victory might have encouraged even English Jacobites to rise. But if the Forty-Four invasion failed, it helped to inspire the Forty-Five.

35

The Irish Dimension – Fontenoy, Spring 1745

I knew well by the cold
And the fury of Thetis by the shore,
By the tuneful, merry singing of the birds
That my Caesar would return ...
That the Gaels will not be sadly fettered much longer.

Piaras Mac Gearailt, *Rosc Catha na Mumhan*, 1745[1]

The Penal Laws had made Ireland a time bomb, with most of the population hoping that the Stuart army in exile would rescue them. As a modern historian Eamonn Ó Ciardha says, 'With the landing of a sizeable and well-armed contingent of the Irish Brigade, Jacobites would certainly have provided a more formidable threat than their Scottish and English contemporaries.'[2]

What happened on a distant battlefield in Flanders became the spark that lit the Forty-Five. To understand why, we need to know something of conditions in Ireland at the time.

Contemplating vast new mansions built with rents from confiscated Catholic estates, a poet of the old language lamented,

Oh! who can well refrain from tears
Who sees the hosts of a thousand years
Expell'd from this, their own green isle,
And bondsmen to the base and vile![3]

Corruption was even more blatant than in Walpole's England, the spoils of perpetual office greedily divided among the new aristocracy.

The religion of the majority was outlawed. 'There is no instance, even in the ten persecutions [of Roman Christians] of such severity as that which the Protestants have exercised against the Catholicks', was Dr Johnson's comment. 'Did we tell them we have conquered them, it would be above board; to punish them by confiscation and other penalties were monstrous injustice.'[4]

Some who lost their estates became 'gentlemen graziers', breeding cattle and sheep on a big scale which they sold on the hoof at Dublin or Cork so profitably that they made fortunes. Barred from the professions, others became doctors or wine merchants or served with the Irish Brigade.

Forced to pay exorbitant tithes to Protestant rectors, sometimes at gun point, in addition to those paid voluntarily to their own parish priests, peasants were equally resentful. The hold over them of the surviving old gentry and the priests was strengthened by the inability of the new landlords and rectors, whom Ó Rathaille calls 'foreign devils' (*diabhal na-iasachta*), to speak Irish. Because James III nominated Catholic bishops, all priests were Jacobites and their activities show 'they did not cultivate Irish "independence" but loyalty to the regal rights and pretensions of the exiled Stuart'.[5]

However, contrary to popular belief, over ten per cent of tenant farmer land stayed in Catholic hands until the twentieth century. Some landowners bequeathed their estate intact by having an only son each generation, like the Lords Kenmare who kept over 100,000 acres. Others gave land in trust to a Protestant neighbour who leased it back to them on a peppercorn rent. Many made false conversions, crypto-Catholics such as the poet Piaras Mac Gearailt who conformed to the Church of England, but in secret practised his old faith.[6]

There were enclaves of wealthy Catholic landowners in Munster and Connacht whose children intermarried, such as the 'Nagle Country' along the beautiful Blackwater Valley of North Cork.[7] Here, four branches of the Nagle family, each with its own estate, still spoke and read Irish, welcoming poets like Eoghan Rua Ó Súilleabháin, whom for a time they employed at Annakissy as a tutor. (However, Munster's Till Eugenspiegel soon lost his post, apparently for making advances to a daughter of the house.) They also recruited, discreetly, for the Irish Brigade in which their sons served as officers – to return with the polished manners of *ancien régime* France. All descended from Sir Richard Nagle, James II's Secretary for Ireland or from his brother James, the Patriot Parliament's sergeant-at-arms.

Catholics of all classes hated the new Protestant Ireland. But the young men who might have led a rising were overseas.

The Irish Brigade

The Irish soldiers who went into exile after Limerick or joined Irish regiments in the armies of Catholic Europe, dubbed the 'Wild Geese' (*Géanna Fiáine*), were Jacobites to a man. For officers, it meant a profession barred to them at home, though dangerous, badly paid and insecure – they might starve in times of peace. For other ranks, it meant the same risks yet also an escape from toiling on the soil and a chance to serve under men who spoke their own language. Above all, it was an opportunity to fight for the rightful king, perhaps one day on Irish soil.

In 1745 the best of them were with the French army in the Irish Brigade, which contained six regiments of foot – Rothe's, Berwick's, Bulkeley's, Clare's, Dillon's and the newly formed Lally's – each a single battalion of 685 men. There was also a cavalry regiment, FitzJames's Horse, with two squadrons – 240 troopers in all. Red coats and colours bearing the Cross of St George made the foot almost indistinguishable from that of Hanoverian England, but its fifes and drums played 'When the King enjoys his Own again' or 'The White Cockade'. Officers and men swore allegiance to James, to whom every regimental appointment or promotion was submitted for approval.

They were generally acknowledged to be magnificent troops, with an impressive list of battle honours. In 1731 Dean Swift wrote to Sir Charles Wogan, 'I cannot but highly esteem those gentlemen of Ireland who, with all the disadvantages of being exiles and strangers, have been able to distinguish themselves by their valour and conduct in so many parts of Europe.'[8]

Many officers were born in exile, like Thomas Lally of the Dillon Regiment, whose father, Sir Gerald Lally from Tuam, was a general in the French service. In 1737 Thomas crossed the Channel, to gauge the strength of Jacobitism in all three kingdoms. Next year he was sent on a mission to St Petersburg, to ask the Russians to exchange their English alliance for one with France. In 1744 he became colonel of the new Irish regiment bearing his name.

The Ascendancy was terrified of the Irish Brigade. A Dublin pamphleteer, Charles Forman, wrote in 1728:

As long as there is a body of Irish Roman Catholic troops abroad, the chevalier will always make some figure in Europe by the credit

they give him; and being considered as a prince that has a brave and
well-disciplined army of veterans at his service ... Should France
grow wanton with power, forget her engagements and obligations
to Britain, can she anywhere find such a proper instrument as the
Irish regiments to execute such enterprises as she may undertake in
favour of the chevalier's pretensions when they square with her own
interests?[9]

In the first years of his reign George II, who was anxious to keep on good
terms with France allowed the Brigade to recruit in Ireland. However, during
the 1730s the Dublin authorities reacted furiously, executing several recruiting agents. They had reason for alarm.

Besides invading Ireland and returning confiscated estates to their owners,
the Brigade's officers were planning to ensure the Restoration's survival, as
may be seen from a memorandum King James received from Colonel the
Hon. Ulick Burke (the Earl of Clanricarde's younger son) in 1737. As well as
bringing back the Scots Parliament and making the Irish Parliament independent, it urged him to give Scotland and Ireland armies that could put
down any resurgent English opposition to a new Stuart order.[10]

In the spring of 1745 Catholic Irishmen, whether at home or abroad,
rejoiced at news that came from the Austrian Netherlands (Belgium). The
British commander-in-chief there was the twenty-three year old Duke of
Cumberland, George II's younger son, who, in spring 1745, had marched
south with 50,000 English, Hanoverian and Austrian troops to relieve
Tournai – besieged by the French. He hoped to crush Marshal Saxe who,
with an army the same size, had taken up a strong position at Fontenoy, five
miles outside the city.

On 30 April, after his cavalry had been repulsed several times,
Cumberland launched a massive, head-on attack with his infantry, a huge
Anglo-Hanoverian column bludgeoning its way into the French centre.
Counter-attacked in the flank by the French horse, they formed squares and
beat them off, before resuming their advance – seemingly on the point of
victory.

However, Saxe then mowed down the column's front ranks with grapeshot, the French and Swiss Guards charging its left. But it was the charge by
the Irish Brigade that won the day. Their bands playing 'The White Cockade',
roaring '*Cuimhnídh ar Luimneach agus ar fheall na Sasanach*' ('Remember

Limerick and English treachery'), they tore into the enemy's right flank with the bayonet, Bulkeley's Regiment capturing a colour from the Coldstream Guards. The entire Brigade covered itself with glory.

Accepting he was beaten, Cumberland ordered his troops to retreat, leaving (as Tobias Smollet sardonically puts it) his sick and wounded 'to the humanity of the victors'. That evening he shed tears of rage. He had suffered 7,500 casualties, not many more than the French, but the battle enabled Marshal Saxe to capture Tournai and overrun the entire Austrian Netherlands.

The Irish Brigade had lost ninety-eight officers and 400 other ranks killed or wounded. Immediately after Cumberland's withdrawal, King Louis went in person to congratulate each regiment, making Colonel Lally and Lieutenant-Colonel Walter Stapleton brigadier-generals on the battlefield.[11]

For English and Scots Jacobites, Fontenoy meant that the Hanoverian princeling had received a bloody nose. It was much more for Irish Jacobites, giving them back their pride. The victory was a catalyst, inspiring Irishmen abroad to make every effort to help the Prince of Wales regain his father's throne.

36

'I am come home, Sir', summer 1745

'Then', said Mr Hugh, 'what number of men has he brought along with him?' 'Only seven', said Kenlochmoydart. 'What stock of money and arms has he brought with him then?' said Mr Hugh. 'A very small stock of either,' said Kenlochmoydart. 'What generals or officers fitt for commanding are with him?' said Mr Hugh. 'None at all,' replied Kenlochmoydart. Mr Hugh said he did not like the expedition at all.

Bishop Forbes, *The Lyon in Mourning*[1]

Although Prince Charles remained in France, the French government took little notice of him. In desperation, he decided he would invade Scotland by himself, although the Associators were unable to find money for even the smallest force – MacGregor of Balhaldie fled the country because he could not pay a bill for £50.

There had always been communities of Catholic Irish merchants on France's Atlantic shore. Some in Brittany were smugglers and privateers as well, which meant there were Irishmen with fast ships well used to outrunning pursuit by British patrols. Lord Clare, who had led the Irish Brigade at Fontenoy, introduced the prince to three of them.

Nantes' leading shipowner, Antoine Walsh – a former French naval officer – was rich from privateering and the slave trade. James II had sailed back to France after the Boyne on board a ship skippered by his father Philip, a Waterford merchant who became a St Malo corsair. Walsh was a key figure in the local Irish community and a fanatical Jacobite. The other two were Walter Rutledge and Pierre-André d'Heguerty. Rutledge, from Connacht, was a banker who owned a Dunkirk privateer. D'Heguerty, a former colonial governor, was the son of an officer in Dillon's Regiment.

Sir John Murray of Broughton went to Paris in August 1744. Meeting Charles behind the stables of the Tuileries Gardens, he warned him that no more than 5,000 Scots would rise – and only if he brought 3,000 French troops. The Prince replied that he would try if he had a single footman.

In spring 1745 Charles borrowed money from two Irish bankers in Paris, Messers Waters, and from a Scots banker there Aeneas MacDonald (who later described the expedition as 'entirely an Irish project'). With other funds lent by Walsh, Rutledge and d'Heguerty, this was spent on Charles's behalf by a Captain O'Sullivan, to buy weaponry. Walsh offered to take him to Scotland on one of his own ships, the *Du Teillay*, a frigate of eighteen guns he would skipper himself while Rutledge hired a redundant warship from the French navy, the *Elisabeth* of sixty-four guns, pretending he wanted her as a privateer.

The *Du Teillay* carried 1,500 muskets, 1,800 broadswords and £4,000 in gold coin. On the *Elisabeth* were more muskets and broadswords, 20 small cannon, and 100 picked volunteers from Clare's Regiment – veterans of Fontenoy, who included a large proportion of officers.

Also on board the *Elisabeth* was a group who were later immortalised in Scottish myth as 'the Seven Men of Moidart'. In fact, four were Irish, one was English and only two were Scots. One of the Irishmen, Charles's tutor Sir Thomas Sheridan was over seventy – 'a drooping old man' – and another, Colonel Sir Jean MacDonnell of FitzJames's Horse, was elderly, while 'Parson' Kelly had been Atterbury's secretary. The Englishman, Colonel Francis Strickland, was a Yorkshire recusant and the Prince's major-domo. The two Scots were the gouty Duke of Atholl, nearly sixty, who had been out in the Nineteen, and Aeneas MacDonald the banker.

The one genuinely useful member of the seven was John William O'Sullivan, an officer on the French general staff who, besides seeing active service in Flanders and in Italy, had taken part in France's conquest of Corsica and understood guerilla warfare. Highly professional, but jovial and fond of a drink, he quickly endeared himself to Charles.[2] Later a Whig moaned that 'to the abilities of this man we may justly attribute the success with which a handful of banditti have long been able to overrun and plunder a large part of this opulent and powerful nation'.[3] In 1747, at King James's request, O'Sullivan was to compile a vivid, first-hand account of the Forty-Five.

When it was too late to stop him, Charles wrote to his father and King Louis, explaining his plan. The little expedition sailed from Belle Isle on 5 July, with the Prince disguised as a French abbé – wearing a black suit.

Four days later, a hundred miles west of the Lizard it was intercepted by HMS *Lyon* of fifty-eight guns. Fearing she might be joined by another warship, the *Elisabeth* began a ferocious duel, reducing the *Lyon* to a floating wreck. However, the *Elisabeth* suffered crippling damage herself. Charles wanted the *Du Teillay* to go to her assistance during the engagement, which lasted five or six hours, but Walsh refused, threatening to order him to his cabin.

The *Elisabeth* was forced to put back to France, taking the Irish regulars on whom Charles had depended to capture Fort William and other strongholds, with half his muskets and broadswords. Undaunted, he made Walsh hold course for Scotland, fog saving the *Du Teillay* from interception by two more British men-of-war, who belonged to the same patrol as HMS *Lyon*. They did not realise she was carrying Prince Charles – the *Lyon*'s crew thought they had been fighting French ships bound for America.

On 23 July Charles landed on the island of Eriskay, between South Uist and Barra, in Clanranald country. The wind from Fontenoy, together with Irish money and seamanship, had brought him this far. Now it was up to the Scots – the other sons of the Gael.

The day after he landed, Charles sent for Alexander MacDonald of Boisdale, Clanranald's uncle, who lived on the adjoining island of South Uist. When he revealed who he was, Boisdale told him to go home. 'I am come home, Sir, and I will entertain no notion at all of returning to that place from whence I came', replied the Prince. 'I am persuaded my faithful Highlanders will stand by me.'

Next day, the *Du Teillay* sailed into Loch nan Uamh, anchoring off Borradale in Moidart, which was also in Clanranald country. The Prince was safe enough here. He soon found he had been right about the Highlanders.

'There entered the tent a tall youth of a most agreeable aspect, in a plain black coat, with a plain shirt, not very clean, and a cambrick stock fixed with a plain silver buckle, a plain hatt with a canvas string having one end fixed to one of his coat buttons: he had black stockins and brass buckles in his shoes,' recalled an eyewitness in a famous description. The writer (a Clanranald MacDonald) adds, 'I found my heart swell to my very throat.'[4] Many felt the same. Years later Sir Walter Scott met elderly men who remembered the Prince's magnetism – and at this particular moment he needed all of it.

Understandably, the clan chiefs were reluctant to rise. When Cameron of Lochiel arrived, he told the Prince they were under no obligation to do so, because he came without the French troops they had stipulated. Since there was not the slightest chance of success, he advised him to go back to France.

'In a few days, with the few friends that I have, I will erect the royal standard, and proclaim to the people of Britain, that Charles Stuart is come over to claim the crown of his ancestors, to win it, or to perish in the attempt,' was Charles's reply. 'Lochiel, who, my father has often told me, was our firmest friend, may stay at home and learn from the newspapers the fate of his prince.'

'No,' said Lochiel, 'I'll share the fate of my prince, and so shall every man over whom nature or fortune hath given me power.'[5] This was a far from predictable reaction since Lochiel was one of the new entrepreneurial chiefs, a tough, hard business man. Had he refused, no other chief would have joined. Knowing that a warrant for his arrest had been issued, for corresponding with King James, may have helped him make up his mind.

Inspired by Lochiel who could bring 500 fighting men, other clans, mainly the various septs of MacDonalds – Clanranald, Glengarry, Keppoch, Glencoe – pledged support, although MacDonald of Sleat refused. After the arms and ammunition on board the *Du Teillay* had been unloaded, on 4 August Charles ordered Walsh to take the little frigate home to France, to show he would never turn back. (King James created Walsh an earl for his services.)

More clansmen joined the prince. So did two Lowlanders, old Gordon of Glenbuchat and Murray of Broughton who became his secretary. On 19 August Charles arrived at Glenfinnan, a narrow river valley in Lochaber. Until 4 p.m., there was no sign of Lochiel and his men. Then they arrived, fully armed.

The Duke of Atholl unfurled the royal standard which was blessed by the pessimistic 'Mr Hugh', Catholic bishop for the Highlands. The clansmen named it the *Bratach Bàn* – the White Banner. After this, King James's commission appointing Charles prince regent was read. He made 'a short but very Pathetick speech', in which he said he had always known he would find in the Highlands brave gentlemen fired with 'the noble example of their predecessors, and jealous of their own and their Country's honour, to join with him in so glorious an enterprise'.[6] He ordered brandy casks to be broached, for everybody to drink the health of James VIII.

Charles's timing could not have been better. Most of the Hanoverian army was in Flanders, with less than 4,000 of its troops (including garrisons) stationed in Scotland. Many Scots still detested the Union and few of the Whigs were ready to risk their lives for George II.

The prince stayed long enough at Glenfinnan for O'Sullivan – his only staff officer whom he promoted to colonel – to hand out what arms there were. From Glenfinnan, Charles went to Invergarry from where, on Murray of Broughton's advice, he led the little army – now about 1,200 strong – towards Edinburgh.

The enemy's first definite news that he had landed reached the Duke of Argyll on 6 August, sent by the Presbyterian minister at Ardnamurchan. Lieutenant-General Sir John Cope, who was King George's commander in Scotland, marched with 1,500 foot from Stirling towards Fort Augustus, intending to intercept the prince, but then learned the Highlanders were waiting in ambush at the Corrieyairack Pass. Aware that he risked another Killiecrankie, Cope withdrew to Aberdeen and shipped his men to Edinburgh, which he hoped to reach before Charles.

Stronger every day, the Jacobites entered the Lowlands unopposed. En route, the prince received a letter from Lord Lovat, asking to be made Lord Lieutenant of Inverness-shire and Duke of Fraser, and for permission to murder his neighbour Duncan Forbes of Culloden (with whom he had been on seemingly friendly terms since 1715). Charles sent Lovat a commission as lieutenant-general, but only a warrant to arrest Forbes.

The prince soon endeared himself to the Highlanders whose dress he wore – tartan doublet, trews and plaid. En route, at Lude House near Blair Atholl in Perthshire, he held a ball, calling wryly for 'This is no mine ain house' as the first reel, which he danced with zest. He marched on foot at the head of the army, eating the same rations (sometimes dry bread) and sleeping on straw, 'which encouraged prodigiously the men', says O'Sullivan. On 26 August, 'He marched that day at least five and twenty miles, with the cruellest rain that could be seen.'[7] When they waded across rivers, he waded too, ensuring there was a glass of gin for everyone on the far bank. He began to learn Gaelic and sing Gaelic songs.

On 4 September he entered Perth, ordering that his father be proclaimed. Here he was joined not only by Robertsons and MacGregors, but by grandees who included the Duke of Perth, Lord Ogilvy, Lord Strathallan, Oliphant of Gask and Lord George Murray. They were followed by Lord Elcho – son and heir to the Earl of Wemyss, a great Fifeshire landowner,

Described by Horace Walpole as 'a silly horse racing boy', the Duke of Perth has been dismissed as a lightweight. Yet, if not over intelligent or a natural soldier, and crippled (from being run over by a barrel as a child), he was a devout Catholic who saw loyalty to the Stuarts as part of his faith. After evading a Whig attempt to arrest him, he had raised his own regiment.

In contrast, a big, tall man, fifty but fit, a younger brother of Atholl, Lord George Murray had fought for King James in the Fifteen and the Nineteen, then made his peace with the Hanoverians and would become the Forty-Five's flawed mainspring. No one denies his bravery – before leading a charge he told his Highlanders, 'I do not ask you, my lads, to go before, but merely to follow me.' His elegant memoir, *Marches of the Highland Army*, portrays a reasonable, even engaging, human being (who pities a Swedish prisoner of the Jacobites because the Swede is a gentleman and speaks good Latin).

Yet his behaviour showed otherwise, that of a very difficult personality who was vain, touchy and tricky-tempered. He knew how to lead the rank and file, but not how to lead officers. Even his admiring aide-de-camp, the Chevalier de Johnstone, admits he had faults – 'proud, haughty, blunt, and imperious, he wished to have the exclusive ordering of everything'.[8]

At Perth Charles gave Lord George, the Duke of Perth and the Duke of Atholl joint command of his army, all three ranking as lieutenant-generals. Other appointments were O'Sullivan as adjutant-general and quarter-master general, and Sir Jean McDonnell as inspector-general of cavalry. This meant trouble since Murray did not care for Irishmen. Much worse, Lord George and Charles found they disliked each other.

On Wednesday 18 September 1745 the Jacobite army entered Edinburgh without a shot fired, only the castle holding out for Hanover. As Charles marched in, 'the demonstrations of joy that both gentle and simple showed him, can't be expressed, the roads were so crowded for near upon a mile before he came to the Canongate that he could hardly make his way'.[9] At midday, the Ross Herald proclaimed James VIII as king and Charles as prince regent at the Mercat Cross in the High Street.

'He was in the prime of youth, tall and handsome, of a fair complexion', is how a Whig eyewitness describes the prince. 'He had a light-coloured peri-wig with his own hair combed over the front; he wore the Highland dress, that is, a tartan short coat without the plaid, a blue bonnet on his head, and on his breast the star of the order of St Andrew.'[10]

When he entered Holyroodhouse, the first royal prince to do so since his grandfather in 1681, a gentleman emerged from the crowd, James Hepburn of Keith, who, drawing his sword and holding it high, walked before him in token of loyalty. An 'Associator', Keith had fought in the Fifteen and hated the Union because it 'made a gentleman of small fortune nobody'.[11] That night 'Ladies of Fashion came to kiss his hand.'

Meanwhile, O'Sullivan summoned the city authorities to a tavern in Writers' Close, warning that if a shot were fired from any window, he would burn the house down. Always the staff officer, he ordered them to ensure that bakers went on baking and butchers slaughtering, and see that the troops were given bread and beer – everything would be paid for. He had the city scoured for muskets, but only 1,200 were found, mostly of poor quality.[12]

Prestonpans

Next day, Charles learned that Cope had landed at Dunbar and was twenty miles away. In inimitable prose O'Sullivan recalls his address to the chiefs. '"Now gents" says he, "the sword is drawn, it won't be my fault, if I set it in the scabbard, before you be a free and happy people."'[13] Then Charles and his 2,400 Highlanders marched to meet Sir John.

Tacksmen and gentry in the front rank carried broadsword, targe and pistols. O'Sullivan had given Lochaber axes (supplied by Perth's bodyguard) to a handful of men, but some carried clubs or scythes on poles. Those who had muskets or fowling-pieces were untrained, with no idea of volley fire.

By contrast, Cope's army, who numbered about the same, were regulars though few had yet seen action. They included two regiments of dragoons led by the veteran Colonel James Gardiner. Sir John also had eight small cannon (1.5-pounders) and several mortars. An experienced commander, he occupied a strong position five miles from Edinburgh in flat, open country at Prestonpans – sometimes called Gledsmuir – near the village of Tranent, that was protected by a marsh on one flank, and by ponds, ditches or stone walls on the others.

However, under cover of darkness and thick mist the Jacobites crossed the marsh by a little known path, silently moving round it to face Cope's left, and then lay down in the stubble. When they rose to their feet at daybreak on the morning of 21 September, they were barely 200 yards away from their enemy.

Cope tried to regroup facing left, but did not have time. The Highlanders fired a single volley, then charged. 'The left, composed of the Camerons,

Stewarts of Appin and the Duke of Perth's Regiment which were almost all MacGregors, behaved most gloriously', says O'Sullivan, 'for they rushed in with such fury upon the enemy, after their first discharge, that they had not time to charge their cannon, and then the broadswords played their part, for with one stroke, arms and legs were cut off, and heads split to the shoulders, never such wounds were seen.'[14]

It was over in five minutes, the dragoons behind Sir John's infantry bolting like rabbits. Colonel Gardiner, who dismounted and fought with a half-pike in an attempt to rally them, was killed by a Lochaber axe. More than 300 government troops lay dead on the field, with 73 officers and nearly 1,500 men taken prisoner. Cope escaped with a handful of cavalry, to inspire the song 'Hey, Johnnie Cope, are ye wauking yet?' Only thirty of Charles's men had fallen.

Next day, the Jacobites marched back to Edinburgh in triumph, pipers playing 'When the King enjoys his Own again', brandishing swords and guns acquired on the battlefield, waving the enemy's colours. Behind them came captured cannon and prisoners, then carts with enemy wounded. The prince gave orders that the prisoners should be well treated, paroling their officers from captivity. Over 150 men joined Charles's army.

Yet there were signs of disunity. Murray had angrily countermanded O'Sullivan's decision to post an out-guard near Tranent before the battle so as to keep a close eye on the enemy, as well as his equally sensible placing of two battalions on the Edinburgh road in case Cope tried to break through to the city during the night. Nor, against the Irishman's advice, did he place marksmen in the steeple of Tranent village church.

37

Building an Army, Autumn 1745

I am here Adjutant-General, Inspector and all sorts of other
things ... Our army increases daily. We are expecting the Duke
of Atholl who is 3 days march away from us with two thousand
of his people.

Colonel O'Sullivan to Colonel Daniel O'Bryen,
6–7 October 1745[1]

Prestonpans was the spectacular victory the Cause needed. Recruits flooded
in. Of Scotland's strongholds only Edinburgh Castle and Stirling Castle and
the Highland forts remained in Whig hands, while many burghs stayed loyal
to George.

There is a mistaken belief that throughout the Forty-Five the Jacobite army
consisted exclusively of clansmen. In its entirety, it eventually numbered
6,750 Highlanders and 5,400 Lowlanders, with 830 Irish troops and 300
Englishmen.[2] Most of the Lowlanders came from Episcopalian areas such
as Aberdeenshire and Banff, 'Piskies' who saw a Presbyterian Kirk and a
German king as blasphemies – gentlemen, farmers, weavers, blacksmiths,
cobblers.

Nearly seventy and a frail asthmatic, the saintly, much respected Lord
Forbes of Pitsligo, a veteran of the Fifteen who was known as the 'oracle'
by Lowland gentry, had ridden all over Aberdeenshire asking other
Episcopalian lairds to rise for King James. (The Baron of Bradwardine
in Sir Walter Scott's *Waverley* is modelled on Pitsligo.) Having gathered
120 mounted men and 150 foot, he gave the order, 'Oh Lord, Thou knowest
our Cause is just. Gentlemen, march!' Arriving in Edinburgh on 8 October,
he found that Lords Balmerino, Kenmure, Kilmarnock, Nithsdale and
Ogilvy had followed his example.

The proportion of Scots who came out was less than in 1715 and fewer clans rose – eighteen instead of twenty-six – which did not necessarily mean a dramatic decline in support. Far more than those who came out wanted 'the auld Stuarts back again', if only because their return would restore Scotland's freedom, while, as in England, there was anger at Whig corruption.

Contemporary estimates of support for a Restoration are generally dubious. However, that by the Presbyterian divine Alexander Carlyle, a staunch Whig who as a young man fought as a volunteer for Cope at Prestonpans (and whom Scott thought 'a shrewd old carle'), is plausible. He recalls that, 'The Commons in General, as well as two-thirds of the Gentry at that period, had no aversion to the Family of Stuart, and could their Religion have been Secur'd, would have been very glad to see them on the Throne again.'[3]

Many who stayed at home did so because earlier attempts had failed. Some landowners stopped their eldest son and heir from embarking on such a dangerous gamble, but sent a younger son, although sometimes the elder insisted on going instead. Ever since 1715 there had been two Dukes of Atholl, one Hanoverian and the other Jacobite, as a result of this policy. In the Hebrides, MacLeod of Raasay joined after handing over his estate to his heir to avoid forfeiture in case of defeat.

Although scarcely devoted to the Hanoverians, on the whole Presbyterians, who formed the majority of Lowlanders besides including many Highlanders, tended to be Whigs. This was because a Jacobite victory would end the Kirk's dominance and bring in prelacy and Popish liturgy. Nevertheless, a surprising number fought for Charles. (Some regiments had Presbyterian as well as Catholic and Episcopalian chaplains.)

Morale soared on 7 October when a French ship reached Montrose, followed by three others soon after. On board were 2,500 French army muskets, six 'Swedish' light cannon, £5,000 in gold coin and the Marquis d'Éguilles who was the unofficial French ambassador. The ships also brought specialist officers from the Irish Brigade – notably Colonel Grante, a gunnery expert, and the cavalryman Major Baggot.

On 13 October Louis XV signed the Treaty of Fontainebleau with James, formally recognising him as King of Scots.

During the six weeks that Charles occupied Edinburgh, the city became a capital again, just as Dublin had in 1689. Even Whigs were delighted when as prince regent he dissolved the 'Pretended Union' with England. Meanwhile, George Kelly and Sir James Steuart of Coltness went to beg France to send regular troops as soon as possible.

In his novel *Waverley*, Scott describes balls and receptions in 'the long-deserted halls of the Scottish palace'. However, when some ladies organised a ball at Holyrood, the prince looked in only briefly, complimented them on their dancing, and said 'I have now another air to dance – until that be finished I'll dance no other.' O'Sullivan remembered his sleeping on the ground among the troops, never more than four hours, spending the day drilling and exercising them. He comments, 'It is very strange that a Prince of that age who really liked dancing and fowling, never thought of any pleasures, and was as retired as a man of sixty.'[4]

This must be qualified. We know from Lord Elcho that Charles dined in public every day before reviewing his army, after which he received 'ladies of fashion'. He also supped in public, with music, and often there was a ball even if he was absent. He found time to sit for Allan Ramsay who was summoned to paint him at Holyrood, producing a likeness with a fresh young face. Intended for use as an official portrait after the Restoration, this was immediately engraved by Robert Strange. It was only rediscovered in 2016, still in the possession of Lord Elcho's family.[5]

At first Charles's council met in Holyrood at nine o'clock every morning. It consisted of the Dukes of Perth and Atholl, Lord George Murray, Lords Pitsligo, Nairn, Ogilvy and Elcho, Lord Lewis Gordon, the clan chiefs and Mr Secretary Murray, with Sheridan and O'Sullivan. Then, angered by Perth's questions, Lord George demanded the exclusion of Catholics (by which he meant the dukes, Sheridan and O'Sullivan) from the council, arguing that England would be shocked to learn there were 'Papists' among the Prince's advisers.

Charles disagreed, pointing out that not just Perth but several of the clan chiefs were Catholics, while O'Sullivan was 'the only military man in the army, and that everybody was satisfied with [him]'.[6] After this, the council met only on urgent matters. The decision how and when to invade England was postponed until the troops had become a proper army and there were more recruits.

After the rising, Lord George blackened O'Sullivan's name so effectively that he was not rehabilitated until 1996 when Stuart Reid demonstrated that he was actually the better soldier of the two. Reid's view is shared by Murray Pittock, one of the most authoritative of modern Jacobite scholars.

David Morier's painting, *An Incident in the Rebellion of 1745*, portrays wild clansmen with broadswords or Lochaber axes. Yet although the Highland charge was still used to break enemy formations, after Prestonpans most of Charles's men carried a 'Brown Bess' musket and bayonet, later replaced by French or Spanish muskets that fired a 16.5mm ball.

During their time at Edinburgh they received training in drill, battle-field manoeuvres and musketry – volley firing by ranks – from the few Scots who had been regular officers and one or two regulars from the Irish Brigade.

'Somebody – almost certainly one of the Irish officers – organised the Jacobite forces of the '45 into the standing Highland and Lowland Divisions', explains the Sandhurst historian Christopher Duffy, who be-lieves the 'higher organisation' of Charles's army was probably the most advanced in Europe and that whoever was responsible must have been famil-iar with the current debate on the subject in France. It gave a tremendous operational advantage, enabling rapid troop movement, since instead of having to issue orders to each regiment, the commander-in-chief need only deal with the two divisions. These 'moved as coherent entities along separate axes', converging on a chosen objective where they joined up – bewildering opponents.[7] It is hard to think of anyone other than O'Sullivan who could have been the architect.

Thirteen infantry regiments were formed, many of them only a single battalion, although some were four. Rejecting O'Sullivan's proposal for a more logical organisation, Highland chiefs insisted on a regiment for each clan (such as Lochiel's or MacDonald of Keppoch's), all with two captains, two lieutenants and two ensigns. 'Gentlemen privates' – tacksmen or clan gentry who fought in the front rank – received double pay. Discipline was rudimentary. Even so, regimental adjutants daily reported the men's numbers and condition to headquarters, receiving the new password.

To avoid confusion, Lowland regiments wore Highland dress with blue bonnets, the regiment raised by Lord Ogilvy in Forfarshire wearing a red and black tartan, but trews instead of the kilt. Everybody from the prince to the humblest private sported a white cockade in his bonnet. Pay was 6d a day for privates, half-a-crown for captains.

'Colonel John Roy Stewart's Edinburgh Regiment' (mainly Perthshire men), was named after its swashbuckling colonel from Strathspey – the model for Robert Louis Stevenson's Alan Breck in *Kidnapped* – who had served in the Scots Greys as an NCO and then as a captain of grenadiers in the Royal Ecossais at Fontenoy. The Irish possessed no monopoly of fine Gaelic poets, for John Roy wrote verse in Scots Gaelic that gives a fascinating insight into a Jacobite soldier's mind.

Daunting staffwork was involved in assembling an army. Troops had to be fed, billeted and paid, weapons and ammunition, wagons and horses provided, duties alloted, rosters issued. The one man with the skills to organise this was O'Sullivan, which was why Charles called him the army's 'only military man'. In his narrative, O'Sullivan mentions making an inventory of munitions, tents and vehicles captured at Prestonpans, buying horses and tents, with shoes and food cannisters for each man.

Charles constantly asked advice from O'Sullivan, who became his unofficial chief-of-staff. To avoid upsetting the Scots, the prince received his words in secret, later pretending it was his own opinion.[8] Guessing how much he listened to the Irishman, Lord George grew increasingly angry, trying several times to oust him as quarter-master general. He failed mostly because only O'Sullivan knew anything about staffwork.[9]

But building this war machine from scratch, and maintaining it, needed cash. The £4,000 Charles brought from France was soon spent. So was £5,500 (much of it in bank notes) levied on a resentful Glasgow by Charles's treasurer John Hay of Restalrig, the £5,000 landed at Montrose, £4,000 in Cope's captured military chest and 1,500 guineas lent by Lord Elcho. A half-crown levy on every pound sterling of Edinburgh rents was not going to be easy to extract. The situation was made worse by both the Bank of Scotland and the Royal Bank of Scotland having withdrawn as many bank notes from circulation as possible

In areas under their control, the prince's supporters ordered people pay their taxes to King James instead of George, but revenue from this source would obviously be slow to come in. The solution was found by Mr Secretary Murray.

Murray ordered the cashier of the Royal Bank of Scotland, John Campbell – a Breadalbane, not an Argyll, Campbell – to exhange the bank notes from Glasgow into gold and silver, or else the effects of the bank's directors and managers would be seized. The cashier explained that all the bank's coin and specie had been moved to the castle, which still held out for King George. What not even Murray seems to have understood was that Campbell was a secret and very canny Jacobite who never revealed his political sympathies.

Under a white flag of truce, the cashier went up to the castle and told the governor that, if it was to survive, his bank must have coin to continue doing its ordinary day-to-day business. Seeing no harm, the governor allowed him to withdraw well over £7,000 in gold. Discreetly, this went into the prince regent's war chest, enabling him to invade England.[10]

James II welcomed to St Germain-en-Laye in January 1689 by Louis XIV, who gave him the château for his residence and a large pension. His son, the Duke of Berwick, is at his left. By Nicholas Langlois. (Bibliothèque Nationale de France)

The dynamic James Graham of Claverhouse, Viscount Dundee ('Bonnie Dundee'), who routed the Williamite General Mackay at Killiecrankie but was killed at the moment of victory. By the Scots miniaturist David Paton. (National Galleries Scotland)

'Fighting Dick' Talbot from Co. Kildare, the Duke of Tyrconnell, who as a young man had plotted to murder Cromwell after escaping from the massacre at Drogheda, and who in 1689 raised Ireland for King James. By François de Troy. (© National Portrait Gallery, London)

The heroic Patrick Sarsfield, Earl of Lucan. A grandson of Rory O'More (one of the leaders of the Irish rising of 1641), Sarsfield became a cavalry general who during the War of the Two Kings personified Irish Jacobitism. Attributed to Hyacinthe Rigaud (1659–1743). (NGI.4166, National Gallery of Ireland Collection. Photo © National Gallery of Ireland)

Mary of Modena, James II's queen, whose political skills as regent for her son James III and considerable powers of persuasion have been under estimated by historians. After a portrait by Kneller. (© National Portrait Gallery, London)

Lord George Murray, 'out' in the Fifteen and the Nineteen as well as the Forty-Five. He was a brave but unbalanced commander whose overbearing arrogance hampered the Jacobite high command during 1745–46. Artist unknown.

A great priest politician, Dr Francis Atterbury, the High Church Bishop Rochester and Dean of Westminster who during 1721–22 organised a little-known but potentially formidable plot to seize London and restore the Stuarts. After a portrait by Kneller. (© National Portrait Gallery, London)

Flora Macdonald saved Prince Charles by disguising him as an Irish maid, 'Betty Burke'. Under house arrest in London, she holds handcuffs in token of her captivity. After a portrait of 1747 by J. Markuin. (National Galleries Scotland)

Wrongly suspected of spying for George II, poor Clementina Walkinshaw (named after Queen Clementina) was Prince Charles's ill-treated mistress for eight years, shown here in 1760 aged forty at the end of their unhappy affair. Artist unknown. (ART Collection/ Alamy Stock Photo)

Dr William King, Master of St Mary Hall, Oxford, a Jacobite agent who at the opening of the Radcliffe Camera in 1748 used amid wild applause the word *redeat* ('may he return') six times, referring to Charles – who visited him in London in 1750. Later, he turned against the prince. After a portrait by Thomas Hudson.

Although he did not fight for Prince Charles in the Forty-five as sometimes suggested, Dr Samuel Johnson – in his day England's foremost man of letters – always remained a discreet Jacobite who distinguished between George III as *de facto* king and Charles III as *de jure* king. By Sir Joshua Reynolds. (Classic Image/ Alamy Stock Photo)

Robert Burns's 'Bonnie Lass of Albany' – Charles's daughter by Clementina Walkinshaw, Charlotte, whom he legitimised and created Duchess of Albany. She nursed him devotedly during his last years. By Hugh Douglas Hamilton. (ART Collection/ Alamy Stock Photo)

38

Charles Invades England, Winter 1745

Our cavalry can't be here before February and the Pretender
may be crowned at Westminster by that time.

Duke of Richmond, 5 December 1745[1]

The next move was finally decided at a meeting of the prince's council at
Holyrood on the night of 30 October.

Charles wanted to invade north eastern England, arguing that Marshal
Wade's troops, who had just returned from Flanders, would reach Newcastle
only a little before the Jacobite army and, exhausted by their long march
north, should be easy to defeat. Capturing Newcastle would cut off London's
coal supplies, causing panic in the capital. It would also encourage English
Jacobites to join – there were many recusants in Northumberland and northern Yorkshire.

Lord George disagreed, saying they must on no account risk a battle –
defeat meant ruin, with at best a very difficult retreat. Instead, he wanted
to build up their position in Scotland and wait until the French landed.
However, this would give the enemy time to bring back still more troops
from Flanders.

In the end, the council agreed by one vote to invade England, but by way
of Carlisle. The chiefs thought the mountainous Lake District better suited
for Highland tactics, while it would let English supporters join without fear
of interception. Knowing the clansmen might desert if they thought their
chiefs unwilling, Charles reluctantly accepted their opinion.[2]

A fortnight earlier he had written to his father, 'As matters stand, I must
either conquer or perish in a little while.' He added that he would have nearly

8,000 foot and 300 cavalry. What he did not say was that he needed to move fast – he was running out of money to pay them. However, he still hoped for reinforcements from France while, aware of the English Jacobites' support for the previous year's abortive invasion, he was confident his numbers would double when he crossed the border, especially in Catholic areas.

Before leaving Edinburgh, the prince issued a proclamation, asking if people were better off because of his family's fifty-seven year exile? He targeted Whig corruption. Why had nothing been done about parliamentary abuses – venal placemen, penal laws? As soon as King James was restored, these would be dealt with by a free parliament.

The army that set out to conquer England on 31 October 1745 was a little over 5,000 infantry with about 450 cavalry. At least a third of the foot and an even greater proportion of the horse were Lowlanders.

The new divisional structure made possible a two-pronged invasion. Under the joint command of Atholl and Perth, the Lowland Division went westward via Peebles, Moffat and Lockerbie with the artillery and provision wagons. Charles and Lord George led the Highland Division south through Roxburghshire, to link up with the slower Lowlanders just north of Carlisle on 9 November, the timing planned by O'Sullivan who provided march tables. (The Highlanders could trot like ponies.)

The object was to make Marshal Wade think they were aiming at Newcastle. Undeceived, Wade sent his troops west to Morpeth, but heavy snow forced them back. The invaders were helped by the terror they inspired. 'Gentlemen, I suppose you have done with your murdering today', an old lady enquired of officers quartered at her house. 'I should be glad to know when the ravishing begins.'[3]

When they invaded Carlisle on 13 November it was vile weather, O'Sullivan recalling that on parade he could hardly see his horse's ears through the fog. However, the garrison, local militia, were faint-hearted. After four days the city capitulated, as did the castle when Charles refused to grant terms for the citizens unless it did so. In their robes, the mayor and the aldermen presented the keys of the city to him on their knees, then proclaimed James III in the market place.

This success resulted in histrionics by Lord George, who resigned as an army commander because Perth had been allowed to direct the siege, but graciously accepted reinstatement. Despite his gallantry in battle he was a liability. His arrogance made it hard for him to work with others while as a pessimist he was the opposite of Charles, always too prone to optimism.

O'Sullivan says the Prince 'went always a foot ... notwithstanding the rigor of the season we were in, he never came to his lodgings until he saw the guards posted, and the men quartered, and to cause no jealousy marched alternatively at the head of each regiment; every man had access to him ... He was never heard to say a rash word to any man, praised most graciously those that served well, and treated very mildly those that did not.'[4]

A Lancashire gentleman, John Daniel, recalled 'the brave Prince marching at their head, like Cyrus or a Trojan hero'. Daniel was drinking their health at a tavern when the Duke of Perth walked in and invited him to become an ensign in the Perth regiment. He accepted with alacrity, recruiting forty men.[5]

Yet Charles's commanders grew increasingly worried at the lack of recruits. Although the little army was cheered as it entered Preston, bells pealing, with cries of 'God bless the King and the Prince!', only sixty Preston men joined – even though Mr David Morgan from Merthyr-Tydfil, who was one of the Duke of Beaufort's lawyers, rode in to do so accompanied by two recusant gentlemen from Herefordshire. The prince insisted that large numbers would enlist as soon as they reached Manchester.

He failed to appreciate that unlike Scots the English did not see the Union as a threat to survival as a nation or that surveillance in England was closer than in Scotland. English Jacobites remembered the disembowelments after the Fifteen, the confiscated estates. Few were ready to risk their lives without support from a substantial force of foreign regulars.

Caution was evident even at Manchester, which was famous for loyalty to the Stuarts. A sergeant went ahead to drum up recruits for the 'yellow-haired laddie', accompanied by a girlfriend and a drummer-boy. When they arrived, a hostile crowd surrounded them, but they were rescued by other Mancunians.[6] The army followed next day, 29 November, amid cheering and pealing bells. That evening houses were illuminated in rejoicing. Yet only 200 from a population of 20,000 joined a new 'Manchester Regiment', instead of the 1,500 expected by Charles.

Like the Lowlanders, the regiment wore tartan. Its colonel, Francis Towneley, once a captain in the French army, was a recusant whose brother had fought for Tom Forster at Preston. The other senior officers were Catholics too, but junior officers were High Churchmen or nonjurors. They included young 'Jemmy' Dawson, who had just left St John's College,

Cambridge, without a degree and dared not tell his father, and Thomas Sydall, a wigmaker whose Jacobite father had been executed in 1716. As for rank and file, 'The typical sergeant or private in the Manchester Regiment was a native Lancastrian artisan, Roman Catholic in religion, about twenty years old', Paul Kléber Monod tells us. 'The younger soldiers in the regiment may have been seeking adventure or trying to escape from the miseries of apprenticeship.' [7]

The march south continued. Given flexibility by O'Sullivan's two-divisional structure, Murray used the fast moving Highland Division to trick Cumberland's scouts into thinking the prince meant to cross the River Mersey en route for Wales. The feint sent the duke on a wild goose chase to block the ford, while the Lowlanders crossed the Mersey higher up. The Highlanders then rejoined Charles. Lord George has been much praised for this manoeuvre, but it would have been impossible without O'Sullivan's organisation.

At 11 a.m. on 4 December, Charles's cavalry, in blue coats faced with red and scarlet waistcoats laced with gold, rode into Derby. They had met no opposition, the Derbyshire Yeomanry having mistaken a herd of cattle for them and fled. The infantry arrived towards 4 p.m., 'six or eight abreast, with about eight standards, most of them white flags and a red cross; their bagpipers playing as they marched along'. The bridges being down they had forded the Mersey, led by the prince although the water rose to his middle.

Charles himself arrived in the dusk, on foot as usual, and was escorted by his men to lodgings at Exeter House, a mansion in Full Street, after he had ensured they were given beer, bread and cheese, and straw. That evening he discussed whether to wear Highland dress when entering London.

Meanwhile, Kilmarnock's Horse Grenadiers had caught a Whig spy, Captain Weir, who alarmed his captors by producing a newspaper with details of Cumberland's army. They learned that the duke was in hot pursuit and would soon reach Lichfield.

Next day, the prince held a council at the Virgin's Inn. Supported by the Duke of Perth and Lord Nairn, Charles proposed they continue their advance on London which was only four days march away. David Morgan told the council there were just 3,000 troops between their army and the capital – dragoons and undisciplined militia.

Suddenly a gentleman entered the council chamber to report that General Ligonier was waiting for them on the road to Northampton with 9,000 regulars. No such force existed – the gentleman, 'Captain Williams', was a Whig agent, an Irish pimp and card sharp whose true name was Bradstreet. However, the council believed him. 'That fellow will do me more harm than all the Elector's army!' shouted Charles, ordering him to be thrown out.

Lord George told the prince, 'it was the opinion of Every body present that the Scots had now done all that could be Expected of them', recalls Lord Elcho. 'The Counties through which the Army had pass'd had Seemed much more Enemies than friends to his Cause, that their [sic] was no French Landed in England, and that if there was any party in England for him, it was very odd that they had never so much as Either sent him money or intelligence or the least advice what to do.'

Murray argued that even if the prince's army evaded Ligonier and defeated Cumberland, they would lose men and then have to deal with a Hanoverian army of 7,000 troops when they reached London. He added, '4,500 Scots had never thought of putting a King upon the English Throne by themselves'.[8] (The true figure was nearer 6,000.)

Charles replied they would reach London before Cumberland and be warmly welcomed. In any case, he had letters proving the French were on the way. Since November they had been assembling troops and transports at Calais and Boulogne. King Louis's envoy, the Marquis d'Éguilles – so enthusiastic for the cause that he wore Highland dress – bore the prince out, offering to be shot if they did not land within a fortnight. But there was no recent communication with France and the council did not realise they were telling the truth.

Murray and the Scottish chiefs, who had lost their nerve, insisted on turning back. Even O'Sullivan thought it the only possible decision 'according to all the rules of war, and prudence'. He had suggested doing so at Manchester, 'finding that not a man of any consequence appeared'. (So much for charges of sycophancy on his part.) He felt sorry for the prince: 'I never saw anybody so concerned as he was for this disappointment, nor never saw him take anything after so much to heart.'[9]

Only Perth, Atholl and Clanranald were in favour of going on. That evening, in front of several officers, Atholl called his brother Lord George 'the most infamous of traitors'. That great historian of Jacobitism, Eveline Cruickshanks, believes the chiefs 'threw in their hands when they held most of the trump cards', a mistake that she attributes to 'a narrow kind of Scottish nationalism', citing the Chevalier de Johnstone's wish for a 'national war' between England and Scotland.[10]

'After this, I know that I have an army that I cannot command any farther than the chief officers please, and, therefore, if you are all resolved upon it, I must yield,' Prince Charles told them furiously. 'But I take God to witness that it is with the greatest reluctance, and that I wash my hands of the fatal consequences.'

'It is all over, we shall never come again,' moaned old Sir Thomas Sheridan. Sir Jean MacDonnell told an embarrassed Lochiel, 'if we are to perish, it were better to do so with our faces to London than to Scotland'.[11] The Irishmen knew the Scots could never achieve an independent Scotland. So did Charles, who in any case wanted all three kingdoms.

The council's assessment of the situation seemed logical, yet there were some good arguments for marching south, even if it would be a gamble. One was the speed of the Jacobite army, able to cover an astonishing amount of ground in only a few days. Another was the panic in London, which gave Charles a potent psychological advantage.

Moreover, help was coming from France, as George Kelly reported in a letter of 1 December to Sir Thomas Sheridan. (Kelly had reached Paris safely, despite enemy agents trying to seize him in the Netherlands.) He reports that the Earl Marischal and Lord Clancarty are taken very seriously indeed at the French court, Lord Bulkeley hopes to raise supporters in Wales and Lord Clare may go to Scotland. Best of all, 12,000 Irish troops commanded by the Duc de Richelieu have received orders to sail for Kent on 14 December.

The council might also have decided differently had they been able to read Cumberland's mind. A dispatch of 5 December from the Duke of Richmond (who was his second-in-command) shows that Cumberland thought Prince Charles could reach London first. In the same dispatch Richmond declared, 'the rebels will certainly be two days march before us'.

In Murray Pittock's view, Charles's strategy 'was the right one; to take London as rapidly as possible'. After retreat was forced on him, 'there was no real strategy left, only tactics'.[12] Early on 6 December, his army began its march back to Scotland. Two days later a letter arrived from Lord Barrymore and Sir Watkin Williams-Wynn. It informed the prince that they were ready to join him at London with what forces they could muster or else to rise in their own area – whichever he wanted.

39

The Forty-Five behind the Lines

Look down on us, poor Whigs, O Lord,
  For we are full of trouble.

Bishop Forbes, *The Lyon in Mourning*[1]

Eveline Cruickshanks and Paul Kléber Monod have shown how wide support was for Charles in England during the Forty-Five. There was even greater enthusiasm in Ireland. Had the French landed, large numbers would have joined him in both countries.

Hanoverian England's reaction to Sir John Cope's defeat at Prestonpans was one of dismay, but not of fear as it had no doubt that regular troops would soon chase the Highlanders back to their mountains. In his interminable *Night Thoughts*, Edward Young (a favourite poet of Frederick, Prince of Wales) referred scornfully in October 1745 to a 'Pope-bred Princeling' who led 'ragged Ruffians of the North'.[2] Horace Walpole was equally sure that such 'banditti' could never conquer a kingdom – 'raw ragamuffins'.

Later, Walpole was not so certain, 'Now comes the Pretender's boy, and promises all my comfortable apartments in the Exchequer and Custom-house to some forlorn Irish peer, who chooses to remove his pride and poverty out of some large unfurnished gallery at St Germain's', he wrote jokingly but uneasily. 'I shall wonderfully dislike being a loyal sufferer in a thread-bare coat, and shivering in the ante-chamber at Hanover, or reduced to teach Latin and English to the young princes at Copenhagen . . . Will you ever write to me at my garret at Heerenhausen?'

On 21 October, Walpole wrote still more uneasily to Horace Mann that in London the previous night, 'information was given of an intended insurrection and massacre by the Papists; all the Guards were ordered out, and the Tower shut at seven'. Shortage of beef due to a widespread cattle murrain was attributed to Catholics poisoning the wells as part of the Jacobite war effort. Soon Walpole was groaning, 'I still fear the rebels beyond my reason'.

Any pretence at confidence vanished when on 6 December (a date later known to the Jacobites as 'Black Friday') a report reached London of Charles's arrival at Derby, only 120 miles away, and that he had outmaneouvred Cumberland and was on his way south. Henry Fielding, a vociferous anti-Jacobite, says in his newspaper *The True Patriot*, that 'when the Highlanders, by a most incredible march, got between the duke's army and the metropolis, they struck a terror into it scarce to be credited'.

Lord Chancellor Hardwicke informed his brother, who was with the Duke of Cumberland's army, that the capital had been panic stricken by the thought of the prince slipping past Cumberland as he had Wade and reaching London. 'Our alarm was much increased by the news of a large embarkation at Dunkirk, which was intended for the south and in concert with the Young Pretender to land near the capital.'[3]

Tobias Smollett tells us that Whig citizens were terrified of a revolution – the entire Establishment was in danger of being overthrown. Learning that the French invasion was about to sail, they feared 'an insurrection of the Roman Catholicks, and other friends of the House of Stuart'. Above all, they dreaded the Highlanders who were only four days' march away, their faces showing 'the plainest marks of horror and despair'. In contrast, 'Jacobites were elevated to an insolence of hope, which they were at no pains to conceal.'[4]

At night, proclamations in the name of the 'Prince Regent' were posted all over the capital, increasing the terror. Shops and playhouses were shut, business at a standstill. There was a run on the banks on 6 December (although it is not true that they delayed it by paying out in red-hot sixpences). Captain Nagle of Lally's Regiment, who was there, reported that should the prince's army reach London or the French land, many secret Jacobites would declare for him.

George, who had returned from Hanover, was described by his prime minister, Henry Pelham, as 'frightened yet impracticable'. There were false rumours, spread by Jacobites, that his bags were on board the royal yacht, lying at anchor in the Thames in readiness for his flight home to Germany. Walpole thought that should Charles look like winning, George might give up the Crown if he could keep Hanover.

In the north, people believed the Highlanders would murder, rape and burn. There were fears of cannibalism. At Carlisle, the prince had found a child of seven hiding under his bed. The mother begged him to spare it – she thought it would be roasted on the spit as there was nothing else in the house to eat.

Hardwicke told his brother 'The same terror [as in the capital] but in a higher degree (as the strength to resist was less) has spread itself through all parts of the kingdom and to every great town, on every road which it was possible for the rebels to take on their way to London.' 'Loyal associations' sprang up to raise money for recruiting extra troops – Tories who did not join were arrested. In *Tom Jones*, Fielding recalls wild suspicions 'when the late rebellion was at its highest'.

While Charles was invading England, Brigadier-General Lally, a hero of Fontenoy, crossed over to Sussex in a smuggler's boat. Disguised as a sailor, he enlisted a force of 'free traders' who called themselves 'Prince Charles's Volunteers', wore a red uniform and were ready to fight for the Cause when the French landed. They never saw action, but rumours of their existence added to the terror.[5]

'Roman Catholick' gentry were rounded up, such as the blameless Thomas Weld of Lulworth Castle in Dorset. Suspicions about Catholic neighbours were not always unjustified, however – in Yorkshire two recusant squires, Tempest of Broughton and Scrope of Danby, had each purchased fifty brace of horse pistols. Mr Harry Wells of Little Somborne in Hampshire, who maintained a Jesuit 'mission' on his estate, was prosecuted for drinking a toast in a Winchester tavern. It ran,

> A health to him that was turn'd out;
> Not to him that turn'd him out.
> And the Devil turn him inside out,
> That will not put this health about.[6]

Some Catholics joined loyal associations to avoid prison, the ninth Duke of Norfolk attending a royal levée at St James's to pretend he loved the Hanover family, although secretly he remained a Jacobite until his death in 1777.

In Scotland, many burghs stayed loyal to Hanover, Edinburgh reverting as soon as the prince marched out. Lieutenant-General Roger Handasyde, who arrived there on 14 November, only a week after Charles crossed the border into England, had no difficulty in recruiting an Edinburgh regiment to fight for King George, or in raising militia at Glasgow, Paisley and Renfrew, but they amounted to a mere 1,700 foot and 500 horse.

Charles failed to recognise what a handicap it was for him to be a Catholic. He did not convert because he saw no need, the Palazzo del Re's nonjuror chaplains having neglected to tell him about English and Scots fear of Catholics. Had he accepted the Prayer Book he would have disarmed many enemies. His religion did not matter so much in areas where Episcopalians were strong – Aberdeenshire, Banffshire, Kincardineshire, Atholl and Eastern Perthshire – yet even they disliked Popery.

It is easy to forget that many Highlanders were Whigs, their strongholds being Inverary and Inverness. The Campbells, who by now had become farmers rather than cattle raiders, formed themselves into the Argyll Militia, routing MacGregor of Glengyle when he threatened them. MacKays, MacLeods, Munroes and Grants likewise supported George, but contributed little. MacDonald of Sleat and MacLeod of Dunvegan were special cases. They had kidnapped young men, selling them as indentured labour to American or Caribbean planters (like David Balfour, the hero of Stevenson's *Kidnapped*), which the Whig government overlooked in return for their support. Convinced Jacobites, these two powerful chiefs would otherwise have joined Charles.[7]

His one really formidable opponent in Scotland was Duncan Forbes of Culloden, Lord President of the Court of Session and the country's senior legal officer, who did his best to organise support for George among his long cultivated network. Yet Forbes's only reliable ally, the Earl of Loudon, proved hopelessly inept. Occupying Inverness in December, Loudon arrested old Lord Lovat, who, despite being infirm, escaped on a ghillie's back to raise the Frasers for Charles. When Loudon sent 500 MacLeods to capture Aberdeen, they were easily routed by Lord Lewis Gordon.

Aberdeen, an Episcopalian stronghold, stayed firmly loyal to the Stuarts until Charles evacuated the city at the end of February 1746. Fittingly, this was the birthplace of the hero in the Jacobite song 'The White Cockade':

> But aye the thing that blinds my e'e
> Is the white cockade aboon the brae

Its stirring tune became the Jacobite battle march, played menacingly on pipes and drums during the Highlanders' charge.

The Forty-Five in Ireland

One morning in autumn 1745 an Anglican bishop burst into the bedroom of the viceroy, the Earl of Chesterfield, at Dublin Castle, shouting, 'The Papists are all up!' 'I am not surprised at it, my lord', replied the viceroy. 'Why, it is ten o'clock – I should have been too, had I not overslept myself.'

Chesterfield did not anticipate a Jacobite rising in Ireland. He treated Catholics tactfully, but warned that if they rose, 'I will be worse than Cromwell',[8] offering a reward for Charles's capture.

Yet the Hanoverian loyalty of Lord Chesterfield, a professional cynic, may not always have been so unwavering. In 1740, five years before becoming viceroy, he had gone secretly to Avignon, for a meeting with the arch-Jacobite Duke of Ormonde, who lived there in pleasant retirement with his 'ladies'. Neither Chesterfield nor Ormonde, who died in November 1745, has left any record of what they discussed, but one cannot rule out a Restoration.

When during the crisis the beautiful Miss Ambrose, called the 'dangerous Papist' and well known to be a Jacobite, appeared at a Dublin Castle reception dressed in orange, Chesterfield merely asked her

Tell me, Ambrose, where's the jest
Of wearing Orange on the breast,
When, underneath, that bosom shows
The whiteness of the rebel rose?[9]

The Ascendancy's terror

The presence of Irish officers in Scotland did not go unnoticed in Ireland, or that others were spying in England. No one watched Charles's progress more fearfully than the Ascendancy, which equated Highlanders with Raparees. Far from sharing the viceroy's serenity, the Dublin Parliament decreed the death penalty for any Irish Brigade officer who came home, while the Lord Mayor of Dublin issued a proclamation offering £50,000 'for apprehending the Pretender and his Eldest Son, or either of them that shall attempt to land in Ireland'. Pipers were banned – singing 'The White Cockade' became a criminal offence.

As in England, a Protestant Association was formed, pledging loyalty to George, while several regiments of militia were raised. In October the viceroy reviewed 4,000 of them, horse and foot, at a parade on St Stephen's Green. Rumours spread – Lally and two officers of Dillon's had been seen in

Connacht, troops from the Brigade were going to land on the Antrim coast The spy Bradstreet reported how at Derby he had heard Jacobite leaders talk of sending forty agents to western Ireland.

In reality, weakened by a famine that had killed nearly half a million in 1740–1 and held down by strong garrisons, strategically sited, Catholic Ireland had no plans for a rising. 'The roads [were] spread with dead and dying bodies', an eyewitness recalled of 1741, 'with mankind the colour of the docks and nettles which they fed on; two or three, sometimes more on a car going to the grave for want of bearers to carry them, and many buried in the fields and ditches where they perished.'

Even so, her people were thrilled by the advent of Prince Charles, as Irish poets demonstrated. Piaras Mac Gearailt wrote a tribute to the prince, *Rosc Catha na Mumhan* (Battle Cry of Munster), sung to a stirring tune that would have made a fine national anthem. In another poem he refers to Charles as *Mo léoghan lannach láidir* (My strong brave lion).[10]

The mood of Whigs everywhere changed wonderfully, however, when Charles and his army turned back from Derby. Horace Walpole wrote smugly on 9 December, 'the spirit against the rebels increases every day ... here in London, the aversion to them is amazing'. At playhouses in all three capitals – after the scare was safely over – Whig audiences sang fervently 'God Save the King!', which they had stolen from the Jacobites. No less ironically, it was a version rearranged by a Catholic, Thomas Arne.

40

Withdrawal to Scotland, Winter 1745

Rather than go back, I would wish to be twenty feet under ground

Prince Charles before leaving Derby

Although the decision to go back to Scotland doomed the Honest Cause, its army's fighting retreat was a fine achievement during which, plodding through snow and slush, they turned and savaged their pursuers.

Leaving Derby on 6 December, instead of marching on foot at their head Charles rode a horse among them, sunk in gloom. His troops were equally cast down, if few deserted – they knew they would be lynched by a Whig mob before reaching Scotland. David Morgan confided in Sir John MacDonnell that he was sure the cause was lost and left for Wales (only to be arrested en route). Travelling the way they had come, the army was greeted with sullen hostility, even by an occasional bullet.

The men recovered their spirits, believing they were going home to build a free Scotland. Charles revived, too. At Lancaster he told Murray it was time to turn and fight Cumberland, who with only half his troops and not enough infantry was outnumbered. Arguing that there was no suitable ground, Lord George refused – missing a good chance of a Jacobite victory.

'We had the cruellest rain that day, that ever I saw, we had several torrents to pass', is how O'Sullivan recalls leaving Kendal. 'The Prince was always a foot, and forded those torrents as the men did, never would get a' horse-back, and if it was not for the way he acted that day, I verily believe we could not keep half our men together; but not one went off, nor stayed behind – only those that were really sick or old.'[1]

The prince easily evaded Wade's advance guard under General Oglethorpe, who was strangely dilatory in pursuit. Afterwards, a furious Cumberland had Oglethrope (a closet Jacobite) court-martialled and although acquitted he never received another command. However, the duke himself began to snap at Charles's heels. On 18 December, after leaving the tiny town of Shap high up on the fells, the Jacobites captured two enemy troopers who told them Cumberland was just a mile behind, with '4,000 horse'.

Murray sent word to the prince, who had gone ahead with the main body of the army, that here was a chance to give Cumberland a nasty surprise. Charles disagreed, merely sending a handful of reinforcements.

Just after sunset, dismounting in the snow, 300 enemy dragoons took up position behind dry-stone walls on the top of Thrimby Hill near Clifton village and began firing. In response, led by Lord George, sword in hand, shouting 'Claymore!', the Macphersons charged them and they fled. They then waited at Clifton for the enemy's main body. Unaware the Jacobite force was so strong, Cumberland dismounted another 500 dragoons who in the dusk opened fire with their carbines. The MacPhersons charged again and the enemy stumbled off in their jackboots, under fire from a MacDonald regiment. Four Hanoverian officers and thirty troopers were killed, the Jacobites losing a dozen men.

Although a model rearguard action, Clifton was a mere skirmish. More significant was an incident revealing the friction between Lord George and O'Sullivan. Later, George claimed how after the engagement he found the Irishman too busy to issue the orders for next day's march, drinking what he called 'mountain malaga' with the prince.

On the night of 19 December the Jacobite army reached Carlisle. Here Charles received a letter from Lord John Drummond, saying he had landed at Montrose with troops from the Royal Ecossais Regiment and 350 volunteers from all seven regiments of the Irish Brigade under Brigadier-General Walter Stapleton – the 'Piquets'.

When the prince marched out from Carlisle next morning, he left most of his cannon and a garrison including the entire Manchester Regiment. O'Sullivan says this was done to slow Cumberland's pursuit – the duke lacked siege artillery, it was winter and his troops could not live off the country. If the garrison had to surrender, it should be able to obtain good terms.

As it was, the duke reached Carlisle on 21 December, soon followed by siege guns. Nine days later the garrison commander, Sir John Hamilton of

Sandstown, unwisely accepted his terms – 'they will not be put to the Sword, but be reserved for the King's Pleasure'. This turned out to be hanging, drawing and quartering for officers and NCOs, transportation for other ranks.

Shortly afterwards, Cumberland rushed down to London to save his father, convinced that the French had landed. He left General Hawley in command.

On 20 December Charles's troops marched six abreast across an 'unfordable' Esk, as if marching across a field. Holding each other's collars with icy water up to their armpits, they lost only two women camp followers who were drowned. D'Éguilles commented, 'nothing is impossible to those kind of men'.[2]

On Christmas Eve the prince entered Glasgow, where enemy agents had spread reports of his utter defeat, and reviewed his army on College Green. Here, still optimistic, his troops celebrated Hogmanay. The Glaswegians, who had shown rather too much zeal for Hanover, were made to supply 6,000 badly needed new uniforms, blue bonnets and shoes, with 12,000 shirts.

Early in January 1746, reinforced by Lord John Drummond's troops, Charles left Glasgow and occupied Sterling. Here he besieged the castle, which dominated the main road between the Highlands and the Lowlands.

Even after Lord John Drummond's Royal Ecossais arrived, few Scots officers had any military experience. The shortage was overcome with regular officers from the Irish Brigade, most of whom came with Lord John although some had already arrived, such as Colonel Ignatius Browne of Lally's Regiment. Eventually there were nearly sixty of them. (Many others were captured en route by enemy warships.) These gentlemen did not make the journey to waste their talents fighting in the ranks and immediately began to improve the army's discipline and musketry. Born soldiers, the Scots learned quickly.

Some Scottish officers resented what Lord Elcho called 'the preference the Prince gave the Irish', which he attributed to their favouring 'Passive obedience, Absolute monarchy [and] the Roman Catholick Religion'.[3] He could not bring himself to accept that Charles consulted them because of their expertise as highly trained professional soldiers. Whatever Elcho may say, Irish and Scots worked well enough together. They shared the same aims – to restore King James and rescue their countries from English domination.

Veterans of Fontenoy who had beaten England's best troops, they were able to communicate with Highlanders in 'Erse'. (Some clansmen carried

Irish bibles.) The Brigade made an invaluable contribution, Charles himself testifying in a communiqué issued after the Battle of Falkirk how 'Irish officers were of vast use in going through the different posts of the army, and assisting in the various dispositions that were made.'[4]

We know that Captain Browne was (in today's jargon) operations officer of the Duke of Perth's Regiment while, as aide-de-camp to the Duke of Atholl, Colonel Richard Augustus Warren of Rothe's did the same job for the Atholl Brigade. Similarly, Major Nicholas Glascock of Dillon's Regiment was attached to Lord Ogilvy's as operations officer – and to 'discipline' the men.

Irish expertise improved the cavalry. Originally this consisted of Lord Elcho's Life Guards (around 150 men), Lord Pitsligo's Horse (120), Lord Kilmarnock's Horse Grenadiers (100) and Murray of Broughton's Hussars (70). In *Waverley*, Scott, who spoke to survivors, says that despite smart blue uniforms many of the troopers looked more like kennel-huntsmen or grooms than soldiers.

But then Major James Baggot of FitzJames's Horse took over the Prince's Hussars who wore tartan jackets and Tartar fur caps and rode captured horses, turning them into a reconnaissance unit that became the Jacobite army's eyes and ears for fifty miles around. John Daniel says Baggot (from Baggotstown, County Limerick) did the prince 'infinite service' – his men would have ridden to 'hell's gate to fetch away the keys'.[5] The cavalry became still more effective with the arrival of a troop of FitzJames's Horse under Captain Robert O'Shea. Unfortunately, many of their mounts died from lack of winter fodder and were impossible to replace.

The artillery was trained and commanded by Colonel James Grante of Lally's Regiment, Baron of Iverk in County Kilkenny, who was a distinguished mathemetician as well as a gunner.[6] His cannon consisted of the 'Swedish' field guns sent from France and light pieces captured at Prestonpans.

Charles had at least one Irish aide-de-camp, Captain Felix O'Neill of the Fews in Armagh, from Lally's Regiment, who was a future Spanish general. Cumberland's successor in Scotland, the Earl of Albemarle, heard that O'Neill was reckoned to be among the Brigade's most talented young officers.

Shortly before Charles reached Glasgow, the nineteen-year-old Duke of York arrived at Boulogne to accompany the French invasion force that the Duc de Richelieu was to take across to Kent by moonlight. However, York found that Richelieu and his staff had lost contact with his brother. The

French plan had been to join Charles and the English Jacobites, whom they expected to rise in large numbers, then march on London.

When officers from Lally's Regiment, sent over to London to spy, wrongly reported major troop concentrations around the capital, Richelieu contemplated landing in Wales instead of Kent to link up with Charles. Told of his retreat, he thought of joining him in Scotland, then decided against it as his transports would have needed a battle fleet as escort and a major victory at sea. For by now the Royal Navy was waiting in strength outside Boulogne and Calais.

Storm force weather set in, with howling gales, and the invasion was called off on 1 February 1746. Even so, a few French ships slipped through the enemy patrols, landing arms and Irish volunteers.

Leaving Glasgow to besiege Stirling Castle, Charles went down with flu, at Sir Hugh Paterson's house at nearby Bannockburn. He was nursed by his host's blue-eyed niece, Clementina Walkinshaw, the youngest of ten sisters, who belonged to a Jacobite family and had been named after the late queen. Not yet physical, this was the start of a peculiarly unhappy love affair.

As the prince lay sick, Lord George demanded he hand over command to a committee (chaired by himself). Declining, Charles wrote a reply, saying he shared his followers' concern for the future, 'Everyone knew before he engaged in the cause, what he was to expect in case it miscarried, and should have stayed at home if he could not face death in any shape: but can I myself hope for better usage? At least I am the only person upon whose head a price has already been set ...' He ends, 'my authority may be taken from me by violence, but I shall never resign it like an idiot'.[7]

The siege at Stirling made little progress. Colonel Grante wanted to shell the castle from the town cemetery where his men would be under cover, but was overruled and made to site his batteries in a dangerously exposed position. Then, when examining the walls, he was badly wounded by a cannon ball. The half-French, half-Scots officer who took over, Mirabelle de Gordon, was a boastful drunk. Many of the red-coated Irish Piquets who manned the trenches were killed by enemy snipers because of his inefficiency.

41

The Battle of Falkirk, 17 January 1746

a despicable Enimy

General Hawley on Jacobites – before the battle[1]

Although in his mid-sixties (considered advanced old age in 1746), General Henry 'Hangman' Hawley had no doubts about his ability to deal with the Jacobites, whom he swore to drive from one end of the kingdom to the other, ostentatiously building a double gallows at Edinburgh. On 13 January he set off to do so, with 10,000 regulars, pitching camp just outside Falkirk.

Advised by O'Sullivan, Charles marched his 8,000 foot and 360 cavalry on to a ridge known as Falkirk Hill, south west of the town, on the morning of 17 January. At 4 p.m., when it was pouring with rain, Hawley, who had just sat down to dinner convinced the Jacobites would never dare to attack, was warned they were advancing. Without waiting to put on his hat, he sent three dragoon regiments to drive them off the ridge while forming up his infantry. He feared they might escape.

The Battle of Falkirk

Although on a small scale, Falkirk was a confused affair. Hawley thought his enemy's only tactic was charging with the sword but, trained by Irish regulars to use volley fire by ranks, they had become formidable infantry. Some regiments even possessed a grenadier company – men picked for their height and reach, who threw small iron spheres packed with gunpowder, exploded by a short fuse.

The first line consisted of Highlanders – MacDonalds, Camerons, Frasers, MacPhersons, MackIntoshs, Stewarts – the second of Lowlanders. When Hawley's 700 dragoons charged, Lord George ordered the front line to kneel and fire a volley at ten yards' range. They emptied eighty saddles before slipping under the enemy horses to dirk them in the belly. The survivors bolted, riding down their own infantry, those who fled to the right received another volley. The clansmen raced after them, cutting the slower to pieces, then charged Hawley's foot, whereupon his left and centre disintegrated.

Hail and rain blew into the faces of Hawley's infantry on the right, soaking cartridge boxes. Even so, forming a hollow square four battalions strong, supported by dragoons who had reformed, they attacked with the bayonet. Some of Charles's second line broke and ran, but O'Sullivan brought up his reserve, the Irish Piquets and the Royal Ecossais, before whom the enemy fled – 'driven like sheep before a dog'.

Hawley set fire to his camp, retreating to Edinburgh. In just twenty minutes, 350 of his men had been killed or wounded and nearly 300 taken prisoner while he had lost his guns and his baggage – the ultimate disgrace for an eighteenth-century general.

Jacobites losses were fifty men killed with eighty wounded. Their victory might have been complete had they chased the enemy through Falkirk, but the pipers had thrown down their pipes to fight and there was no other way of making the army regroup. 'The Prince would absolutely pursue them', O'Sullivan tells us, 'but the night was drawing on and the men so dispersed and harrassed, by the cruel weather we had, and being under arms all day that there was no possibility of undertaking anything.'[2]

'My heart is broke!', wrote Hawley, who had thirty-one troopers hanged for 'deserting to the rebels', and thirty-two infantrymen shot for 'cowardice'. He blamed Edinburgh's burgesses rather than himself. 'As to your diminishing their numbers, and ridiculing their discipline, you see and I feel the effects of it', he told them. 'I never saw any troops fire in platoons more regularly, make their motions and evolutions quicker, or attack with more bravery than those Highlanders did at Falkirk last week.'[3]

The Jacobites occupied Falkirk, where the prince ate Hawley's supper while his army acquired the enemy officers' baggage, including – as O'Sullivan happily recalled – 'hampers of good wine and liquors'. So many enemy officers had been killed that gold watches were cheap.

Yet the Jacobites had lost useful men. The Stewarts of Appin had two captains killed. Lochiel was wounded in the leg, his brother Archibald Cameron receiving a bullet in the chest that would have gone through his body but for his targe. Other officers were badly hurt. On the following day Colonel Aeneas MacDonald of Glengarry was accidentally shot by a Keppoch MacDonald, who was hanged – causing a spate of desertions by fellow clansmen. Charles had only won some breathing space.

After burying the enemy dead, he returned to besieging Stirling Castle, but he knew very well that his only chance lay in winning a decisive victory over Cumberland, who would come looking for him when the weather improved. Meanwhile, he was again struck down by flu, returning to Sir Hugh Paterson's house – and Clementina.

What became clear was that the Jacobites would never take Stirling Castle. On 29 January the prince received a letter signed by Murray and the chiefs demanding that, in view of 'a vast number' of desertions since Falkirk, he abandon the siege and retreat into the Highlands, where he could capture the enemy forts and in the spring find 'an army of 10,000 effective Highlanders'.

'Can we imagine, that, where we go the enemy will not follow, and at last oblige us to a battle which we now decline?', he wrote in reply. 'What will become of our Lowland friends? Or shall we abandon them to the fury of our merciless enemies?'[4] Nevertheless, the retreat north began on 2 February.

Then Lord George changed his mind. During the retreat he burst in on Charles at dinner and, in 'the most disrespectful and impertinent manner, told him "it was a most shameful and cowardly flight, that they were a parcel of villains that advised him to it; as if he had never consented, nor had any share in it".'[5]

At a council meeting soon after, he would not let anybody speak except those whom he named. When Charles tried to do so, he threatened to leave, saying the prince must not speak until everyone present had given an opinion. Lord Lewis Gordon asked him if he was mad – the prince must speak whenever he thought fit. No, said Lord George, only after everyone else. Charles did as Murray wanted, but such behaviour meant a badly divided command.

On 16 February the prince stayed at Moy Hall near Inverness where his handsome young hostess, known as 'Colonel Anne', had raised her own Lady Mackintosh's Regiment in defiance of her Hanoverian husband. Lord Loudon, defending Inverness, tried to capture Charles here by night, bringing 1,500 troops, but in the dark the local blacksmith and three friends panicked his men into fleeing with a single pistol shot and shouts of 'Advance, Clan Cameron!', 'Advance, Clan MacDonald!' Next day, 200 of Loudon's men deserted.

On 20 February the prince captured Inverness, making Duncan Forbes's comfortable mansion at nearby Culloden his headquarters. A pleasant little city, Inverness was the capital of the Highlands although, so Edmund Burt had heard, the inhabitants did not not think of themselves as Highlanders because their first language was English.

The weather was so bad that Cumberland postponed his campaign. Despite the snow, recruits went on joining Charles, whose army grew steadily. Aberdeen and Montrose were abandoned on 23 February – meaning reinforcements could no longer come by sea. A privateer had landed a squadron of 130 troopers from FitzJames's Horse the day before, with saddles but no chargers. Kilmarnock's Horse became 'Kilmarnock's Foot Guards', to give the Irishmen mounts.

Two more privateers carrying the other squadrons of FitzJames's Horse were captured by the Royal Navy. (Among them was Captain Patrick Darcy, who had been Marshal Saxe's aide-de-camp at Fontenoy.) The last reinforcements to get through were forty-two men from Berwick's Regiment, who landed at Peterhead on 25 February. Four weeks later, the enemy intercepted a ship bringing twenty-one Irish officers, some from as far off as Naples, with £15,000 in gold coin.

Cumberland's first objective was Aberdeen. At Brechin, seeing 'a singularly pretty girl' in the crowd, he bowed from the saddle and raised his hat. 'To his great mortification, and to the no less delight of spectators, the object of his admiration returned the compliment by a contemptuous gesture which does not admit of description.'[6] This was Jacobite country.

Charles concentrated on eliminating enemy strongholds north of the Spey. Fort George and Fort Augustus fell to Brigadier-General Stapleton early in March, a lucky shot exploding the latter's powder magazine, but Fort William held out. When the enemy attacked a ford at Fochabers, they were routed by Major Glascock, who took eighty prisoners. Unfortunately, the Spey was fordable in too many places. All that could be done was to keep a watch for the enemy, posting scouts on the far side. Baggot's Hussars patrolled the banks, assisted by Captain O'Shea with troopers from FitzJames's Horse.

In mid March, Charles fell ill again, this time dangerously, with 'a spotted fever' (probably scarlet fever) that kept kept him in bed for ten days at

Elgin and left him very weak. Meanwhile, new recruits were arriving in large numbers. Unfortunately, he had almost no money to pay them.

On 18 March there was a last Jacobite success. Lord Loudon's troops had seized all the ferries across the Dornoch Firth north of Tain, but in an operation meticulously planned by O'Sullivan, Colonel Richard Augustus Warren collected a fleet of small boats and landed his men unexpectedly on the far side – 'a highly evolved piece of staff work ... which very nearly succeeded in taking Loudon in the jaws of a pincer'.[7] Accompanied by Duncan Forbes, Loudon never stopped retreating until he reached Skye.

42

Culloden, 16 April 1746

We met evil sorcery
We were treated with wiles and deceit
On our own hillsides we scattered,
It was through ill chance that they did prevail.

Colonel John Roy Stewart, *Latha Chul-Lodair*

On 12 April, Cumberland's army crossed the Spey, unopposed. Reduced to just twenty-six troopers owing to the lack of horses, Baggot's Hussars had been unable to keep a proper watch, while at Fochabers Lord John Drummond, who might have inflicted severe casualties, did not have enough men to contest the crossing. As the Jacobites marched out from one end of Nairn their foes marched in at the other.

Charles had 5,400 infantry and 150 cavalry, with twelve poorly served light cannon. Many of his best troops (MacPhersons, Frasers, MacGregors and a fair number of MacDonalds) had not arrived. Yet instead of retreating into the hills, he decided to fight.

He had no option. Lowlanders and Irish regulars would not survive in the Grampian Mountains, and he had run out of money to pay his troops. Nor could he afford to lose Inverness which was his last supply depot. If his army was less than at Falkirk, he believed his Highlanders were invincible – unaware that they had not been fed by his incompetent quarter-master, Hay of Restalrig, despite there being plenty of food at Inverness.

His Scots saw themselves as fighting not just for the Stuarts but against the Union. Their Irish allies – only 300 – fought for a Stuart Restoration and a free Catholic Ireland. What both wanted was, in Murray Pittock's words, 'local independence for Scotland and Ireland, with a loose and multi-kingdom monarchy'.[1]

Supported by ten cannon and six coehorn mortars, Cumberland's army, 9,000 strong, consisted of four regiments of dragoons, fifteen infantry battalions and 1,800 Whig clansmen. They were led by excellent officers who included Major James Wolfe, the future hero of Quebec. An efficient commissariat ensured that they had all been properly fed.

Four months younger than Prince Charles, William Augustus, Duke of Cumberland, was a capable commander who lacked neither courage nor confidence. A leg wound suffered at Dettingen that never healed may have been responsible for his bulk (some eighteen stone) and savage temper. Despite a strong German accent he fancied himself as an Englishman defending his family heritage.

He occupied Aberdeen on 27 February, three weeks after taking Perth, which the Jacobites had held since September. Knowing how fast his enemy could move, he took care to protect his communications. Cavalry units were posted at Bannockburn and Brig of Earn, and Hessian mercenaries – six battallions of whom had landed at Leith on 8 February – garrisoned Perth and Stirling

During his stay at Aberdeen he made his foot soldiers learn a new method of bayonet fighting – to thrust obliquely, not at the man in front but at the man on the right, under his sword arm. He knew that although the Jacobites fought like regular infantry, at one point they would resort to the Highland charge. However, the drill was never put into practice.

On 15 April Lord George tried to mount a night attack on the enemy's camp at Nairn twelve miles away. 'This is Cumberland's birth day, they'll all be drunk as beggars.' Two gallons of brandy per regiment had been issued.

There are conflicting accounts of what happened, but Felix O'Neil, Charles's aide-de-camp, is convincing, although he differs from other versions. He says that when Lord George called it off at 2 a.m., mistakenly fearing that Cumberland had been warned, the enemy was only a mile away.[2] According to O'Neil, the prince rode to the head of the column and begged the chiefs to go on, promising to lead the attack himself. They refused. Tearfully, he told them 'he did not so much regret his own loss as their inevitable ruin'. O'Sullivan believed this had been the one chance of victory.[3]

Charles's troops were exhausted after marching for two days and a night without eating. Some collapsed into the heather despite pelting rain, others tried to find food. During the coming battle many could be seen nodding in the ranks, overcome by fatigue. (The deepest sleepers were to be woken, briefly, by enemy bayonets.) The prince, who had managed to find some bread and whisky at Culloden House, gave orders to kill and cook any cows that could be found but there was no time. The enemy was advancing in battle order.

In a letter to Charles written the day after the battle, Lord George blamed O'Sullivan for choosing to fight on Drummossie Muir (Culloden), and for everything else that had gone wrong. 'He, whose business it was, did not so much as visit the ground where we were to draw up in line of Battle, and it was a fatal error yesterday to allow the enemy so fair a field for their horse and cannon.'[4]

Lord George does not mention how he himself had suggested two alternative sites that would have been far worse. One, near Dalcross Castle, was bounded by a deep ravine across which the enemy could have fired volley after volley into the Jacobites with impunity. The other, on the south bank of the Nairn, would have exposed Charles's army to mortar fire from the other bank and meant abandoning Inverness – letting the Jacobites escape, to starve in the hills.

O'Sullivan, as operational commander, was justified in rejecting both. Yet he 'has been scorned for centuries for not choosing a better one'.[5] He had wanted to fight further west, on better ground than any suggested by Lord George. But the sudden onset of Cumberland's army made it impossible to avoid fighting on Drummossie Muir, whose boggy ground was ill-suited for a Highland charge. The site did at least give some slight protection against a flanking attack – field enclosures at Culloden on the left and at Culwhiniac on the right.

In a lament for Culloden, *Latha Chul-Lodair*, Colonel John Roy Stewart blames the disaster ahead entirely on Lord George, whom he solemnly curses – '*Mo sheachd mallachd air Mhoirear Deòrsa*' ('My sevenfold curse on George Murray'). In another poem he describes Murray as 'an utter blackguard of ranting and lies' who had 'sold his honour . . . for the purse that was fattest'. Convinced of his treachery, during the battle he tried to find and kill him.[6]

Whatever he was, Lord George was definitely not a traitor. Yet the fact that an experienced professional soldier like Stewart could feel as he did about the army's most formidable fighting commander shows how deeply some officers distrusted him.

The battle

Although a short engagement by small armies, there is surprising disagreement among historians over how the battle was fought.

Lord George insisted on putting his Atholl Brigade (Murrays, Stewarts and Fergussons), together with the Camerons on the right of the front line. This was the place of honour previously occupied by the MacDonalds who instead were on the left, despite their protests; the slight did not help MacDonald morale. The cannon were sited in batteries of four at right, left and centre – without the efficient direction of Grante, who was still ill. A scanty body of horse, less than fifty, was on each wing while Charles had a small mounted escort. (Too few cavalry in flat country was going to be a grievous handicap.)

The Irish, the Royal Ecossais and the Lowlanders formed the second line under Brigadier-General Stapleton.There was no proper reserve.

The Jacobites could hear a rolling tattoo from 225 drums coming nearer and nearer through the mist. Cumberland's army was advancing over a front of half a mile. At midday it came in sight, the foot in three lines, cannon at intervals, with two dragoon regiments on each wing.

Riding up and down his own front as the pipes played, Charles encouraged his men. 'Here they are, coming, my lads, we'll soon be with them. They don't forget Gledsmuir nor Falkirk and you have the same arms and swords ... Go on, my lads, the day will be ours and we'll want for nothing!' O'Sullivan, who tells us this, admired the prince's self-control. 'Not the least concern appeared on his face', he records, 'in the greatest concern or danger, it's then that he appears most cheerful and hearty.'[7]

At 1 p.m. enemy artillery fired a cannonade that continued for twenty minutes, targeting Charles whom they just missed. When his groom was decapitated and he himself was spattered with mud and blood, he took his usual place in the second line. Jacobite cannon responded ineffectively, although Charles's infantry fired twice as many volleys as their opponents.

After half an hour of fruitless manoeuvring to outflank each other, the armies engaged at close quarters. Within another half hour the battle would be over.

The Atholl men and the Camerons on the prince's right began to drop beneath the cannonade and from musketry by the Campbell militia on their flank. Inexplicably, Lord George did nothing, despite Charles sending O'Sullivan,

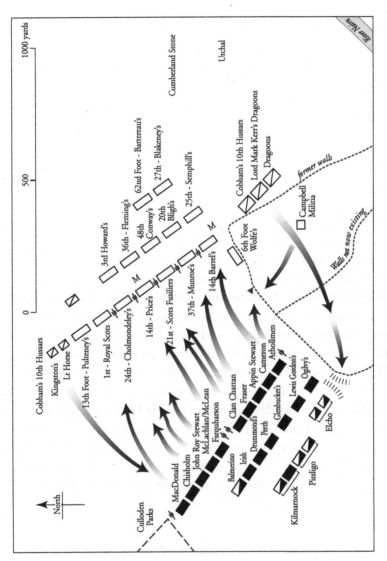

1000 yards

500

0

River Nairn

Cumberland Stone

Urchal

Cobham's 10th Hussars

Kingston's

Lr Horse

13th Foot - Pulteney's

1st - Royal Scots

24th - Cholmondeley's

14th - Price's

21st - Scots Fusiliers

37th - Munroe's

14th Barrel's

3rd Howard's

36th - Fleming's

48th Conway's

62nd Foot - Battereau's

27th - Blakeney's

20th Bligh's

25th - Semphill's

M

M

M

6th Foot Wolfe's

Cobham's 10th Hussars

Lord Mark Kerr's Dragoons

Dragoons

Campbell Militia

former walls

Walls not now existing

MacDonald

Chisholm

John Roy Stewart

McLachlan/McLean

Farquharson

Clan Chattan

Fraser

Appin Stewart

Cameron

Athollmen

Balmerino

Irish

Drummond's

Perth

Glenbucket's

Lewis Gordon's

Ogilvy's

Kilmarnock

Pitsligo

Elcho

Culloden Parks

North

Cobham's 10th Hussars

The Battle of Culloden, 16 April 1746

then Stapleton, to him with orders to charge immediately. By now the clouds were thickening and there were squalls of rain, hail and snow – 'From the sky came a third of our ruin', says John Roy Stewart.[8]

The Jacobite front line had been properly facing the enemy at the wrong angle. Officers were slow in obeying Lord George's order to correct this, and did so imperfectly. Finally, he felt able to launch an attack.

His brigade and the Camerons hurled themselves at Cumberland's army but boggy ground, with wind and rain in their faces, slowed them down, lessening the charge's impact. Even so, two enemy regiments were overwhelmed, losing a colour and one-third of their men killed or wounded. But, backed up by cannon, another regiment counter-attacked, firing at point blank range, which decimated the attackers. The Atholl men and the Camerons turned and ran, carrying Lochiel whose ankles had been broken by grapeshot. The Chevalier de Johnstone says that if only they had held their ground for three minutes more until their comrades came up, Cumberland's army 'very much shaken . . . would soon have been put to flight'.[9]

In the centre, Mackintoshes hacked their way through the English front line, but were checked by the second. Then they too ran.

On the left, the MacDonalds, whose charge was even slower because of a longer distance to cover and heavily waterlogged ground, met a still hotter reception from musketry and cannon – Keppoch was killed at the head of his clan and Clanranald was badly wounded, while Colonel Lachlan MacLachlan of Inchconnel who charged with them had his head removed by a cannon ball. The MacDonalds disintegrated, bolting back across the heather.

Breaking through the enclosure walls and charging the Jacobite flanks, Cumberland's dragoons decided the battle. The Highlanders fled. Too much had been expected from men who were worn out by lack of sleep and food, and a night march worse than any they had made in England. The few Jacobite horse tried to hold off the dragoons but there were not enough of them and they were overwhelmed almost at once, Baggot being taken prisoner. This left the prince's fleeing infantry at the dragoons' mercy.

Defeat

While Charles was trying to rally the right, O'Sullivan galloped over to O'Shea who commanded his escort and yelled, 'All is going to pot!', telling him to get the prince away. Charles however refused to leave the field of battle, shouting, 'They won't take me alive!' Then he saw the moor was covered with Jacobites fleeing from Hanoverian dragoons, with no cavalry of his own to protect them. Reluctantly, he accepted that it was time to leave.

Not all Jacobites ran, Lowland units driving back the dragoons. Charging Cumberland's men with a handful of troopers, Viscount Strathallan was run through the body – dying, he took Communion from an Episcopalian chaplain in the form of whisky and oatcake. More than one body of clansmen left the moor with pipes playing, flying the prince's standard. So, on the right, did the two battalions of Ogilvy's Regiment who kept their ranks and forded the River Nairn, repeatedly turning to form squares and fire at pursuing cavalry. They reached Forfarshire in safety.

The MacDonalds were saved by Brigadier-General Stapleton's 150 Irish Piquets, who let them run back through their ranks, then closed up to maintain a steady volley fire that held off the enemy horsemen. (Captain O'Neil says that Charles had ordered them to cover the MacDonalds' flight, his last command.[10]) They were supported by a Frenchman, Captain de Saussay, who went on working a 4-pounder cannon before he and his crew were hit by a mortar shell. Two-thirds of the Wild Geese were killed or wounded, but the rest stood their ground heroically until their ammunition ran out. Carrying a mortally wounded Stapleton with them, the survivors marched off to Inverness next day, obeying his dying command to surrender.

Clan Chisholm's standard-bearer, William Chisholm, was another who refused to run, killing sixteen redcoats with his claymore until shot down from behind. 'His widow composed a Gaelic song in his memory, "*Mo run geal òg*", in which she says he was the handsomest, bravest, kindliest man in Strathglass, the best swordsman, and had the sweetest kisses and the strongest head [for drink] in the Strath.'[11]

The road from Culloden to Inverness was littered with dead men cut down by dragoon sabres while Cumberland, who refused to recognise Jacobites as belligerents, gave orders to bayonet their wounded as they lay on the battlefield. Some were piled in heaps into which cannon were fired. Over thirty prisoners were burned alive in a bothy and nineteen captured officers were clubbed to death with musket butts.

Next day another seventy were shot, while murder squads were sent to search every dwelling for miles around and kill fugitives out of hand. Over 1,000 Jacobites had died during the battle, another 500 or more being slaughtered in the aftermath. Cumberland's casualties may have been about

200 killed, with 200 gravely wounded – most of whom died of their injuries – and another 800 less seriously wounded.

The duke issued a communiqué informing his army that the enemy's regiments had been ordered not to give them quarter. Before the end of the month an order to this effect, signed by Lord George, was printed and widely circulated. Designed to excuse attrocities, it was a forgery, presumably by an officer on Cumberland's staff.

Two days later, Johnstone found '4,000 Highlanders' in excellent spirits at Ruthven, with Lords George, Atholl and Perth. 'We were masters of the passes between Ruthven and Inverness', the chevalier recalls. 'Our numbers increased every moment, and I am thoroughly convinced that in the course of eight days we should have had a more powerful army than ever.'[12]

In reality they were, at most, only 1,500 men. Then a letter arrived from the prince, telling them it was all over. This was the right decision – they might have waged a guerilla war until autumn, but would have been starved into surrender.[13] 'The Highlanders gave vent to their grief in wild howlings and lamentations', says Johnstone, 'the tears flowed down their cheeks when they thought that their country was now at the discretion of the Duke of Cumberland.'[14]

There was a last flicker of defiance after two French ships landed 3,000 muskets and £36,000 in gold at Loch nan Uamh that were hastily hidden at Loch Arkaig. On 8 May Lochiel, Cluny, Glenbuchat and others met nearby at Murlaggan, signing a resolution to gather a new army at Achnacarry on 15 May, but only 400 clansmen came to the rendezvous. Then Hanoverian forces recaptured Fort Augustus, threatening the territory of Lochiel who was the scheme's main advocate. It was the end.

'We are outlaws now and must take to the hills', sighs John Roy Stewart in *Latha Chul-Lodair*, 'with little food or fire on the rocks where cold mist lies.'

43

Hanover's Revenge

They've killed my father, they've killed my brothers,
They've savaged my kindred and plundered my kinsfolk,
They've burned my country and raped my mother –
Yet if Charles had won, no one would hear me grieving.

Anon, *Achadh nan Comhaichean*[1]

Cumberland nursed a deep hatred for the nation that dared dispute the Hanover family's right to rule her, saying, 'I tremble for fear that this vile spot may still be the ruin of this island and *our family*.'[2] He did all he could to ensure the Scots would not dispute it again. No doubt a few Jacobites were still waging a guerilla war, but that did not justify his methods.

For two months he stayed in the Highlands, sending out parties to shoot men without trial, to rape and loot, to burn castles and cabins, to wreck fishing boats and to drive off cattle and sheep, making sure the population would starve. At home in mountain country, Whig Campbells of the Argyll Militia took a full part. Tobias Smollett, no Jacobite but a Scots patriot, sums it up – 'in a few days there was neither house, cottage, man nor beast, to be seen in the compass of fifty miles; all was ruin, silence and desolation'.[3]

Episcopalian chapels were targeted. 'Her oratories have been profan'd and burnt, her holy altars desecrated, her priests outrigiously [sic] plundered and driven from their flocks', Robert Lyon, chaplain of Lord Ogilvy's Regiment, wrote just before his execution. Cumberland 'by wilful fire and sword, by every means of torment and distress – barbarity exceeding Glencoe massacre itself – has brought a dreadful desolation upon my dear country.'[4]

Defiantly, small groups of Jacobites went on ambushing Hanoverian troops in the Highlands and raiding Whig landowners until well into 1748.[5]

Jacobites filled the gaols from Edinburgh down to London, the 'ordinary sort' crammed below decks on prison hulks.[6]

Lords Derwentwater, Kilmarnock, Balmerino and Lovat were beheaded. A brother of the earl executed in 1716, Derwentwater, who had been captured at sea on his way to join the prince, 'suffered decapitation with the most perfect composure and serenity'.[7] Kilmarnock died bravely, but declared he was guilty of treason, saying he was so short of money that, 'if Mahommed had set up his standard in the Highlands I had been a good Mussulman for bread'.

When Kilmarnock and Balmerino were on their way to be tried, there was an argument over whose coach should carry the axe, until Balmerino cried, 'Come, come, put it in with me!' Horace Walpole thought Balmerino 'the most natural brave old fellow I ever saw: the highest intrepidity, even to indifference. At the bar he behaved like a soldier and a man.'[8] For his execution, he wore the blue uniform of the prince's Life Guards. Before laying his head on the block he declared 'I was brought up in true, loyal Anti-Revolution principles', asking God to bless the king, the prince and the duke. He also praised Charles's good nature, affability, compassion and courage.[9]

Lovat had been caught on a remote Highland island while being received into the Catholic Church. On his way back to the Tower after the trial, a hag screamed, 'You'll get that nasty head of yours chopped off, you ugly old Scotch dog!' and he shouted back, 'I believe I shall, you ugly old English bitch!' As he was about to kneel at the block, a stand for spectators fell down, killing or maiming eighteen. He laughed, 'The more mischief, the better sport!'

Over eighty commoners were hanged and disembowelled at Kennington Common, Carlisle, York, Penrith and Brampton. On the scaffold they proclaimed their loyalty to King James, Colonel Towneley denouncing the 'Oppression of a German Hanoverian Usurper'. (Perhaps explaining why he was cut down before he was dead, so able to feel his disembowelment.)[10] A song, 'Towneley's Ghost', has him appear in a nightmare to Cumberland, crying 'Nero himself would blush to own the slaughter thou hast made.' A ballad by the poet William Shenstone, 'Jemmy Dawson', tells how Jemmy's betrothed insisted on watching his butchery, then died of shock.[11]

A few were pardoned, notably the Earl of Cromartie who was a friend of Prince Frederick. Some died in prison, including the Duke of Atholl at the Tower, but most were transported to work as indentured (semi-slave) labour on the American or Caribbean plantations.

In contrast, officers and men of the Irish Brigade and the Royal Ecossais suffered a brief, if unpleasant, confinement before being shipped back to France in exchange for British prisoners-of-war. A surprising number of the leaders escaped abroad, but the Duke of Perth died at sea. Lord George made his way to Holland, then to Rome where King James settled a pension on him.

Mr Secretary Murray had deserted before Culloden, feigning illness. After the battle, he hastened to Loch Arkaig, hoping to steal the gold left there, but was caught. Turning King's Evidence, his testimony enabled the government to condemn Lovat, for which Murray received a full pardon. However, 'Evidence Murray' never dared go back to Scotland and his wife abandoned him.

Despite Murray's revelations, English and Welsh Jacobite leaders such as Beaufort, Hynde Cotton and Williams-Wynn avoided punishment. Burning letters made it impossible to prove anything against them in court.

In 1746 an Act anent Heritable Jurisdictions took away the power of chieftains and great Lowland lairds over clansmen and tenants, which meant an end to 'pit and gallows'. An Act of Proscription deprived a clansman of his right to bear arms, while a Dress Act forebade him to wear Highland dress – both acts enforced by imprisonment or transportation.

As a Highlander himself, Duncan Forbes, despite having had his house at Culloden wrecked and plundered, and his valuable livestock stolen, did his best to soften the laws' impact, especially the Dress Act. Again and again, he pleaded for leniency. Infuriated, Cumberland refused – the lord president was 'arrant Highland mad', an 'old woman who spoke to me of humanity!' This may explain why Forbes was never repaid the large sums he had contributed to the 'Black Cockade', the cause of Hanover. He died in 1747, a ruined man.

Yet it would be long before clan loyalties disappeared. There were many Scots who were ready to fight for the prince again.

But where was he?

44

'Skulking', Summer 1746

He called for a dram; and when the bottle of brandy was
brought, he said he would fill the glass for himself; 'for', said
he, 'I have learn'd in my skulking to take a hearty dram'.

Prince Charles, June 1746[1]

In Glen Corodale on the island of South Uist, in May 1746, Hugh MacDonald
of Balshair came upon some men who had not seen him approaching through
the mist. One, fat and middle aged, spoke in French to another, taller man,
who ran into a nearby bothy. A third shouted that Balshair was harmless. He
was able to explain that he had come to warn of troops on nearby Eriskay.
The fat man – O'Sullivan – took Balshair inside the hut, presenting him to
Charles, Prince Regent of Great Britain and Ireland, who wore a dirty kilt
and a soot-stained nightcap.

Offering Balshair a dram, the prince invited him to dinner – a leg of
beef spotted with soot and eaten off a wooden chest. They were joined by
MacDonald of Boisdale who warned that a search party might come at any
moment. But Charles said 'it was but seldom he met with friends he could
enjoy himself with', insisting on their staying for a bowl of punch.

'At last I starts the question if his Highness would take it amiss if I should
tell him the greatest objections against him in Great Britain,' recalled
Balshair. 'I told him that Popery and arbitrary government were the chiefest.'
The prince answered, 'it was only bad constructions his enemies put on it' –
meaning they distorted what he stood for. He added that most of Europe's
rulers 'had little or no religion at all'.

'We continued this drinking for three days and three nights. He still had
the better of us, and even of Boisdale himself, notwithstanding his being as
able a bowlsman, I dare say, as any in Scotland.'[2] On the morning after the

carouse ended, everyone except Charles had a monumental hangover, lying on their beds. 'His Royal Highness was the only one who was able to take care of the rest, in heapng them with plaids, and at the same time merrily sung the *Te Deum*.'[3]

Hoping to find a ship to France Charles had made for the coast after Culloden, with O'Sullivan and Captain O'Neil. At the end of April, aware the enemy were hunting him, he left the mainland for the Outer Hebrides, wandering from island to island, keeping just ahead of his pursuers, often on the edge of starvation and nearly drowning at sea. He then moved to Skye with the aid of the heroic Flora MacDonald, who helped to smuggle Charles, disguised as her Irish maid 'Betty', from Benbecula to the island. Returning to the mainland early in July he spent weeks slipping through cordons of Whig troops, only escaping by crawling through them on hands and knees across the heather at night.

In *Kidnapped*, Robert Louis Stevenson (who had read the accounts in Bishop Robert Forbes's *The Lyon in Mourning*) recreates what it felt like to be chased through the Highlands: 'There were the tops of mountains all round . . . from whence we might be spied on at any moment; so it behoved us to keep in the hollow parts of the moor, and when these turned aside from our direction to move upon its face with infinite care. Sometimes, for half an hour together, we must crawl from one heather bush to another. . .'

When it rained, 'By day, we lay and slept in the drenching heather; by night, incessantly clambered upon breakneck hills and among rude crags. We often wandered; we were often so involved in fog that that we must lie quiet till it lightened. A fire was never to be thought of. Our food was only drammach [oatmeal and water] and a portion of cold meat we had carried . . . the mist enfolding us as in a gloomy chamber.' There was further torment from dysentery and midges.

The prince's feet were cut and bleeding, his legs ulcerated from scratching at midge bites. Even so, shelter in a Highland shieling – a windowless, one-room, heather-thatched hovel of turf and stones, barely six foot high, swarming with vermin, that had a hole in the roof instead of a chimney and was thick with peat smoke – could be worse than exposure on the hills. Rain came through the roof, mixing with soot and falling like drops of ink on those inside. But as it was summer he did not have to share his quarters with cows or chickens.

Often a pudding of blood from cattle on the hoof was served as a meal, while other guests might have their heads capped in tar to kill lice. (On one occasion 'four score' of these were picked off Charles.) Sleeping on a bare earth floor, he would wake to find himself blinded by smoke, demented from itching and spotted with rain-soaked soot. Just outside, standing conveniently near the door, a gigantic midden served as a house of easement.

Shielings were luxurious, however, compared with the bothies in the high mountain pastures where the prince sometimes took refuge – 'the most miserable huts that ever were seen', according to Duncan Forbes.

Perhaps understandably, the prince drank brandy or whisky whenever he could find them, sometimes a bottle a day. He also took to tobacco, smoking the clay pipe shared by his companions, 'every one at his turn, so many whiffs', according to O'Sullivan, although he later acquired his own, its broken stem bound with thread. What he disliked most, he told O'Sullivan, was his escort's good manners when they came across water, which they scooped up and drank from their bonnets. They would never let him do the same, but insisted on his drinking from one of theirs – 'greasy and God knows what else'.[4]

Whether in the Grampians or on the Hebridean islands, the prince knew he was being hunted for his life by over a thousand enemy troops. If captured, as he nearly was several times, the Hanoverians were not going to miss the chance of extinguishing so deadly a threat – a block and an axe awaited Charles Stuart. (Although Boswell heard he expected poison or the assassin's knife.) Yet his high spirits astonished his companions. More than once he danced in the heather, crooning Gaelic songs, to make them forget their danger.

Incidents stand out, such as his escape from the mainland to Skye as Flora MacDonald's maid, 'Betty'. In a flowered linen gown and a brown, hooded mantle, he looked unusually tall for a Scots maiden, an unconvincing cross-dresser whose long strides with skirts hitched up too high caused scandal. One lady said she never saw 'such an impudent looking woman', another called him 'an odd muckle trallop'.[5] Quite apart from what might happen to her if caught, Flora (a demure young lady whom James Boswell describes as 'uncommonly well bred'), cannot have enjoyed the performance.

Then there were 'the Seven Men of Glenmoriston' who ignored the £30,000 offered for his capture when they ran into him by chance in the heather. A few days before, they had routed sixty redcoats whom they forced to hand over a herd of cattle, while they had also killed a spy – placing his head on a tree by a high road as a warning for others. None of them could speak English so Charles's ability to communicate (there was a heated argument when he declined to go the way they wanted) shows that he must have picked up basic Gaelic.

After hiding Charles in a grotto with a purling stream that he compared to a palace, they took him through his pursuers on a hair-raising trek until, in September, they reached 'Cluny's Cage' on Ben Alder, the refuge of the chief of the MacPhersons – 'a very romantick, comical habitation' built over a tree platform on a mountainside and masked by bushes.

At other times he thrived. John Cameron, once a Pesbyterian chaplain with the prince's army who met him in August, recalled, 'He was then barefooted, had an old black kilt coat on, a plaid, philabeg and waistcoat, a dirty shirt and a long red beard, a gun in his hand, pistol and dirk by his side. He was very cheerful and in good health and, in my opinion, fatter than when he was in Inverness.'[6]

Others, too, were impressed by his ability to endure hardship. 'We travell'd in this manner three days and nights without much eating or any sleep, but slumbering now and then on a hillside', wrote Lochgarry, recalling how they evaded an enemy search patrol. 'Our indefatigable Prince bore this with greater courage and resolution than any of us, nor never was there a Highlander born cou'd travel up and down hills better or suffer more fatigue. Show me a king or prince in Europe cou'd have borne the like.'[7]

Charles was just one of many fugitives who were hunted after Culloden. Pursued by the Argyll Militia, Colonel John Roy Stewart had to skulk for months in the heather, sheltering in caves and even under a waterfall. He wrote a Psalm:

> The Lord's my targe, I will be stout.
>   With dirk and trusty blade,
> Though Campbells come in flocks about,
>   I will not be afraid . . .

He joined the Prince at Ben Alder, fainting with emotion on seeing him again.

Colonel O'Sullivan, who could not cope with mountains or fifty mile treks over the heather, had left the prince at the end of June and found a ship that took him to Bergen in Norway. Upon finally reaching France, he begged Louis XV to rescue Charles. Louis responded by sending Colonel Warren (who had returned) and two other Irish officers with *L'Heureux* and *Le Prince de Conti* – frigates of thirty and twenty guns respectively.

When the prince heard of their arrival in Loch nan Uamh, he told his companions, 'I hope you are now out of misery, but for my part I'd willingly undergo more dangers and hardships than I have done, if I could be of any use to you and my poor country.'[8] He then made his way to Loch nan Uamh, which he reached on 19 September.

Joined by Lochiel, Sir Thomas Sheridan and twenty Scottish gentlemen who included John Roy Stewart, together with a hundred Highlanders, he went on board, in trews and plaid. Notwithstanding the robust impression he made on John Cameron and Lochgarry, Smollett heard that 'the Prince Pretender' had looked haggard – 'His eye was hollow, his visage wan, and his constitution greatly impaired by famine and fatigue.'[9]

They sailed at 2 a.m. the next morning, heavy mist enabling them to pass undetected through a cordon of enemy warships, and landed at Roscoff in Brittany on 30 September.

45

Europe's Hero, 1746–1748

All Europe was astonished at the greatness of your enterprize, for tho' Alexander and other heroes have conquered kingdoms with inferior armies, you are the only one who ever engaged in such an attempt without any.

Frederick II of Prussia, letter to Prince Charles,
12 January 1747[1]

Louis XV invited Charles to Versailles, where he arrived in a coach as Britain's prince regent with Lochiel as his Master of Horse, and courtiers following in two others. 'His dress had in it, I thought, somewhat of uncommon elegance', an officer in the cortège dryly recalled. 'His coat was of rose-coloured velvet embroidered with silver and lined with silver tissue; his waistcoat was of a rich gold brocade . . . in short, he glittered all over like the star which they tell you appeared at his nativity.'[2]

Frederick the Great wrote asking for his portrait, declaring that his adventure had all the hallmarks of an epic, save a happy ending. Voltaire, too, believed he was a hero. In Britain, pamphlets and even an anonymous novel, *Ascanius*, applauded his Highland odyssey.[3] 'If this young gentleman should declare himself a Protestant and another [Frederick, Prince of Wales] should not act suitable to the great and good examples he has had before him, the Lord knows how matters may end,' thought Prime Minister Henry Pelham.[4]

Old-fashioned historians say that Culloden ended Jacobitism, yet for Charles it was just the end of the beginning. He wanted another rising, soon, begging Louis XV to invade England. Louis suggested Scotland, offering 6,000 French troops, but the prince had set his heart on capturing London. However, by now France could not afford a full-scale invasion. A visit to King

Ferdinand VI at Madrid in 1747 was unproductive, although the Spaniards were courteous.

Sixty Scots gentlemen were given French commissions but Lochiel, who received a colonelcy, opposed a scheme for a Scots Brigade, arguing it would deprive Scottish Jacobites of leaders at home, as it did in Ireland. Strongly in favour of another Highland rising, Lochiel might have persuaded Charles to change his mind about invading Scotland had he not died of meningitis in 1748.

At Paris, 'When the Prince came out of his coach to go into the Opera there was such a clapping of hands, such a cry of "*Vivat!*", such demonstrations of joy, which continued for some time after in the box, that the like was never seen,' recalls O'Sullivan.[5] The prince lived magnificently, running up debts for Louis's government to pay.

O'Sullivan belonged to a hard-drinking Irish côterie around the prince that included the Reverend George Kelly, who, although a parson, procured girls for him. Another luminary was Robert MacCarthy, Earl of Clancarty – known as 'Cyclops' from having had an eye knocked out with a bottle by General Braddock during a tavern brawl – who did not appear to be entirely sane.

Shocked by his brother's way of life, in 1747 the Duke of York, who had joined the prince in Paris, fled back to Italy and, encouraged by James, entered the Church, to be made a cardinal before becoming a priest and so depriving Charles of an heir. To know that his father and brother no longer expected a Restoration was, Charles declared, a dagger through his heart. Averse to visiting Rome for fear of hurting his image in England, he never saw his father again.

By now the king was a shadowy figure. As long ago as the 1730s Bolingbroke had suggested he abdicate in favour of Charles and during the Forty-Five many had thought that he might. However, he continued to 'reign', holding court at Palazzo del Re and creating peers as late as 1761. The palace acted like a modern consulate, giving small cash handouts to Britons in Rome who were down on their luck. But his health was cracking and he suffered from severe bouts of depression. After 1746 he opposed another rising in the Highlands, convinced it would be defeated. Yet he always remained devoted to 'dearest Carluccio', as he lovingly referred to Charles.

Meanwhile, Charles was enjoying the Paris of Rameau, Madame de Pompadour and Casanova. In 1747 he began a torrid romance with Marie Louise, the Duchesse de Montbazon, a young brunette whose mother had been Queen Clementina's sister – a portrait after Lancret shows her as a wilful rococo shepherdess. She bore him a son who lived only a few months, but early in 1748 her family made her end the affair.

Charles had already acquired a new mistress, the fiery Polish Princesse de Talmont (née Marie Jabłonowska) who was forty-seven and highly intelligent, with many leading intellectuals among her friends. He called her *La Reine de Maroc*. Their stormy liaison lasted for three years.

He contemplated marriage, not with Marie, but with a daughter of Louis XV. King James advised him not to aim so high, suggesting instead a daughter of the Duke of Modena who was reputed to be the greatest beauty in Italy. In 1747 he even considered proposing himself as a consort for the Russian Tsarina.

The French victory at Laffeldt in July 1747 during the ongoing War of the Austrian Succession, in which Marshal Saxe defeated Cumberland, who was nearly taken prisoner, seemed a good omen. The Irish Brigade fought like devils, spurred on by rumours that Charles was with the French army in disguise. Sadly, the Marquis d'Argenson, who believed a Stuart Restoration would benefit France, had been replaced as foreign minister by the Marquis de Puysieux whose priority was peace at any price.

In October 1748 the Treaty of Aix-la-Chapelle (immortalised by Handel's fireworks music) ended the war but also stipulated that neither James III nor his children could live in France. Charles declined to leave. One November evening, alighting from his carriage at the Paris opera he was seized by royal guardsmen before he could draw the pistols he always carried and was bundled into a coach. After three days in a cell at the Château de Vincennes he agreed to go. Never again would he trust the French – the people most likely to help him.

He took refuge in Avignon, where he received a regal welcome and spent the winter. Joined by Madame de Talmont, he outraged his hosts by organising a gigantic fête in his own honour that included a Grand Ball and fountains running with wine – leaving the Pope to foot the bill. Early in 1749, at the risk of disappearing into the Bastille, he returned to Paris. Here he lived in a convent in the rue Saint-Dominique where Marie had a discreet apartment reached by a secret staircase.

A master of disguise, from now on he impersonated a courier, a merchant, a Neapolitan officer, an Irish captain in the Spanish army, a one-eyed abbé with an eyepatch and a false nose, or a friar whose hood hid his face. Even among those who knew him, he used an alias – Baron Douglas, Mr Benn, Mr Williams, Comte d'Albany or Dr Smith. French police and Hanoverian spies were baffled. Not knowing where he was, mistaken sightings and wild rumours of plots kept George II's government in a state of constant alarm.

46

Jacobite Revival, 1746–1750

Many eyes, formerly cold and indifferent, are now looking
towards the line of our ancient and rightful monarchs.

Sir Walter Scott, *Redgauntlet*

The Honest Cause began to revive. Jacobites convinced themselves that the
Forty-Five had nearly succeeded – forgetting how heavy had been the odds.

Reports of Cumberland's atrocities circulated all over Europe, Voltaire
alleging that 800 of Charles's supporters had had their hearts torn out and
thrown in their faces. From a conquering hero, the duke was transformed
into a monster for whom even Whigs felt revulsion. In the first flush of
enthusiasm, the Butchers' Company had made him an honorary livery-
man, and he became 'Butcher Cumberland' – a name that stuck. In 1757,
humiliatingly defeated by the French army at Hastenbeck in the Seven Years
War, he panicked, surrendering large areas of Hanover. His infuriated father
disowned him, ending his military career.

Charles, in contrast, was admired even by enemies. Everybody, friend
or foe, expected another rising. In winter 1746, Sussex Jacobites (recusant
gentry and smugglers) invited Charles to invade their county, while City of
London aldermen sported tartan waistcoats. The Independent Electors of
Westminster held a dinner at the Vintners' Hall in 1747 at which, says *The
Gentleman's Magazine*, 'The following toasts were drunk. The King (each
man having a glass of water on the left hand, and waving the glass of wine
over the water), the Prince [Charles], the Duke [Henry] ... and that the
naturalisation bill be kicked out of the House and the foreigners out of the
kingdom.'[1]

There were Jacobite riots at the Staffordshire county elections with a
demonstration at Lichfield races in September where Dr William King,

the flamboyant principal of St Mary's Hall, Oxford, James's new agent in England, counted 275 supporters among gentlemen present. They included Sir Watkin Williams-Wynn, who wore a tartan waistcoat and a white cockade. King James's health was drunk and 'When the King Comes Home Again' was sung. They were cheered on by a mob from Burton-on-Trent with tartan ribbons around their hats.[2]

Oxford rioted in February 1748, the mob yelling 'King James! King James!' – a minister grumbled that the university was a 'sanctuary of disaffection'. At the opening of the Radcliffe Camera in April 1749, Dr King delivered a Latin oration in which he lamented Oxford's decay and, to wild applause, used no less than six times the phrase *redeat ille genius Britanniae*, 'restore the genius of Britain'. Everyone knew he meant Prince Charles.

'*Redeat*' appears on a portrait medal of Charles by Roettiers the Younger, struck in France in 1745. Without a wig, his hair fairly long, he has a receding chin yet is clearly very handsome. The reverse shows Britannia gazing longingly at a fleet of ships, with the inscription *amor et spes* – 'Hope and Love'. Medals like this were used as propaganda throughout the Cause.

Engravings and sculpture also played a part in propaganda, such as Louis Tocqué's flattering portrait of 1748 in which Charles wears armour – a general's garb in eighteenth-century iconography. (Tocqué was France's most fashionable portraitist, having painted the queen and the dauphin.) Jean-Baptiste Lemoyne's head-and-shoulder's portrait bust of about the same date was thought by many people, including Charles himself, to be the best likeness. Casts of the bust were on sale at London shops, making him easy to recognise – which explains why he went everywhere in disguise

Wine glasses, rings, watches, snuffboxes, fans, punchbowls, even teapots, bore a likeness of Charles or Jacobite symbols, with mottoes such as *Audentior ibo* ('I shall go more boldly'), implying there would be a next time. Everything possible was pressed into service to remind people of the King over the Water.

On Restoration Day (29 May) 1750, 300 artisans hanged George II in effigy at Walsall, tying turnips and an orange round its neck with a label – 'Evil to him that Evil think, it is this that makes the Nation Stink'.[3] Pro-Stuart riots spread to Birmingham, Wednesbury and Shrewsbury. Troops put them down in July, several soldiers being killed, some rioters finding shelter with local landowners. Paul Monod suspects that behind the disturbances lay plans for a rising, but it was not what he calls 'the last great Jacobite gambit'.[4]

There was plenty of life left in the Honest Cause and not just among Midlanders. In June 1750 Charles was proclaimed King at Newcastle in front of a crowd of 6,000 cheering colliers.

Long after the Duke of Cumberland's departure, his troops treated all Scotland and not just the Highlands as an occupied country. Even Whigs resented their brutishly arrogant behaviour, especially that of English officers, and began to feel sorry for the defeated. Everywhere, there was evidence of sympathy.

John Campbell, the Royal Bank's crypto-Jacobite cashier whose role in helping Charles was never discovered, felt so strongly that in 1749 he commissioned William Mosman to paint him in full Highland regalia, complete with dirk and claymore. This was three years after the Dress Act had outlawed it. What may be significant is that he wears a red and black tartan, which had been the uniform of many in the prince's army.

In 1749, Sir Hector Maclean of Duart produced a plan approved by Louis XV and the Duc de Richelieu, regardless of the Treaty of Aix-la-Chapelle. Some 5,000 French troops would land in eastern Scotland and 4,000 Swedish in western Scotland, joined by a further 10,000 clansmen. A war chest was available – the gold landed at Loch Arkaig in 1746, of which Cluny Macpherson was trustee. At the same time, Lord Clancarty with volunteers from the Irish Brigade would sail up the River Lee into County Cork and raise all Munster.

But Charles was only interested in England. In any case, the 'Loch Arkaig Treasure' was proving to be a curse, though the prince retrieved part of it in 1749 and Cluny used most of the remainder to relieve victims of Cumberland's attrocities. Alasdair Ruadh MacDonell of Glengarry (of whom more will be heard), then accused Cluny and Dr Archibald Cameron, Lochiel's brother, of embezzling £6,000 from it, which, although untrue, was believed by many in the Highlands.[5]

47

The Elibank Plot, 1752–1753

We have had two rebellions ... besides plots and conspiracies
without number ... But the claims of the banished family,
I fear, are not yet antiquated; and who can foretell, that their
future attempts will produce no greater disorder.

David Hume, *Of the Protestant Succession*[1]

In spring 1749 Alexander MacDonald of Lochgarry reported to King James
that the clansmen were ready to rise. Accordingly, in May, Charles placed a
large sum of money with his Paris bankers, instructing James Dormer, his
agent at Antwerp, to buy 6,000 Highland broadswords and 26,000 muskets.
(The son of a recusant peer, Dormer also supplied him with pornography,
such as *The Nun in the Chemise*.) He obtained a new commission as Prince
Regent from his father.

Despite Lochgarry's invitation, he decided that England took precedence
over Scotland. On 16 September 1750 he arrived in London, accompanied
by John Holker, a Lancashire recusant who had been an officer of the
Manchester Regiment. At a conference in Pall Mall (at the Cocoa Tree club
with its discreet exit) he told the Duke of Beaufort, the Earl of Westmorland,
Colonel Arthur Brett, Dr King and fifty other English Jacobites that he
would lead a rising in England if 4,000 men would join.

Disappointingly, they insisted the campaign must start in Scotland.[2]
However, he took the opportunity to stroll down the Mall, just as his grandfather James II had done when at Whitehall. Escorted by Colonel Brett (a
military fossil cashiered in 1715) he also inspected the Tower of London's
defences, declaring that a gate could be blown in with a petard.

Summoned to the house of a prominent London Jacobite, Lady Primrose,
in Essex Street off the Strand, Dr King – a florid, Hogarthian figure – was

astounded to find himself presented to the prince in her dressing room. Charles explained that he had come to England to discuss 'a scheme', but nothing was ready so he was leaving. Dr King recalled,

> As to his person, he is tall and well-made, but stoops a little, owing perhaps to the great fatigue which he underwent in his northern expedition. He has a handsome face and good eyes. I think his busts which about this time were commonly sold in London are more like him than any of the pictures which I have yet seen . . . He hath a quick apprehension, and speaks French, Italian and English, the last with a little of a foreign accent. As to the rest, very little care seems to have been taken of his education. He had not made the belles lettres or any of the finer arts his study.

In modern terms, Charles was no intellectual.

Dr King adds that before the prince left England, 'He came one evening to my lodgings [in the Temple] and drank tea with me.' King must have been alarmed when his servant remarked that his guest looked just like the busts of the Young Chevalier for sale in a nearby shop window.[3]

Charles would not have amassed his Antwerp arsenal without a plan. He told King it came from 'friends who were in exile'. No details survive, only the English Jacobites' refusal to rise. The historian Frank McLynn believes he was in England because he thought George II was on his deathbed and Cumberland might try to make himself regent – on the grounds that his older brother Frederick, Prince of Wales, was too feeble to rule – and the ensuing chaos would be ideal for a coup d'etat.[4]

During his five day stay, Charles was received into the Church of England by the nonjuror Bishop Robert Gordon, renouncing Catholicism at a ceremony that probably took place in the chapel of Gordon's house in Theobald's Row. 'With the catholics he is a catholic; with the protestants he is a protestant', observes Dr King. 'To convince the latter of his sincerity, he often carried an English Common Prayer-book in his pocket.'[5]

Charles had not forgotten Frederick II's flattering letter so, in 1751, he visited Berlin where he was well received, his host suggesting that he hire Swedish troops. At the same time, purely by concidence, Frederick appointed Lord Marischal, now a Prussian officer, as his ambassador at Paris, alarming George II's government who were unaware that the Marischal had no time for Charles. (He wanted a Scottish republic run by grandees like himself.) Doron Zimmermann argues convincingly that 'the Elibank conspiracy cannot be understood apart from the ambivalent collusion of Frederick II', who 'had ample reason to consider the Jacobite card'.[6]

In his journal, Lord Elcho says that Alexander Murray, younger brother of Patrick Murray, Lord Elibank, had enlisted a hundred Jacobites who would seize St James's Palace and the Tower, and kill the entire Hanover family – perhaps by poison. Lords Westmorland and Denbigh were in the plot, with 'persons of rank', who included Lord Marischal. Some of this cannot be true. Charles forebade assassination while the Marischal would never have helped. Yet the rest is plausible. According to Horace Walpole, Murray and Elibank were 'active Jacobites', but so cautious that nothing could be proved.

Elcho adds that Charles intended to come to London for the coup, hiding in Lady Primrose's house. Donald MacDonell of Lochgarry and Dr Archbibald Cameron (who had escaped with the prince on board *L'Heureux*) would go to Scotland and raise the clans. They were to stress that Charles had become a Protestant.

What may have been an alternative scheme is described by the eccentric adventurer Philip Thicknesse:

> Mr Seagrave, an Irish officer with only one arm, formerly well known at the Café de Condé, at Paris, assured me that he had been with the Prince in England between the years 1745 and 1756, and that they had laid a plan of seizeing the person of the King, as he returned from the play, by a body of Irish chairmen, who were to knock [down] the servants from behind his coach, extinguish the lights, and create a confusion, while a party carried the King to the water side, and hurried him away to France.

Given the period's poor lighting and lack of policing, a coup of this sort might have worked. George 'often returned from the theatres in so private a manner, that such an attempt was not impracticable, for what could not a hundred or two desperate villains effect at eleven o'clock at night, in any of the public streets of London? Twelve minutes start would do it . . .'[7]

Elcho and Thicknesse omit to name the coup's mainspring, George Heathcote, a Jamaica merchant, former City alderman and MP, who was in his fifties. There had been careful planning – how to enter St James's Palace from the park, a note of times when the guard changed, how to storm the Tower – using the prince's suggestion of blowing in a gate with a petard.

In September 1752, Dr Cameron and MacDonald of Lochgarry met the prince at Menin, in Flanders. He told them Prussia was going to help, powerful Englishmen hitherto hostile were ready to rise and Swedish troops would land in Scotland. Charles may even have visited England to inspect preparations, given a hiding place at Godalming by the Oglethorpes. Madame de Mézières (Eleanor Oglethorpe) had come over from France and was staying there, perhaps to entertain him.

Betrayal

Timed for 10 November 1752, the attempt was suddenly postponed until May or June the following year. Probably the leaders guessed they were under surveillance, Alexander Murray fleeing to France and a twenty year exile. The scheme was finally abandoned after Archie Cameron was arrested in spring 1753.

The plot had long been known to the prime minister, Henry Pelham, from Alasdair Ruadh MacDonnell of Glengarry, once an officer in the Royal Ecossais. Captured en route for the Forty-Five, he had gone back to Scotland in 1749 to steal some of the Loch Arkaig gold, after which he offered Pelham his services. A gentlemanly looking man, very good company, he quickly became a crony of the prince, who presented him with a gold snuffbox.

The identity of 'Pickle' (his codename, taken from Smollett's *Peregrine Pickle*, the fashionable novel of the day), remained unknown until 1897 when Andrew Lang spotted that the spy and Alasdair both wrote 'how' instead of 'who'.[8] He had been suspected by Dr Cameron, whose wife wrote to warn King James, but her warning reached Charles too late

The only person to suffer for the Elibank Plot was Cameron, who on a tip-off from Pickle was caught in Scotland, sent to the Tower and found guilty of treason. Pronouncing sentence, the judge stressed he would be conscious when butchered – hanged 'but not until you are dead'. (The real motive for killing him was to stop him revealing Pickle's identity.)

The night before he died, without proper writing materials he pencilled notes on slips of paper. On one he praised Charles, 'always the same, ever affable and courteous, giving constant proofs of his great humanity and of his love for his friends and his country'. On another, he prayed God to restore the royal family 'without which this miserably divided nation can never enjoy peace and happiness', and to 'defend the King, the Prince of Wales, and the Duke of York from the power and malice of their enemies'. He forgave 'the Elector of Hanover and his bloody son'.[9]

At Tyburn on 7 June 1753, despite the judge's instructions Cameron was allowed to hang until he was dead. Smollett says the crowd were impressed by his 'deportment . . . which they could not help admiring as the standard of manly fortitude and decorum'.[10]

Pickle was never paid. His patron Pelham died in 1754, as did his father whom he succeeded as chief of the clan, to inherit nothing save debts and the ruined castle of Invergarry at Loch Oich. He spent the rest of his life in abject poverty, in a hovel where he died in 1761.

Clementina Walkinshaw

The plotters suspected there was a mole and thought they knew who it was. 'When he was in Scotland [Charles] had a mistress, whose name is Walkinshaw, and whose sister was at that time, and is still housekeeper at Leicester House', Dr King tells us, writing about 1762. (Leicester House was the residence of the Hanoverian Princess of Wales.) Later, 'he sent for this girl [Clementina], who soon acquired such a dominion over him, that she was acquainted with all his schemes and trusted with his most secret correspondence'.[11]

Over thirty and penniless, Clementina had gone to the Low Countries in 1752, hoping to enter a convent. The only alternative, if she was lucky, was a post as an upper servant. Hearing she was still at Dunkirk, Charles, who had recently left Marie de Talmont, sent her 50 louis d'or and a message to come and live with him. They were together for eight years. There was little affection on the part of Charles who kept her only to satisfy his sexual needs, the poor woman staying with him because she was penniless and had nowhere to go. She may have had a short-lived son by him while in 1753 she certainly bore him a daughter, Charlotte. Frank McLynn believes she had already had a child by, of all people, Colonel O'Sullivan.[12]

Full of drunken quarrels, the affair brought little happiness to either. O'Sullivan witnessed what he called 'a devilish warm dispute' between them at a café in the Bois de Boulogne while Lord Elcho says that Charles thrashed her with a walking stick.

In 1760 she would bolt into a convent with her daughter, King James coming to the rescue with a pension.

Suggestions that she was a spy were nonsense but, wrongly assuming that 'Mrs Walkinshaw' was informing on them, in 1754 England's Jacobite leaders sent an envoy to Paris, Daniel Macnamara, who begged the prince 'to part with an harlot, whom, as he often declared, he neither loved nor esteemed'. He replied he would not get rid of a dog to please them, shouting that the £5,000 a year they paid him was not enough – if they did not do what he wanted, he would send their names to George.[13]

According to Elcho, Charles never received another halfpenny from England where his friends became too frightened to plot. Yet although Dr King and Lady Primrose turned against him, Elcho exaggerates. Most of the Jacobite old guard in England and Wales had left the scene, or would very soon – Lord Barrymore and Sir Robert Abdy died in 1748, Sir Watkin Williams-Wynn in 1749, Sir John Hynde Cotton in 1752 and the Duke of Beaufort in 1756. For the moment, the Earl of Westmorland and Sir John Philipps stayed loyal.

It is hard to reconcile Charles in the 1750s with the hero of the Forty-Five. He anticipated those young officers of the twentieth-century World Wars who could not adapt to civilian life. '*De vivre et pas vivre est beaucoup plus de mourir*', he wrote in about 1760 – meaning that a living death is worse than dying. Bred to be a king, he could see no other reason for his existence.

48

'The Fifty-Nine'?

I firmly believe, that, on very little encouragement from abroad, as great numbers wou'd appear in the pretender's cause, as did in the year 1745 . . .

The Earl of Findlater and Seafield, 1755[1]

Despite the Elibank Plot's failure, support for James III survived and the Whigs still felt threatened. 'When the newspapers swarm with our military preparations at home, with encampments, fire-ships, floating castles at the mouths of the great rivers, &c., in short, when we expect an invasion', moaned Horace Walpole in October 1755. In his view, the French were bound to invade and 'perhaps invite the Pretender to be of the party'.[2]

Although hostilities had not been declared, the Seven Years War had begun and, like Walpole, the Duke of Newcastle's government feared another pro-Stuart rising. They were worried by the way their spies lost track of the prince. Lord Elcho tells us he lived incognito with Clementina, 'Sometimes in Switzerland & sometimes in Flanders, and now and then making trips to Paris where no Soul of Fashion ever Saw him.'[3]

The situation started to change with the official outbreak of war in 1756 when France found herself fighting England and Prussia. It changed totally in December 1758 after Madame de Pompadour's friend the dynamic Duc de Choiseul became Louis's foreign minister.

Regardless of Clementina, most English Jacobites celebrated every 29 May and every 10 June, drinking healths to the King over the Water, days when white roses sold for a high price. New dining clubs sprang up, even at supposedly Whig Cambridge where the True Blue Club (which still exists) was founded in 1756 and drank a toast to 'Our Old Friend' – King James.[4]

When Pitt the Elder was out of office in 1757, the Tory pamphleteer John Shebbeare complained in *A Sixth Letter to the People of England* that 'the present grandeur of France and calamities of this nation are owing to the influence of Hanover on the councils of England'. Besides a three-year prison term Dr Shebbeare had to stand in the Charing Cross pillory for an hour – throughout, he was cheered by the crowd.

By now in early middle age, Prince Charles was described by Walter Scott in *Redgauntlet* as 'a man of middle life, about forty, or upwards; but either care, or fatigue, or indulgence, had brought on the appearance of premature old age, and given to his fine features a cast of seriousness or even sadness'. This must be based on first-hand accounts from people who had actually met the prince at this time. Scott also insists on his 'stately' air – that of a king in exile.

The war went badly for the French in America and India while, subsidised by England, Frederick II waged a brutally effective campaign against France's ally, the Habsburg Empress Maria Theresa. At the same time, the French were humiliated by English raids on their coastline. Something had to be done, not just to turn the tide but to save their possessions overseas.

Choiseul revived plans for invading England – if he evicted George II, the Anglo-Prussian coalition would collapse. Previous expeditions had been thwarted by storms, but he believed that by waiting for good weather he could send troops across the Channel in specially designed flat-bottomed boats escorted by gun-ships. His enthusiasm won fellow ministers' support.

He thought that Charles would be more effective leading a campaign in Scotland instead of accompanying the expedition to England. A decade after the Forty-Five, Scottish gaols were still full of men who had been imprisoned for wearing tartan, causing widespread anger, and Lochgarry reported that 10,000 Highlanders were ready to rise.[5]

But the prince insisted on England. His agent, Lord Blantyre, recommended Wales or Cornwall as the best place to land, with Bristol and Oxford as key objectives for securing the capital – a smaller landing in the Clyde near Glasgow should concentrate on capturing Edinburgh.[6] Charles thought he had gained his point when in January 1759 Louis XV promised his envoy, Colonel Wall of FitzJames's Regiment, that there would be a full-scale invasion of England. He also agreed that James should abdicate in Charles's favour.[7]

In February, Choiseul invited the prince to his house in Paris, to discuss the plan. Charles, who had refused to attend previous meetings or even come to Paris, arrived late. Some said he was drunk but this may just have been his truculent manner. (Zimmermann thinks he was 'more likely just exhausted'.)[8] Distrustful of Louis and his ministers, Charles suspected the French of wanting to relegate him to a sideshow in Scotland or Ireland.

Later that month Choiseul reassured the prince that in the event of the invasion's success he would replace George on the throne of Great Britain. He omitted to say that Charles was not going to play an active role in the invasion.

Although near bankruptcy from maintaining the world's largest army, France was determined to evict the Hanoverians, building over 300 transports that by June were anchored in harbours along the coast from Dunkirk to Nantes. Almost 50,000 men – including five Irish Brigade regiments – were on standby to invade England, trained to disembark in seven minutes. Smaller forces would invade Scotland and Ireland.

Aware of the threat, the Royal Navy blockaded France's north-western ports and in July British warships sailed into Le Havre, destroying several transports. In August, Paris ordered Admiral de La Clue-Sabran to bring twelve warships from Toulon to Brest, reinforcing Admiral Marquis de Conflans's twenty-one, which would form an unbeatable armada. But before he could reach Brest, La Clue-Sabran's fleet was caught and destroyed by Admiral Boscawen off the Algarve, the French flagship being driven ashore.

France then made the expedition to Scotland her priority instead of England. If it worked, they would land troops at Maldon and Portsmouth. They waited for favourable weather, which came on 20 October when gales disrupted the blockade. However, Conflans lost his chance and within a week the enemy's ships were back in position.

When the blockade was again momentarily dispersed by a gale Conflans led his fleet out of Brest and sailed for Quiberon Bay where the invasion force had assembled. Admiral Hawke intercepted him and on 20 November 1759, despite foul weather, blew Conflans's ships out of the water. The invasion was over.

Hopes had remained high in what O'Sullivan called 'that mournful and unhappy kingdom of Ireland' where poets referred cryptically to Charles as the shepherd, the roving hawk or the wanderer. There had been rumours of an invasion in 1752 and again in 1756. The French wanted campaigns in all three countries as did the Irish Brigade.[9] In 1759, 18,000 troops under the

Duc d'Aiguillon and Marshal the Earl of Thomond assembled at Vannes, ready to land in Munster and Connacht. They brought with them a 'Mr Dunn', who would impersonate Charles.

Their expedition was cancelled but a small force sailed, commanded by François Thurot, a half-Irish privateer who was credited with capturing sixty British merchantmen. (His grandfather Captain O'Farrell had served in James II's army and in the Irish Brigade.) Thurot took 1,300 picked troops to attack Ulster, besides arms for local supporters. After weathering storms during which half the troops died, he landed 600 men at Kilroot, County Antrim, in February 1760, seizing Carrickfergus with its castle. However, he had too few men to occupy Belfast, his real objective.

Sailing home, his squadron was intercepted by three British warships and he was killed in the ensuing engagement. Madame de Pompadour's comment on this last fragment of a grand design was that the French might have won at Quiberon had Thurot been in command. At least one bard, Liam Dall Ó hlfearnáin, was thrilled by his landing in Ulster, writing verses headed *Failtiughadh Righ Searlas* – 'A Welcome for King Charles'.

An earlier Trafalgar, Quiberon Bay's impact on France was devastating. Despite fighting on for three more years, she could no longer defend her own coast or merchant shipping and defaulted on public debt. In 1763 the Treaty of Paris confirmed that she had ceased to be a great power in the New World.

For Jacobites the defeat was total, ending all chance of an invasion or another rising. France, their greatest ally, could no longer help them. It was Quiberon Bay, not Culloden, that doomed the Honest Cause.

49

The Death of James III and VIII,
1 January 1766

...born the most unfortunate of princes, destined to
seventy-seven years of exile and wandering, of vain projects, of
honours more galling than insults, and of hopes such as make
the heart sick.

Thomas Macaulay, *The History of England*

During the 1750s King James had grown disillusioned with a son who never
came to see him. Well-informed about Charles's chaotic way of life, he was
deeply upset by his abandonment of Catholicism. Yet even now the king did
not despair of a Restoration because he genuinely believed that rule by 'our
family' would be beneficial for Britain.

After a stroke in 1762 James was not expected to live. He recovered, but
two years later was again struck down, lingering bedridden at Palazzo del
Re. By now even Whigs accepted him as a fact of life, almost an institution
– he had entered 'the pantheon of English folk heroes'.[1] Even so, the Honest
Cause was in serious decline.

One September afternoon in 1762, Edward Gibbon, still working on *The
Decline and Fall of the Roman Empire*, strolled down St James's Street to the
Jacobite stronghold of the Cocoa Tree in Pall Mall where he was a member,
although no Jacobite himself. It being the time for dinner he saw, 'Twenty or
thirty, perhaps, of the first men in the kingdom in point of fashion and fortune
supping at little tables covered with a napkin, in the middle of a coffee-room,
upon a bit of cold meat, or a sandwich, and drinking a glass of punch.'

What astonished Gibbon was their politics. 'At present we are full of
King's counsellors and lords of the bedchamber, who, having jumped into

the ministry, make a very singular medley of their old principles and language with the modern ones.'[2]

Why had Jacobites turned into Hanoverians?

For a start, George III, who had become king in 1760, was very different from his grandfather George II. 'This Sovereign don't stand in one spot, with his eyes fixed royally on the ground, and dropping bits of German news', noted Walpole. 'He walks about and speaks to everybody.' Twenty-three years old, he had been born and bred in his adopted country. Here was a king who saw himself as an Englishman, declaring, 'I glory in the name of Briton.' The Hanoverians had become home grown – as Boswell put it, 'the Brunswick graft now flourishes like a native shoot'.

Before, the Jacobites had boasted of younger, more personable leaders. Now the reverse was true. At forty, Charles was ageing badly, a drunk with, until recently, a drunken mistress. In contrast, George III was a thoroughly decent young man, driven by a sense of duty.

Twentieth-century historians concentrated on George's attempt to recover powers the Crown had lost under his predecessors, and how he replaced Whigs by Tories to regain control of Parliament. They ignored his other reason for bringing Tories into government for the first time since 1714, which was to wean them away from Jacobitism.

'Sir Francis Dashwood, a man of slender parts, of small experience, and of notoriously immoral character, was made Chancellor of the Exchequer, for no reason that could be imagined, except that he was a Tory, and had been a Jacobite,' splutters Macaulay. 'The royal household was filled with men whose favourite toast, a few years before, had been the King over the Water.' [3]

The Earl of Westmorland, a former pillar of Jacobitism, was promoted to general, Sir John Philipps became a privy counsellor and Lord Elibank (of the Plot) was offered an English peerage. Tory Oxford was preferred to Whig Cambridge, while Dr Johnson and Shebbeare the pamphleteer received pensions.

This explains the new atmosphere at the Cocoa Tree. George's policy had ended parliamentary Jacobitism. The Honest Cause survived outside Parliament but on an increasingly small scale. Even the most loyal were disheartened by Charles's failure to marry and beget an heir – there was no point in fighting for a dynasty without a future.

It is said that a disguised Charles went to George's coronation in September 1761, and that when the Champion rode into Westminster Hall during the coronation banquet and threw down his steel gauntlet, challenging anyone who disputed the new sovereign's right to the crown, an unknown lady picked it up and left a glove in its place in token of defiance, then vanished among the crowd. Another version says that Charles hurled a white glove at the Champion from the gallery. There was certainly some sort of discreet protest. So many guests passed their glasses 'over the water' at the banquet that finger bowls, ubiquitous elsewhere, were banned from royal palaces.

But nothing shook the prince's faith in his destiny. In August 1762 he dictated a message for Oliphant of Gask to take home: 'Assure my friends in Britain that I am in perfect good health and that they must not lose hopes, for that I expect all things will go well. That [the Restoration] will come some day like a Thunderbolt.'[4]

James succumbed to a final stroke on New Year's Day 1766. Although he had wanted a simple interment, Clement XIII insisted on a royal funeral.

The king lay in state at his palace for five days, in royal robes, a crown on his head and a sceptre in his hand. Then, escorted by the Swiss Guard and the Papal Militia his body was taken to his parish church, the Church of the Holy Apostles, whose interior was hung in black and filled with silver skeletons bearing wax tapers.

Here he lay on a catafalque lit by another 1,100 tapers while Cardinal Albani celebrated the requiem Mass, sung by the papal choir. (The Pope wanted to officiate, but was prevented by icy weather and a bout of asthma.) Among the congregation were twenty-two cardinals, the heads of the English, Scots and Irish colleges at Rome, several hundred seminarians and the Order of Malta's Grand Prior of England. After lying in state for three more days, the body was transferred with great pomp to St Peter's for interment in the crypt.

King James was a far better, far more decent man than the first two Hanoverians and one of awesome integrity, sacrificing three crowns for his faith. It is odd that he has not been canonised by the Church to whom he was so loyal. Despite crushing disappointments, he remained undaunted by his sad destiny, too sensible to let his life become a tragedy – unlike his elder son.

PART FIVE

Charles III and George III

50

King Charles III, 1766

... reared from infancy never to forego the desire or the hope
of recovering the Crown.

Giulio Cordara, *Commentary*[1]

Charles was en route for Rome, from whim and not because he expected his
father to die, when news reached him of King James's death. Held up by snow
and icy roads, he only arrived on 23 January.

Greeted by his brother, he installed himself at Palazzo del Re, where
Cardinal Henry had gathered a small crowd outside who shouted '*Viva il
Re!*' as he entered. Visiting the English, Scots and Irish Colleges, rectors and
seminarians paid homage to him as sovereign, singing *Te Deum* – for which
they would be expelled by the Pope. His father's secretary of state, Andrew
Lumisden, wrote how the new king 'charms everyone who approaches him'.
(Lumisden had been Charles's secretary during the Forty-Five and was a
veteran of Culloden.)

Unfortunately Pope Clement was an exception, refusing to recognise
Charles as king and listening to slanders by Cardinal Albani who, despite
celebrating James's requiem, was in Hanoverian pay. Clement was told that
should he recognise Charles, British warships would shell Civitavecchia
and Catholics would be expelled from Canada. The College of Cardinals
rejected Charles's claims, which meant that all Europe's Catholic sovereigns
did so too. Priests in Britain were instructed to pray for the Hanoverian king
at Mass.

Clement continued to pay Charles King James's pension, but never missed
an opportunity of snubbing him. The Papal Guard no longer posted sentries
outside Palazzo del Re and police removed the royal arms from over the main
door, confiscating his father's state carriage because it bore royal insignia.

Invited to a private audience, he was treated as a nobleman, not as a king. Cardinals and Roman nobles were forbidden to receive him.

Nonetheless, he remained at Palazzo del Re which provided a dignified setting for his court, while Palazzo Savelli enabled him to shoot in the Campagna. He lived in comfort. Besides the papal pension, his father had left him large sums in cash while his brother gave him an allowance.

Andrew Lumisden, James III's secretary of state, continued in office. As master of the household Charles appointed John Hay of Restalrig (once disastrously in charge of the commissariat at Culloden), whom he made a baronet. Among his gentlemen in waiting were Captain Adam Urquhart and Lachlan Mackintosh, also veterans of Culloden. Colonel John Roy Stewart (not to be confused with the Strathspey poet), who had been with him since 1745, became Groom of the Chambers. The late king's Protestant chaplain, Mr Wagstaffe, was kept on.

The little court did not lead an easy life, as appears from a letter Lumisden wrote to his sister during late autumn 1766:

> Almost from break of day to midnight I am employed about the king. Besides serving him as his secretary, I am obliged to attend him as a gentleman of the bedchamber when he goes abroad, both morning and evening, and after dinner I retire with him into his closet. Add to this the time we sit at the table, and you will see I have not a moment to myself. I am never in my apartment but either to sleep or write ... We have been five of the nine months since the king's coming into Italy either at Albano or other parts of the country, a' shooting, and which kind of wandering life is more likely to increase than diminish.

As if talking to himself, Lumisden says 'I have lived for many years in a sort of bondage; but I may name these past few months a mere slavery. Yet I readily submit to every convenience, when honour and duty call on me to do so.'[2]

What made the household's life unbearable were Charles's drunken rages, during which he grossly insulted them. Mackintosh left in 1767 and the rest, including Lumisden, in December 1768. Hopelessly drunk, Charles had ordered them to acompany him to the theatre – when they declined, he dismissed them. Next morning, he changed his mind, but even so they left. Only Stewart and Wagstaffe stayed. Four Italian noblemen took their place, one of whom was Master of the Horse, while in 1771 the household acquired two Irish gentlemen in waiting – officers or ex-officers of the Irish Brigade.

By this time hard drinking had become chronic alcoholism. At luncheon, taken at about 10 a.m., Charles drank whisky while during dinner, at 4 p.m., he switched to wine – six bottles in an evening. (His favourite was a sweet vintage from Cyprus.) Prone to wild rages when sottish, sober he was charming and dignified. Often his face grew red and bloated, covered in pimples, but at other times he looked healthy enough, perhaps because he drank in binges, with intervals between his sprees.

After an audience in 1767 Bishop Gordon reported with relief that there was not a spot on his face, not even a pimple – he was 'jolly and plump, though not to excess, being still agile and fit for undergoing toil'.[3] Yet his brother was in despair at his enslavement by 'the nasty bottle', to the point of writing a treatise on *The Sins of the Drunkard*.

George III grew less popular because of a widely disliked prime minister, the Earl of Bute, while when the costly Seven Years War ended in 1763 England gained nothing but Voltaire's 'barren waste' – Canada. Marriage to a German, even to one who acclimatised, did not help his image as a 'Briton'.

'We then fell upon political topics and all agreed in our love of the Royal Family of Stuart and regret at their being driven from the throne', James Boswell wrote in his journal after a dinner party in London in January 1761. 'That by the Revolution we got a shabby family to reign over us, and that the German War [the Seven Years War], a consequence of having a German sovereign was the most destructive thing this nation ever saw.'[4] Normally, Boswell concealed his Jacobitism, just as he would tone down Johnson's in his biography of the great man.

'The zeal of our non-juror grows more furious as he grows in years', wrote the renegade Dr King in 1763, a tacit admission that the Cause still flourished. 'I don't know whether he would be a martyr; but no man is a greater enthusiast in religion than he is in the Jacobite cause.'[5]

Whatever Rome said, recusants went on praying for Charles III at their chapels. In Advent they sang John Wade's *Adeste Fideles* ('O Come all ye Faithful') whose composer had left England hurriedly after the Forty-Five. Written as a birthday ode for Charles it looked forward to his coronation, 'joyful and triumphant' – as coded references reminded the singers.

Dining clubs continued to drink the King over the Water's health, passing glasses (engraved with a rose, a thistle, a shamrock, an oak tree or Charles's portrait) across finger bowls. More were founded, such as the oddly named Parched Pea Club at Catholic Preston in 1771.

Jacobite opinions were not limited to gentry. Since 1756 John Holker, once of the Manchester Regiment, had been France's 'Inspector General of Foreign Manufactures' – a polite name for top industrial spy – and played a big role in improving French cotton production by importing British machinery and textile experts. As such, he gained an insight into the minds of England's workers and in 1768, hearing of unrest among colliers, suggested that Charles should recruit them. However, the king showed no interest.

During the year Charles III succeeded his father a Scots Gaelic poet, Duncan Bàn MacIntyre from Glen Orchy, wrote a poem whose imagery would have been familiar to the Munster bards, in which he praises his patron's lavish hospitality at a fine Highland mansion. The last verse pays tribute to the new Stuart King:

> Glad tidings to cheer me would be
> If I were to see thee tomorrow
> Invested with the Crown,
> Amid rejoicing and pomp,
> Instead of King George.

Revealingly, the poem's title was 'Song to John Campbell, Banker' – the same man who had secretly helped to finance Charles's army in 1745.[6]

The Hanoverian regime long remained fearful of the Highlands. Major Caulfield continued building his military roads until 1762 and huge sums were spent until 1769 on strengthening Fort George, on the Moray Firth near Inverness. Designed to cow the clansmen, it cost over £200,000, more than Scotland's annual revenue. Yet in 1770 Campbell spies reported that Clan Maclean was 'stirring'. Nor was a rising entirely impractical. The Seven Years War was over, the British army had grown smaller and there were many Jacobites in its Scottish regiments.

Against all odds, little groups went on hoping for a Restoration, like that around Bishop Forbes of Ross and his friend at London, Bishop Gordon, who had received Prince Charles into the Anglican Church. Robert Forbes compiled *The Lyon in Mourning* – memoirs of the Forty-Five by men who had taken part, including accounts of the prince's flight through the heather.

In a letter to Gordon, Forbes mentions the Royal Oak Club, founded at Edinburgh in 1772, that met every month (dinner cost a shilling). The club's loyalties are clear from its house anthem:

Ye true sons of Scotia, together unite,
And yield all your senses to joy and delight;
Give mirth its full scope, that the nations may see
We honour our standard, the royal oak tree.[7]

This was the first song in *The True Loyalist; Or Chevalier's Favourite*, a book of Jacobite ballads published in 1779, presumably at the club's expense.

Dublin Castle grew less fearful of the Irish Brigade, letting its officers come home. But there were other Irish Jacobites, such as the Tipperary 'Whiteboys', founded in 1759 to co-operate with Conflans's invasion, who took an oath 'to restore Prince Charles to the throne of his ancestors'. In white cockades and white smocks (to imitate French uniforms), armed to the teeth, they regularly marched past government barracks, pipers defiantly playing 'The White Cockade', as at Capoquin in 1762.[8] As peasants, their main business, which spread to neighbouring counties, was a savage resistance to turning arable land into grazing, Church of Ireland tithes and rack-renting.

In 1767, James Nagle of Garnavilla near Cahir in County Tipperary, a 'gentleman grazier' who belonged to the Jacobite family, was charged with high treason because of involvement in a Whiteboy plot for a rising all over Ireland – the last time a man was tried for his life on account of loyalty to the Stuarts. The Whiteboys hated graziers and the plot never existed. Even so, like James Cotter in 1720, Nagle was facing legal murder. However, a young barrister cousin called Edmund Burke easily secured his acquittal.[9] The episode shows how 'conservative [Irish] Protestants still feared Jacobitism into the late 1760s and 1770s'.[10]

Oliver Goldsmith, an Anglo-Irishman, always remained a Jacobite, insisting that only the banished dynasty's return could save the country – by which he presumably meant the three kingdoms. In 1773, referring to the Whigs he told Dr Johnson, 'They have hurt our constitution, and will hurt it, till we mend it by another HAPPY REVOLUTION.'[11]

In 1769 a new pope was elected, Clement XIV, who as a young man had been one of James III's chaplains. At an audience in June, he embraced Charles, explaining that, while personally he would gladly recognise him as king, he was under pressure from hostile foreign powers. If he called himself Baron Renfrew, however, he would be treated with respect by the papal court. After this, Charles was overwhelmed with invitations from the Roman nobility.

In 1770 he started to travel again, visiting Florence where he was received by the first minister, and touched for the Evil at Pisa.

John Baptist Caryll, Lord Caryll, who became his secretary of state shortly after, was a Sussex recusant – once of Knepp Castle. An admirer of Charles since meeting him in France in 1744, he believed a Stuart Restoration would be good for England and was still feasible. He impressed Charles, who made him a Knight of the Thistle.

51

The Last Stuart Queen, 1772

The silver rose her drooping head shall rear.

Anon, 'Upon the marriage of the King with the Princess Louisa'[1]

In January 1771 Lady Miller, a 'poetess', was presented to Charles in Rome at the Duchess of Bracciano's reception and again at Princess Palestrina's. Tall, stooping, in a gold-laced red coat, he wore the blue ribbon of the Garter. She says he was 'bloated and red in the face' from drinking, but must have been handsome when young. She noticed his dignified manner and 'melancholic, mortified appearance'.

At their second meeting he produced a pack of tarot cards. Running through them, he held up one with the Pope and another with the Devil. Laughing, he told her, 'There is only one of the trio missing now and you know who that should be.'[2]

Later that year Lord Caryll went to Paris where he told Louis XV's ministers that if Charles had a son his dynasty would be France's ally for centuries to come. He needed diplomatic assistance to choose a bride and marry. He also required the help of an eloquent officer in the Irish Brigade, Colonel Edmund Ryan of Berwick's Regiment. The French agreed to both requests.

Charles arrived in Paris as 'Mr Smith', his departure from Italy in August having given London a nasty fright. Mann's spies had lost track of him at Modena and another Forty-Five was feared. Always a martyr to imagination, Horace Walpole believed a Jacobite armada was on its way from Spain.

George's government also suspected Charles of planning to be a candidate for the Polish throne, in place of King Stanisław whose enemies were trying to depose him. This was not entirely unreasonable in view of his Sobieski blood. However, the French foreign minister soothingly explained that

Charles's visit had nothing to do with politics but concerned marriage to 'a rich heiress, a woman in Germany'.[3]

His cousin, the Marquess of Jamaica, had suggested his sister-in-law as a bride, Princess Louise of Stolberg-Gedern, which was a tiny principality in the Hartz mountains. Her late father had been among the innumerable sovereign princes of the Holy Roman Empire (of the sort that Empress Maria Theresa's chancellor, Wenzel Anton, Prince of Kaunitz, called 'humming-bird kings') so it was a passable match.

Nineteen years old but precociously worldy, a brunette with a pretty face despite too much rouge, watchful blue eyes and a good figure, she was the reverse of rich. The alternative, becoming a nun, persuaded the penniless girl to accept a man old enough to be her father. However, she was told his position would be regularised by the Pope and she would reign over Roman society as 'Her Majesty'. She also thought that France still meant to restore him.

Queen Louise

They were married by proxy at Paris in March 1772, renewing their vows when they met at Macerata in the Papal States on 14 April. It was Good Friday, but Louise's mother insisted on their marrying at once. Even so, it was a cheerful wedding, in the chapel of Palazzo Marefoschi which belonged to the Cardinal of York's friend, Cardinal Marefoschi, with crowds outside shouting '*Viva il Re!*' On Easter Sunday there was a reception for the nobility from miles around that went on into the small hours of the morning.

When they reached Rome Louise's brother-in-law presented her with a gold snuffbox set with diamonds – inside was a cheque for £10,000 and a document for an annuity of £4,000 a year. A medal was struck, bearing the heads of 'King Charles III of Great Britain, France and Ireland' and his new queen. In London, Bishop Gordon wrote to his friend Bishop Forbes in Scotland, 'the Lady's name is Louisa, and a most amiable princess by all accounts she is'.[4] From France the Duke of Melfort (great-grandson of James II's secretary of state) sent Louise an elegant petition begging her to give the Honest Cause an heir.

For two years the couple seemed happy enough at Palazzo del Re, lionised by Roman society who called Louise 'the Queen of Hearts'. Even Mann admitted the Pretender stayed sober for months. A Catholic again, Charles felt sure Clement XIV would recognise him as *de jure* king. But Clement was frightened of upsetting George who still felt threatened. (When in 1774

Prince Charles of Mecklenburg-Strelitz asked Queen Charlotte to help Lord Elcho obtain a pardon, she replied he 'must not think of doing a favour to anyone engaged in the late rebellion')[5]

In 1774 the 'Count and Countess of Albany' left Rome for Florence to live in the Casino Corsini just outside the city walls, moving in 1776 to Palazzo Guadagni (now Palazzo Clemente), a fine Renaissance palace inside. But they were ostracised by Grand Duke Pietro Leopoldo and the Florentine nobility.

Louise did not bear a child and, with nothing to occupy her, was reduced to breeding rabbits. Her one pleasure, she said, was reading Montaigne's essays in bed. She declared that a woman should have an intellectual friend by day and a carnal friend by night. Her husband was neither.

Later, Charles claimed that Horace Mann had given Louise thousands of Venetian gold sequins to administer a 'potion' which rendered him impotent. Dropsical and asthmatic, with suppurating sores on his legs, drinking more than ever, it is hard to imagine a less loveable husband. When the couple went to the theatre he took flasks of wine in his pockets, leaving his box to vomit in the corridor, before being carried in a stupor to his coach.

In Britain, nonjurors were dying off or conforming, recusants losing interest. Yet on 16 February 1774, a letter from 'A South Briton' appeared in a London daily paper, *The Public Advertiser*, that damned the Revolution for encouraging rebellion and perjury, called William and Mary 'two undutiful children' and blamed 'our governors [who] by their wicked example of bribery, corruption, dissipation, gambling, and every species of wickedness ... have so debauched the morals of the people'.[6] This what every Jacobite had always believed and a thousand copies were reprinted in Scotland.

Outraged, the House of Commons resolved 'the said letter is a false, scandalous, and traitorous libel upon the constitution of this country, and tending to alienate the affections of his Majesty's subjects from his Majesty and his royal family'. The printers received a prison sentence.

Despite many members turning Hanoverian, the Cocoa Tree stayed a bastion of Jacobite conviviality. In September 1774 London newspapers reported that, strolling down St James's 'such as call themselves the King's Friends ... would stop of an evening under the windows, and appear highly delighted with the old favourite songs'. These included 'When the King enjoys his Own again'.[7]

Charles had not inherited the right to appoint bishops in Ireland and in 1774 Irish Catholics were permitted to swear allegiance to George III, renouncing 'any allegiance, or obedience, to the person assuming the title of "Charles III". The following year Lord Trimleston led sixty prominent Dublin Catholics in taking the oath and Irish priests began to pray for George in their chapels.

Many among the Irish diaspora stayed faithful, however, like Count Patrick Darcy from Galway, a maréchal de camp (brigadier-general) in the French army who was a member of the Académie des Sciences. His house in Paris was always open to Jacobite exiles until he died in 1779. By then most of the Irish Brigade were Frenchmen. An exception was General Count O'Connell of Derrynane in Kerry who had joined Clare's Regiment in 1757 as a boy of fourteen, fought against George III at the Siege of Gibraltar and died only in 1833. (His nephew was the 'Liberator', Daniel O'Connell.)

Dr Samuel Johnson, Jacobite

Although Johnson worshipped in mainstream Anglican churches, the 'Great Cham' (Khan) of English letters avoided taking the oaths of allegiance or abjuration and was spiritually a nonjuror, veering between a de facto king who paid him a pension and loyalty to the *de jure* king.[8] While conceding that the new dynasty held the throne by 'long consent', he called the Forty-Five 'a noble attempt' and insisted 'The First Whig was the Devil'. Dining with the Lords of Session at Edinburgh in 1774, he declared 'George the 1st was a robber, George the 2nd a fool, and George the 3rd is an idiot.'[9]

In 1777 he claimed that 'If England were to be fairly polled, the present King [George] would be sent away tonight.' In his view,

> The people, knowing it to be agreed on all hands, that this King has not the hereditary right to the Crown, and there being no hope that he who has it can be restored, have grown cold and indifferent upon the subject of loyalty, and have no warm attachment to any King. They would not therefore risk any thing to restore the exiled family. They would not give 20 shillings a piece to bring it about. But, if a mere vote could do it, there would be 20 to 1; at least, there would be a very great majority of voices for it.

He added, 'all those who think a King has a right to his crown, as a man has to his estate . . . would be for restoring the King [Charles], who certainly has the hereditary right, could he be trusted with it; in which there could be no danger now, when laws and everything else are so much advanced.'[10]

The doctor spoke not only for many English people, but for Scots and Irish, and for some across the Atlantic Ocean. In 1775 he had been to Paris, visiting the English monastery of St Edmund's, where James II's coffin still lay in state and whose Benedictines remained loyal to Charles III. In 1779 he helped one of the monks find a publisher for a translation of the Duke of Berwick's memoirs, a book demolishing much of the Whig myth about the Revolution.[11]

Yet Charles was half the King over the Water his father had been, unrecognised by other Catholic sovereigns, unable to appoint bishops in his nominal realms, unable to call on an Irish 'army in exile'. In March 1775, Lord Caryll despaired, resigning his post as secretary of state. Another Jacobite had commented, 'He has not even dog's wages for his trouble but does all for stark love and kindness.' Charles found it impossible to replace him.

52

An American Dream? 1775

> In America we are not yet republicans ... What more potent
> appeal to American pride than to say: 'We have got rid of King
> George; we choose of our own free will the older line and
> King Charles'?
>
> John Buchan, *The Company of the Marjolaine*[1]

There were Native Americans who fought for the Stuarts. These were the tribes of the Wabanaki Confederation on the coast of what is now south-eastern Canada and the northern United States (the tribes included the Abenaki, Mi'kmaq, Passamaquoddy) who, as converts to Catholicism, adapted surprisingly well to colonial inroads. Seafarers by tradition, not merely did they learn how to crew the newcomers' merchantmen and whalers, but they acquired their own fleet of brigs and ketches for trading and even piracy.

Fluent in French and English, well-informed of events in Europe, the Wabanaki deplored the Glorious Revolution's dethronement of a great Catholic chief, no doubt influenced by a dislike of the Protestant seamen of New England, and for decades remained loyal Jacobites. Throughout the Franco-British struggle for North America they served with Louis XV's troops, providing them with valuable scouts. They only abandoned the Honest Cause in the 1760s after the French were driven out of Canada.[2]

As for American patriots, in 1774 *The St James's Chronicle* for 1–3 September reported 'The Chevalier ... has had pressing invitations to America for which he will not embark unless assisted by the Crowns of France and Spain.'[3] Two months later, English Jacobites informed Charles they were ready to help if he wanted to lead a rising in North America. He replied that it had already been suggested but thought it inadvisable. Yet King George's government suspected he might do so.

Nevertheless, when the Massachusetts Militia fought the redcoats at Lexington in 1775 their fifes and drums played the Jacobite battle march, 'The White Cockade'.[4] This was painfully familiar to veterans in the King's Own Royal (4th) Foot who were there, having suffered more casualties at Culloden than any other English regiment.

Did the Militia, or at any rate someone in the Militia, see Charles as the alternative to George III?

In September 1775 the Earl of Dartmouth, Secretary for the Colonies, discovered 'a traitorous correspondence' with 'rebels in North America', carried by American ships. Filed next to his report are details of letters found at Prince's Coffee House, Prince's Street, Leicester Fields (today's Leicester Square). Run by a Mrs Leslie, this was frequented by Jacobites. One letter was from 'N.B.' to a 'Mr Statuvell' [Hatwell?], addressed care of Mrs Leslie.

'N.B.' says he is at the 'D.of N's' [the Duke of Norfolk's?], who assures him money will be ready at a moment's warning and 'if his Highness had received the intelligence . . . of the landing at Milford Haven, the day will be ours'. The writer has been sent a letter by the 'D. of Q' [Duchess of Queensberry?] who says all is going to plan and that 'George looks very sour mouthed especially at his regiments'. When examined, Mrs Leslie claimed the Pretender was in England and she had spoken to him.[5] Then she disappears from history.

What can we make of this? All we can say is that Charles, tenth Duke of Norfolk, a Catholic, remained discreetly loyal to the Stuarts, while the Duchess of Queensbery was a sister of the Lord Cornbury who forty years before had plotted a Restoration. Whatever lay behind Mrs Leslie's letters, the timing indicates that George III's government feared a link between Jacobites and Colonists – even that Charles might have gone to Milford Haven to sail for America.

Had the Forty-Five succeeded, a restored Stuart state with semi-independent governments in Scotland and Ireland could well have given America a similar government. There might never have been an American revolution – perhaps not even a French one. The counter-factual possibilities are dazzling. Thirty years later, there were Americans who would have liked Charles to replace George III. 'Almost certainly, some kind of invitation was made by the Bostonians in 1775 that he should be the figurehead of a provisional American government.'[6]

Until then Americans had seen themselves as loyal subjects of the Crown, but a Jacobite leavening must have existed, especially among Episcopalian Scots. A member of Washington's army who may have been a Jacobite was General Hugh Mercer (killed at the Battle of Princeton in 1777), once a surgeon in Charles's army.

Admittedly, there had been deep dislike of Charles's Catholicism. In 1745 the Bostonians had burned his effigy with one of the Pope, while Benjamin Franklin had feared that everyone in Britain's domains would have to become a Catholic if the Jacobites won. In 1774, *A Letter to the People of Great Britain* from the Continental Congress claimed that Catholicism has 'deluged your island in blood and dispersed impiety, bigotry, persecution, murder, and rebellion throughout every part of the world'.[7]

However, Charles could argue that he had become a Protestant in 1750, despite his recent return to Rome. A coronation at Boston or Philadelphia may even have been mooted – Episcopalian prelates could be brought over from Scotland to crown him.

It took time for the idea of a president to evolve and, until then, American Jacobites must still have regarded Charles as their king. Early in 1776 Tom Paine published *Common Sense*, a pamphlet denouncing George III as 'the Royal Brute of Great Britain' and attacking the entire institution of monarchy. But this was too radical for many, not just for Jacobites. A Stuart king could well have appealed to conservative Patriots as well as Tories – and to the French who eventually intervened in America. Dr Johnson believed that a fundamental reason for colonial rejection of British rule was the ancient dynasty's replacement by the Hanover family, which had weakened respect for the monarchy. In 1783 he told General Oglethorpe, a former governer of Georgia and a Jacobite at heart, that the rift was due to George III's 'want of inherent right'.

In theory, Charles would have made a useful figurehead for the Patriots. Much has been written on Highland regiments fighting their way back into Hanoverian favour during the war – whether they would have fought quite so keenly against the hero of the Forty-Five is questionable. A coronation at Boston and an American court that looked down on the court of St James's with its German Pretender might well have hastened King George's collapse into insanity.

On the other hand, given Charles's alcoholism and temperament, it is unikely that an American adventure of this sort would have lasted very long. It was fortunate for everybody that he declined the invitation.

Writing thirty years later, the philologist Louis Dutens said the Abate Angelo

Fabroni, rector of Pisa University, had told him of letters sent to Charles in 1775 by Bostonians, assuring the king of their loyalty and asking him to come and lead them. Monsignor Fabroni was a distinguished historian who translated Gibbon's *Decline and Fall* into Italian. As a friend of Cardinal York and a frequent visitor to Palazzo del Re, he was well-informed about the Honest Cause. He had even delivered the eulogy at James III's funeral.

Another witness for American support is Washington Irving, who in *Abbotsford and Newstead* (1835) records how Sir Walter Scott had told him of seeing among the Stuart Papers at Carlton House 'a memorial to Charles from some adherents in America, dated in 1778, proposing to set up his standard in the back settlements'. Although the document has never been found, it must have existed – Scott was not a man to tell lies.

Most of this has been long, if not widely, known. In 1908 it inspired John Buchan to write a haunting short story, *The Company of the Marjolaine*. This relates how after Yorktown four American gentlemen visit Charles in Italy to offer him a throne in North America, but change their minds on seeing him lying on the floor in a drunken stupor, surrounded by bottles.

The reality behind the rumours seems to be that on their own authority some monarchically minded Americans did indeed ask Charles to lead them, but later preferred to forget the scheme – which would explain why so little evidence survives.

The reason for his refusal was not so much ill health as determination to regain the three kingdoms on this side of the Atlantic, which – to him at least – did not seem impossible, especially if France intervened in the American war. He still hoped for a French invasion of England that would bring a Restoration.

Since reverses for George III's troops would make French intervention more likely, Charles followed the American campaigns on a large map that his agent, Dom Gregory Cowley, Prior of St Edmund's at Paris, obtained for him.[8] The prior also supplied any information from the front that he could glean from French sources. Regarding himself as their king, Charles rejoiced at the colonists' victories – perhaps seeing the campaign as a re-run of the Forty-Five.

If nothing came of the plans to crown Charles king in North America, former Stuart supporters made an enduring contribution to the new United States. When Dr Samuel Seabury, the High Church rector of Hempstead, Long Island, came to Britain in 1784 to be consecrated as an American bishop, he could not ask Anglican prelates to officiate as they would insist on his swearing allegiance to George III. But because he had studied at Edinburgh in the early 1750s, he knew where to find a solution, confirmed in his opinion by Dr Martin Routh of Magdalen College, Oxford, who was also a High Churchman.

Seabury then had himself consecrated at Aberdeen as 'Bishop among the Americans' by three Episcopalian prelates who although they had ceased to pray for Charles in 1780, were still viewed with suspicion by the government at London. Alarmed by the prospect of a Jacobite Church across the Atlantic, it quickly brought in provision for the consecration of non-English bishops.

While Bishop Seabury abandoned the prayer for Charles, he introduced the Scottish liturgy instead of the Book of Common Prayer. 'The sacramental soul of Jacobitism', it has been claimed in consequence, 'put down deep roots in America, where its legacy lives and thrives today.'[9]

53

The Last Years of Charles III

While the life of Charles Edward was gradually wasting in
disappointed solitude, the number of those who had shared
his misfortunes and dangers had shrunk into a small band of
veterans, the heroes of a tale which had been told.

Sir Walter Scott, *Redgauntlet*

In 1776 Count Vittorio Alfieri was presented to the king and queen, a
red-headed young Piedmontese poet whose play *Cleopatra* had won him
the name 'father of Italian tragedy'. He soon decided Louise was the love of
his life. Charles, who did not see the danger, allowed Alfieri to pay constant
visits to Palazzo Guadagni and act as her *cavaliere servente* in the Italian fashion – a Platonic escort. At some time during 1778 the fascinating Vittorio, an
accomplished seducer, became Louise's lover.[1]

Her husband's health was worse than ever. Writing from Florence in May
1779 Mann reported that he had 'a declared fistula, great sores on his legs,
and [is] insupportable in stench and temper, neither of which he takes the
least pains to disguise to his wife, whose beauty is vastly faded of late'. Mann
commented, 'She has paid dear for the dregs of royalty.'

On St Andrew's Night 1780, which he celebrated in his usual way, her
husband beat her, tore hair from her head and tried to throttle her. Louise
fled to Rome, installing herself at a convent and asking her brother-in-law,
the cardinal, for help, while secretly continuing her affair with Alfieri – telling Henry that Vittorio was just a friend. Henry let her live at his palazzo
and spoke to the Pope, who put her under his personal protection, paying
her half Charles's pension.

Infuriated, Charles quarrelled violently with his brother. Only when
he fell gravely ill and Henry visited him at Florence in March 1783 did the

cardinal learn the truth. Alfieri then made a hasty departure. Ludicrously, Charles hoped his wife would return and do public penance.

In December 1783 as 'Count Haga', Gustav III of Sweden arrived in Florence, an impressive figure who had restored Sweden to her place as a great power. He not only visited Charles but stayed with him at Palazzo Guadagni, treating him as a fellow sovereign. He also offered to buy the hereditary grand-mastership of all 'Templars' (freemasons) throughout the world that he mistakenly supposed belonged to Charles. In return for 4,000 rix thaler, Charles, who was not even a mason, signed a document appointing Gustav as his successor.[2]

He was delighted with even this small sum, having developed a terror of poverty despite his brother's readiness to bail him out. His finances were always in chaos – on one occasion he pawned a cherished pair of jade-handled pistols. Yet when someone suggested he sell an enormous ruby inherited from the Sobieskis he replied that he was going to make it a crown jewel as soon as he returned to England. Until the day he died, he never doubted there would be a second Restoration – not even in 1784 when Parliament restored the Scottish estates confiscated after the Forty-Five.

Genuinely sorry for the wreck who had once been Europe's hero, King Gustav negotiated a decree of separation that gave Louise a comfortable financial settlement. She left Rome, living with Alfieri until his death in 1803. Despite Charles's treatment of Louise, one cannot disagree with Frank McLynn's assessment of her – 'an accomplished liar, cold, cynical and egotistical'.[3]

For a moment, Gustav's recognition of Charles as king horrified Horace Mann, who suspected another rising. His worries were quickly dispelled. Even so, George III's government still feared the exiled family.

We know from Louise that Charles kept 12,000 gold sequins under his bed at Palazzo Guadagni in case of another Forty-Five. In September 1783, heartened by George III's defeat in America he had written to the Comte de Vergennes, Louis XVI's foreign minister, pleading for France to make another effort to restore him – 'the moment was never more favourable'.[4]

He still had supporters in all three kingdoms. As late as 1785 one or two English tourists made a point of seeing James II's catafalque at Paris. Although he never expressed his opinions in public, the Honourable Richard Barry, who had brought a letter promising help from Sir Watkin Williams-Wynn to

Charles at Derby in 1745 and was afterwards MP for Wigan, stayed a Jacobite until his death in 1787.[5] Another lifelong Stuart supporter was Francis Hurt Sitwell of Renishaw in Derbyshire, president of the local Church and King Club, who died in 1793.[6] Like Mr Sitwell, recusant squires continued to display portraits of the Kings over the Water in their houses.

There were even recruits from the younger generation. In 1778 a youthful antiquarian from County Durham, Joseph Ritson, published a genealogical tree of the Kings of England which showed Charles III as the country's sovereign. In 1790, in *Ancient Songs and Ballads*, he claimed 'When the King enjoys his Own again' was 'the most famous and popular air ever heard in this country'.

The Scottish remnant would still have fought for Charles. When the ban on tartan was lifted in 1782 a Caithness laird, John Sinclair of Ulbster, began to wear full Highland dress. Passing through Logierait in Perthshire, he left his carriage to walk in the hills. Suddenly he realised he was being followed by a large crowd who were talking excitedly in Gaelic. An old Highlander came up to him. 'Sir,' he said in a low voice, 'If you are come in the good old cause, I can give you to understand that there are a hundred good men ready to join you within the sound of the bell of Logierait.'[7]

In 1786 a tourist, Alexandre de La Rochefoucauld, met a boatman near Fort William, a MacDonald, who spoke a little English. Showing a long scar on his wrist he called 'a Culloden memento', he told him. 'If King Charles has need of 20,000 lives they're here, at his disposal.' Then he asked if he was still alive and had children. Learning he was alive but childless, he exclaimed, 'All our hopes are finished! Ah, if only we'd had the 6,000 French we were waiting for in Scotland, George would have been chased back to Hanover!' La Rochefoucauld adds that throughout the Highlands men spoke of 'King Charles' – referring to 'George' or 'the governor', never as king.[8]

In Ireland, Catholic gentlemen, especially veterans of the Irish Brigade, still sighed for the Honest Cause while peasants spoke of *an fánagh Righ gan ainm* – 'the wandering king without a name'. Furthermore, 'A residual loyalty to Charles Stuart survived in the Irish literary tradition into the 1770s and 1780s.'[9]

Shortly before his own death in 1782 Eoghan Rua Ó Súilleabháin, last of the great Munster poets, wrote a tribute to Charles. It ends defiantly, *Sláinte mo Rex!* – 'A health to my King!'

The Duchess of Albany

In 1784 Charles's daughter by Clementina Walkinshaw joined him at Florence. Thirty-five, a big, dark-haired woman, plain but warm hearted, Charlotte looked after him for the rest of his life, giving him care he badly needed. She hid a lurid past (three children born to the Archbishop of Cambrai) of which her father always remained unaware.

He told Charlotte to call herself 'Her Royal Highness', creating her Duchess of Albany besides legitimising her under French law and making her a Knight (not Dame) of the Thistle. For a short period, he gave balls for her three times a week at Palazzo Guadagni. He may even have seen Charlotte as his successor. 'I mention with regrate' [sic] commented Oliphant of Gask, 'that the late King... conveyed as far as he could his Crown and effects to his Legitimate Daughter.'[10]

Charlotte aroused widespread interest, not only in committed Jacobite circles, Robert Burns writing 'The Bonny Lass of Albany':

> This lovely maid's of royal blood
> That ruled Albion's kingdoms three
> But oh, alas! for her bonnie face.
> They've wranged the lass of Albany.

Admittedly, Burns's Jacobitism is debatable.

The end of Charles III

A likeness of Charles painted at Rome about 1785 by the Irish artist Hugh Douglas Hamilton (now in the Scottish National Portrait Gallery) shows a man broken by disappointment. When he moved back into Palazzo del Re the same year he was dying from dropsy and asthma – footmen had to carry him from his carriage to morning Mass. An English visitor, Bertie Greatheed, pursuaded him to talk about the Forty-Five but he became so excited that he had a seizure and fell on the floor. The tune 'Lochaber No More' reduced him to tears.

Yet George III still felt menaced by the King over the Water. When in 1787 Captain Arthur Philip was entrusted with founding a penal settlement at Botany Bay and made its governor, he had to swear an oath that he would not further the cause of 'the man called Charles Edward Stuart'.[11]

The end came early in 1788 when Charles suffered a stroke. Given the last rites by his brother, he died on 31 January. Had he done so on the day before, it would have been the anniversary of his great-grandfather stepping out from a window in Whitehall Palace onto the scaffold.

Fearful of upsetting the British government, the Holy See refused a royal funeral at Rome. However, the Cardinal of York – now Henry IX – had his brother's body brought to Frascati where he celebrated a magnificent requiem. Later, Charles was interred in St Peter's Basilica. Charlotte, who attended the service at Frascati, remained on affectionate terms with her new sovereign, until her own death from cancer in November 1789. (Even at this late date the master of her household had been an English Jacobite, a Benedictine monk from Paris.)

For all his sottishness and callous treatment of women, it is hard not to pity Charles in his last years – 'The decadence was too tragic to prose about, the decadent too human to moralise on.'[12] He is best remembered as the 'Prince Adventurer' of the Forty-Five. In October 1746 one of the Glenmoriston men, Patrick Grant, a monoglot Gaelic speaker, had come to Edinburgh, swearing to go beyond seas and seek him. He told Bishop Forbes, 'Meet when we will, the Prince and I shall never part again.'[13]

PART SIX

Twilight

54

Henry IX, 1788–1807

'Wo's me! For the faithful are minished from among the children of men, and are much upon the decrease.'

Bishop Forbes, *The Lyon in Mourning*[1]

The new King over the Water, the Cardinal Duke of York, had spent his life at Rome or in his bishopric of Frascati. Although there were still a few diehard Jacobites, his 'reign' was a shadowy postscript. Henry IX was no more than the living ghost of the Honest Cause.

A portrait of a dashing young man in armour, painted by Quentin de La Tour during the Forty-Five, was long thought to be his elder brother, but the Duc de Luynes recalls the young Henry as quite different from Charles. 'He talks more, laughs a lot, is very lively and has a deep love of music. He is much smaller.'[2] The free-thinking Duc de Richelieu, who saw a lot of him in 1744, was irritated by a piety verging on religious mania, although this matured. Even so, his decision to enter the Church had been a surprise.

In 1747, the year he became a cardinal, he moved into the queen's former apartments at Rome. He lived there until 1764, giving weekly *conversazioni* to which invitations were much coveted. 'In this way the Palazzo del Re maintained its social distinction and continued to provide concerts performed by some of the best musicians in the city.'[3] He shocked King James by inviting his choir master, the Venetian Baldassare Galuppi – composer of the opera *Enrico* – to dine with him.

In 1769 Bishop Forbes heard that Scots visitors had been pleasantly surprised by his lack of hauteur – 'frank and free, more like a companion than a superiour'.[4] Usually, however, Henry was noticeably reserved, if garrulous with a few close friends. Spare, middle-sized, dark skinned, he looked distinguished rather than handsome.

Writers such as James Lees-Milne think he may have been homosexual,[5] but despite a liking for good-looking young men and one or two emotional friendships it seems improbable that he ever slept with anybody. What he wanted was companionship, which he found in 1769 when he appointed Monsignor Angelo Cesarini as his major-domo. Loyal, good natured, Cesarini retained the post until his patron's death.

There was a seminarian at Frascati, Marchese Ercole Consalvi, a young Roman noble whom he treated as a son. Henry secured his entry into the Curia and then his appointment as a monsignor, furthering what became a brilliant career in every way he could. Consalvi always remained close, spending summer holidays with him at Frascati.

Appointed archpriest (administrator) of the Vatican Basilica in 1751, the Cardinal Duke became titular Archbishop of Corinth in 1758, Bishop of Frascati in 1761 and Vice-Chancellor of the Holy Roman Church in 1763, which gave him the magnificent Palazzo Cancelleria as a residence in Rome, to where he commuted daily from his palace at Frascati.

He found no difficulty in coping with Curia politics and in 1775 organised the conclave that elected Pius VI (it dragged on for months) without making enemies. By 1788 his income from clerical posts all over western Europe and Latin America came to £40,000 a year. Much of this went on helping the poor in his diocese or rebuilding and improving its seminary which acquired a theatre, a concert hall, a library and even a printing press.

His journeys between Rome and Frascati were always at full gallop in a coach-and-six, escorted by running footmen in livery. Frascati was his real home, where he kept an impressive collection of books. He relaxed there, exchanging his cardinal's cassock for a black coat lined with red silk, black velvet breeches, red silk stockings and a red silk waistcoat.

To remind the world he was Britain's *de jure* sovereign, he commissioned medals with on one side his profile under a clerical skull cap and on the other a woman holding a cross with St Peter's in the background – the inscription stating that he was 'King Henry IX... not by men's desire but by the will of God.' His staff wore the royal livery, addressing him as 'Your Majesty'. So did British visitors who wished to please.

He regularly touched for the Evil, laying his hands on sufferers to whom he gave touch-pieces. There was a rumour that among those who came to be healed was George III's half-witted brother William Henry, Duke of Gloucester – bizarre behaviour for Butcher Cumberland's nephew.

He made few political gestures apart from a memorial sent to the royal courts of Europe announcing his accession. When in 1792 the Holy See's gazette styled George III *Re di Gran Bretagna* instead of *Duca di Hannover*, he protested to Pius VI – 'O God, what a blow' – reminding him of what the Stuarts had sacrificed for their faith. Till the day he died, he referred to George as 'the Elector of Hanover'.

In the same year, 1792, Edmund Burke mocked Irish Protestants for still being frightened of the Pretender, the Pope and the French king, their 'bugaboos'. Perhaps they thought that Rome would 'send over the Cardinal of York to rule them as his Viceroy' and impose Popery.[6] Ironically, Burke came of Jacobite stock. It has even been argued that 'his defence of the old monarchical system in Europe was the last flare of the Irish Jacobite dream of a restored monarchy, in which Catholic Ireland would play its full part and regain its lost privileges'.[7]

During the 1790s Irish Jacobitism transformed itself into Jacobinism and republicanism, if not without backward glances. There were Jacobite echoes among the 'Defenders' (heirs of the Whiteboys) who fought to protect their fellow peasants against Protestant 'Peep o' Day Boys'. In 1793 the lord lieutenant, the Earl of Westmorland, informed the prime minister, William Pitt, that 'The Defenders have been frequently heard to declare that the King [George III] is not the Catholic King.'[8]

The last Jacobites

The Honest Cause did not vanish overnight. A few men in all three kingdoms saw Henry as their king, such as the nonjuror Bishop Mansfield who was Bishop Gordon's successor. As too did the High Master of Manchester Grammar School in 1801, according to his pupil, Thomas de Quincy.

The younger Laurence Oliphant of Glask, a survivor from the Forty-Five, exhorted his son to stay loyal to King Henry and his Sardinian heirs, adding, 'Passive obedience and non-resistance is our unalterable duty.'[9] By then, most Episcopalians prayed for George at their services, but Glask made his chaplain pray for Henry IX.

In August 1794, while on the Grand Tour, George III's sixth son, the twenty-one-year-old Duke of Sussex, found his carriage blocked by another vehicle in a narrow street at Frascati. Realising it was Henry's carriage, he jumped out to introduce himself, addressing his cousin as 'Your Royal Highness' throughout. Both were charmed by each other.

During the previous year even Whigs had been shocked by the news that in Paris a revolutionary mob had thrown James II's skeleton into the Seine – the last prior of St Edmund's kissing its bony hand as it was carted off. In 1798 the French compounded the atrocity by occupying Rome. Henry fled to Naples, then Sicily, before going to Venice in 1799 for the conclave to elect a new pope. Destitute, he took refuge in a monastery, selling his few remaining valuables.

By now the Hanover family had developed a conscience about the Stuarts. George III had let Louise, Countess of Albany, use the royal opera box when she came to London in 1791 and was presented to him. (Walpole was amazed by her self-possession, but Louise knew she was a queen.) After Henry died, George's daughter, Princess Augusta, would confide in the Irish diarist John Wilson Croker that only then did she feel herself to be a real princess. Learning of his plight, George arranged for Henry to be paid £4,000 a year. If grateful, he saw it as part of his grandmother Mary of Modena's dowry to which he was legally entitled – by that date amounting to several million pounds. Though Henry still referred to George as 'the Elector of Hanover'.

George's view of his own right to the throne emerged in his refusal to grant Catholic emancipation. He believed that to do so would break his coronation oath to uphold the Protestant religion. 'If I violate it, I am no longer legal sovereign of this country, but it falls to the House of Savoy' – meaning Henry's heir, Charles Emmanuel, King of Sardinia.[10]

In 1796 the French Directory considered making Henry king of Ireland, but Wolfe Tone, the United Irishmen's leader, rejected the idea. (Yet in 1803 Lord Cloncurry, released from imprisonment as a United Irishman, visited Frascati and showed no hesitation in addressing Henry as 'Your Majesty'.)[11] When France's General Humbert landed in Mayo in 1798 and set up a short lived 'Republic of Connacht', he found 'ghosts that had been born in the Ireland of Anne and George I coming back to haunt the age of Pitt and Napoleon'.[12] Clearly, these were Jacobite ghosts.

In 1799 the Stuarts made a brief reappearance in European diplomacy. When Napoleon offered peace following the War of the First Coalition that had disrupted all Europe, Britain demanded that France should restore her legitimate sovereign, the exiled Louis XVIII. The French foreign minister, Talleyrand, pointed out that Britain's legitimate monarch was an exile in Italy.

Eventually, Henry returned to Frascati where he was rapturously greeted by its inhabitants. He found a new friend in Charles Emmanuel who after abdicating had become a priest. There were many British visitors, including the Duke of Sussex. In 1804, unlike other cardinals he refused to attend Napoleon's crowning by Pius VII – as a *de jure* sovereign, he could not give his blessing to a usurper. It was a gesture that needed courage.

After an Indian summer King Henry, who had grown senile and lost his mind, died at Frascati on 13 July 1807 from catching a chill. He was buried at St Peter's with his parents and his brother.

As papal secretary of state, Henry's protégé Cardinal Consalvi (best known from Sir Thomas Lawrence's portrait in the Waterloo Chamber at Windsor), played a key role at the Congress of Vienna that rebuilt Europe after the Napoleonic Wars. He warmly supported the alliance between Throne and Altar, in which 'legitimism' – a monarch's inalienable right to his throne – was crucial. In the world of Metternich and of apostles of reaction, such as Bonald and de Maistre, Jacobitism, especially passive obedience, made sound sense. Consalvi had not forgotten what he had been told by King Henry.

55

The Heirs

Ye know ye King of England never dies, & were Henry the 9th
to do so, unquestionably the King of Sardinia is our Lawfull
Prince.

Laurence Oliphant of Gask, 1788[1]

In his will (signed 'Henry R') the king bequeathed his claims to Charles
Emmanuel who, as senior descendant of James II's sister Henrietta, Duchess
of Orleans, became head of the House of Stuart. The suggestion that Henry
left his 'crown jewels' to the future George IV to show he recognised
Hanover's right to the throne is nonsense. Purely as a token of goodwill his
executor, Monsignor Cesarini, sent Prince George his badges of the Garter
and the Thistle.

Charles's widow, Queen Louise, spent her last years at Florence, and after
Alfieri's death found a devoted companion in the painter François-Xavier
Fabre who was fourteen years her junior. Money was no issue – when King
Henry died she extracted a pension of £1,600 from George III. Seated on a
throne-like chair, she held court at Casa Alfieri, with a *salon* that included
the poet Ugo Foscolo and the historian Simonde de Sismondi. Tactful guests
addressed her as 'Your Majesty'. She died in 1824.[2]

In 1810 Napoleon asked Louise whether or not she had given King Charles
a son. When she told him they were childless, the Emperor expressed regret,
saying that if she had, he would have restored him to the throne of Great
Britain. Even under Bonaparte, France had not forgotten the Stuarts.

Six years later, a Russian army officer, Charles Edward Roehenstart
('Rohan-Stuart'), wrote to seek the prince regent's help in obtaining Mary of
Modena's dowry, as he was the Duchess of Albany's son. He claimed, untruth-
fully, that Charles had married Clementina Walkinshaw, his grandmother,

and that his mother in turn had married a Swedish Count Roehenstart. Lord Liverpool's cabinet was sufficiently worried to investigate the claims and try, unsuccessfully, to extradite him from France.

The Stuart succession

Privately, even the British government admitted that Henry IX's heir had been Charles Emmanuel of Sardinia. When Charles Emmanuel's brother, King Victor, died in 1824 the foreign secretary asked the prime minister if the court should go into mourning. Lord Liverpool replied that it should, as some thought Victor had been 'lawful King of Great Britain to the day of his death' – Liverpool meant that there were still Jacobites.

The Hanoverians tried to take over the Jacobite tradition, the prince regent contributing in 1819 to the cost of a monument to the exiled kings at St Peter's by Antonio Canova, and by buying as many of the Stuart Papers as he could. In 1821, by now George IV, Butcher Cumberland's great-nephew visited Edinburgh wearing a tartan kilt and pink silk tights in a pageant stage-managed by Sir Walter Scott. Yet he wept when he signed the Catholic Emancipation Act of 1829, aware like his father that he reigned only because he was not a Catholic.

Sympathy in a new age

Divine right 'has now come back to us, like a thief from transportation, under the alias of Legitimacy', grumbled Macaulay in 1825 since it was the creed of those who believed in 'Throne and Altar.[3] Romanticism and revulsion against the French Revolution made many sympathise with the Jacobites. In France, both Legitimists and Orléanists were to be fascinated by the similarities between what happened in their country in 1830 and in England in 1688.

'He was sprung from a Jacobite family & entered [public] life with the hereditary opinions of his class', Disraeli wrote of his friend Sir Francis Burdett, who campaigned for the Reform Bill of 1832. 'He was against the Boromongers, that is to say the new Capitalist classes which Wm the 3d & the House of Hanover had introduced: he was for annual Parliaments & universal suffrage.' But as a result of the French Revolution, 'he was looked upon as a Jacobin, when in reality he was a Jacobite'.[4] (Perhaps significantly, Lord Cloncurry was one of Burdett's closest friends.)

Tractarian Churchmen, who did not care for Parliament meddling with Anglican beliefs, venerated the nonjurors – so much that in 1836 Dr Thomas Arnold grumbled that Jacobitism had returned when Edward Pusey, a prominent Tractarian, claimed in a sermon that the root cause of strife between government and Church was the Glorious Revolution. Meanwhile Scott's novels, Burns's verse and James Hogg's *Jacobite Reliques of Scotland* kept alive the memory of the Honest Cause.

As did Lady Nairne, author of *The Scottish Minstrel* (1821–4), who came from an impeccably Jacobite background. In the Fifteen and the Forty-Five her grandfather, Oliphant of Gask, had fought for James III, as had her maternal grandfather Robertson of Struan in 1715. Her husband's grandfather had led the second Highland line at Prestonpans. Born in 1766, she was named 'Caroline', growing up in a house whose chaplains prayed for King Charles and then for King Henry. Her nostalgic songs – such as 'Charlie is my Darling' or 'Wha'll be King but Charlie' – recapture something of Jacobitism's appeal.

The Duke of Modena, Head of the House of Stuart

The period's romanticism and the cult of the tartan was exploited by two personable and highly articulate charlatans. These were the 'Sobieski Stuart' brothers, who in the 1840s pretended to be Charles's grandsons. Many people were taken in, including several Scottish peers.

The true heir of the Stuarts, however, was King Victor's daughter Mary, who married Francis IV, Duke of Modena. In 1831 during a debate on repealing the oath of abjuration, an MP argued that the oath was the only obstacle between the House of Sardinia and the British throne. At Mary's death in 1840, her claim passed to her son, the future Francis V of Modena whom Queen Victoria created a Knight of the Garter when he visited England in 1855.

Absolute monarch of his little state, Duke Francis was genuinely benevolent, filling Modena with free hospitals and free schools, with homes for the poor, giving audiences twice a week to humble petitioners. When he was deposed by the Risorgimento in 1859 and Modena became part of Italy, his tiny army, the Brigate Estense – 3,600 strong – was so loyal that it marched en bloc with him into exile in Austrian territory.

In 1861 the Marquess of Normandy, rebutting Gladstone's wild accusations against the duke, stressed that 'Francis V, is by his mother the eldest lineal descendant of our kings of the House of Stuart . . . the eldest of the lawful blood of our own exiled dynasty.' People had not forgotten his claim. Disraeli was rumoured to toast in secret, 'The King over the Water, the Duke of Modena', while in Anthony Trollope's *Barchester Towers* (1857) the High Tory Miss Thorne cherished 'a dear unmentioned wish for the restoration of some exiled Stuart'.

'Young England' and the reinvention of Toryism revived interest in Jacobites as the first Tories. When Benjamin Disraeli gave working men the vote in 1867 he believed he was acting in the Jacobite tradition. In his novel *Endymion* (published in 1880 but set in the 1850s) Lord Waldershare, 'one of the old rock, a real Jacobite', declares 'Are not the principles of Toryism those popular rights which men like Shippen and Hynde Cotton flung in the face of an alien monarch? . . . I saw a great deal of the Duke of Modena this year . . . He is our sovereign lord.'

The last Hanoverian monarch pretended to be a Stuart even more enthusiastically than George IV. 'Lord John, sometimes I think you place your loyalty to Parliament before your loyalty to your sovereign', Victoria told her charmless Whig Prime Minister Lord John Russell – to receive the biggest put-down of her entire life. 'Ma'm' he replied, 'my answer to a sovereign of the House of Hanover can only be in the affirmative.'[5]

She nonetheless continued to cherish her fantasies, holidaying at Balmoral, wearing tartan, dressing her sons in kilts and giving a 'Royal Stuart Ball'. Later, however, she grew more realistic, writing in her journal how it was common knowledge that her family had been put on the throne to stop Popery. Intriguingly, she would not allow finger bowls at Buckingham Palace – banned since George III's coronation and re-introduced only after her death. Did she fear that some guest might drink the health of a sovereign over the water?

The Jacobite Revival

The life of Francis's niece and heir, 'Mary III' (whose husband became King Ludwig III of Bavaria in 1913) coincided with a Jacobite revival. This began in London in 1889, with an 'Exhibition of the Royal House of Stuart' that consisted of paintings and memorabilia, many lent by Jacobite families. Another donor was Queen Victoria, who did not appreciate that the exhibition's aim was to whip up support for a Stuart restoration. An Order of the

White Rose was founded, followed in 1891 by a Jacobite Legitimist League with a strongly right-wing political programme. A short-lived newspaper was started, the *Whirlwind*, illustrated by J. M. Whistler and Walter Sickert, who was its art critic. Several Jacobites stood for Parliament, without success.

The movement's history remains to be written. In some ways, not unlike the intellectual wing of *Action Française*, its eccentric yet far from insignificant members numbered university dons and poets, as well as Scottish and Irish nationalists, who included Andrew Lang and W. B. Yeats.

In 1898 an American journalist identified several other groups of Jacobites. The most important were a few Scottish lairds, Roman Catholic peers and Irish country gentlemen, who cherished Jacobitism as a pious opinion, but were fully aware of the hopelessness of their cause. As their head, he singled out the fifth Earl of Ashburnham, founder of the White Rose Club. An ardent Legitimist, in 1899 Asburnham bought rifles for an abortive Carlist coup in Madrid and was probably behind the posting of placards outside Buckingham Palace proclaiming 'Mary III' just before Edward VII's coronation. (Kaiser Wilhelm II, who was staying at the palace, advised his uncle to shoot those responsible.)

The Great War put an abrupt end to the new Jacobitism. 'I remember my surprise in 1915 in Flanders when I found that Prince Rupprecht of Bavaria, the commander opposite, was the gentleman whom we had been wont to salute by telegram on his birthday as Prince Robert of Wales,' wrote John Buchan, a former member of the White Rose Club.[6]

During the war Mary's son, Crown Prince Rupprecht, served as a highly effective German army commander. After Germany's defeat he tried to re-establish Bavaria as an independent kingdom and was later hunted by the Gestapo. Always very popular, when he died in 1955 the Federal Government allowed the Bavarian crown to be placed on his coffin during his funeral procession through Munich. He neither asserted nor denied his Stuart claims, but sometimes wore the Stuart tartan.

Shortly after his death, the Royal Stuart Society (successor to the White Rose Club) placed a monument to Rupprecht in the former Royal Bavarian Chapel in Warwick Street, Westminster – to the 'Head of the Royal Houses of Wittelsbach, of Cerdicing, of Plantagenet, of Tudor and of Stuart'. Fittingly, this is now the central church of the (Catholic) Anglican ordinariate whose members are the heirs to the nonjurors.

Today, Rupprecht's grandson HRH Duke Francis of Bavaria, born in 1933, is regarded as *de jure* king of Great Britain by Jacobite diehards of the Royal

Stuart Society, who refrain from making any claim on his behalf that he does not make himself. Like all Stuart Pretenders since the death of Henry IX he has never claimed the British throne. As the duke is unmarried, his eventual successor as senior heir of the House of Stuart will be his niece Sophie, Hereditary Princess of Liechtenstein.

Epilogue

Jacobite traditions – even Jacobite instincts – have contributed substantially to the independence movements in both Scotland and Ireland.

During the nineteenth century when a politically independent Scotland was unthinkable, the Jacobite novels of Walter Scott and Robert Louis Stevenson played a vital role in keeping alive the country's sense of nationhood. Today, the cult of Culloden, whose battlefield has become a place of pilgrimage, is a potent expression of nationalism, while members of the SNP sometimes wear the White Rose as a symbol of their country.

Irish Jacobitism morphed into Jacobinism and republicanism during the French Revolution, although Daniel O'Connell and, for a time, even Arthur Griffith (founder of Sinn Féin) thought – like the Jacobites – that dual monarchy was a better solution than a republic. A distinguished modern Irish historian has written, 'For those minded to see it, some irreducible continuity persisted from Jacobite monarchists, through Jacobin republicans, O'Connellite Repealers, Fenians, Home Rulers and so on.'[1]

Despite losing most of Ireland, today's federal British Isles with parliaments at Edinburgh, Belfast and Cardiff as well as London – even if they do not yet have full indepence under the crown – are not so very unlike the multinational monarchy that the Jacobites had hoped to build.

One can also argue that the dispute between the families of Stuart and Hanover underlined the Crown's indispensability as a focus of unity between the nations of these islands. The magic of direct descent and divine right may have gone, but squatters' rights have been transformed by the alchemy of long tenure. Stuart blood has even reappeared in royal veins, down a bastard line. Through his mother, the Duke of Cambridge will be the first of our monarchs since Queen Anne to descend from James II – by way of Arabella Churchill, she with the beautiful legs.

Appendix
Novels about Jacobitism

Sir Walter Scott

Sir Walter Scott wrote the first. In *Waverley; or 'Tis Sixty Years Hence* (1814) a young English army officer brought up on Jacobite principles joins Prince Charles's army in 1745 and fights at Prestonpans. Although a magnificent novel (admired by Goethe) and though Scott obtained details from men who had actually fought in the Forty-Five, it has a subtly pro-Hanoverian bias that implies the Cause was always doomed and, unconvincingly, credits Cumberland with magnanimity.

Rob Roy (1817), set in 1715, contains romanticised portraits of the bandit Rob Roy MacGregor and his outlawed clan, as well as caricaturing a Jacobite family of Northumberland Catholic squires, tragi-comic relics of the past, who are inevitably swept away.

Redgauntlet (1824), is the Elibank Plot moved to the 1760s. Scott's secret bias is evident again, depicting plotters as fanatics and Hanoverian rulers as supremely merciful. Yet there are convincing descriptions of Charles in middle age and of Dr William King ('Dr Grumball').

Robert Louis Stevenson

The real hero of *Kidnapped* (1886) is a Jacobite officer on the run in the 1750s, modelled on Colonel John Roy Stewart. It conveys the smouldering resentment in the Highlands after the Forty-Five's defeat but is best at recreating what it felt like to be hunted through the heather – based on first-hand accounts of Charles's experiences in 1746 in Bishop Forbes's *The Lyon in Mourning*.

Although the sinister hero of *The Master of Ballantrae* (1888), one of Stevenson's weirder novels, is a Jacobite who fought at Culloden he belongs

to the same genre as Mr Hyde in the author's *Jekyll and Hyde*. The early part
has an excellent evocation of how the Honest Cause divided a family – who
should join the prince in the Forty-Five and who should stay at home.

Catriona (1893) is the slightly disappointing sequel to *Kidnapped*, with a
plot centring around the injustices committed after the Forty-Five and with
Jacobite characters who really existed.

John Buchan

Even if certain the Honest Cause was always doomed, Buchan had considerable sympathy for it. *A Lost Lady of Old Years* (1899) recounts the adventures
during the Forty-Five of a Jacobite youth training for the Law, who meets
Prince Charles and tries to save the appalling Lord Lovat of whom there is a
good portrait. There is a lively, if inaccurate, description of Culloden, with
the implied message that defeat on Drummossie Moor meant the end of the
old Scotland.

A better book, *Midwinter* (1923) is built around a Highland officer's
unsuccessful mission to persuade England's Jacobite magnates to rise for the
prince in 1745, with a fascinating picture of Lord Cornbury (of the Cornbury
Plot) as a supporter of the Stuarts who regretfully decides that Charles cannot
win. A ruthless double agent, Mr Kyd from the Lowlands, embodies the
constant treachery undermining Jacobitism. Best of all is the young Samuel
Johnson, arming himself with a sword and determined to fight for the King
over the Water.

J. M. Barrie

His strange novella of 20,000 words, *Farewell Miss Julie Logan* (1931) has
been described as 'Scottish Gothic', even as aligning Jacobitism with sexu-
ality. Set in a lonely Highland glen haunted by Jacobite ghosts, Miss Julie
herself is a phantom who has sheltered the fugitive Prince Charles.

Naomi Mitchison

Her pleasant romance *The Bull Calves* (1947) concerns a Jacobite family
whose estates have been forfeited because its head was 'out' in the Fifteen.
Although he recovers them, he does not join the Forty-Five apart from sheltering fugitives. There is much grumbling about the Union with England.

D. K. Broster

In its time her Jacobite trilogy – *The Flight of the Heron* (1925), *The Gleam in the North* (1927) and *The Dark Mile* (1929) – enjoyed huge popularity. The novels are set in the Forty-Five and the uneasy Scotland of the 1750s, with a hero who is a passionate supporter of the banished family.

IRELAND'S JACOBITE VERSE

One should mention, too, the Irish verse inspired by Jacobitism, notably that of Thomas Moore and Thomas Osborne Davis, and above all of Emily Lawless in her wonderful *The Wild Geese* (1902).

Acknowledgements

I realise only too well my rashness in trying to fit into a short space a full account of such a vast subject, whose different aspects are covered in depth by many distinguished historians – by Eveline Cruickshanks, Jonathan Clark, Daniel Szechi, Murray Pittock, Paul Kléber Monod and Christopher Whatley. But I feel general readers as well as academics should have a story that surveys the Jacobite movement as a whole, which is what this book attempts to do. Anyone wishing to learn more should consult titles listed in the bibliography.

For Ireland I owe a special debt to the writings of the late J. G. Simms, and to those of Éamonn Ó Ciardha, whose work has been crucial in making known Ireland's neglected role in the Jacobite story. Similarly, for Scotland I am indebted to Whatley and Patrick's seminal *The Scots and the Union*, and to Ronald Black whose anthology of eighteenth-century Scottish Gaelic verse, *An Lasair*, helps us to see into the mind of Highlanders such as Colonel John Roy Stewart.

I am also most grateful to the abbot and community of Douai Abbey (heirs of the Jacobite St Edmund's priory at Paris) for letting me see the letters from James III and Prince Charles that are preserved in their library.

For invaluable help over many years, I should like to thank the staffs of the British Library, the Cambridge University Library and the London Library.

In particular, I must thank my copy-editor James Rose for greatly improving the book's readability, Stella Lesser for reading the proofs, Deborah Warner for finding the pictures and, as usual, my agent Andrew Lownie for his unfailing encouragement.

Notes

Quotations from Horace Walpole are referenced by date and may be found in:

W. S. Lewis (ed.), *The Yale edition of Horace Walpole's Correspondence*, 48 vols (New Haven, Yale University Press, 1937–83)

Un-numbered quotations from Lord Macaulay are in:

T. B. Macaulay, *The History of England From the Accession of James II* (Cambridge University Press, 2011)

Numbered quotations from Macaulay are from his essays, for which source references are given.

EPIGRAPH

1 Charles I, *Eikon Basilike, or The King's Book*, ed. E. Almack, p. 206

PROLOGUE

1 Ailesbury, *The Memoirs of Thomas, Earl of Ailesbury*, ii, p. 233

INTRODUCTION

1 Charles I, *Eikon Basilike*, p. 231

CHAPTER 1

1 *Macchabees*, 1, xi:10
2 Burnet, *A History of My Own Time*, iv, p. 539
3 Ailesbury, i, p. 31

CHAPTER 2

1 Ailesbury, i, p. 126
2 Barclay, 'James II's "Catholic Court"', in *Ideas, aesthetics and enquiries in the early modern era*, viii
3 Miller, *James II, a study in kingship*, p. 173
4 Ailesbury, i, p. 127
5 Clarke (ed.), *The Life of King James the Second, King of England*, ii, pp. 617–21
6 Sowerby, *Making Toleration: The Repealers and the Glorious Revolution*, p. 3
7 Halifax, 'A Letter to a Dissenter' in *The Complete Works*, p. 130
8 Sowerby, p. 55

CHAPTER 3

1 Burnet, iii, p. 344
2 Shield and Lang, *The King over the Water*, p. 202
3 *Gentleman's Magazine* (2), pp. 42, 99–100, 323–4, 339, 430, 533
4 Childs, *The Army, James II and the Glorious Revolution*
5 Callow, *The Making of King James II*
6 Charles I, *Eikon Basilike*, p. 263
7 Ailesbury, i, pp. 195–7
8 Burnet, iii, p. 408
9 Ailesbury, ii, p. 496
10 Ailesbury, i, pp. 224–5

CHAPTER 4

1 Corp, *A Court in Exile: The Stuarts in France 1688–1718*, p. 20
2 Macky, *A View of the Court of St Germain from the Year 1690, to '95*
3 Lord G. Murray, 'Letter to Lady Amelia, 9 September 1745', in *The Jacobite*, No. 116 (Perth, 2004), pp. 14–15
4 Macaulay, *Lord Macaulay's Essays*, pp. 91–2
5 Miller, *The Life and Times of William and Mary*, p. 20
6 Charles I, *Eikon Basilike*, p. 246
7 Monod, *Jacobitism and the English People, 1688–1788*, p. 347
8 Linehan, *St John's College Cambridge: A History*, p. 167
9 Macaulay, *Essays*, p. 588

10 Dalrymple, *Memoirs of Great Britain and Ireland*, i, p. 286

11 Monod, *Jacobitism*, pp. 138–45

12 Burnet, iv, p. 3

13 Monod, *Jacobitism*, p. 55

14 Burnet, iii, p. 406

15 Evelyn, *The Diary of John Evelyn*, 21 February 1689

16 Pittock, M., *Poetry and Jacobite Politics*, p. 46

17 Burnet, iv, p. 3

18 Ailesbury, ii, pp. 264–5, 298

19 Doebner, *Memoirs of Mary, Queen of England, 1689–93*, p. 48

20 Stevens, *Journal*, pp. 13, 27

21 Dryden, *Works*, v, p. 281 – cit. Pittock, *Poetry and Jacobite Politics*, p. 103

22 *A Form of Prayer and Humiliation . . .*, 1690

CHAPTER 5

1 Ailesbury, i, p. 250

2 Balcarres, *An Account of the Affairs of Scotland*, p. 66

3 Dalrymple, i, p. 287

4 Francis, *Romance of the The White Rose*, p. 37

5 Dundee, *Letters of John Grahame of Claverhouse*, pp. 40–1

6 Macpherson, *Original Papers*, i, p. 360

7 Mackay, *Memoirs of the War Carried on in Scotland and Ireland*, p. 52

8 Dryden, *Works*, iii, p. 22

CHAPTER 6

1 Clarke (ed.), *The Life of King James*, ii, pp. 622–3

2 Ibid., ii, pp. 636–7

3 Simms, 'Dublin in 1685', in *War and Politics in Ireland 1649–1730*, pp. 49–63

4 Gilbert (ed.), *A Jacobite Narrative of the War in Ireland 1688–91*

5 Lenihan, *The Last Cavalier, Richard Talbot (1631–91)*

6 Foster, *Modern Ireland 1600–1972*, p. 143

7 D'Avaux, *Negotiations*, pp. 292–3

8 Berwick, i, p. 95

9 Lenihan, p. 131

10 Stevens, *The Journal of John Stevens*, pp. 61–2

11   Simms, *Jacobite Ireland*, p. 159
12   Berwick, i, p. 95
13   D'Avaux, p. 433
14   Ibid., pp. 390–1
15   Lenihan, p. 188
16   Story, *An Impartial History of the Wars in Ireland*, p. 22
17   Ailesbury, i, pp. 252–3

CHAPTER 7

1   Scott (ed.), *A Collection of Scarce and Valuable Tracts*, vii, p. 97
2   Clarke (ed.), *The Life of King James*, ii, pp. 392–3
3   Burnet, iv, p. 90
4   Clarke (ed.), *The Life of King James*, ii, p. 47

CHAPTER 8

1   Stevens, p. 193
2   Story, p. 124
3   Stevens, p. 193

CHAPTER 9

1   Ó Bruadair, *Duanaire Dháibhidh Uí Bhruadair*, iii, p. 141
2   Ibid., iii, p. 152
3   Ibid., iii, p. 167
4   Wauchope, *Patrick Sarsfield and the Williamite War*, p. 213
5   Stevens, pp. 208–9
6   Stevens, p. 21
7   Cox (ed.), 'A diary of the siege of Athlone, 1691'
8   The best acount is McNally's, *The Battle of Aughrim 1691*
9   Claudianus, *The Irish Mars*, pp. 1–3
10   Gilbert (ed.), *A Jacobite Narrative*, p. 166
11   Ó Rathaille (O'Rahilly), *Dánta Aodhagháin Uí Rathaille*, p. 7
12   Ó Buachalla, 'Irish Jacobite Poetry' in *Irish Review*, vii, no 2 (1992), p. 40
13   Ó Ciardha, p. 85
14   Translation James Clarence Mangan

CHAPTER 10

1 *A Complete Collection of State Trials and Proceedings for High Treason*, xii, cols 817–19
2 Evelyn, v, p. 27
3 Châteaubriand, *La Vie de Rancé*, p. 290
4 Monod, *Jacobitism*, pp. 270–1
5 Bastian, *Daniel Defoe's Early Life*, p. 152
6 Ailesbury, i, p. 105
7 Ibid., p. 333
8 Ibid., p. 344

CHAPTER 11

1 Evelyn, v, p. 148
2 *Complete Collection of State Trials*, xiii, cols 137–139
3 *Complete Collection of State Trials*, xiii, col. 757
4 Evelyn, v, p. 233

CHAPTER 12

1 Hopkins, *Glencoe and the End of the Highland War*, p. 328
2 *Great Britain's Just Complaint For Her Late Measures, Present Sufferings, and the Future Miseries . . .*, Oxford 1692
3 Burnet, iv, p. 6
4 Hume, *Essays*, p. 73
5 Burnet, iii, pp. 364–5
6 Campbell, *The Doctrines of the Middle State*, p. ii, cit. Nimmo, 'The Sacramental Soul of Jacobitism', in *Living with Jacobitism*, ed. McInnes, German and Graham
7 Defoe, *A Tour through the Whole Island of Great Britain*, iii
8 Defoe, *A Tour*, iii
9 Burt, *Letters from a Gentleman in the North of Scotland*, i, p. 23
10 Ibid., ii, pp. 109, 115
11 Ibid., pp. 64, 107
12 Forsyth, *In the Shadow of Cairngorm*, p. 146
13 Whatley and Patrick, *The Scots and the Union*, p. 142
14 Nimmo, p. 53

CHAPTER 13

1 Rancé, *Letters of Armand de Rancé*, ii, p. 161
2 Callow, *King in Exile: James II, Warrior, King and Saint*, p. 326
3 Earbery, *An Historical Account of the Advantages that have Accru'd to England . . .*, pp. 7–10
4 Burnet, iv, p. 538
5 *An Act for the further Security of his Majesties Person and the Succession of the Crown in the Protestant line* (London, 1701)
6 *The Weekly Journal or British Gazeteer*, 21 January 1716

CHAPTER 14

1 Guthrie, 'Johnson's Touch-piece and the "Charge of Fame"', in Clarke and Erskine-Hill, *The Politics of Samuel Johnson*
2 Szechi, *Britain's Lost Revolution?*, p. 80
3 Shield and Lang, p. 62
4 Lockhart, *'Scotland's Ruine'*, p. 56

CHAPTER 15

1 MacQuoid (ed.), *Jacobite Songs and Ballads*, p. 30
2 Ibid., p. 49
3 Shield and Lang, p. 60
4 The best account is Whatley and Patrick, *The Scots and the Union*
5 Whatley and Patrick, p. 277
6 Stephen, *Scottish Presbyterians and the Act of Union*
7 Whatley and Patrick, p. 276
8 Lockhart, *'Scotland's Ruine'*, pp. 209–10
9 MacQuoid (ed.), p. 30
10 Lockhart, *'Scotland's Ruine'*, p. 210

CHAPTER 16

1 MacQuoid (ed.), p. 56
2 Szechi, *Britain's Lost Revolution?*, p. 198
3 Hooke, *The Secret History of Colonel Hooke's Negotiations in Scotland*, p. 83
4 Forbin-Gardanne, *Mémoires du Comte de Forbin*

5 Defoe, preface to *The History of the Union*
6 Tayler, A. and H., *1715: The Story of the Rising*, p. 7
7 Lockhart, 'Scotland's Ruine', p. 232
8 Szechi, *Britain's Lost Revolution?*, pp. 200–1
9 Ibid., p. 111
10 Ibid., pp. 32–3

CHAPTER 17

1 Ó Rathaille (O'Rahilly), p. 166
2 Chenevix Trench, pp. 52–9
3 Ó Ciardha, p. 127
4 Ó Rathaille (O'Rahilly), pp. xviii, 106–7
5 O'Conor, in Hooke, pp. 120–6; Ó Ciardha, pp. 122–44
6 Drake, *The Memoirs of Capt. Peter Drake*, p. 151
7 Hooke, *Correspondence of Colonel N. Hooke*, i, p. 307

CHAPTER 18

1 Swift, 'Journal to Stella', in *The Works of the Rev. Jonathan Swift*, i, p. 195.
2 *Complete Collection of State Trials*, xv, cols 116, 127, 130
3 Shield and Lang, p. 153
4 Mahon, *History of England from the Peace of Utrecht to the Peace of Versailles 1713–1783*, i, p. 79
5 MacQuoid (ed.), p. 70
6 Ibid., p. 262
7 Macknight, *Life of Henry St. John, Viscount Bolingbroke*, pp. 399, 400
8 Shield and Lang, p. 161
9 Szechi, *Jacobitism and Tory Politics*, p.173
10 Macpherson, *Original Papers*, ii, pp. 385–6
11 'Letter from Mr Lesly to a Member of Parliament in London', in *A Collection of Scarce and Valuable Tracts*, iv, p. 213
12 Somerset, *Queen Anne*, p. 501

CHAPTER 19

1 Lockhart, p. 479

2   St John, *Works of the late Right Honourable Henry St John, Lord Viscount Bolingbroke*, i, pp. 53–4
3   Szechi, *Jacobitism and Tory Politics*, p. 173
4   Tayler, A. and H., *1715*, p. 312
5   Miller, *The Stuarts*, p. 228
6   Monod, *Jacobitism*, p. 58
7   Pittock, *Poetry and Jacobite Politics*, p. 66
8   Ellis (ed.), *Poems on Affairs of State*, p. 613

CHAPTER 20

1   Mahon, *History of England*, i, Appendix, p. xix
2   St John, *Works*, i, p. 113
3   Ibid., pp. 53–4
4   Ibid., p. 53
5   Ibid., p. 38
6   Szechi, *1715, The Great Jacobite Rebellion*, p. 65
7   St John, *Works*, i, p. 36
8   MacQuoid (ed.), p. 82
9   Berwick, ii, pp 208–9
10 Stuarts, *Calendar of the Stuart Papers*, i, p. 425
11 St John, *Works*, i, p. 59

CHAPTER 21

1   MacQuoid (ed.), p. 41
2   Lockhart, p. 381
3   MacQuoid (ed.), p. 125
4   Tayler, A. and H, *1715*, pp. 43–6
5   Sinclair, *Memoirs of the Insurrection in Scotland*, p. 93
6   Ibid., p. 34
7   Macky, *Memoirs of the Secret Services of John Macky*, p. 199
8   Lenman, *Jacobite Risings in Britain 1689–1746*, p. 416
9   Patten, *The History of the Late Rebellion*, i, p. 46
10 Ibid., p. 100
11 Szechi, *1715*, p. 197
12 Sitwell, *Letters of the Sitwells and Sacheverells*, pp. 113–14
13 Patten, i, p. 39

CHAPTER 22

1 Lenman, p. 154
2 Sinclair, pp. 213, 214
3 Campbell, *The Life of the Most Illustrious Prince, Duke of Argyll and Greenwich*, p. 189
4 Patten, i, p. 48
5 Tayler, 'John, Duke of Argyle, and Greenwich', p. 101
6 Mar, *Report on the Manuscripts of the Earl of Mar and Kellie*, pp. 516–17
7 Clarke, *A Journall of Severall Occurences from 2d November 1715, in the Insurrection*
8 Oates, *The Last Battle on English Soil, Preston 1715*, p. 58
9 Patten, i, pp. 120–3
10 Ibid., p. 100
11 Oates, p. 142
12 Szechi, *1715*, p. 196
13 Baynes, *The Jacobite Rising of* 1715, p. 204

CHAPTER 23

1 *A True Account of the Proceedings at Perth*, p. 443
2 Seton, 'Itinerary of King James III', pp. 249–66
3 Mahon, *History of England*, i, Appendix, p. xxxiv
4 Ibid., Appendix, p. xxxv
5 *Weekly Journal or British Gazeteer*, 21 March 1719
6 *A True Account of the Proceedings at Perth*, pp. 44–7
7 Liria's diary in Petrie, *The Jacobite Movement* (1959), p. 263
8 *A Journal of the Earl of Marr's Proceedings*, p. 8
9 Ibid., p. 9
10 Browne, *A History of the Highlands*, ii, pp. 340–2
11 Sinclair, p. 377
12 Lenman, p. 287

CHAPTER 24

1 *A Faithful Register of the Late Rebellion*, p. 325
2 *A Journal of the Earl of Marr's Proceedings*, p. 16
3 British Museum MSS 38851

4 Coxe, *Memoirs of the Life and Administration of Sir Robert Walpole, Earl of Orford*, ii, p. 307

5 Stuarts, *Calendar of the Stuart Papers*, ii, p. 25

6 *Complete Collection of State Trials*, xv, col. 802

7 Stuarts, *Calendar of Stuart Papers*, ii, p. 35

8 Bogle, 'Lord Nithsdale's Escape' in *Royal Stuart Papers*, lxx

9 Wogan, *Mémoirs sur l'enterprise de Innspruck en 1719*, p. 106

10 Menzies, *Report on the Menzies Manuscripts*, p. 703, No. 172 – letter of 8 May

11 Szechi, 'The Jacobite Theatre of Death' in Cruickshanks and Black (eds), *The Jacobite Challenge*, pp. 57–73

12 *A Faithful Register*, p. 325

13 Menzies, *Report on the Menzies Manuscripts*, p. 703, No. 172

14 Oates, p. 182

15 Ibid.

16 Ibid., p. 170

17 Ibid., p. 176

18 Ibid., p. 179

19 Monod, *Jacobitism*, p. 326

CHAPTER 25

1 MacQuoid (ed.), p. 110

2 Szechi, *1715*, p. 213

3 Cruickshanks, 'Charles Caesar', in Sedgwick (ed.), *The History of Parliament: The House of Commons 1715–1754*

4 Ibid.

5 Wills, *The Jacobites and Russia 1715–1750*, p. 60

6 MacQuoid (ed.), p. 110

7 Wills, pp. 41, 52

8 Ibid., p. 57

CHAPTER 26

1 *The Lockhart Papers*, p. 17

2 Ormonde, *The Jacobite Attempt of 1719. Letters of James Butler, second Duke of Ormonde*

3 Ibid.

4   Keith, *A fragment of a Memoir of Field-Marshal James Keith, written by himself, 1714–34*, p. 51

5   *The Historical Register*, iv (1720), p. 283

6   Mahon, *History of England*, i, p. 504

7   Ó Ciardha, pp. 376–7

8   O'Callaghan, pp. 319–20

9   Ibid., p. 320

10 Ó Buachalla, 'The Making of a Cork Jacobite' in O'Flanagan and Buttimer, *Cork History and Society*

CHAPTER 27

1   Wogan, *Female Fortitude Exemplified . . .*

2   Sedgwick (ed.), *The History of Parliament: The House of Commons 1715–1754*

3   Shield and Lang, p. 295

4   Corp, *The Stuart Court at Rome*, pp. 251–2

5   Cruickshanks and Erskine-Hill, *The Atterbury Plot*, p. 92

CHAPTER 28

1   *Historical Manuscripts Commission*, 14th Report, Appendix ix, p. 504

2   Walpole, *Letters*, i, p. 78

3   *Historical Manuscripts Commission*, Various, v, pp. 242–3

4   Monod, *Jacobitism*, p. 269

5   Bennett, *The Tory Crisis in Church and State 1688–1730*

6   Walpole, *Letters*, i, p.84

7   Atterbury, *English Advice to the Freeholders of England*

CHAPTER 29

1   Cruickshanks and Erskine-Hill, *The Atterbury Plot*, p. 112 (Royal Archives Stuart Papers 53/48)

2   Ibid., (Royal Archives Stuart Papers, 52/141)

3   Cruickshanks and Erskine-Hill, 'The Waltham Blacks' in *Journal of British Studies*

4   *A Letter from an English Traveller at Rome to his Father of 6th May 1721* (London, 1721)

5 Szechi, 'The image of the court', in Corp (ed.), *The Stuart Court at Rome*, pp. 49–64
6 Atterbury, *Second and Last Advice to the Freeholders*
7 Earbery, *Advantages that have Accru'd to England*, pp. 7, 11, 18
8 Szechi, *The Jacobites: Britain and Europe 1688–1788*, pp. 12 n.14 (citing Monod), 92
9 Cruickshanks and Erskine-Hill, *The Atterbury Plot*, p. 140
10 Ibid., p. 121
11 O'Callaghan, p. 369
12 *Complete Collection of State Trials*, xvi, p. 463
13 *Historical Manuscripts Commission*, 14th Report, Appendix ix, 513
14 Stuarts, *Calendar of the Stuart Papers*, vii, p. 39

CHAPTER 30

1 Hervey, *Some Materials towards Memoirs of the Reign of King George II*, i, p. 250
2 Bennett, p. 290
3 Hervey, i, p. 69
4 Ibid., p. 250
5 Lockhart, ii, p. 403
6 Hervey, i, p. 6
7 Ibid., p. 9
8 Burt, ii, pp. 265–307

CHAPTER 31

1 Hervey, i, p. 206
2 Whatley and Patrick, 'Contesting Interpretations of the Union of 1707: The Abuse and Use of George Lockhart of Carnwath's Memoirs'
3 Macaulay, *Essays*, p. 759
4 Szechi, *The Jacobites*, p. 26
5 Pittock, *Poetry and Jacobite Politics*, p. 108
6 Cruickshanks, *Political Untouchables*, pp. 18–19
7 Monod, *Jacobitism*, pp. 286–7
8 Freebairn, *The Miserable State of Scotland*, p. 1
9 Burt, i, p. 23
10 Ó Rathaille (O'Rahilly), p. 22 (an aisling)

CHAPTER 32

1 Gregg, 'The Politics of Paranoia' in Cruickshanks and Black (eds), *The Jacobite Challenge*, pp. 42–56
2 Hooke, *Correspondence of Colonel N. Hooke*, i, p. 196
3 Gregg, 'The Politics of Paranoia', p. 51
4 Shield and Lang, p. 367
5 Corp, pp. 156–63
6 Gregg, 'The Politics of Paranoia', pp. 48–50
7 Gregg, 'The financial vicissitudes of James III in Rome' in *The Stuart Court at Rome*, p. 76
8 Corp, 'All Roads lead to Rome' in Forsyth (ed.), *Bonnie Prince Charlie*, p 74

CHAPTER 33

1 Macaulay, *Essays*, p. 278
2 Black, 'Jacobitism and British Foreign Policy, 1731–5' in Cruickshanks and Black (eds), *The Jacobite Challenge*, pp. 142–60
3 Pollnitz, *The Memoirs of Charles-Lewis, Baron de Pollnitz*, ii, pp. 55–7
4 Hervey, i, p. 171
5 Ibid., pp. 181–2
6 Cruickshanks, 'Lord Cornbury, Bolingbroke and a plan to restore the Stuarts, 1731–1735' in *Royal Stuart Papers*, xxvii
7 Watney, *Cornbury and the Forest of Wychwood*
8 Black, 'Jacobitism and British Foreign Policy 1731–5', p.156
9 Hervey, ii, pp. 565–6
10 *The True Loyalist*, p. 80
11 Ó Ciardha, p. 378
12 Sedgwick (ed.), *The History of Parliament: The House of Commons 1715–1754*

CHAPTER 34

1 MacQuoid (ed.), p. 70
2 Murdoch, 'Tilting at Windmills: The Order of Toboso as a Jacobite Social Network' in Monod, Pittock & Szechi, *Loyalty and Identity*, p. 243
3 Murray, *Memorials*, p. 330

4 Emerson, *An Enlightened Duke*, p. 257

5 Anon (G. Lyttleton), *A Letter to the Tories*, 1748

6 Cruickshanks, *Political Untouchables*, p. 5

7 Lenman, p. 287

8 Monod, *Jacobitism*, p. 271

9 Namier, *Crossroads of Power, Essays on Eighteenth Century England*, p. 45

10 Sedgwick (ed.), *The History of Parliament: The House of Commons 1715–1754*

11 Ibid.

12 Cruickshanks, *Political Untouchables*, pp. 47–8 (Stuart MSS vol 254/92)

CHAPTER 35

1 O'Foghludha, *Amhráin Phiaris Mhic Gearailt*

2 Ó Ciardha, p. 378

3 Seán Ó Tuama, translation James Clarence Mangan

4 Boswell, *Life*, ii, p. 255

5 Ó Ciardha, p. 51

6 Whelan, 'An underground gentry?' in Donnelly and Miller (eds), *Irish Popular Culture*

7 Cullen, 'The Blackwater Catholics and County Cork Society and Politics in the Eighteenth Century' in O'Flanagan and Buttimer (eds), *Cork History and Society*

8 Swift, *Works*, xii, p. 436

9 Forman, *Letter to Sir Robert Sutton*, 1728

10 Ó Ciardha, p. 267

11 Skrine, *Fontenoy*, pp. 158–202 (the best account)

CHAPTER 36

1 Forbes, *The Lyon in Mourning*, iii, p. 50

2 O'Sullivan, *1745 and After*

3 Duffy, *Fight for a Throne*, p. 320

4 *Lockhart Papers*, ii, p. 479

5 Home, *Memoirs of the Rebellion of 1745 and 1746*, p. 42

6 Murray of Broughton, *Memorials*, p. 168

7   O'Sullivan, *1745 and After*, pp. 62, 63

8   Johnstone, *Memoirs of the Rebellion*, p. 48

9   O'Sullivan, *1745 and After*, p. 73

10 Home, *Memoirs*, p. 99

11 Ibid., p. 99

12 O'Sullivan, *1745 and After*, pp. 73–4

13 Ibid., p. 75

14 Ibid., p. 81

CHAPTER 37

1   O'Sullivan, *1745 and After*, pp. 34–5

2   Pittock, *The Myth of the Jacobite Clans*, p. 60

3   Carlyle, *Anecodotes and Characters of the Times*, p. 69

4   O'Sullivan, *1745 and After*, p. 88

5   Drummond, 'Bonnie Prince Charlie returns to Edinburgh' in *Country Life*, 11 May 2016

6   O'Sullivan, *1745 and After*, p. 87

7   Duffy, p. 321

8   O'Callaghan, p. 377

9   'besides Sullivan, and one or two of us who had come from France, there was no one who knew anything about it', says Sir Jean MacDonnell, O'Sullivan, p. 89

10 Gibson, *Diary of John Campbell*, pp. 14–21

CHAPTER 38

1   Cruickshanks, *Political Untouchables*, pp. 92–93

2   Murray, *Memorials*, p. 231

3   Elcho, *A Short Account of the Affairs of Scotland*, p. 310

4   O'Sullivan, *1745 and After*, p. 99

5   Daniel, 'John Daniel's Account' in Blaikie, *Origins of the 'Forty-Five*, ii, p. 168

6   Johnstone, p. 49

7   Monod, *Jacobitism*, pp. 338–9

8   Elcho, p. 337–8

9   O'Sullivan, *1745 and After*, p. 103

10 Cruickshanks, *Political Untouchables*, p. 100

11   O'Sullivan, *1745 and After*, p. 1
12   Pittock, *Culloden*, p. 33

CHAPTER 39

1   Forbes, ii, 62
2   Erskine-Hill, 'The Political Character of Samuel Johnson' in Cruickshanks and Black (eds), *The Jacobite Challenge*, p. 173
3   Yorke, *Life and Correspondence*, i, p. 477
4   Smollett, *A Complete History of England*, iii, pp. 169–70
5   O'Callaghan, p. 421
6   Monod, *Jacobitism*, p. 135
7   McLynn, *The Jacobites*, p. 61
8   Ó Ciardha, p. 310
9   O'Callaghan, p. 418
10   O'Foghludha, p. 30

CHAPTER 40

1   O'Sullivan, *1745 and After*, p.106
2   Ibid., p. 111
3   Elcho, pp. 416–18
4   Browne, iii, p. 197
5   Blaikie, *Origins of the 'Forty-Five*, ii, p. 202
6   O'Callaghan, p. 386
7   Blaikie, *Itinerary of Prince Charles Edward Stuart*, pp. 74–5

CHAPTER 41

1   Elcho, p. 460
2   O'Sullivan, *1745 and After*, p. 119
3   Browne, iii, p. 193
4   Blaikie, *Itinerary*, pp. 76–7
5   O'Sullivan, *1745 and After*, p. 125
6   Duffy, p. 372
7   Ibid., p. 31

CHAPTER 42

1 Pittock, *Culloden*, p. 32
2 Forbes, i, p. 102
3 O'Sullivan, *1745 and After*, p. 154
4 Tayler, *Jacobite Epilogue*, pp. 63–4
5 Pittock, *Culloden*, p. 65
6 '*Clann Chatain an t'Sròil*', in *An Lasair*, p. 167
7 O'Sullivan, *1745 and After*, p. 160
8 '*Clann Chatain an t'Sròil*', in *An Lasair*, p. 167
9 Johnstone, p. 195
10 Forbes, i, p. 103
11 Mackay, *Gaelic Place Names of Upper Strathglass*, p. 5. But Ronald Black questions the story in *An Lasair*, p. 444
12 Johnstone, p. 201
13 For an alternative scenario, see Zimmerman, *The Jacobite Movement in Scotland and in Exile, 1746–59*
14 Johnstone, p. 201

CHAPTER 43

1 Translation Ronald Black, *An Lasair*, pp. 184–5
2 Henderson, *The Life of William Augustus, Duke of Cumberland*, p. xxv
3 Smollett, iii, pp. 183–5
4 Forbes, 'Last and Dying Speech', pp. 15–16
5 Macinnes, 'The Aftermath of the 'Forty-five' in Woosnam-Savage (ed.), *1745*
6 Seton and Arnot, *Prisoners of the '45*, ii
7 Smollet, iii, p. 189
8 Forbes, iii, pp. 54–55
9 Letter to Sir Horace Mann, 1 August 1746
10 Monod, *Jacobitism*, p. 336
11 MacQuoid (ed.), p. 253

CHAPTER 44

1 Forbes, i, p 119
2 Ibid., ii, pp. 95–7

3   'Neil Maceachain's Narrative' in Blaikie, *Itinerary*, p. 101
4   O'Sullivan, p. 215
5   Forbes, i, pp. 118, 298
6   Ibid., i, p. 9
7   'Lochgarry's Narrative' in Blaikie, *Itinerary*, p. 125
8   O'Sullivan, p. 215
9   Smollett, iii, p. 185

CHAPTER 45

1   Forbes, iii, pp. 253–4
2   *Lockhart Papers*, ii, p. 565
3   Griffiths, *Ascanius, or the Young Adventurer*
4   Cruickshanks, *Political Untouchables*, p. 112
5   O'Sullivan, p. 209

CHAPTER 46

1   Cruickshanks, *Political Untouchables*, p. 108
2   Monod, *Jacobitism*, p. 199
3   Ibid., p. 205–6
4   Ibid., p. 209
5   Zimmerman, pp. 77–81

CHAPTER 47

1   Hume, *Essays*, p. 494
2   McLynn, *Charles Edward Stuart*, , p. 398
3   King, *Political and Literary Anecdotes of His Own Times*, pp. 196–200
4   McLynn, *Charles Edward Stuart*, p. 397
5   King, *Political and Literary Anecdotes*, p. 201
6   Zimmermann, pp. 164–5
7   Thicknesse, *Memoirs and* Anecdotes, pp. 341–2
8   Lang, *Pickle the Spy*: Zimmermann, p. 83
9   *Complete Collection of State Trials*, xix, 739–42
10   Smollett, iii, p. 3
11   King, *Political and Literary Anecdotes*, pp. 205–10
12   McLynn, *Charles Edward Stuart*, pp. 423–5
13   King, *Political and Literary Anecdotes*, pp. 205–10

CHAPTER 48

1 Zimmermann, p. 149
2 Letter of 27 October 1757
3 Elcho, p. 499
4 Roberts, *The Family: The History of a Dining Club*
5 Zimmermann, p. 149
6 Ibid., p. 131
7 Ibid., p. 143
8 Ibid., p. 143
9 Ó Ciardha, p. 299

CHAPTER 49

1 Monod, *Jacobitism*, p. 68
2 Gibbon, *Journal*, 24 November 1762
3 Macaulay, *Essays*, p. 759
4 Oliphant, *The Jacobite Lairds of Gask*, p. 235

CHAPTER 50

1 Cordara, *Commentary on the Expedition to Scotland made by Charles Edward Stuart*, ed. Sir B. Seton, p. 18
2 Strange, *Memoirs of Sir Robert Strange*, ii, p. 197
3 Forbes, iii, p. 232
4 Boswell, *Boswell's London Journal 1762–1763*, p. 146
5 King, *Political and Literary Anecdotes*, pp. 192–3
6 Gibson, p. 27
7 MacQuoid (ed.), pp. 28 and 280 (n. iv)
8 Musgrave, *Memoirs of the Different Rebellions in Ireland*, i, pp. 210–12
9 Conor Cruise O'Brien, *The Great Melody*, p. 51–2
10 Ó Ciardha, p. 375
11 Boswell, *Life*, ii, p. 224

CHAPTER 51

1 Forbes, iii, p. 275
2 Miller, *Letters from Italy*, ii, pp. 140–1

3 Ewald, *The Life and Times of Prince Charles Stewart, Count of Albany, commonly called the Young Pretender*, ii, pp. 266–7

4 Forbes, iii, p. 263

5 Elcho, appendix E, p. 459

6 Forbes, iii, pp. 295–6

7 Ibid., iii, pp. 325–6

8 Clark, 'Religion and Political Identity: Samuel Johnson as a Nonjuror', in Clark & Erskine-Hill (eds), *Samuel Johnson in Historical Context*, pp. 79–145

9 Forbes,   iii, p. 292

10 Boswell, *Life*, iii, p. 196

11 Clark, 'Samuel Johnson: The Last Choices. 1775–1784', in Clark & Erskine-Hill (eds), *The Politics of Samuel Johnson*, pp. 190–4

CHAPTER 52

1 Buchan, *The Complete Short Stories*, ii, pp. 115–16

2 Bahar, *Storm of the Sea: Indians and Empires in the Atlantic's Age of Sail*

3 Forbes, iii, p. 324

4 Ryan, 'A Jacobite Tune at the North Bridge', in *The Lincoln Minute Men Dispatch*

5 *Manuscripts of the Earl of Dartmouth*, pp. 368–9

6 McLynn, *Charles Edward Stuart*, p. 519

7 *Journal of the Continental Congress*, i, 1774

8 Dom Gregory Cowley, in Scott, *Gothic Rage Undone*, p. 198

9 Nimmo, p. 53

CHAPTER 53

1 Alfieri, *La Vita di Vittorio Alfieri da Asti*

2 Nordmann, *Grandeur et Liberté de la Suède*, p. 424

3 McLynn, *Charles Edward Stuart*, p. 538

4 *Archives Etrangères, Mémoires et Documents*, French Foreign Ministry Archives, Quai d'Orsay, *Angleterre*, 81, f. 45

5 Monod, *Jacobitism*, p. 187

6 Sitwell, *The Hurts of Haldworth*, p. 225

7 Sinclair, pp. 91–2

8 Scarfe (ed.), *To the Highlands in 1786*, pp. 181–2

9 Monod, *Jacobitism*, p. 42: Pittock, *Poetry and Jacobite Politics*, p. 213
10 Oliphant, p. 297
11 Clark, *A Short History of Australia*, p. 25
12 Buchan, *Short Stories*, ii, p. 107
13 Forbes, iii, p. 105

CHAPTER 54

1 Forbes, iii, p. 262
2 Luynes, *Mémoires sur la cour de Louis XV*, vii, p. 462
3 Corp, 'All Roads lead to Rome' in Forsyth (ed.), *Bonnie Prince Charlie*, p. 73
4 Forbes, iii, p. 234
5 Lees-Milne, *The Last Stuarts*, pp. 151–4
6 Burke, *Letter to Sir Hercules Langrishe on the Roman Catholics of Ireland*
7 S. Deane, 'Edmund Burke' in *Field Day Anthology of Irish Writing*, p. 808
8 'Defenders and Defenderism in 1795' in *Irish Historical Studies*, xxiv (1985), p. 388
9 Oliphant, p. 295
10 Jesse, *Memoirs of the Life and Reign of King George the Third*, iii, p. 246
11 Cloncurry, *Personal Recollections*, p. 198
12 Connolly, *Religion, law and power*, p. 249

CHAPTER 55

1 Oliphant, p. 297
2 Lacretelle, *La Comtesse d'Albany*
3 Macaulay, *Essays*, p. 16
4 Disraeli, *Disraeli's Reminiscences*, p. 37
5 Lord Annan, 'The Whig Tradition' in P. Ziegler and D. Seward (eds), *Brooks's, a Social History* (Constable, 1991), p. 200
6 Buchan, *Memory Holds the Door*, p. 5

EPILOGUE

1 Lenihan, p. 18

Bibliography

PRINTED PRIMARY SOURCES

An Act for the further Security of his Majesties Person and the Succession of the Crown in the Protestant Line (London, 1701)

Ailesbury, Earl of, *The Memoirs of Thomas, Earl of Ailesbury*, ed. W. E. Cooke, 2 vols (Roxburghe Club, 1890)

Alfieri, V., *Memoirs of the life and writings of Victor Alfieri; written by himself*, trans. H. Colburn (London, 1810)

Atterbury, Francis, *English advice to the Freeholders of England* (London 1715)

——, *Second and Last Advice to the Freeholders of England* (London, 1722)

Avaux, Comte d', *Negotiations* [sic] *de M. Le Comte d'Avaux en Irlande (1689–90)*, ed. J. Hogan (Dublin S. O., 1958)

Balcarres, Earl of, *An Account of the Affairs of Scotland relating to the Revolution in 1688* (London, 1714)

Berwick, Duke of, *Memoirs of the Marshal Duke of Bewick*, 2 vols (London, 1779)

Black, R. (ed. and trans.), *An Lasair: Anthology of 18th Century Scottish Gaelic Verse* (Edinburgh, Birlinn, 2001)

Boswell, James, *Boswell's Life of Johnson*, eds G. Birbeck Hill and L. F. Powell, 6 vols (Oxford, Clarendon Press, 1934–50)

——, *The Journal of a Tour to the Hebrides with Samuel Johnson* (London, J. M. Dent, 1935)

——, *Boswell's London Journal 1762–1763*, ed. F. Pottle (New York, McGraw-Hill, 1950)

Bradstreet, D., *The Life and Uncommon Adventures of Captain Dudley Bradstreet* (Dublin, 1755)

Burke, E., *Letter to Sir Hercules Langrishe on the Roman Catholics of Ireland* (Dublin, 1792)

Burnet, Bishop Gilbert, *A History of My Own Time*, ed. M. Routh, 6 vols (Oxford, 1823)

————, *A Supplement to Burnet's History of My Own Time*, eds H. C. Foxcroft and T. E. S. Clarke (Oxford, Clarendon Press, 1902)

Burt, Edmund, *Letters from a Gentleman in the North of Scotland*, 2 vols (Edinburgh, 1822)

Campbell, A., *The Doctrines of the Middle State* (London, 1721)

Campbell, J. L. (ed.), *Highland Songs of the 'Forty-Five* (Edinburgh, 1984)

Campbell, R., *The Life of the Most Illustrious Prince, Duke of Argyll and Greenwich* (London, 1745)

Carlyle, A., *Anecdotes and Characters of the Times* (London, OUP, 1973)

Chambers, R., *History of the Rebellion in Scotland in 1745-6*, 2 vols (Edinburgh, 1827)

————, *Jacobite Memoirs of the Rebellion of 1745* (Edinburgh and London, 1834)

Charles I, *Eikon Basilike*, ed. E. Almack, (London, De La Mare Press, 1904)

Chesterfield, P. D. Stanhope, Earl of, *Letters of Lord Chesterfield*, ed. B. Dobrée, 6 vols (London, 1932)

A Collection of Declarations, Proclamations and Other Valuable Papers. Published by Authority at Edinburgh in the Years 1745 and 1746 (Edinburgh, 1749)

A Collection of Scarce and Valuable Tracts, ed. Sir W. Scott, vii (London, 1814)

Clarke, J. S. (ed.), *The Life of King James the Second, King of England*, 2 vols (London, 1816)

Clarke, P., *A Journall of Severall Occurences from 2d November 1715, in the Insurrection (began in Scotland and concluded at Preston in Lancashire) on November 14, MDCCXV*, Miscellany of the Scottish History Society, i (Edinburgh, 1893)

Claudianus, Andreas, *The Irish Mars*, trans. J. Jordan, in *Journal of the Galway Historical and Archaeological Society*, xxvi (1954-5), pp. 1-13

Cloncurry, Lord, *Personal Recollections* (Dublin, 1849)

A Complete Collection of State Trials and Proceedings for High Treason, ed. T. B. Howell, 33 vols (London, 1816-26)

Cordara, G., *Commentary on the Expedition to Scotland made by Charles Edward Stuart, Prince of Wales, by Padre Giulio Cordara*, ed. Sir B. Seton, Miscellany of the Scottish Historical Society, 3rd series IX (1926)

Cox, L. (ed.), 'A diary of the siege of Athlone, 1691' in *The Irish Sword*, iv, no. 15, p. 88

Crofton-Cooke, T., *Historical Songs of Ireland* (London, 1841)

Culloden Papers (London, 1815)

Dalrymple, J., *Memoirs of Great Britain and Ireland from the Dissolution of the Last Parliament of Charles II until the Sea Battle of La Hogue*, 2 vols (Dublin 1773–88)

Daniel, J., 'John Daniel's Account' in W. B. Blaikie, *Origins of the 'Forty-Five and other papers relating to that Rising* (Edinburgh, Scottish History Society, 1916)

Defoe, D., *The History of the Union between England and Scotland* (London, 1786)

———, *The Secret History of the White Staff. Part II* (London, 1714)

———, *A Tour through the Whole Island of Great Britain* (London, 1726)

Disraeli, B., *Disraeli's Reminiscences*, eds H. M. and M. Swartz (London, Hamish Hamilton, 1975)

Doebner, R., *Memoirs of Mary, Queen of England, 1689–93* (London, 1886)

Drake, P., *The Memoirs of Capt. Peter Drake* (Dublin, 1755)

Dryden, J., *The Works of John Dryden*, ed. W. Frost, vol. v (Berkeley, California, 1987)

Dundee, Viscount of, *Letters of John Grahame of Claverhouse, Viscount of Dundee*, ed. G. Smythe (Edinburgh, 1826)

Earbery, M., *An Historical Account of the Advantages that have Accru'd to England, by the Succession in the Illustrious House of Hanover* (London, 1722)

Elcho, Lord, *A Short Account of the Affairs of Scotland*, ed. E. Charteris (Edinburgh, 1907)

Ellis, F. H. (ed.), *Poems on Affairs of State: Augustan Satirical Verse 1660–1714* (New Haven, 1975)

Evelyn, J., *The Diary of John Evelyn*, ed. E. S. De Beer, 6 vols (Oxford, 1955)

A Faithful Register of the Late Rebellion (London, 1718)

Forbes, R., *The Lyon in Mourning*, ed. H. Patton, 3 vols (Edinburgh Historical Society, 1895)

Forbin-Gardanne, C. de, *Mémoires du Comte de Forbin* (Paris, 1829)

A Form of Prayer and Humiliation for God's Blessing upon His Majesty and his Dominions, and for Removing and Averting of God's Judgements upon this Church and State (London, 1690)

Forman, C., *Letter to Sir Robert Sutton for Disbanding the Irish Regiments in the French Army* (Dublin, 1728)

Freebairn, J., *The Miserable State of Scotland* (Perth, 1720)

Gay, John, *The Poems of John Gay*, ed. F. Bickley (London, Chapman & Dodd, 1923)

The Gentleman's Magazine and Historical Chronicle (London, 1731–1807)

Gibbon, Edward, *Gibbon's Journal to 28 January 1763*, ed. D. M. Low (London, 1929)

Gibson, J. S. (ed.), *The Diary of John Campbell: A Scottish Banker and the 'Forty-five* (Edinburgh, The Royal Bank of Scotland, 1995)

Great Britain's Just Complaint For Her Late Measures, Present Sufferings, and the Future Miseries . . . (Oxford, 1692)

Griffiths, R., *Ascanius, or the Young Adventurer* (London, 1747)

Gyllenborg, Count C., *Letters which passed between Count Gyllenborg, the Barons Gortz, Sparre and Others* (London, 1717)

Halifax, Earl of, *The Complete Works*, ed. W. Raleigh (Oxford, 1912)

Henderson, A., *The History of the Rebellion, 1745 and 1746* (London, 1753)

———, *The Life of William Augustus*, ed. Roderick Macpherson (London, Routledge, 2016)

Hervey, Lord, *Some Materials towards Memoirs of the Reign of King George II*, ed. R. Sedgwick, 3 vols (London, 1931)

The Historical Register. Volume IV. For the Year 1719 (London, 1720)

Hogg, J., *Jacobite Relics of Scotland: Being the songs, airs and legends of the adherents to the house of Stuart*, ed. M. Pittock, 2 vols (Edinburgh University Press, 2001 and 2003)

Home, John, *The History of the Rebellion in the Year 1745* (London, 1802)

Hooke, N., *The Secret History of Colonel Hooke's Negotiations in Scotland, in Favour of the Pretender; in 1707* (London, 1760)

———, *Correspondence of Colonel N. Hooke, agent from the court of France to the Scottish Jacobites, in the years 1703–1707*, ed. W. D. Macray, 2 vols (London, Roxburghe Club, 1870)

Hume, David, *Essays Moral, Political and Literary* (London, Grant Richards, 1903)

———, *History of Great Britain*, London, 1832)

A Jacobite Narrative of the War in Ireland, 1689–91, ed. J. T. Gilbert (Dublin, 1892)

Jacobite Songs and Ballads, ed. G. S. MacQuoid (London, 1887)

Johnstone, Chevalier de, *Memoirs of the Rebellion in 1745 and 1746* (London, 1820)

Journal of the Continental Congress, i (1774)

A Journal of the Earl of Marr's Proceedings, From his First Arrival in Scotland to his Embarkation for France (London, 1716)

Journals and Memoirs of the Young Pretender's Expedition in 1745 by Highland Officers in his Army, in *The Lockhart Papers* (see below)

Keith, J., *A fragment of a Memoir of Field-Marshal James Keith, written by himself, 1714–34* (Edinburgh, Spalding Club, 1834)

King, W., *Political and Literary Anecdotes of His Own Times* (London, 1819)

Leslie, C., *A Letter from Mr Lesly to a Member of Parliament in London* (London, 1714)

A Letter from an English Traveller at Rome to his Father of 6th May 1721 (London, 1721)

Lockhart of Carnwath, George, *The Lockhart Papers; containing Memoirs and Correspondence upon the Affairs of Scotland from 1702 to 1715*, ed. J. Aufrere, 2 vols (London, 1817)

———, *'Scotland's Ruine': Lockhart of Carnwath's Memoirs of the Union*, ed. D. Szechi (Aberdeen, 1995)

Luynes, Albert, Duc de, *Mémoires sur la cour de Louis XV*, ed. L. Dussieux and E. Soulie (Paris, 1860–6)

Lyttleton, G., *A Letter to the Tories* (London, 1748)

———, *Memoirs and Correspondence of George, Lord Lyttleton*, ed. R. J. Phillimore (London, 1845)

Macdonald, Alexander, *Alexius or the Young Adventurer* (London, 1746)

Mackay, H., *Memoirs of the War Carried on in Scotland and Ireland, 1689–91* (Edinburgh, Bannatyne Club, 1836)

Mackechnie, E., *The Poetry of John Roy Stewart* (Edinburgh, 1947)

Macky, J., *A View of the Court of St Germain from the Year 1690, to '95. With an Account of the Entertainment that Protestants meet with there* (London, 1696) in J. Macky, *Memoirs of the Secret Services of John Macky* (London, Roxburghe Club, 1895)

Macpherson, J. J. (ed.), *Original Papers: Containing the Secret History of Great Britain from the Restoration, to the Accession of the House of Hannover: to which are prefixed extracts from the life of James II as written by himself*, 2 vols (London, 1775)

Mahon, Lord (ed.), *Decline of the Last Stuarts. Extracts from Despatches* (London, Roxburghe Club, 1843)

The Manuscripts of the Earl of Dartmouth, Royal Commission on Historical Manuscripts (London, HMSO, 1895)

Mar, Duke of, *A Journal of the Earl of Marr's proceedings: from his arrival in Scotland, to his embarkation for France* (London, 1715)

Mar, Duke of, *Distinct Abridgement of some Materiall Poynts relating to Scots Affairs*, in Oliphant, *The Jacobite Lairds of Gask* (see below)

Mar, H. M. C., *Report on the Manuscripts of the Earl of Mar and Kellie* (London, 1904)

Maxwell of Kirkconnel, James, *Narrative of Charles, Prince of Wales's expedition to Scotland in the year 1745*, ed. G. H. Rose (Edinburgh, 1841)

'Memoirs of the Rebellion in 1745 and 1746 so far as it concerned the Counties of Aberdeen and Banff' in W. B. Blaikie, *Origins of the 'Forty Five and other papers relating to that Rising* (Edinburgh, Scottish History Society, 1916)

Martin, M., *A Description of the Western Isles of Scotland* (London, 1716)

Menzies, H. M. C., *Report on the Menzies Manuscripts* (London, 1877)

Miller, Lady Anne, *Letters from Italy*, 3 vols (London, 1776)

Murray, Lord George, 'Letter to Lady Amelia, 9 September 1745' in *The Jacobite*, No. 116 (Perth, 2004)

——, *Marches of the Highland Army* in Chambers, *Jacobite Memoirs* (see above)

Murray of Broughton, John, *Memorials*, ed. R. F. Bell, Scottish History Society 27 (1898)

Musgrave, Sir R., *Memoirs of the Different Rebellions in Ireland*, 2 vols (London, 1802)

Ó Bruadair, David, *Duanaire Dháibhidh Uí Bhruadair: The Poems of David Ó Bruadair*, trans. and ed. John C. MacErlean, 3 parts (London, 1910–17)

O'Conor, A., *A Translation of the Memorial Presented to the Q. of England (The Wife of the Chevalier de St George) by Father Ambrose O' Conor* (London, 1760), in Hooke, *The Secret History of Colonel Hooke's Negotiations in Scotland . . .* (see above)

O'Foghludha, R., *Amhráin Phiaris Mhic Gearailt* (Dublin, 1905)

O'Kelly, Colonel Charles, *Macariae Excidium or The Destruction of Cyprus* (Dublin, 1850)

Onslow, H. M. C., *Report on the Onslow Manuscripts* (London, 1896)

O'Rahilly, E., *Dánta Aodhagáin Uí Rathaille: The Poems of Egan O'Rahilly*, eds P. Dinneen and T. O'Donaghue (London, 1911)

Ormonde, Duke of, *The Jacobite Attempt of 1719. Letters of James Butler, second Duke of Ormonde*, ed. W. K. Dickinson (Edinburgh, Scottish Historical Society, 1895)

Ó Suilleabháin, E., *Aimhráin Eoghain Ruiadh Uí Shuilleabháin*, ed. P. Dinneen (Dublin, 1923)

O'Sullivan, Sir John W., *1745 and After*, eds A. and H. Tayler (Edinburgh, Nelson, 1938)

Ó Tuama, S. (ed.), *An Duanaire 1600–1900: Poems of the Dispossessed*, trans. T. Kinsella (Portlaoise, 1981)

Patten, R., *The History of the Late Rebellion: With Original Papers and the Characters of the Principal Noblemen and Gentlemen Concern'd in it*, 2nd edn, 2 Parts (London, 1717)

Pennant, T., *A Tour in Scotland and Voyage to the Hebrides* (London, 1772–6)

Philip of Amlerieclose, James, *The Grameid* (Edinburgh, 1888)

Pollnitz, K. L. von, *The Memoirs of Charles-Lewis, Baron de Pollnitz*, 2 vols (London, 1733)

Rae, P., *The History of the Rebellion rais'd against His Majesty King George I by the Friends of the Popish Pretender* (London, 1746)

Rancé, Armand de, *The Letters of Armand de Rancé, Abbot and Reformer of La Trappe*, ed. A. Krailsheimer, 2 vols (Kalamazoo, 1984)

Records of the Parliaments of Scotland to 1707

Richelieu, L. F. A. du Plessis, *Mémoires authentiques du maréchal de Richelieu*, ed. A. de Boilisle (Paris, 1918)

St John, *Works of the late Right Honourable Henry St John, Lord Viscount Bolingbroke*, 8 vols (London, 1809)

Saint-Simon, Louis de Rouvroy, duc de, *Mémoires complètes*, ed. A. de Boilisle (Paris, 1923–30)

Scarfe, N. (ed.), *To the Highlands in 1786* (Woodbridge, Boydell Press, 2001)

Sinclair, Sir John, *Memoirs of the Insurrection in Scotland in 1715. By John, Master of Sinclair, with notes by Sir Walter Scott, Bart.* (Edinburgh, Abbotsford Club, 1858)

Sitwell, Sir G., *Letters of the Sitwells and Sacheverells*, 2 vols (Scarborough, 1901–2)

Smollett, Tobias, *A Complete History of England*, 5 vols (London, 1804)

Spottiswoode Society, *Miscellany: A collection of original papers and tracts*, 2 vols (Edinburgh, 1844–5)

Stevens, J., *The Journal of John Stevens, containing a brief account of the war in Ireland, 1689–91* (Oxford University Press, 1912)

Story, G., *An Impartial History of the Wars in Ireland, with a Continuation thereof* (London, 1693)

Strange, Sir Robert, *Memoirs of Sir Robert Strange, Kt., and of his brother-in-law, Andrew Lumisden*, ed. J. Dennistoun, 2 vols (London, 1855)

Stuarts, *Calendar of Stuart Papers ... at Windsor Castle*, 6 vols (London, 1902–24)

Swift, J., *The Works of the Rev. Jonathan Swift*, 19 vols (London, 1801)

Thicknesse, P., *Memoirs and Anecdotes* (Dublin, 1760)

A True Account of the Proceedings at Perth; the Debates in the Secret Council there; with the Reasons and Causes of the suddain finishing and breaking up of the Rebellion. Written by a rebel (London, 1716)

The True Loyalist; Or Chevalier's Favourite (1779)

Voltaire, F. M. A. de, *Oeuvres completes*, ed. A. J. Q. Beuchot, 72 vols (Paris, 1829–40)

Walpole, H., *Letters of Horace Walpole: Earl of Orford*, 4 vols (Philadelphia, 1842)

Memoirs of King George II, ed J. Brooke, 2 vols (New Haven, 1985)

——, *The Yale Edition of Horace Walpole's Correspondence*, ed. W. S. Lewis, 48 vols (New Haven, 1937–83)

The Weekly Journal or British Gazeteer (London, 1716–20)

Wogan C., *Mémoires sur l'enterprise de Innspruck en 1719*, in J. T. Gilbert, *Narratives of the Detention, Liberation and Marriage of Clementina Stuart* (Dublin, 1894)

——, *Female Fortitude Exemplified in an impartial Narrative of the Seizure, Escape and Marriage of the Princess Clementina Sobiesky* (London, 1722)

Yorke, Philip, *The Life and Correspondence of Philip Yorke, Earl of Hardwicke*, 3 vols (Cambridge, 1913)

SECONDARY SOURCES

Aveling, J. C., *The Handle and the Axe, The Catholic Recusants in England from Reformation to Emancipation* (London, Blond and Briggs, 1976)

Bahar, M. R., *Storm of the Sea: Indians and Empires in the Atlantic's Age of Sail* (Oxford University Press, 2018)

Bastian, F., *Daniel Defoe's Early Life* (London, Macmillan 1981)

Baynes, J., *The Jacobite Rising of 1715* (Cassell, 1970)

Beaven, A. B., *The Aldermen of the City of London*, 2 vols (London, 1908–13)

Bennett, G. V., *The Tory Crisis in Church and State 1688–1730: The Career of Francis Atterbury, Bishop of Rochester* (Oxford, 1975)

Black, J., *British Foreign Policy in the Age of Walpole* (Edinburgh, 1985)

Blaikie, W. B., *Itinerary of Prince Charles Edward Stuart* (Edinburgh, Scottish History Society, 1897)

——, 'Origins of the 'Forty-Five' in *Scottish History Society*, 2nd series, II (Edinburgh, 1916)

Bonnie Prince Charlie and the Jacobites, ed. D. Forsyth (National Museum of Scotland, 2017)

Boulger, D. G., *The Battle of the Boyne* (London, 1913)

Browne, J., *A History of the Highlands and of the Highland Clans*, 3 vols (London, 1853)

Broxap, H., *The Later Non-Jurors* (Cambridge, 1924)

Buchan, John, *Memory Holds the Door* (London, Hodder & Stoughton, 1940)

——, *The Complete Short Stories*, ed. A. Lownie, 3 vols (London, Thistle Publishing, 1997)

Callow, J., *The Making of King James II; the formative years of a fallen king* (Sutton, 2000)

——, *King in Exile: James II, Warrior, King and Saint* (Sutton, 2004)

Chambers, R., *History of the Rebellions in Scotland under the Viscount of Dundee and the Earl of Mar in 1689 and 1715* (Edinburgh, 1829)

Châteaubriand, F.-R. de, *La Vie de Rancé*, ed. J. Benda (Paris, Bossard, 1920)

Chenevix Trench, C., *Grace's Card: Irish Catholic Landlords 1690–1800* (Dublin, Mercier Press, 1997)

Childs, J., *The Army, James II and the Glorious Revolution* (Manchester, 1980)

Clark, J. C. D., *Revolution and Rebellion* (Cambridge, 1986)

——, *English Society 1660–1832*, 2nd edn (Cambridge, 2000)

——, *From Restoration to Reform: the British Isles 1660–1832* (London, Vintage, 2014)

——, and H. Erskine-Hill (eds), *Samuel Johnson in Historical Context* (Basingstoke, Palgrave Macmillan, 2002)

——, and H. Erskine-Hill (eds), *The Politics of Samuel Johnson* (New York, Palgrave, 2012)

Clark, M., *A Short History of Australia* (Sydney, 1963)

Cockayne, G. E., *Complete Peerage*, 14 vols (London, 1910–59)

——, *Complete Baronetage*, 6 vols (London 1900–9)

Connolly, S., *Religion, Law and Power: the Making of Protestant Ireland 1660–1760* (Oxford, 1992)

Corkery, Daniel, *The Hidden Ireland. A Study of Gaelic Munster in the Eighteenth Century* (Dublin, 1925)

Corp, E., *A Court in Exile: The Stuarts in France, 1688–1718* (Cambridge University Press, 2004)

—— (ed.), *The Stuart Court at Rome: the Legacy of Exile* (Aldershort, Ashgate, 2003)

Coxe, W., *Memoirs of the Life and Administration of Sir Robert Walpole, Earl of Orford*, 4 vols (London, 1816)

Cruickshanks, E., *Political Untouchables: The Tories and the '45* (London, Duckworth, 1979)

————, and J. Black (eds), *The Jacobite Challenge* (Edinburgh, John Donald, 1988)

————, and H. Erskine-Hill, *The Atterbury Plot* (London, Palgrave Macmillan, 2004)

Daiches, D., *Charles Edward Stuart* (London, Thames and Hudson, 1973)

D'Alton, J., *Illustrations historical and genealogical of King James's Irish Army List*, 2 vols (Dublin, 1860)

Donnelly, J., and K. Miller (eds), *Irish Popular Culture 1650–1850* (Dublin, 1998)

Douglas, H., *Jacobite Spy Wars* (Sutton, 1999)

Duffy, C., *Fight for a Throne, The Jacobite '45 Reconsidered* (Solihull, Helion, 2015)

Emerson, R. L., *An Enlightened Duke: Life of Archibald Campbell, Earl of Islay, 3rd Duke of Argyll* (Humming Earth, 2013)

Ewald, A. C., *The Life and Times of Prince Charles Stewart, Count of Albany, commonly called the Young Pretender*, 2 vols (London, 1875)

Forsyth, D. (ed.), *Bonnie Prince Charlie and the Jacobites* (Edinburgh, National Museum of Scotland, 2017)

Forsyth, W., *In the Shadow of Cairngorm* (Inverness, 1900)

Foster, R. E., *Modern Ireland 1600–1972* (London, Allen Lane, 1988)

Fothergill, B., *The Cardinal King* (London, Faber and Faber, 1958)

Foxcroft, H. C., *Life and Letters of Sir George Savile, Bart., first Marquess of Halifax*, 2 vols (London, 1898)

Francis, G. F., *Romance of the White Rose* (London, John Murray, 1933)

Haile, M., *James Francis Edward, The Old Chevalier* (London, J. M. Dent & Co., 1907)

Hayes, R., *A Biographical Dictionary of Irishmen in France* (Dublin, Gill, 1949)

Historical Manuscripts Commission, 14th Report, Appendix ix (1895)

Hopkins, P., *Glencoe and the End of the Highland War* (Edinburgh, John Donald, 1986)

Ideas, aesthetics and enquiries in the early modern era, viii (New York, 2003)

Jesse, J. H., *Memoirs of the Life and Reign of King George the Third* (London, 1867)

Lacretelle, A. de, *La Comtesse d'Albany: une égerie européenne* (Monaco, Éditions du Rocher, 2008)

Lang, Andrew, *Pickle the Spy* (London, 1897)

Lecky, W., *A History of Ireland in the Eighteenth Century*, 5 vols (London, 1892)

Lees-Milne, J., *The Last Stuarts* (London, Chatto & Windus, 1984)

Lefèvre-Pontalis, G., *La Mission du Marquis d'Éguilles* (Paris, 1886)

Lenihan, P., *The Last Cavalier, Richard Talbot (1631–91)* (University College Dublin Press, 2014)

Lenman, B., *The Jacobite Risings in Britain 1689–1746* (Aberdeen, 1980)

——, and J. S. Gibson, *The Jacobite Threat: England, Scotland, Ireland, France. A Source Book* (Edinburgh, Scottish Academic Press, 1890)

Linehan, P., *St John's College, Cambridge: A History* (Woodbridge, Boydell Press, 2011)

Lodge, J., *The Peerage of Ireland*, 7 vols (Dublin, 1789)

Macaulay, Lord Thomas, *The History of England from the Accession of James II*, 3 vols (London, 1906)

——, *Lord Macaulay's Essays* (London, 1895)

Mackay, W., *Gaelic Place Names of Upper Strathglas* (Inverness, 1968)

Macknight, T., *The Life of Henry St. John, Viscount Bolingbroke* (London, 1863)

Mcbride, I., *Eighteenth Century Ireland, the Isle of Slaves* (Dublin, Gill & Macmillan, 2009)

McInnes, A. I., K. German and L. Graham, *Living with Jacobitism, 1690–1788: The Three Kingdoms and Beyond* (London, Pickering & Chatto, 2014)

Mclynn, F. J., *France and the Jacobite Rising of 1745* (Edinburgh, 1981)

——, *The Jacobites* (London, Routledge & Kegan Paul, 1985)

——, *Charles Edward Stuart, a tragedy in many acts* (London and New York, 1988)

Mcnally, M., *The Battle of Aughrim 1691* (Stroud, History Press, 2008)

Mahon, Lord, *History of England from the Peace of Utrecht to the Peace of Versailles 1713–1783*, 7 vols (London, 1856)

Miller, J., *The Life and Times of William and Mary* (London, Weidenfeld & Nicolson, 1974)

——, *James II, a study in kingship* (New Haven, 2000)

——, *The Stuarts* (Hambledon and London, 2006)

Monod, P. K., *Jacobitism and the English People, 1688–1788* (Cambridge University Press, 1989)

——, M. Pittock and D. Szechi (eds), *Loyalty and Identity: Jacobites at Home and Abroad* (Basingstoke, Palgrave Macmillan, 2010)

Murray, R. H., *Revolution Ireland and the Settlement* (London, 1911)

Namier, Sir L., *Crossroads of Power, Essays on Eighteenth Century England* (London, Hamish Hamilton, 1963)

Nordmann, C., *Grandeur et Liberté de la Suède* (Paris, 1971)

Oates, J., *The Last Battle on English Soil, Preston 1715* (Farnham, Ashgate, 2015)

O'Brien, C. C., *The Great Melody: A Thematic History of Edmund Burke* (University of Chicago Press, 1992)

O'Callaghan, J. C., *History of the Irish Brigades in the service of France* (Glasgow, 1870)

Ó Ciardha, E., *Ireland and the Jacobite Cause, 1685–1766: A fatal attachment* (Dublin, Four Courts Press, 2002)

O'Flanagan, P. and C. G. Buttimer (eds), *Cork History and Society* (Dublin, 1993)

Oliphant, T. L. K., *The Jacobite Lairds of Gask* (London, 1870)

Ollard, S. L., *The Nonjurors* (London, 1912)

Petrie, Sir C., *The Jacobite Movement. The Last Phase, 1716–1807* (London, Eyre & Spottiswoode, 1950)

——, *The Jacobite Movement* (London, Eyre & Spottiswoode, 1959)

Pittock, M., *Poetry and Jacobite Politics in Eighteenth Century Britain and Ireland* (Cambridge University Press, 1994)

——, *The Myth of the Jacobite Clans, The Jacobite Army in 1745*, 2nd edn (Edinburgh University Press, 2009)

——, *Culloden* (Oxford University Press, 2016)

Plumb, J. H., *Sir Robert Walpole*, 2 vols (London, Cresset Press, 1956 and 1960)

Ranke, L. Von, *History of England, principally in the Seventeenth Century*, 6 vols (Oxford, 1875)

Reading, D. K., *The Anglo-Russian Commercial Treaty of 1734* (Newhaven, Connecticut, 1938)

Reid, S., *1745. A Military History of the Last Jacobite Rising* (New York, Sarpedon, 1996)

Riding, J., *Jacobites: A New History of the '45 Rebellion* (London, Bloomsbury, 2016)

Roberts S. C., *The Family: The History of a Dining Club* (Cambridge Universtity Press, 1963)

Rudé, G., *Hanoverian London 1714–1808* (Gloucester, Sutton Publishing, 2003)

Scott, G., *Gothic Rage Undone: English Monks in the Age of Enlightenment* (Bath, 1992)

Scott, Sir W., 'History of Scotland' in *Lardner's Cabinet Cyclopaedia*, i (Edinburgh, 1829)

Sedgwick, R. (ed.), *The History of Parliament: The House of Commons 1715–1754*, 2 vols (HMSO, 1970)

Sergeant, P. W., *Little Jennings and Fighting Dick Talbot*, 2 vols (London, 1913)

Seton, Sir B. G., and J. G. Arnot, *The Prisoners of the '45* (Edinburgh, Constable, 1929)

Sharp, R., *The Engraved Record of the Jacobite Movement* (Aldershot, Scholar Press, 1996)

Shaw, J., *Political History of Eighteenth Century Scotland* (Macmillan, 1999)

Shield, A., and A. Lang, *The King over the Water* (London, Longmans, 1907)

Simms, J. G., *Jacobite Ireland 1685–91* (London, Routledge & Kegan Paul, 1969)

———, *War and Politics in Ireland, 1649–1730*, eds D.Hayton and G. O'Brien (London, Hambledon Press, 1986)

Sitwell, Sir G., *The Hurts of Haldworth and Their Descendants at Savile Hall, The Ickles and Hesley Hall* (Oxford University Press, 1930)

Skrine, F. H., *Fontenoy* (Edinburgh, 1906)

Somerset, A., *Queen Anne: The Politics of Passion* (London, HarperCollins, 2012)

Sowerby, Scott, *Making Toleration: The Repealers and the Glorious Revolution* (Harvard University Press, 2013)

Speck, W. A., *The Butcher: the duke of Cumberland and the suppression of the 'Forty-Five* (Oxford University Press, 1981)

———, *James II* (Harlow, Pearson Education, 2002)

Spiers, E. M. (ed.), *A Military History of Scotland* (Edinburgh University Press, 2012)

Stephen, J., *Scottish Presbyterians and the Act of Union* (Edinburgh University Press, 2007)

———, *Defending the Revolution: the Church of Scotland 1689–1716* (Ashgate, 2013)

Stewart, M., *The Architectural Landscape and the Constitutional Plans of the Earl of Mar*, (Dublin, Four Courts Press, 2016)

Sullivan, A. M., *The Story of Ireland* (Dublin, 1867)

Szechi, D., *Jacobitism and Tory Politics, 1707–14* (Edinburgh, 1984)

———, *The Jacobites: Britain and Europe 1688–1788* (Manchester University Press, 1994)

————, *1715, The Great Jacobite Rebellion* (New Haven and London, Yale University Press, 2006)

————, *Britain's Lost Revolution? Jacobite Scotland and the French Grand Strategy, 1701–8* (Manchester University Press, 2015)

Tayler, A. and H., *1715: The Story of the Rising* (Edinburgh, Nelson, 1936)

Tayler, H., *Jacobite Epilogue* (Edinburgh, 1941)

————, *The History of the Rebellion in the Years 1745 and 1746* (London, 1944)

————, *Prince Charlie's Daughter. Being the Life and Letters of Charlotte, Duchess of Albany* (London, Batchworth Press, 1950)

Terry, C. S., *John Graham of Claverhouse, Viscount Dundee: 1648–1689* (London, 1905)

Turner, *James II* (London, Eyre & Spottiswoode, 1950)

Watney, Vernon, *Cornbury and the Forest of Wychwood* (privately printed, 1919)

Wauchope, P., *Patrick Sarsfield and the Williamite War* (Dublin, Irish Academic Press, 1992)

Whatley, C. A. and Patrick, D. J., *The Scots and the Union* (Edinburgh, 2006)

Wills, R., *The Jacobites and Russia 1715–1750*, (East Linton, Tuckwell Press, 2002)

Woosnam-Savage, R. (ed.), *1745: Charles Edward Stuart and the Jacobites* (Edinburgh, 1995)

Zimmermann, D., *The Jacobite Movement in Scotland and in Exile, 1746–59* (London, Palgrave Macmillan, 2003)

ESSAYS AND ARTICLES

Barclay, A., 'James II's "Catholic Court"' in *Ideas, aesthetics and enquiries in the early modern era*

Bartlett, T., 'Defenders and Defenderism in 1795' in *Irish Historical Studies*, xxiv (1985)

Black, J., 'Jacobitism and British Foreign Policy, 1731–5' in Cruickshanks and Black (eds), *The Jacobite Challenge*

Bogle, J., 'Lord Nithsdale's Escape' in *Royal Stuart Papers*, lxx (1986)

Clark, J. C. D., 'The Many Restorations of King James: A Short History of Scholarship on Jacobitism, 1688–2006' in Monod, Pittock and Szechi (eds), *Loyalty and Identity*

Corp, E., 'All Roads lead to Rome' in Forsyth (ed.), *Bonnie Prince Charlie and the Jacobites*

Cruickshanks, E., 'Lord Cornbury, Bolingbroke and a plan to restore the Stuarts, 1731–1735' in *Royal Stuart Papers*, xxvii (1986), pp. 4–5

Cruickshanks, E. and H. Erskine-Hill, 'The Waltham Blacks' in *Journal of British Studies*, xxiv (1985), pp. 358–65

Cullen, L. M., 'The Blackwater Catholics and County Cork Society and Politics in the Eighteenth Century' in O'Flanagan and Buttimer (eds), *Cork History and Society*

Deane, S., 'Edmund Burke' in *Field Day Anthology of Irish Writing*, i (Derry, 1991)

Drummond, B., 'Bonnie Prince Charlie returns to Edinburgh' in *Country Life*, 11 May 2016

Eighteenth-Century Ireland, Journal of the Eighteenth-Century Ireland Society (Dublin, 1986–)

Erskine-Hill, H., 'The Political Character of Samuel Johnson' in Cruickshanks and Black (eds), *The Jacobite Challenge*

Gregg, E., 'The Politics of Paranoia', in Cruickshanks and Black (eds), *The Jacobite Challenge*

———, 'The financial vicissitudes of James III in Rome' in Corp (ed.), *The Stuart Court at Rome*

Guthrie, N., 'Johnson's Touch-piece and the "Charge of Fame": Personal and Public Aspects of the Medal in Eighteenth-century Britain' in Clark and Erskine-Hill (eds), *The Politics of Samuel Johnson*

Hynes, A., 'True Religion: Faith and the Jacobite Movement' in Forsyth (ed.), *Bonnie Prince Charlie and the Jacobites*

Macinnes, A. I., '*A' Ghaidhealtachd* and the Jacobites' in Forsyth (ed.), *Bonnie Prince Charlie and the Jacobites*

Maidment, J. (ed.), 'A Hue and Cry after the Pretender' in *Analecta Scotica*, series 1, lxxii (Edinburgh, 1834)

Murdoch, S., 'Tilting at Windmills: The Order of Toboso as a Jacobite Social Network' in Monod, Pittock and Szechi (eds), *Loyalty and Identity*

Nimmo, A. E., 'The Sacramental Soul of Jacobitism' in McInnes, German and Graham (eds), *Living with Jacobitism, 1690–1788*

Ó Buachalla, B., 'Irish Jacobite Poetry' in *Irish Review*, vii, no. 2 (1992)

———, 'A Cork Jacobite' in O'Flanagan and Buttimer (eds), *Cork History and Society*

Ó Ciardha, E., '"A lot done, a lot more to do?": The Restoration and Road Ahead for Irish Jacobite Studies' in Monod, Pittock and Szechi (eds), *Loyalty and Identity*

Petrie, Sir C., 'The Elibank Plot' in *Transactions of the Royal Historical Society*, xiv (1931), pp. 175–96

Riviére, J., '"His little hour of royalty": The Stuart Court at Holyroodhouse in 1745' in Forsyth (ed.), *Bonnie Prince Charlie and the Jacobites*

Ryan, D. Michael, 'A Jacobite Tune at the North Bridge' in *The Lincoln Minute Men Dispatch* (Lincoln, Massachusetts ND)

Seton, W., 'Itinerary of King James III, October to December 1715' in *Scottish Historical Review*, 21 (1923–4), pp. 249–66

Szechi, D., 'The Jacobite Theatre of Death' in Cruickshanks and Black (eds), *The Jacobite Challenge*

——, 'The image of the court: idealism, politic and the evolution of the Stuart Court' in Corp (ed.), *The Stuart Court at Rome*

Tayler, H., 'John, Duke of Argyle and Greenwich' in *Scottish Historical Review*, xxvi (April 1947)

Terry, C. Stanford, 'The Battle of Glenshiel' in *The Scottish Historical Review*, ii (Edinburgh, 1905)

Vaughan, H. M., 'Welsh Jacobitism' in *The Transactions of the Honourable Society of Cymmrodorion* (1920–1), pp. 11–39

Whatley, C. and Patrick, D. J., 'Contesting Interpretations of the Union of 1707: The Abuse and Use of George Lockhart of Carnwath's Memoirs' in *Journal of Scottish Historical Studies*, 27, I (2007)

Whelan, K., 'An underground gentry? Catholic middlemen in eighteenth century Ireland' in Donnelly and Miller (eds), *Irish Popular Culture*

Index